Machiko Sakurai

4

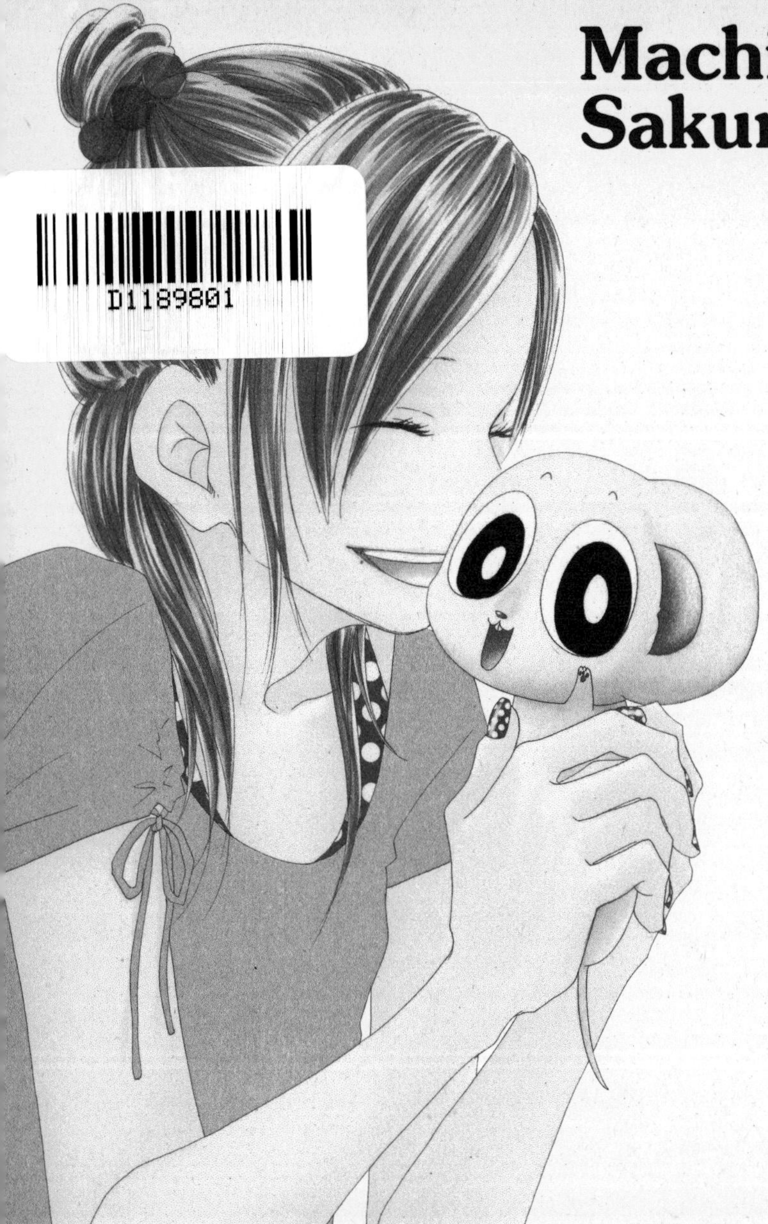

Translated and adapted by Athena and Alethea Nibley

Lettered by North Market Street Graphics

DEL REY

BALLANTINE BOOKS • NEW YORK

A Del Rey Manga/Kodansha Trade Paperback Original

Minimal!, volume 4 copyright © 2008 Machiko Sakurai
English translation copyright © 2009 Machiko Sakurai

Published in the United States by Del Rey, an imprint of The Random House Publishing Group, a division of Random House, Inc., New York.

DEL REY is a registered trademark and the Del Rey colophon is a trademark of Random House, Inc.

Publication rights arranged through Kodansha Ltd.

First published in Japan in 2008 by Kodansha Ltd., Tokyo

ISBN 978-0-345-51072-3

Printed in the United States of America

www.delreymanga.com

9 8 7 6 5 4 3 2 1

Translator/Adapter—Athena and Alethea Nibley
Lettering—North Market Street Graphics

CONTENTS

Honorifics Explained

Throughout the Del Rey Manga books, you will find Japanese honorifics left intact in the translations. For those not familiar with how the Japanese use honorifics and, more important, how they differ from American honorifics, we present this brief overview.

Politeness has always been a critical facet of Japanese culture. Ever since the feudal era, when Japan was a highly stratified society, use of honorifics—which can be defined as polite speech that indicates relationship or status—has played an essential role in the Japanese language. When you address someone in Japanese, an honorific usually takes the form of a suffix attached to one's name (example: "Asuna-san"), is used as a title at the end of one's name, or appears in place of the name itself (example: "Negi-sensei," or simply "Sensei!").

Honorifics can be expressions of respect or endearment. In the context of manga and anime, honorifics give insight into the nature of the relationship between characters. Many English translations leave out these important honorifics and therefore distort the feel of the original Japanese. Because Japanese honorifics contain nuances that English honorifics lack, it is our policy at Del Rey not to translate them. Here, instead, is a guide to some of the honorifics you may encounter in Del Rey Manga.

-san: This is the most common honorific and is equivalent to Mr., Miss, Ms., or Mrs. It is the all-purpose honorific and can be used in any situation where politeness is required.

-sama: This is one level higher than "-san" and is used to confer great respect.

-dono: This comes from the word "tono," which means "lord." It is an even higher level than "-sama" and confers utmost respect.

-kun: This suffix is used at the end of boys' names to express familiarity or endearment. It is also sometimes used by men among friends, or when addressing someone younger or of a lower station.

-chan: This is used to express endearment, mostly toward girls. It is also used for little boys, pets, and even among lovers. It gives a sense of childish cuteness.

Bozu: This is an informal way to refer to a boy, similar to the English terms "kid" and "squirt."

Sempai/Senpai: This title suggests that the addressee is one's senior in a group or organization. It is most often used in a school setting, where underclassmen refer to their upperclassmen as "sempai." It can also be used in the workplace, such as when a newer employee addresses an employee who has seniority in the company.

Kohai: This is the opposite of "sempai" and is used toward underclassmen in school or newcomers in the workplace. It connotes that the addressee is of a lower station.

Sensei: Literally meaning "one who has come before," this title is used for teachers, doctors, or masters of any profession or art.

-[blank]: This is usually forgotten in these lists, but it is perhaps the most significant difference between Japanese and English. The lack of honorific means that the speaker has permission to address the person in a very intimate way. Usually, only family, spouses, or very close friends have this kind of permission. Known as *yobisute*, it can be gratifying when someone who has earned the intimacy starts to call one by one's name without an honorific. But when that intimacy hasn't been earned, it can be very insulting.

Machiko
Sakurai

4

ミニマ

minima!

The story so far...

The plush toy Nicori can talk and move. He was living with Ame, but decided to leave her house in order to protect her from the negative attention that a thoughtless and selfish society is bound to give to a girl with a living toy. Ame was terribly shocked by Nicori's decision. With her friend Midori's words of encouragement in her heart, Ame tries to do her best to fix things, but...!?

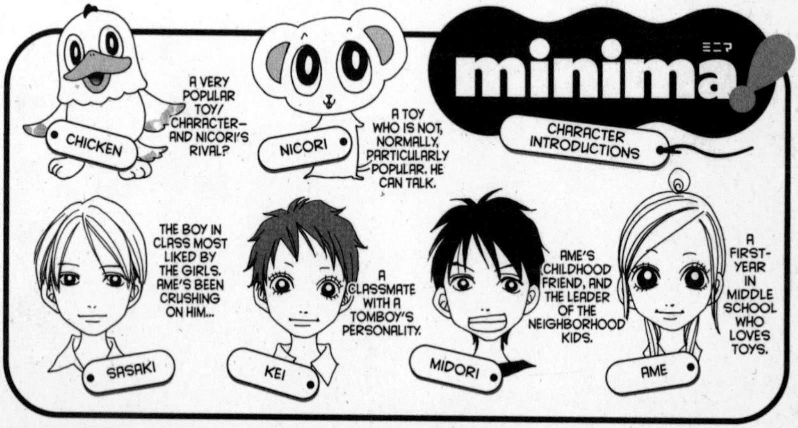
minima!
CHARACTER INTRODUCTIONS
NICORI
A TOY WHO IS NOT, NORMALLY, PARTICULARLY POPULAR. HE CAN TALK.
CHICKEN
A VERY POPULAR TOY/ CHARACTER— AND NICORI'S RIVAL?
AME
A FIRST-YEAR IN MIDDLE SCHOOL WHO LOVES TOYS.
MIDORI
AME'S CHILDHOOD FRIEND, AND THE LEADER OF THE NEIGHBORHOOD KIDS.
KEI
A CLASSMATE WITH A TOMBOY'S PERSONALITY.
SASAKI
THE BOY IN CLASS MOST LIKED BY THE GIRLS. AME'S BEEN CRUSHING ON HIM...

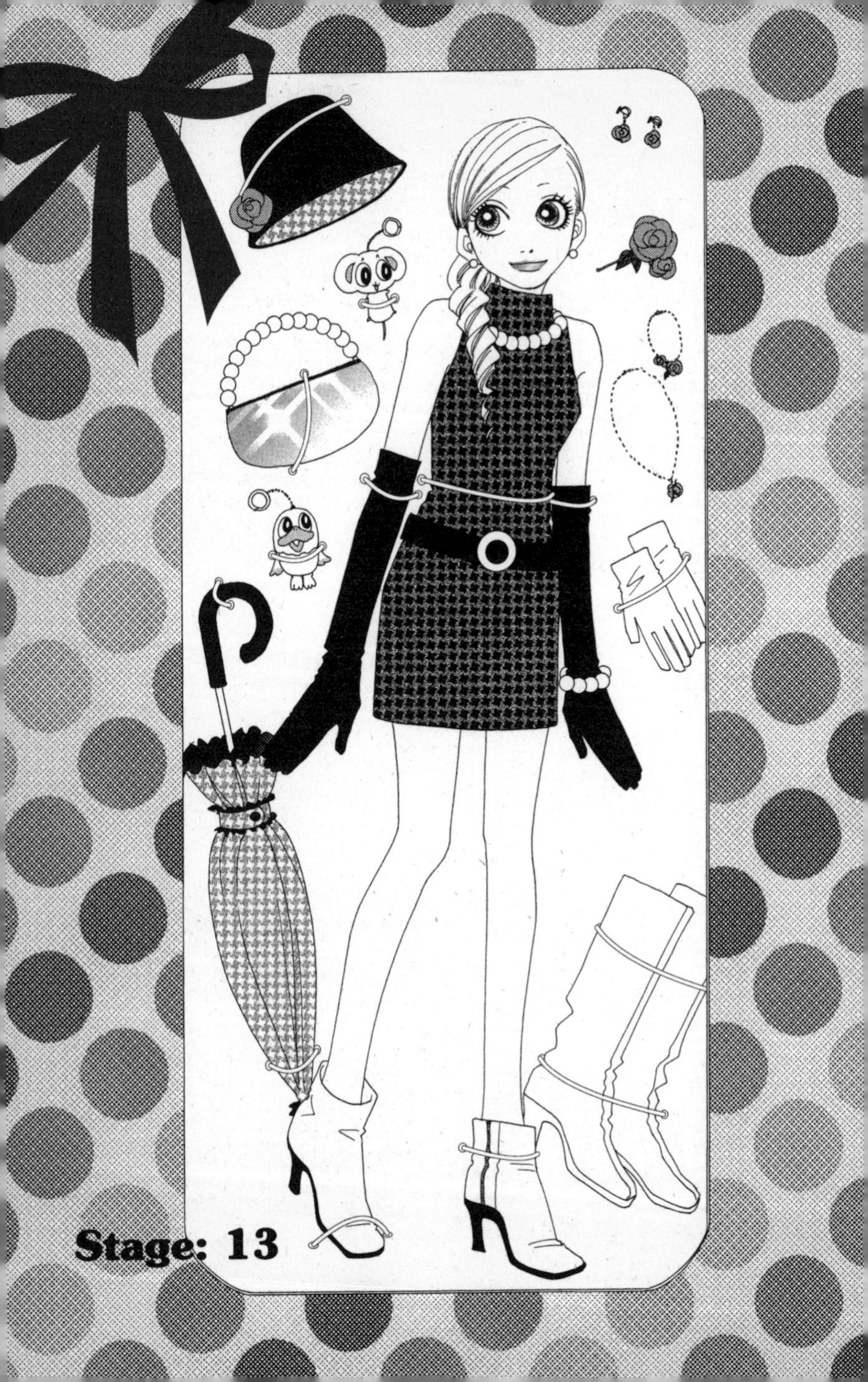

Stage: 13

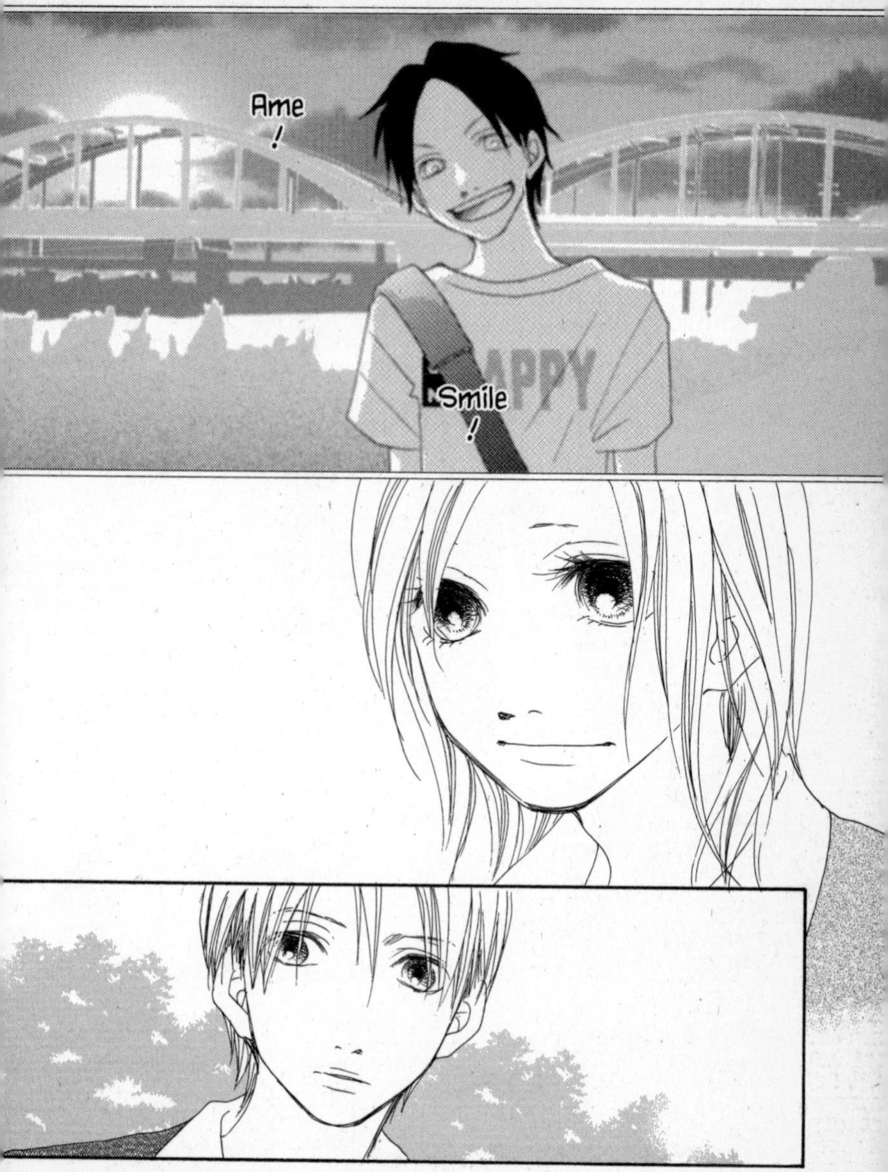
Ame!
Smile!

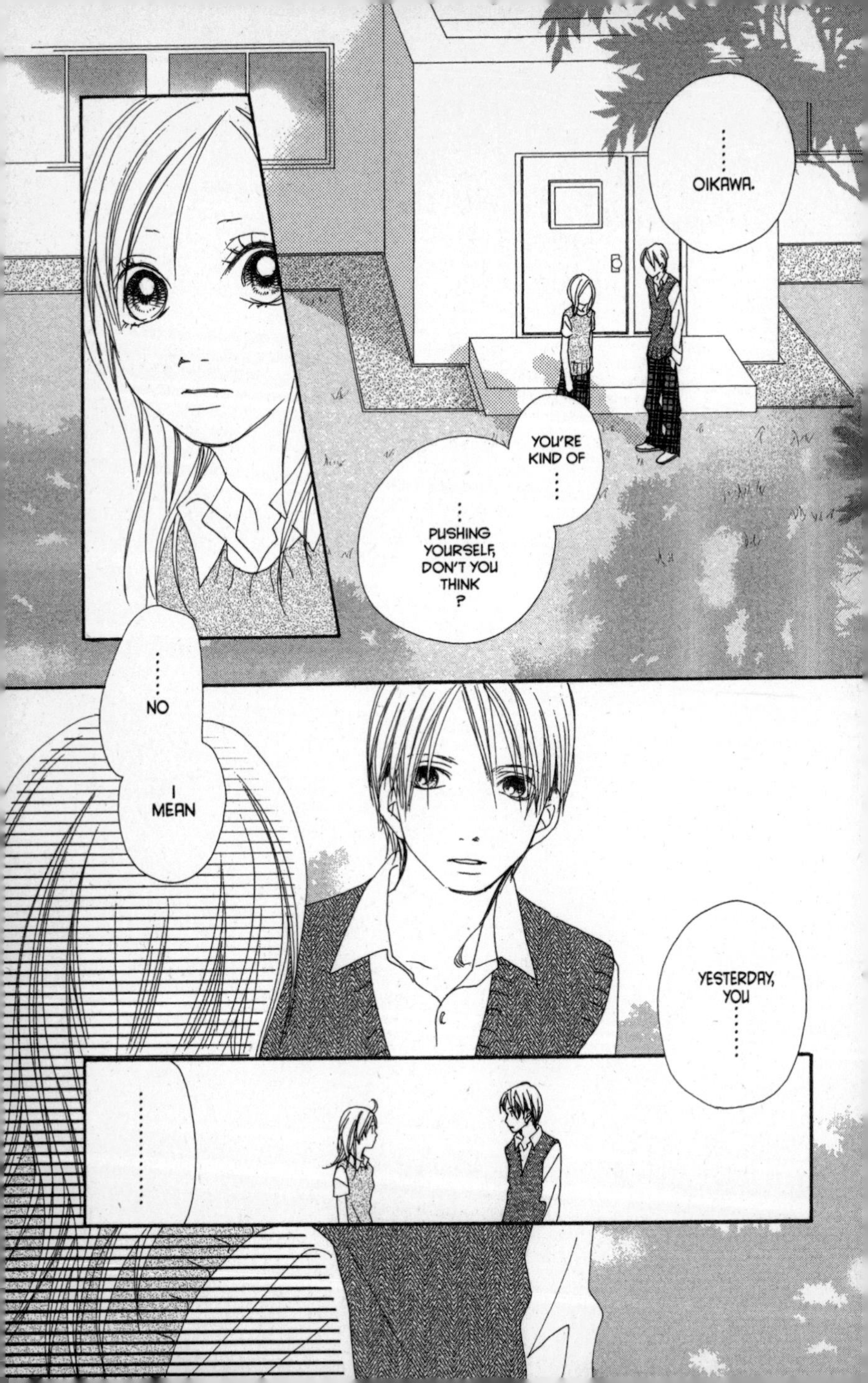
......OIKAWA.
YOU'RE KIND OF ......
......PUSHING YOURSELF, DON'T YOU THINK?
......NO
I MEAN
YESTERDAY, YOU ......
......

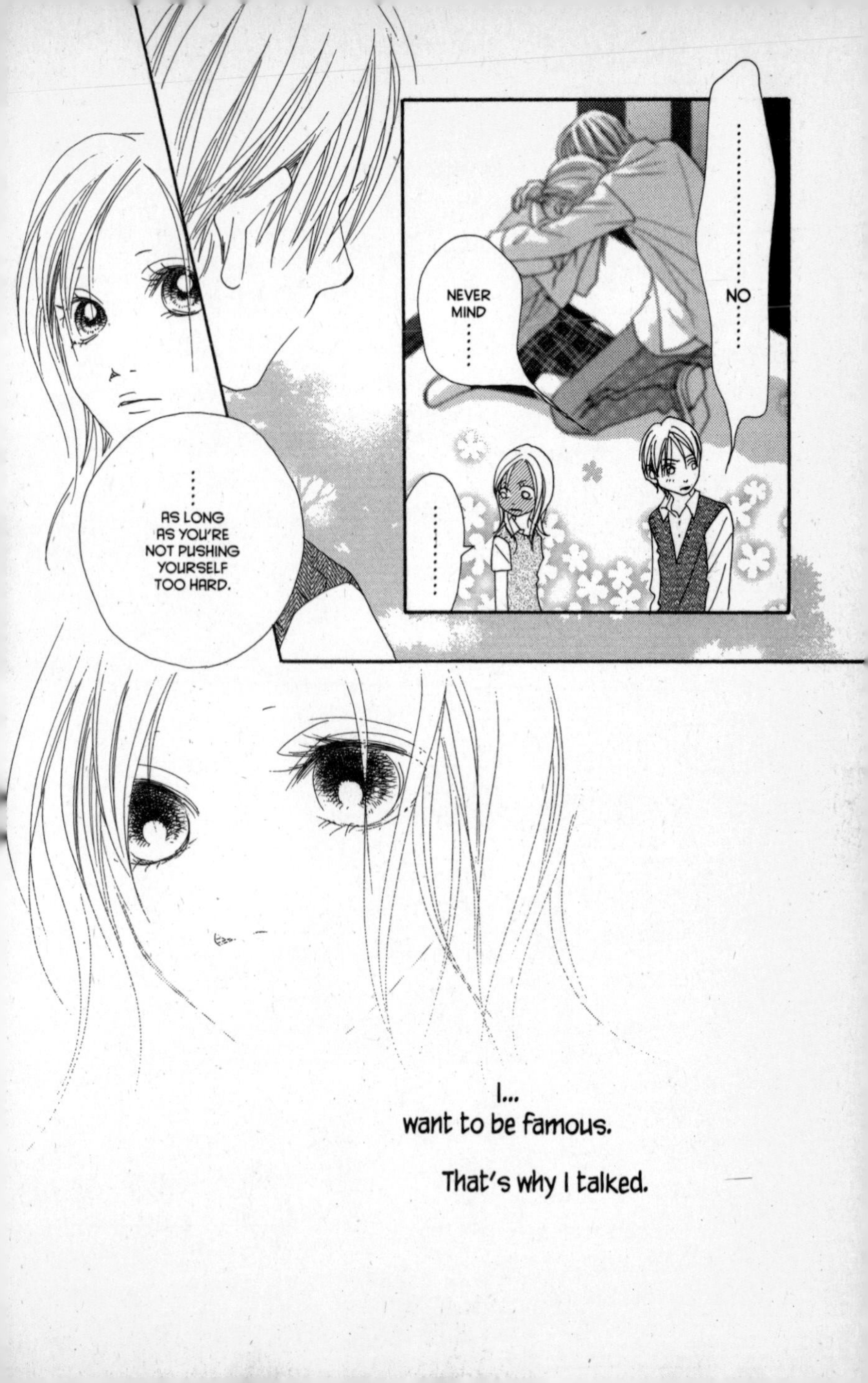
......NO......
NEVER MIND......
....
......AS LONG AS YOU'RE NOT PUSHING YOURSELF TOO HARD.
I... want to be famous.
That's why I talked.

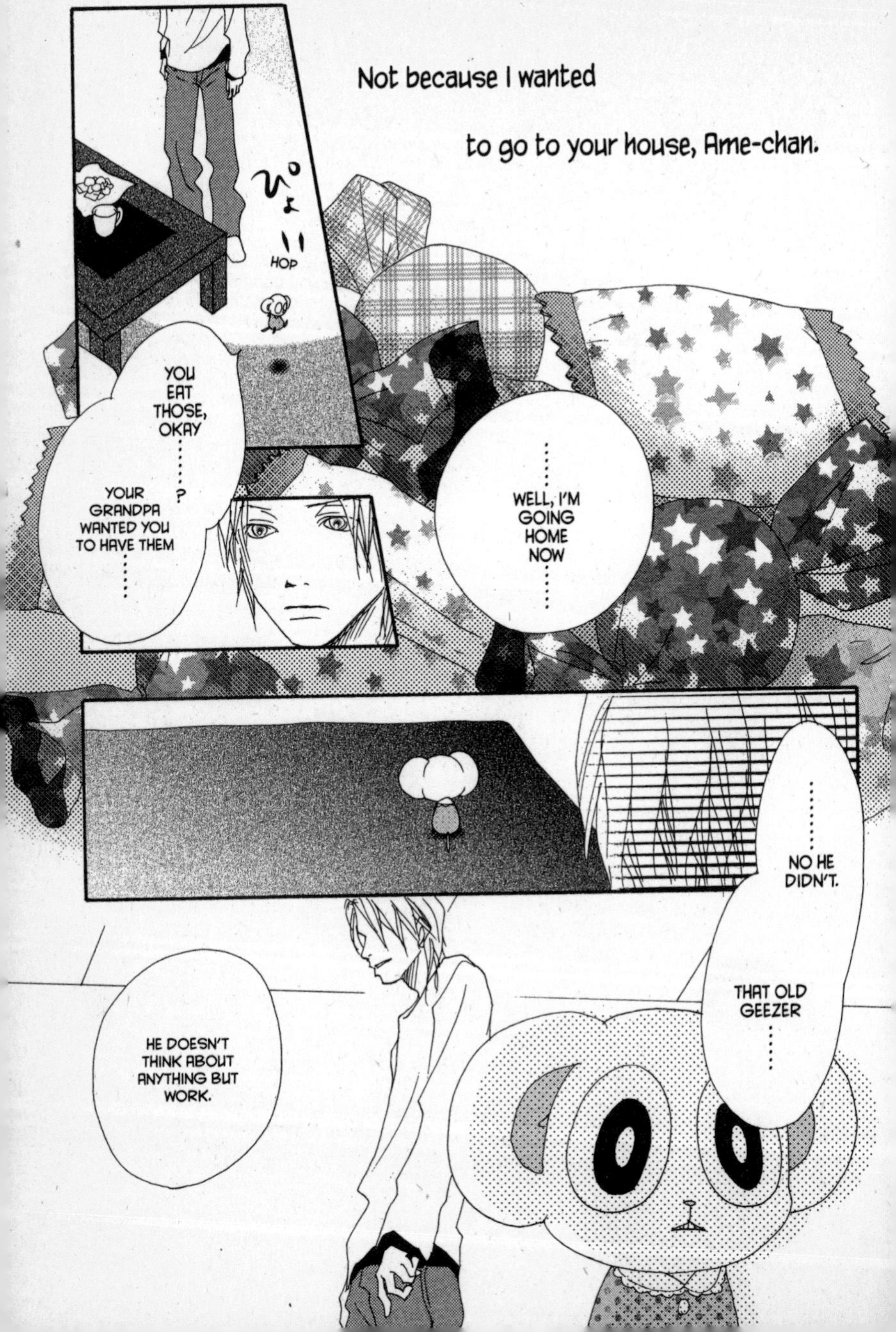
Not because I wanted
to go to your house, Ame-chan.
ぴょい HOP
YOU EAT THOSE, OKAY......?
YOUR GRANDPA WANTED YOU TO HAVE THEM......
......WELL, I'M GOING HOME NOW......
......NO HE DIDN'T.
THAT OLD GEEZER......
HE DOESN'T THINK ABOUT ANYTHING BUT WORK.

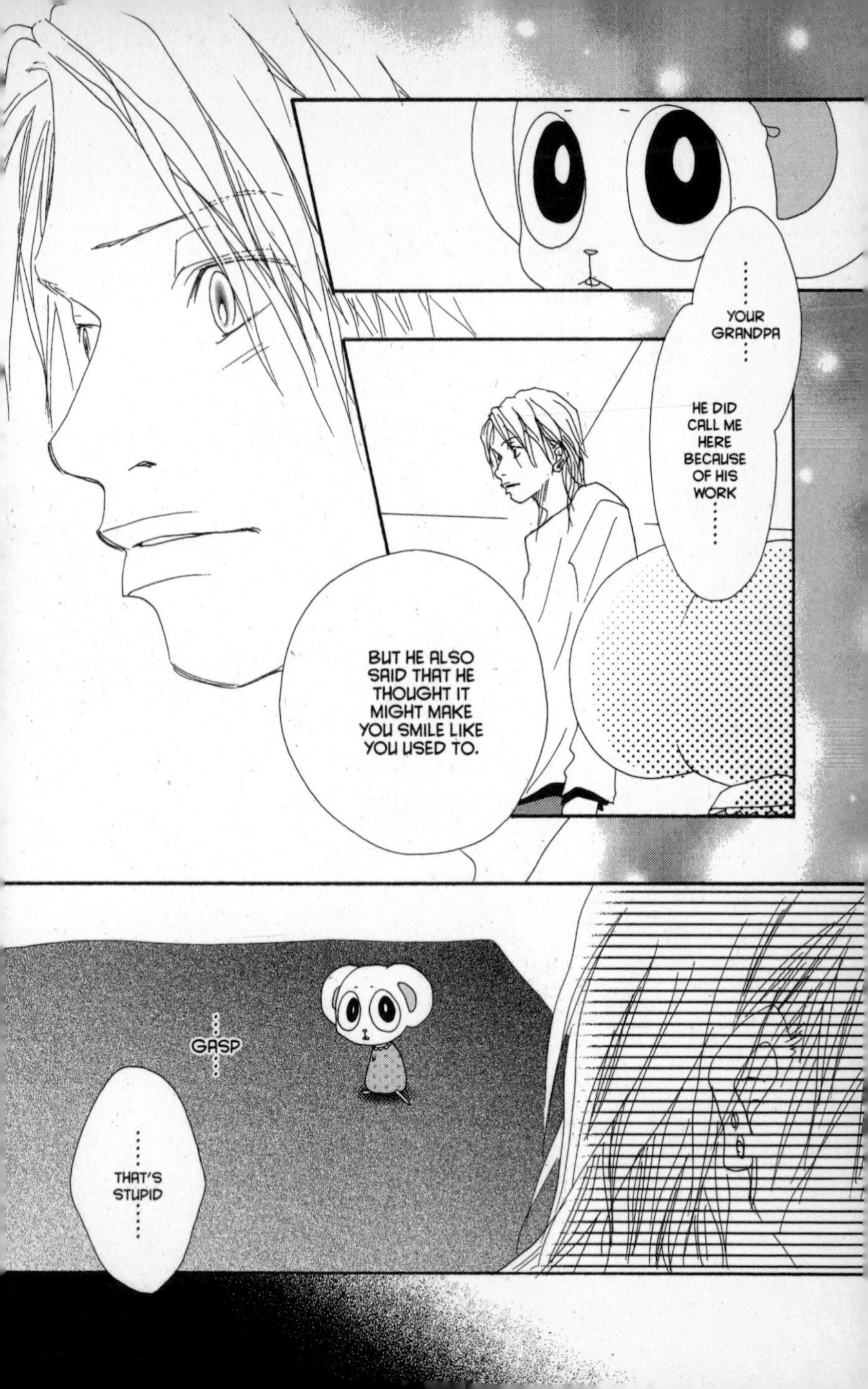
......YOUR GRANDPA......
HE DID CALL ME HERE BECAUSE OF HIS WORK......
BUT HE ALSO SAID THAT HE THOUGHT IT MIGHT MAKE YOU SMILE LIKE YOU USED TO.
......GASP......
......THAT'S STUPID......

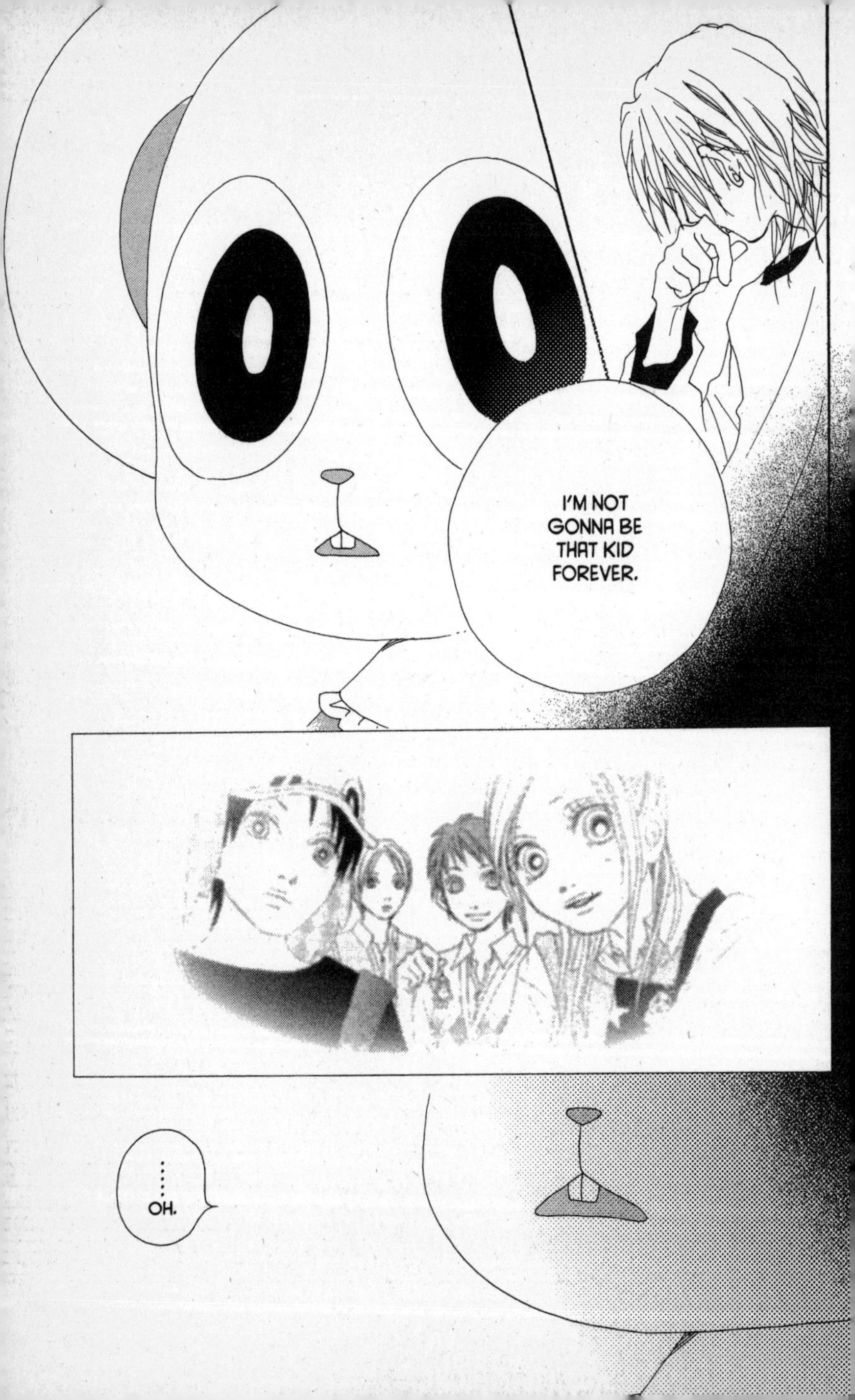
I'M NOT GONNA BE THAT KID FOREVER.
......
OH.

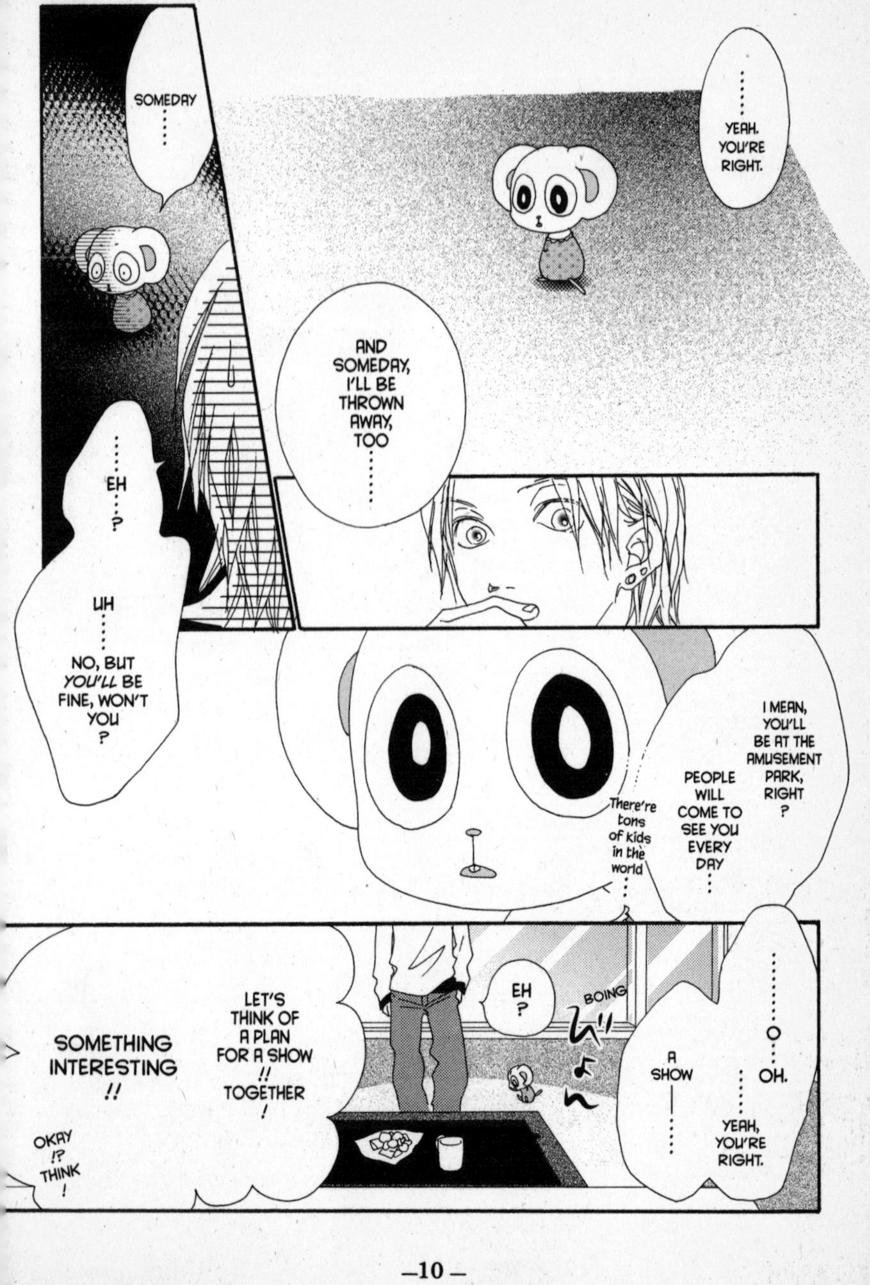
……YEAH. YOU'RE RIGHT.
AND SOMEDAY, I'LL BE THROWN AWAY, TOO……
SOMEDAY……
……EH…?
UH…… NO, BUT *YOU'LL* BE FINE, WON'T YOU?
I MEAN, YOU'LL BE AT THE AMUSEMENT PARK, RIGHT?
PEOPLE WILL COME TO SEE YOU EVERY DAY…
There're tons of kids in the world…
……O…OH.
YEAH, YOU'RE RIGHT.
A SHOW—……
BOING
EH?
LET'S THINK OF A PLAN FOR A SHOW!! TOGETHER!
SOMETHING INTERESTING!!
OKAY!? THINK!

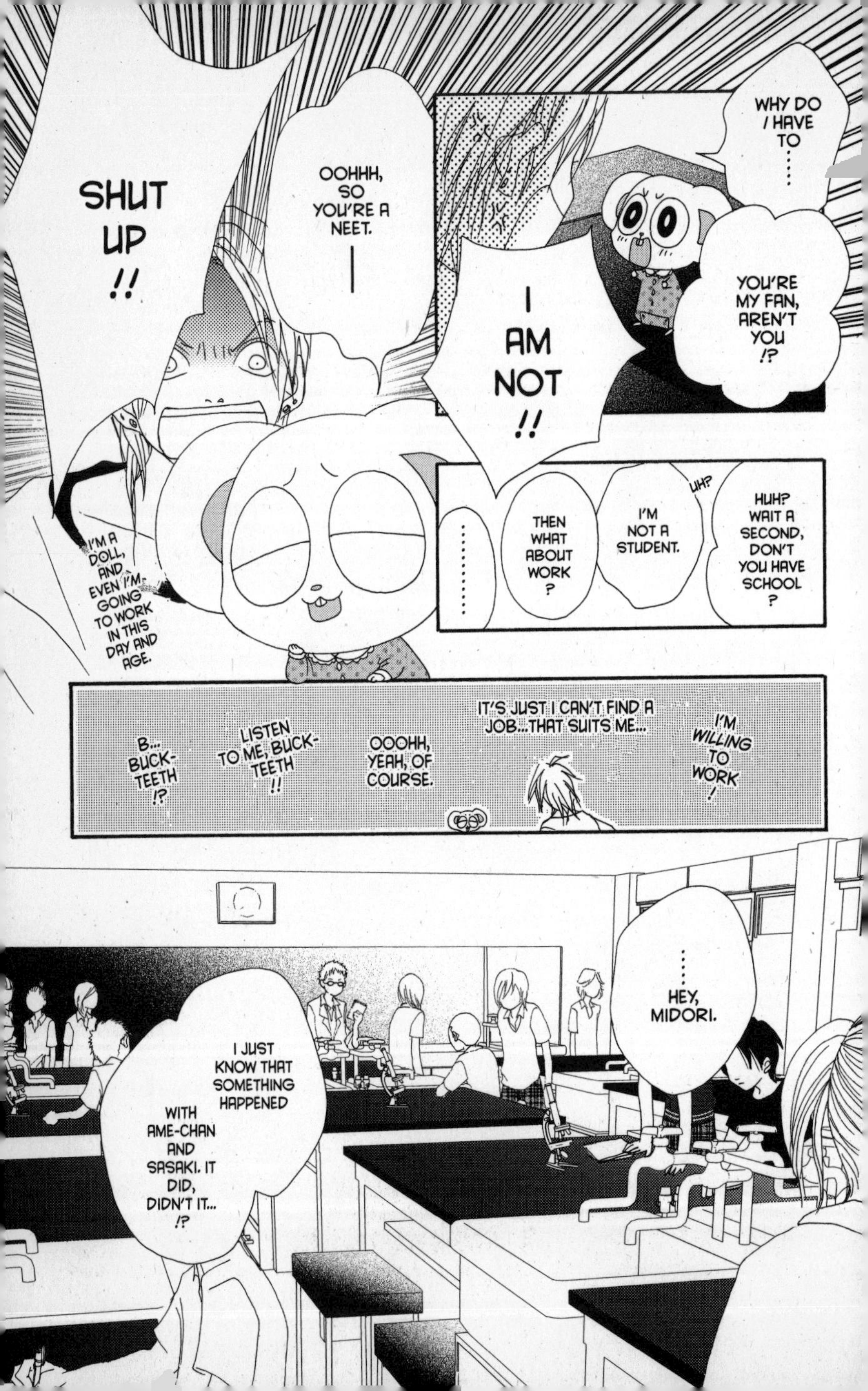
WHY DO I HAVE TO......
YOU'RE MY FAN, AREN'T YOU!?
I AM NOT!!
HUH? WAIT A SECOND, DON'T YOU HAVE SCHOOL?
HUH?
I'M NOT A STUDENT.
THEN WHAT ABOUT WORK?
......
OOHHH, SO YOU'RE A NEET.
SHUT UP!!
I'M A DOLL, AND EVEN I'M GOING TO WORK IN THIS DAY AND AGE.
I'M WILLING TO WORK!
IT'S JUST I CAN'T FIND A JOB...THAT SUITS ME...
OOOHH, YEAH, OF COURSE.
LISTEN TO ME, BUCK-TEETH!!
B... BUCK-TEETH!?
......HEY, MIDORI.
I JUST KNOW THAT SOMETHING HAPPENED WITH AME-CHAN AND SASAKI. IT DID, DIDN'T IT...!?

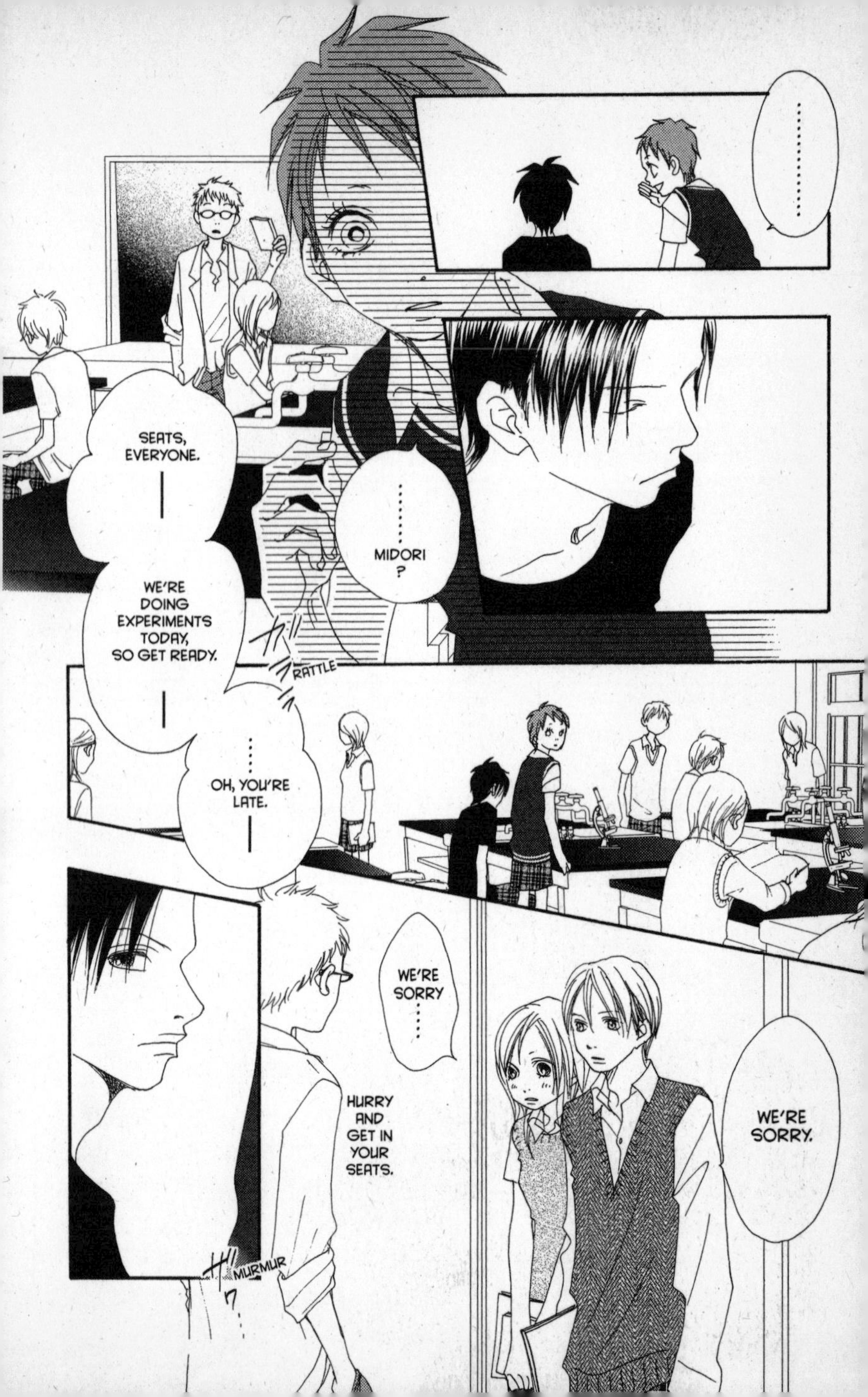
......
...... MIDORI?
SEATS, EVERYONE. —
WE'RE DOING EXPERIMENTS TODAY, SO GET READY. —
RATTLE
...... OH, YOU'RE LATE. —
WE'RE SORRY.
WE'RE SORRY......
HURRY AND GET IN YOUR SEATS.
MURMUR

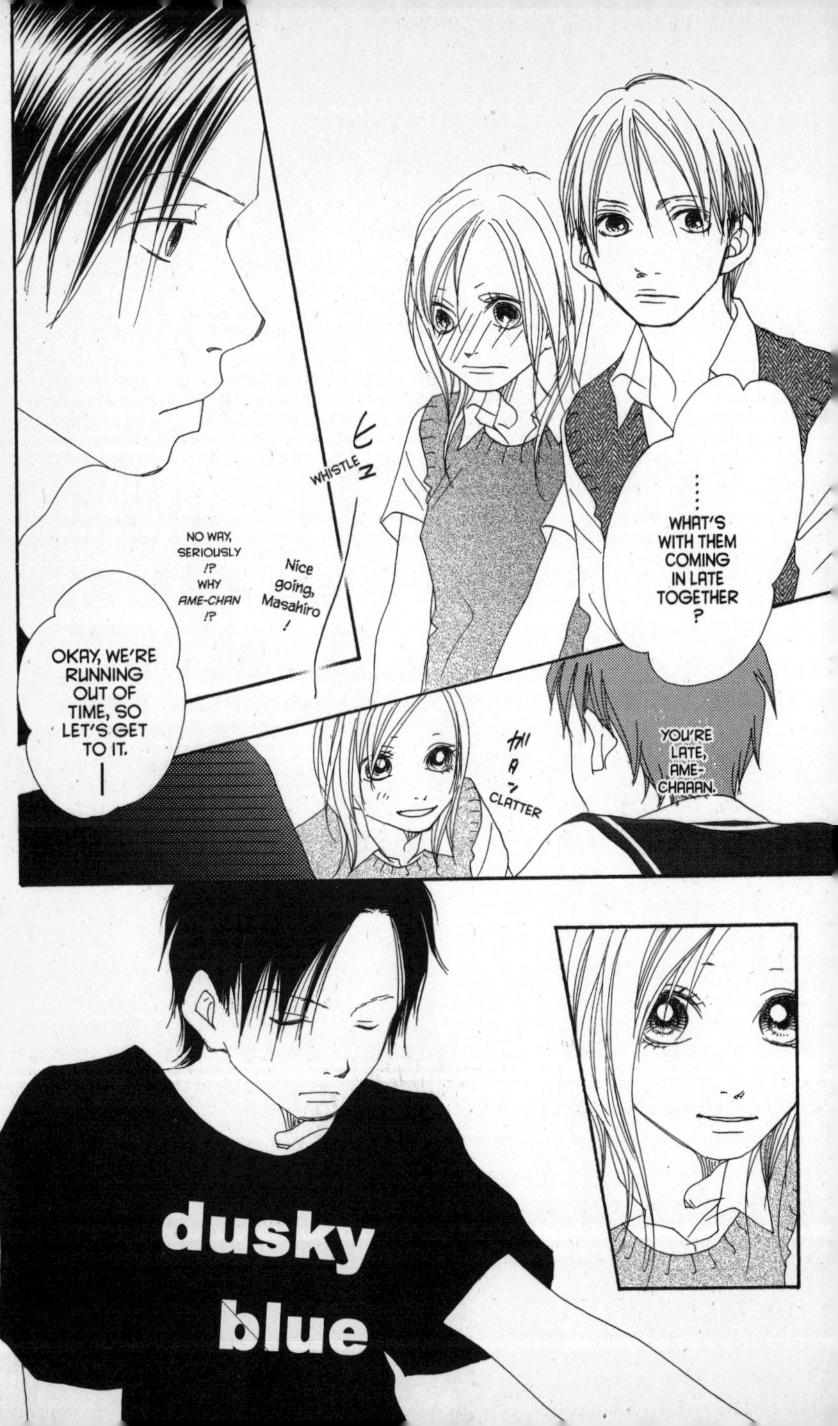

...WHAT'S WITH THEM COMING IN LATE TOGETHER?
WHISTLE
Nice going, Masahiro!
NO WAY, SERIOUSLY!? WHY AME-CHAN!?
YOU'RE LATE, AME-CHAAAN.
CLATTER
OKAY, WE'RE RUNNING OUT OF TIME, SO LET'S GET TO IT.
dusky blue

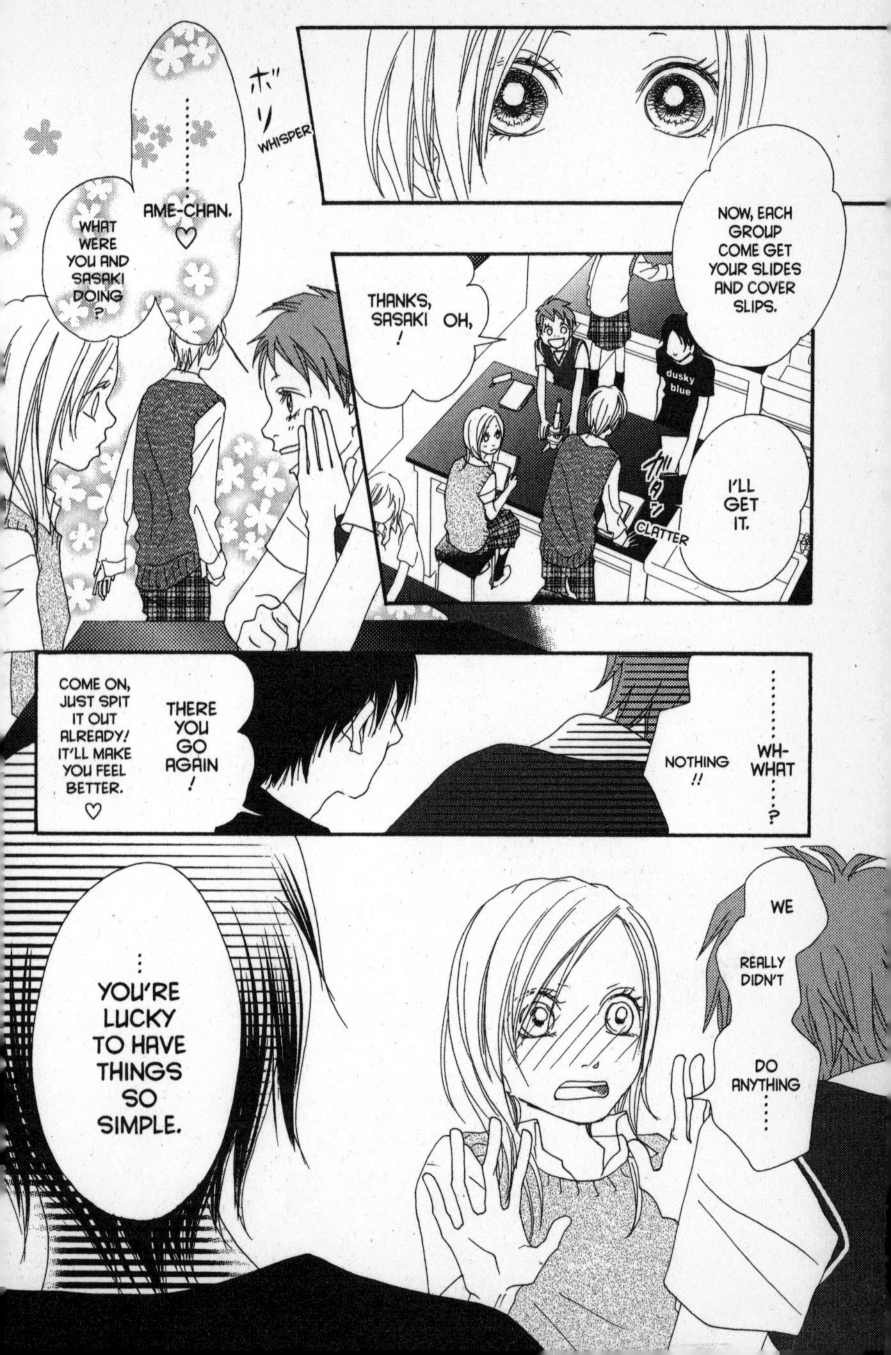
NOW, EACH GROUP COME GET YOUR SLIDES AND COVER SLIPS.
I'LL GET IT.
CLATTER
OH,
THANKS, SASAKI!
ボソ
WHISPER
......AME-CHAN. ♡
WHAT WERE YOU AND SASAKI DOING?
WH-WHAT......?
NOTHING!!
THERE YOU GO AGAIN!
COME ON, JUST SPIT IT OUT ALREADY! IT'LL MAKE YOU FEEL BETTER. ♡
WE REALLY DIDN'T DO ANYTHING......
...YOU'RE LUCKY TO HAVE THINGS SO SIMPLE.

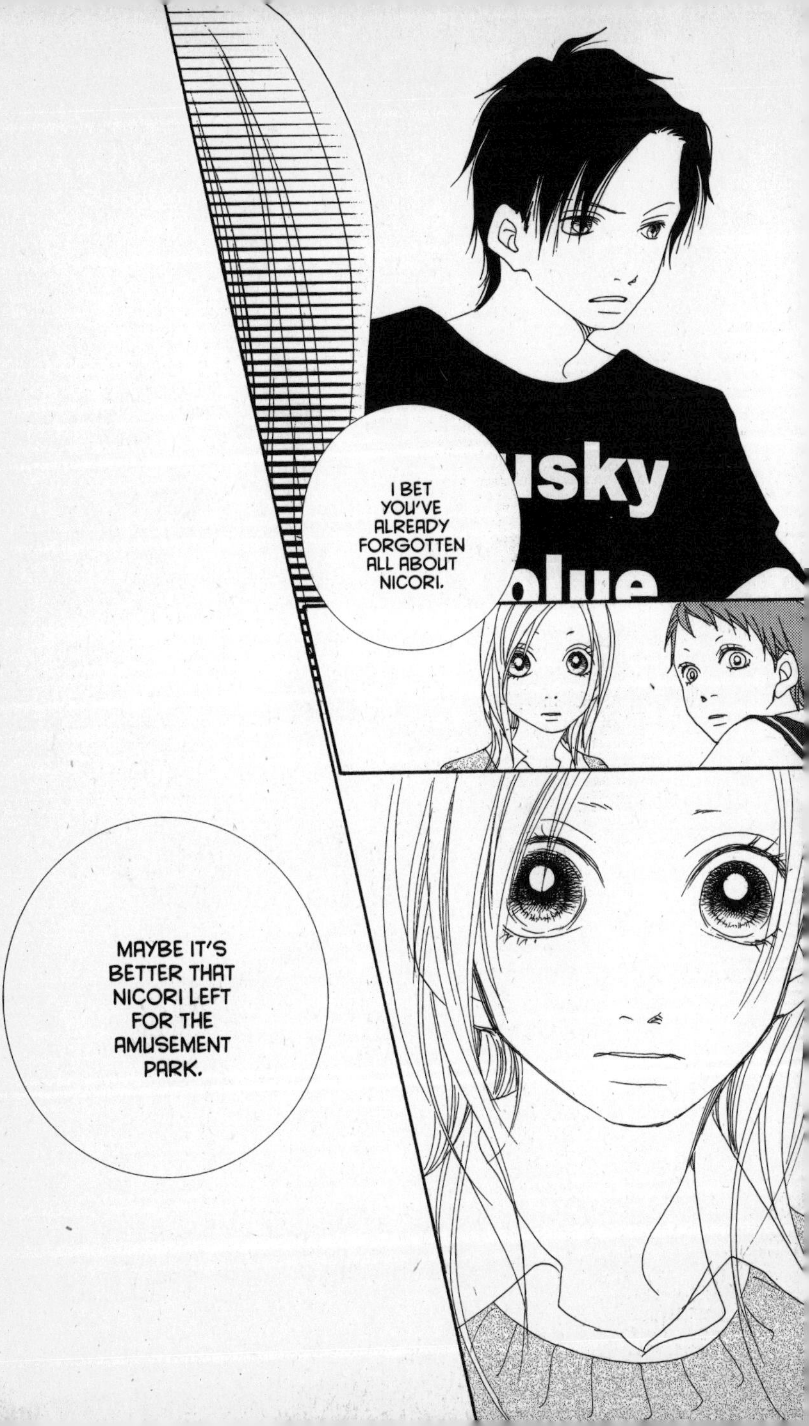

Husky blue
I BET YOU'VE ALREADY FORGOTTEN ALL ABOUT NICORI.
MAYBE IT'S BETTER THAT NICORI LEFT FOR THE AMUSEMENT PARK.

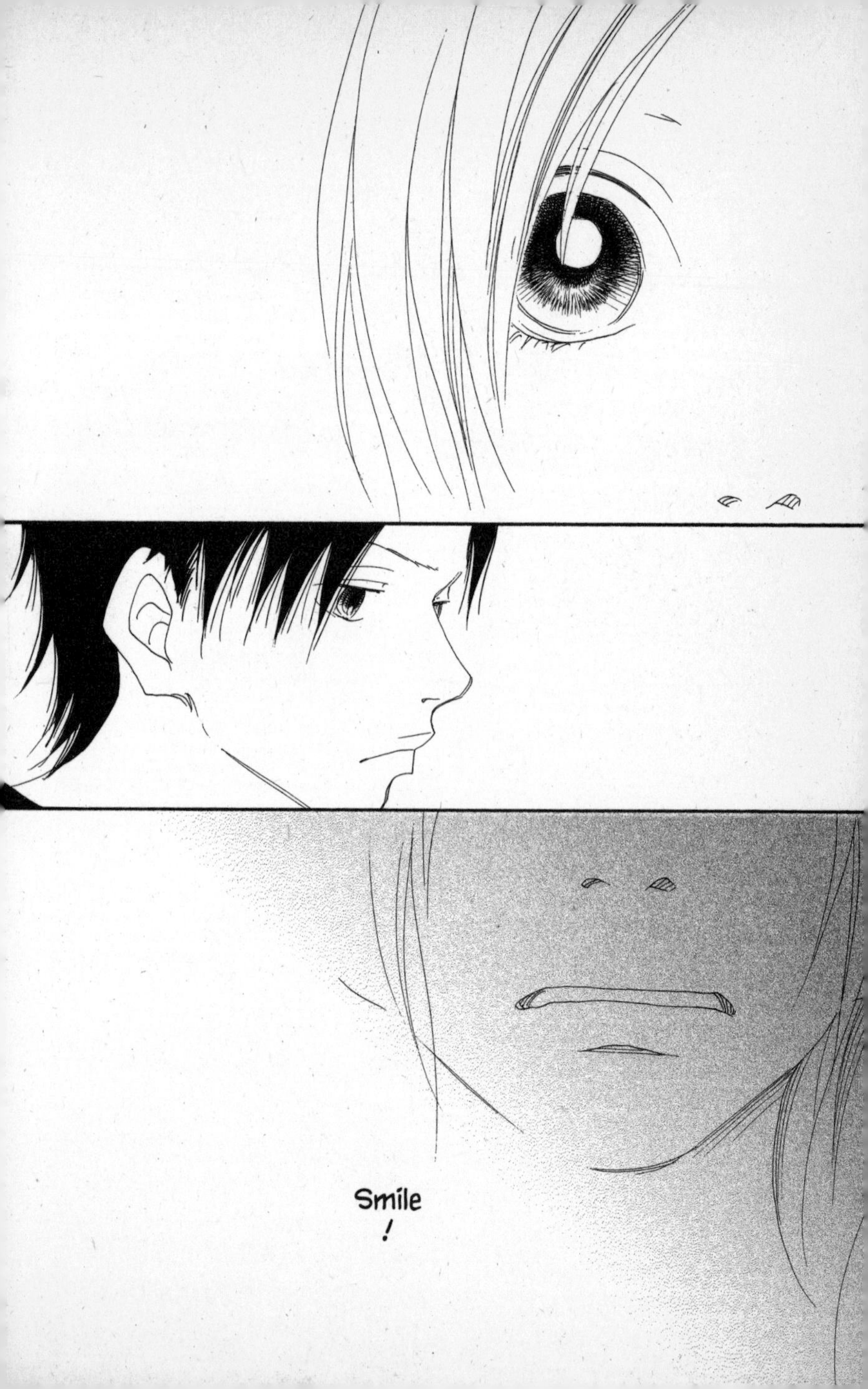
Smile
!

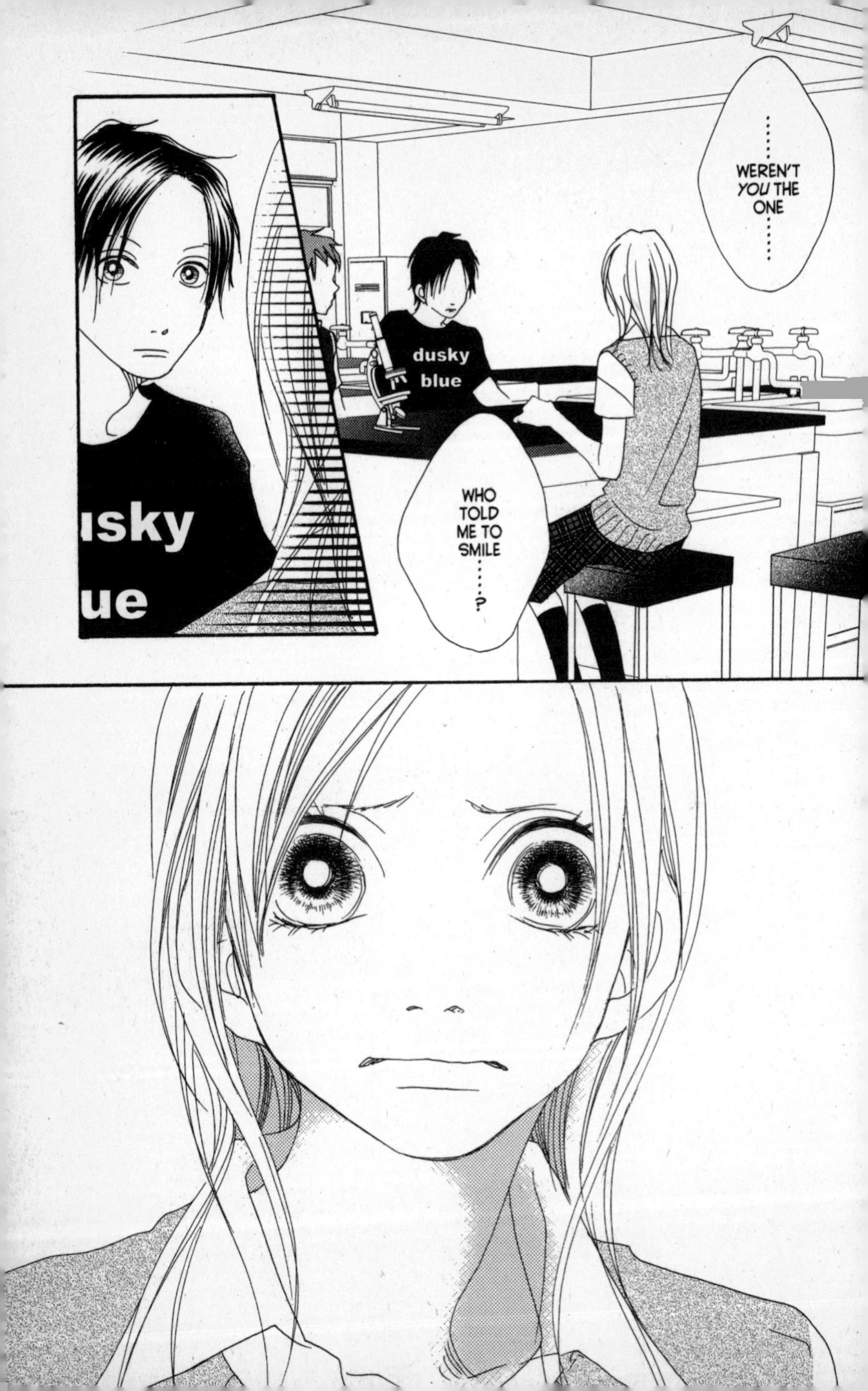
......WEREN'T YOU THE ONE......
dusky blue
WHO TOLD ME TO SMILE......?

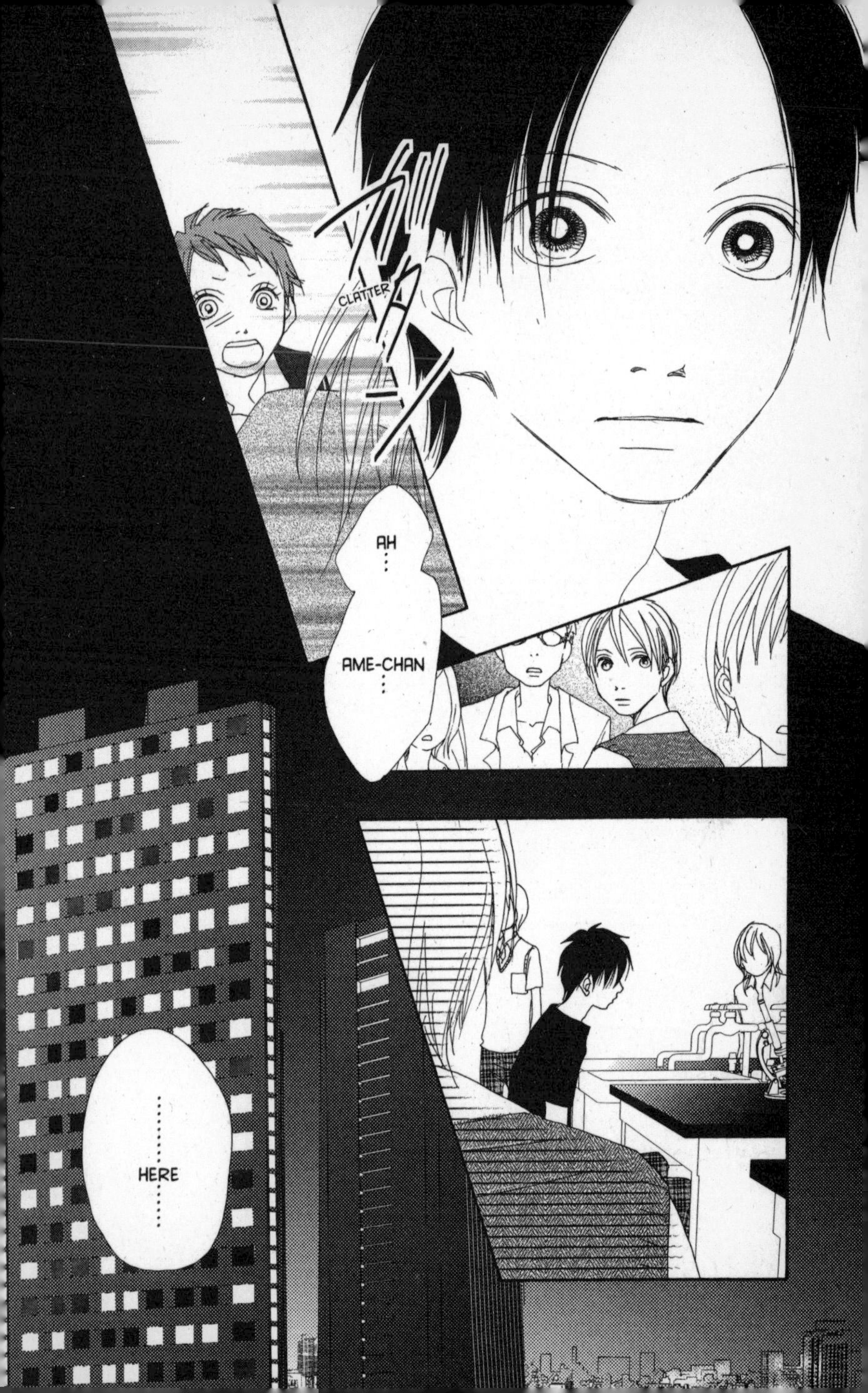
CLATTER
AH... AME-CHAN...
...HERE...

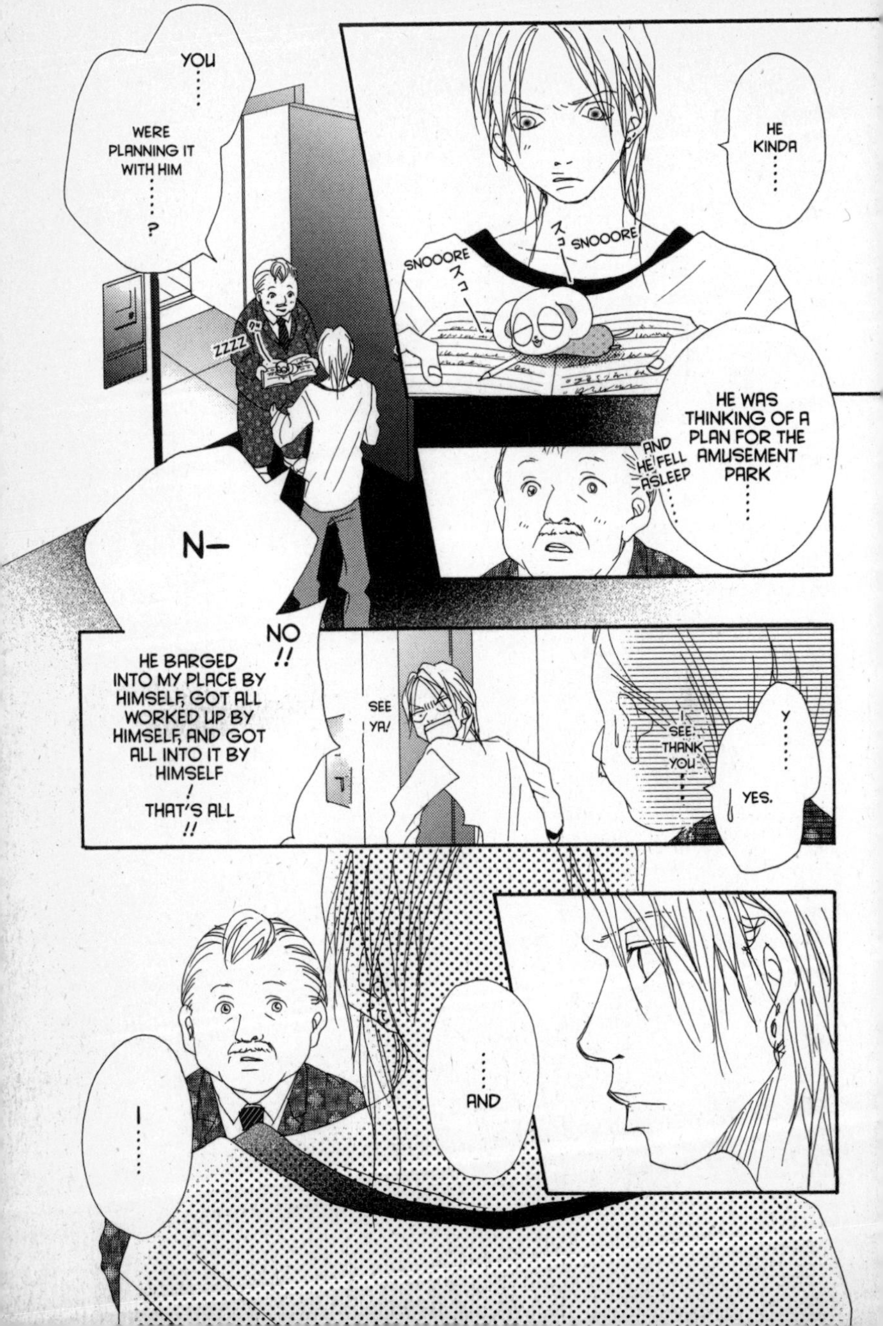

HE KINDA ....
SNOOORE スコ
SNOOORE スコ
HE WAS THINKING OF A PLAN FOR THE AMUSEMENT PARK ....
AND HE FELL ASLEEP ....
YOU .... WERE PLANNING IT WITH HIM .... ?
ZZZZ
N—
Y .... YES.
I SEE. THANK YOU ....
SEE YA!
NO !!
HE BARGED INTO MY PLACE BY HIMSELF, GOT ALL WORKED UP BY HIMSELF, AND GOT ALL INTO IT BY HIMSELF ! THAT'S ALL !!
.... AND
I ....

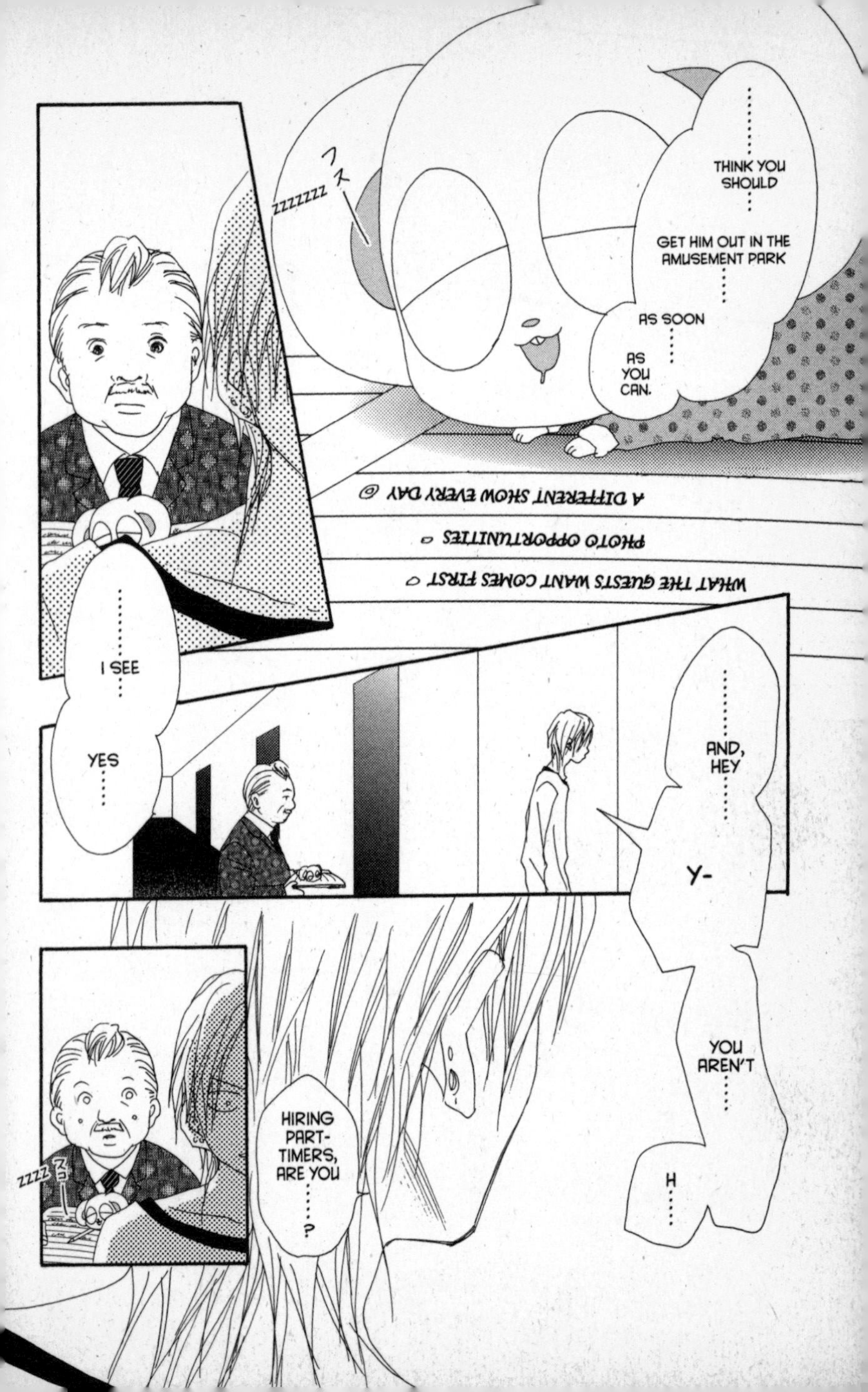
……THINK YOU SHOULD……
GET HIM OUT IN THE AMUSEMENT PARK……
AS SOON…… AS YOU CAN.
フス
ZZZZZZZ
WHAT THE GUESTS WANT COMES FIRST
PHOTO OPPORTUNITIES
A DIFFERENT SHOW EVERY DAY
……I SEE……
YES……
……AND, HEY……
Y-
YOU AREN'T……
H……
ZZZZ
HIRING PART-TIMERS, ARE YOU……?

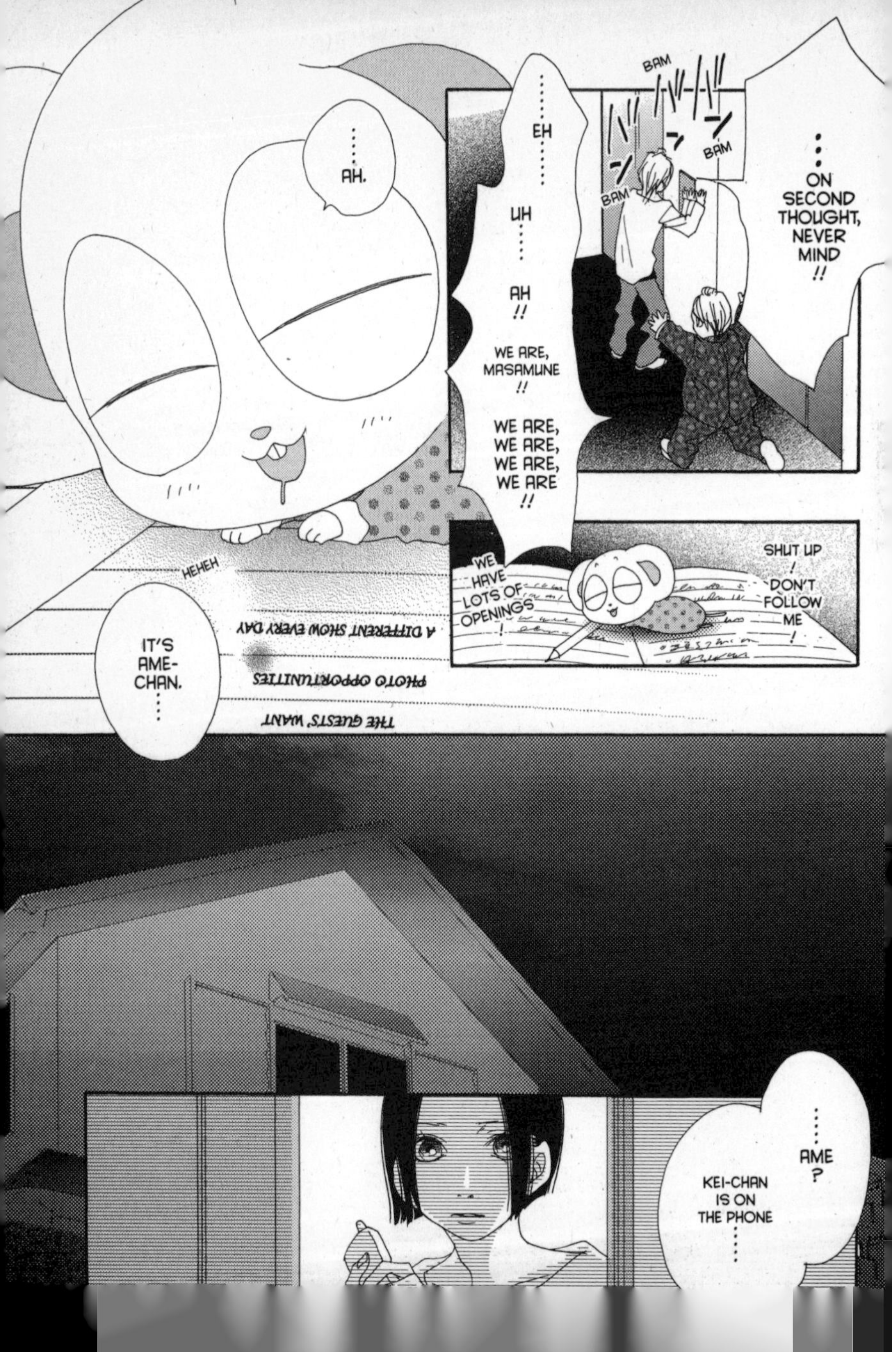
BAM
BAM
BAM
...ON SECOND THOUGHT, NEVER MIND!!
EH...... UH...... AH!! WE ARE, MASAMUNE!! WE ARE, WE ARE, WE ARE, WE ARE!!
...AH.
SHUT UP! DON'T FOLLOW ME!
WE HAVE LOTS OF OPENINGS!
HEHEH
IT'S AME-CHAN....
THE GUESTS' WANT
PHOTO OPPORTUNITIES
A DIFFERENT SHOW EVERY DAY
.....AME?
KEI-CHAN IS ON THE PHONE.....

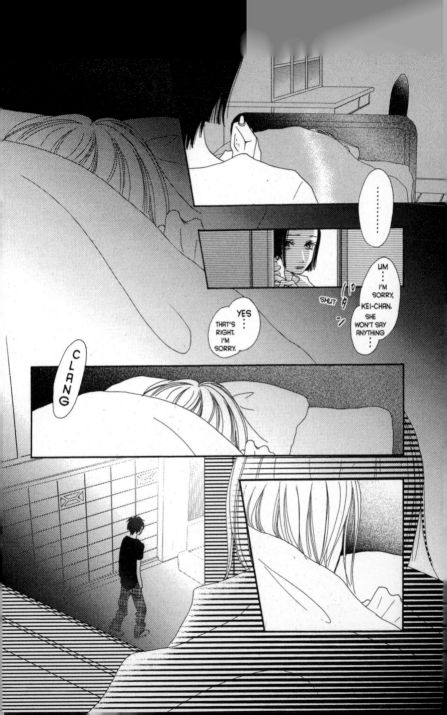

．．．．．．

UM ．．． I'M SORRY, KEI-CHAN. SHE WON'T SAY ANYTHING ．．．

SHUT

YES ．．． THAT'S RIGHT. I'M SORRY.

CLANG

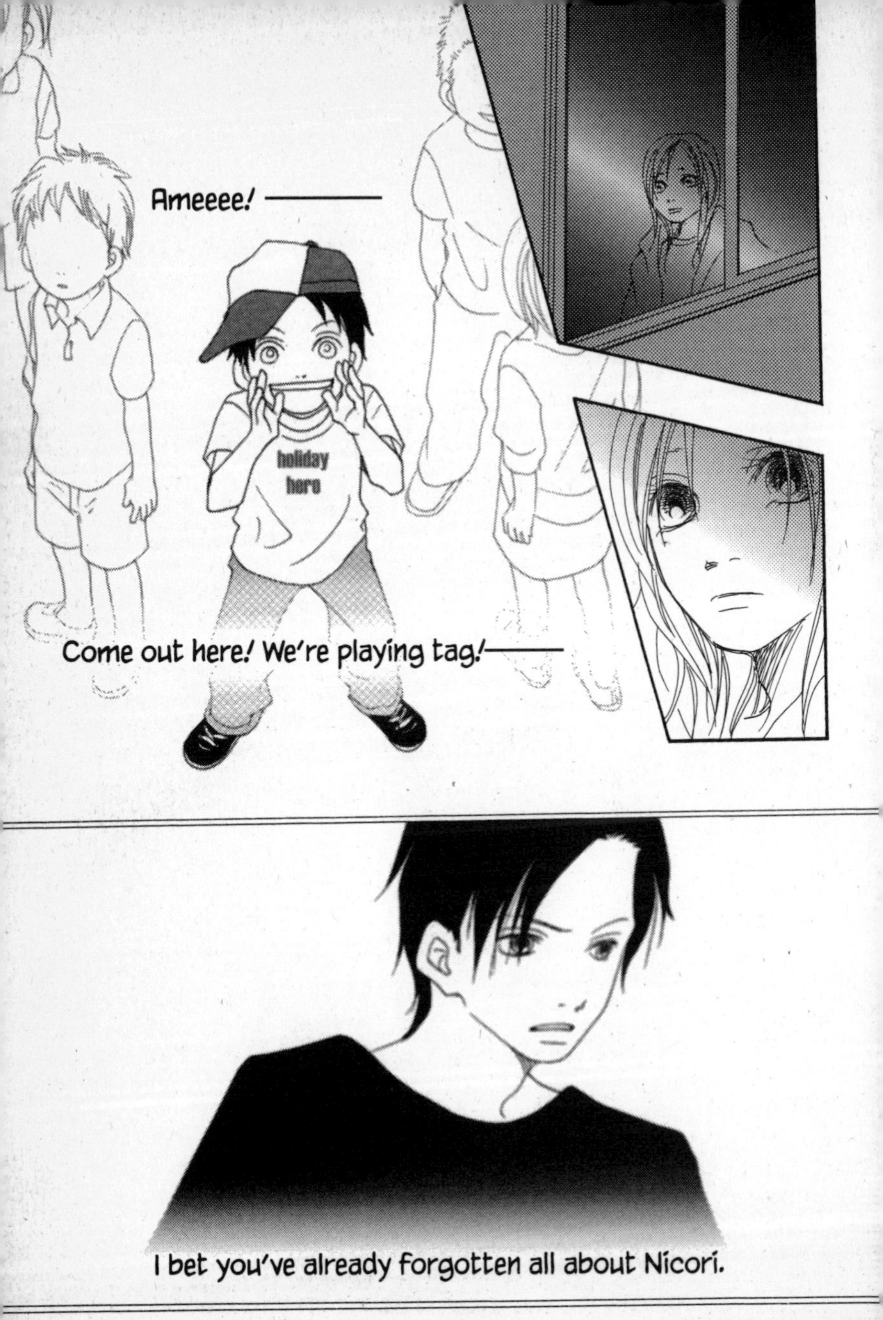
Ameeee! ———
holiday hero
Come out here! We're playing tag! ———
I bet you've already forgotten all about Nicori.

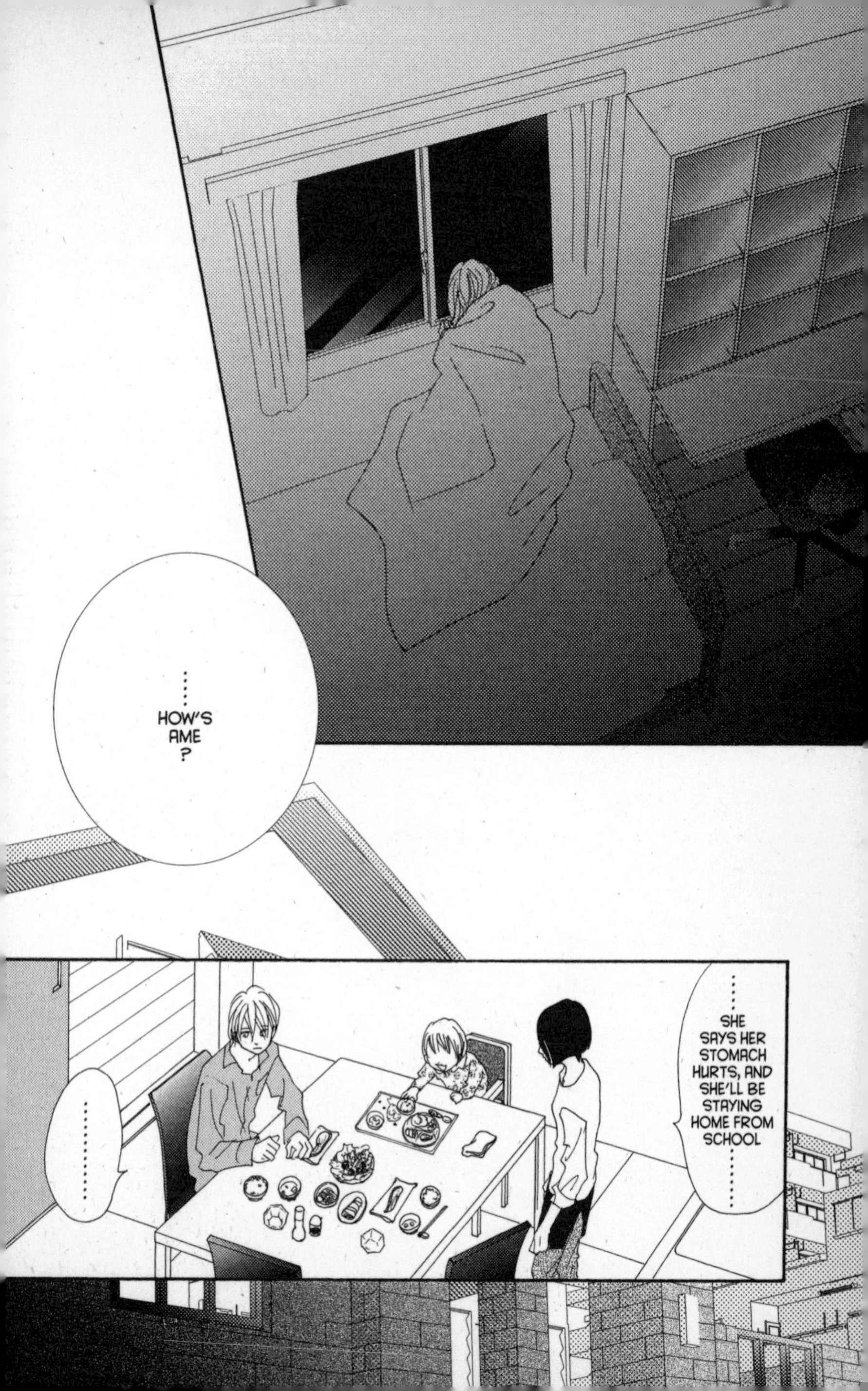

......HOW'S AME?
......SHE SAYS HER STOMACH HURTS, AND SHE'LL BE STAYING HOME FROM SCHOOL......
......

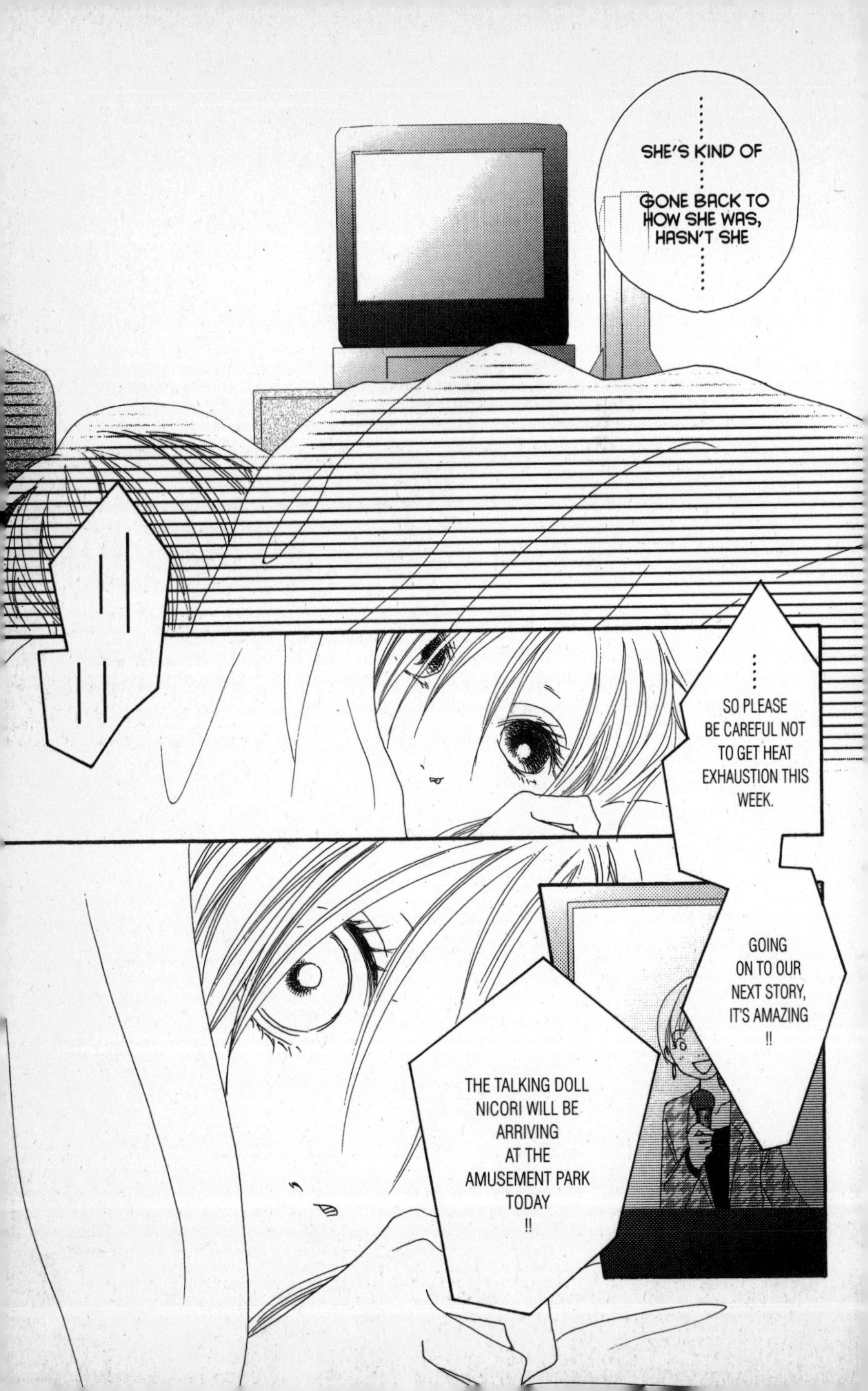
……SHE'S KIND OF ……GONE BACK TO HOW SHE WAS, HASN'T SHE ……
!!
……SO PLEASE BE CAREFUL NOT TO GET HEAT EXHAUSTION THIS WEEK.
GOING ON TO OUR NEXT STORY, IT'S AMAZING !!
THE TALKING DOLL NICORI WILL BE ARRIVING AT THE AMUSEMENT PARK TODAY !!

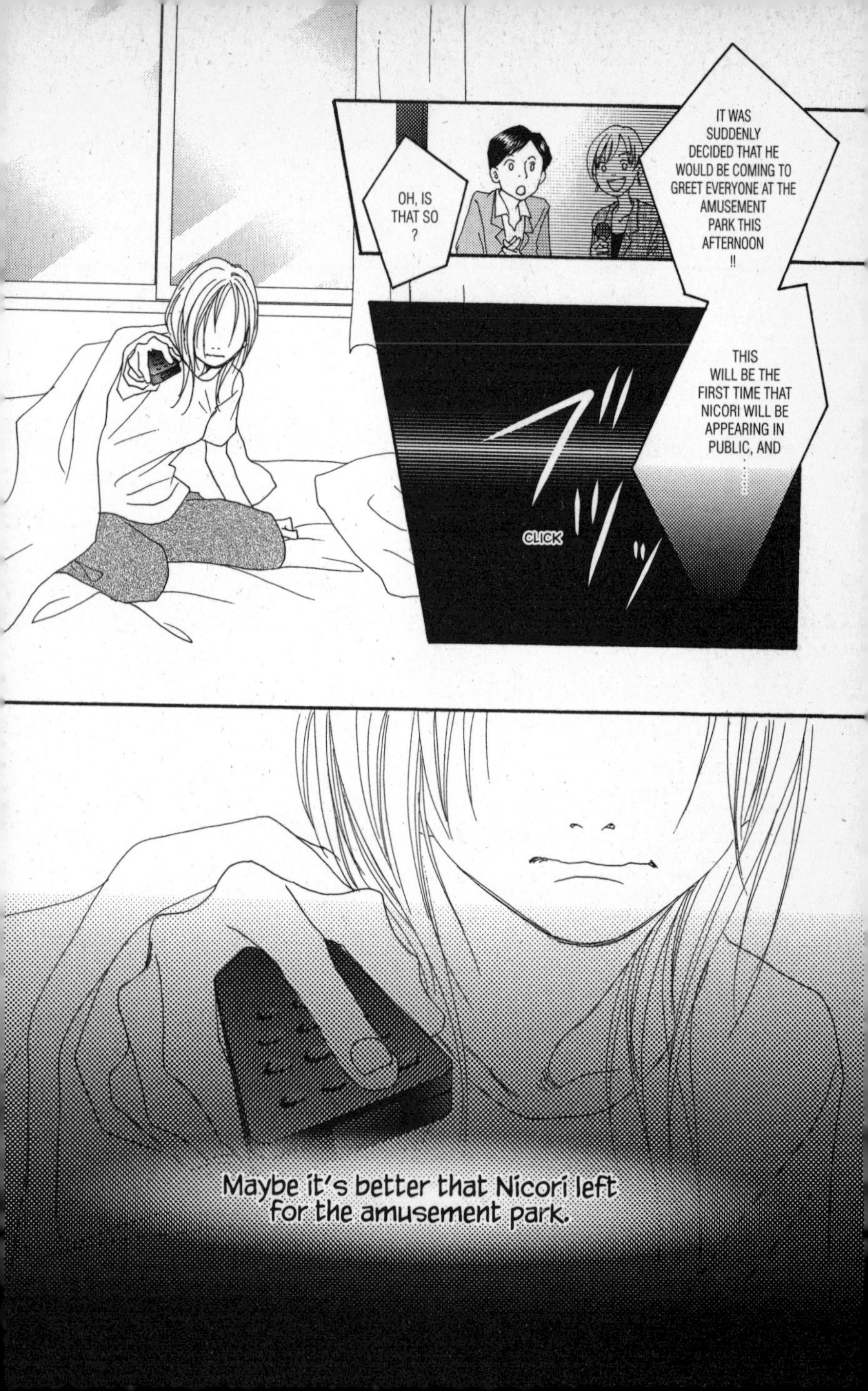
IT WAS SUDDENLY DECIDED THAT HE WOULD BE COMING TO GREET EVERYONE AT THE AMUSEMENT PARK THIS AFTERNOON !!
OH, IS THAT SO ?
THIS WILL BE THE FIRST TIME THAT NICORI WILL BE APPEARING IN PUBLIC, AND ......
CLICK
Maybe it's better that Nicori left for the amusement park.

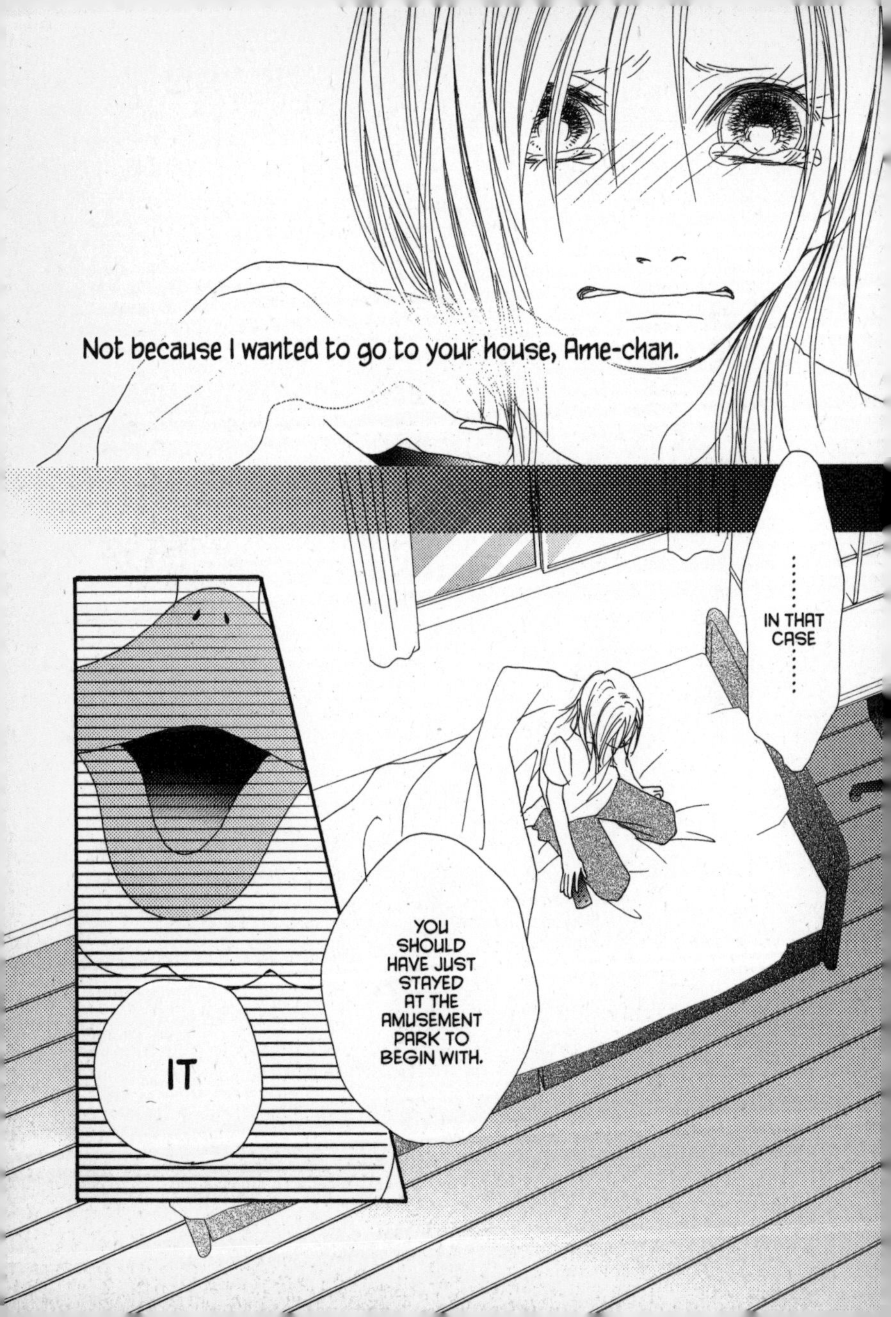

Not because I wanted to go to your house, Ame-chan.
...IN THAT CASE...
YOU SHOULD HAVE JUST STAYED AT THE AMUSEMENT PARK TO BEGIN WITH.
IT

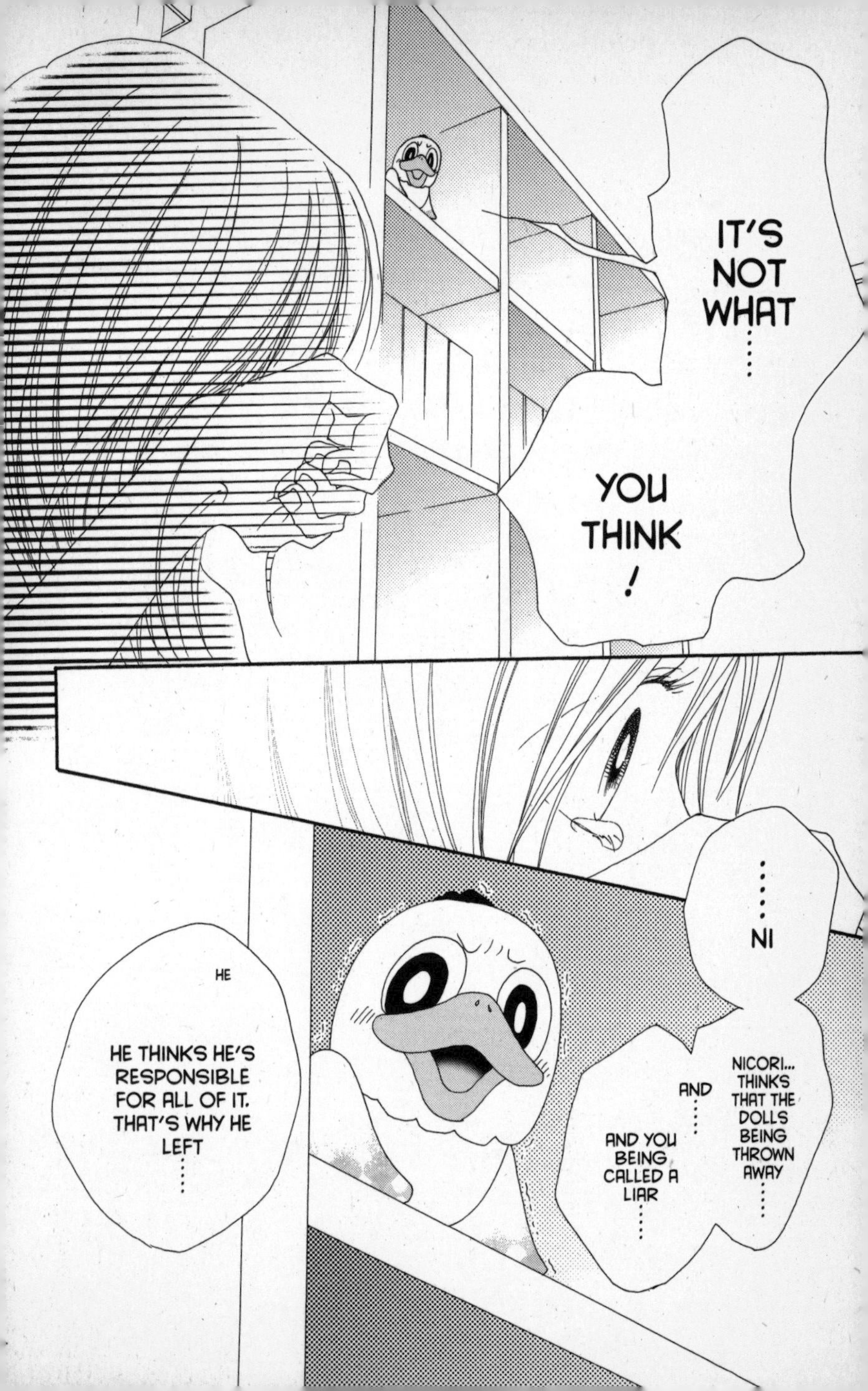
IT'S NOT WHAT ...
YOU THINK!
...NI
NICORI... THINKS THAT THE DOLLS BEING THROWN AWAY ...
AND ...
AND YOU BEING CALLED A LIAR ...
HE
HE THINKS HE'S RESPONSIBLE FOR ALL OF IT. THAT'S WHY HE LEFT ...

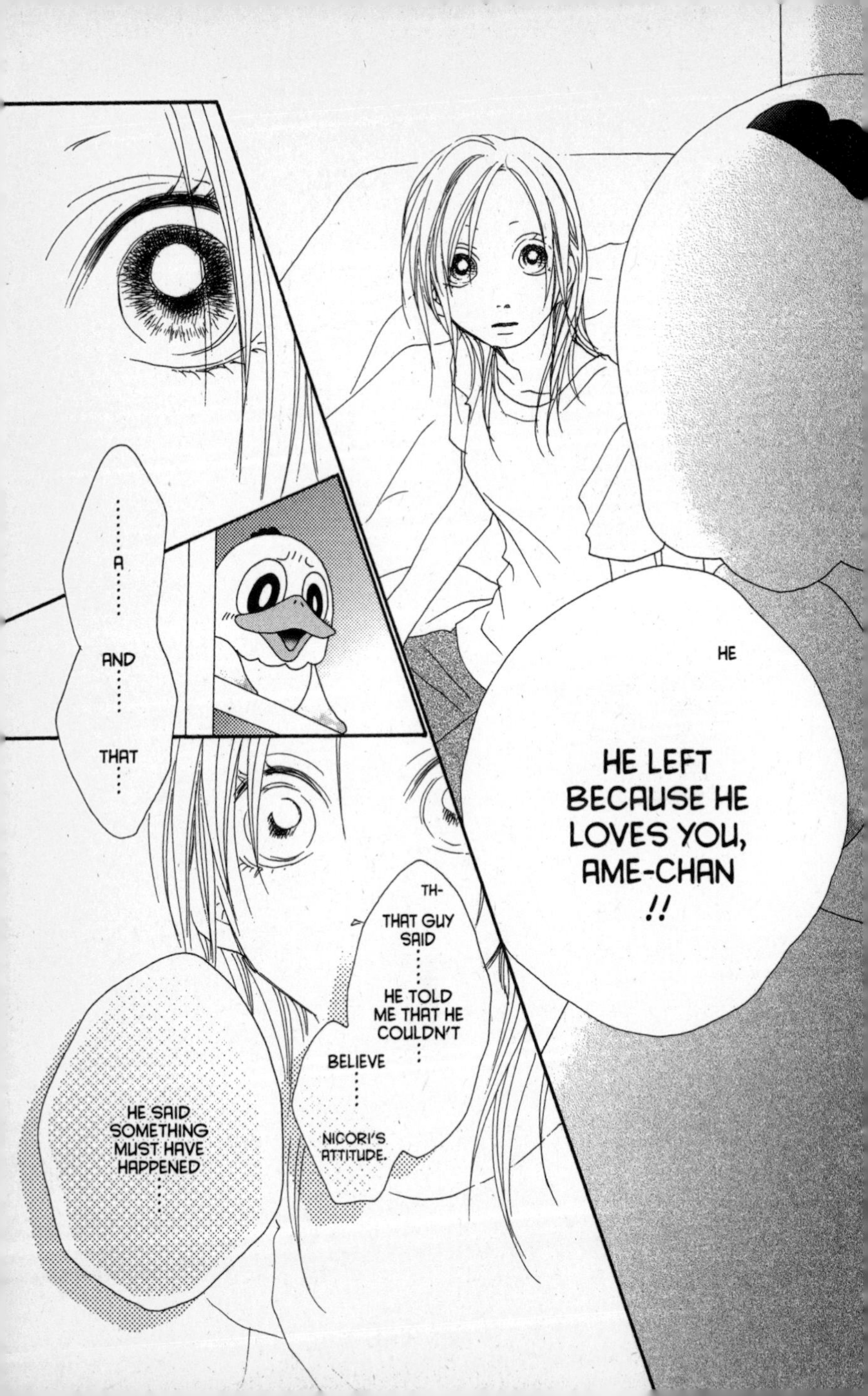
HE
HE LEFT BECAUSE HE LOVES YOU, AME-CHAN !!
......A...... AND...... THAT......
TH- THAT GUY SAID...... HE TOLD ME THAT HE COULDN'T...... BELIEVE...... NICORI'S ATTITUDE.
HE SAID SOMETHING MUST HAVE HAPPENED......

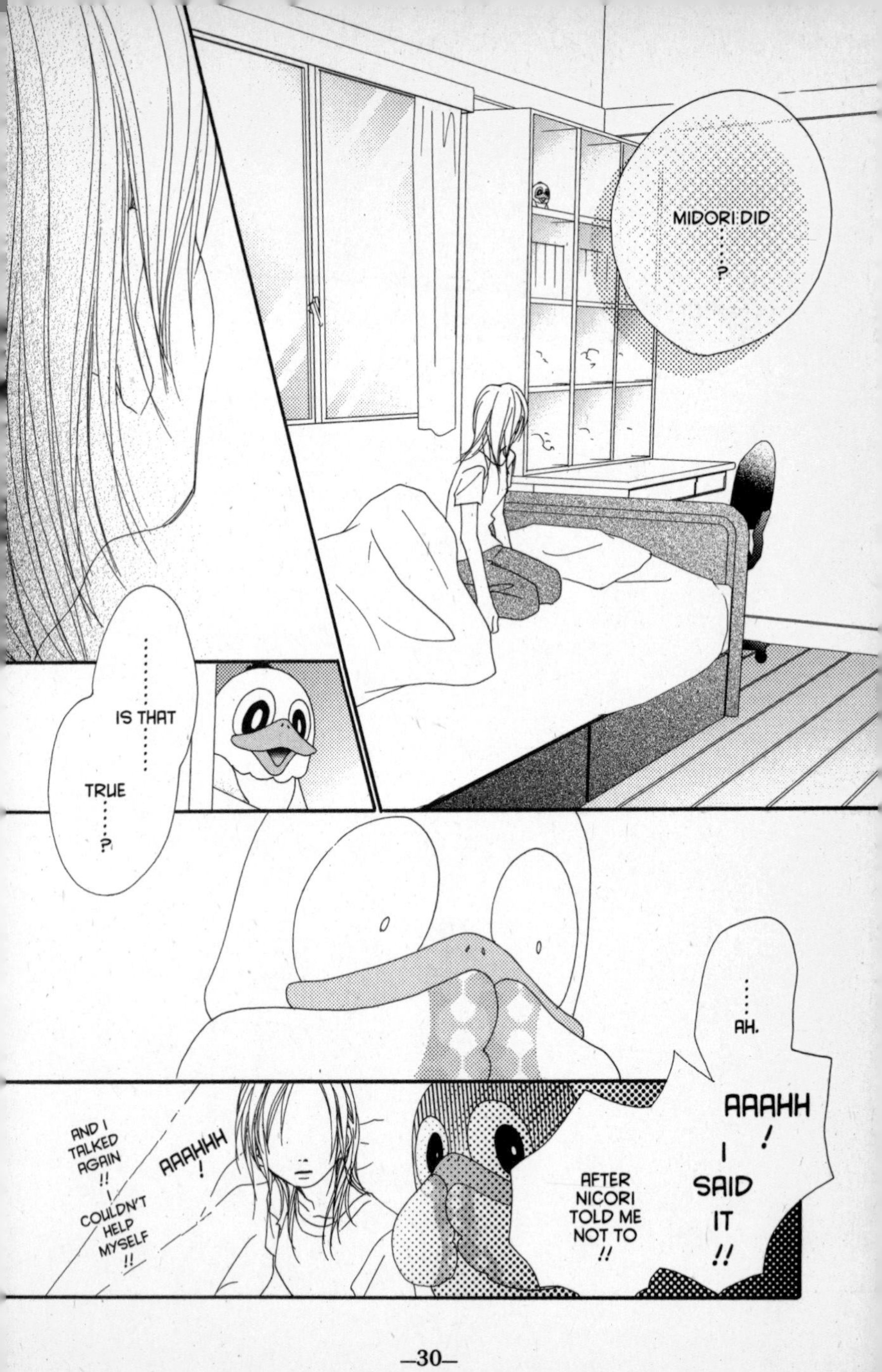
MIDORI DID ......?
...... IS THAT ...... TRUE ......?
...... AH.
AAAHH! I SAID IT!!
AFTER NICORI TOLD ME NOT TO!!
AAAHHH!
AND I TALKED AGAIN!! I COULDN'T HELP MYSELF!!

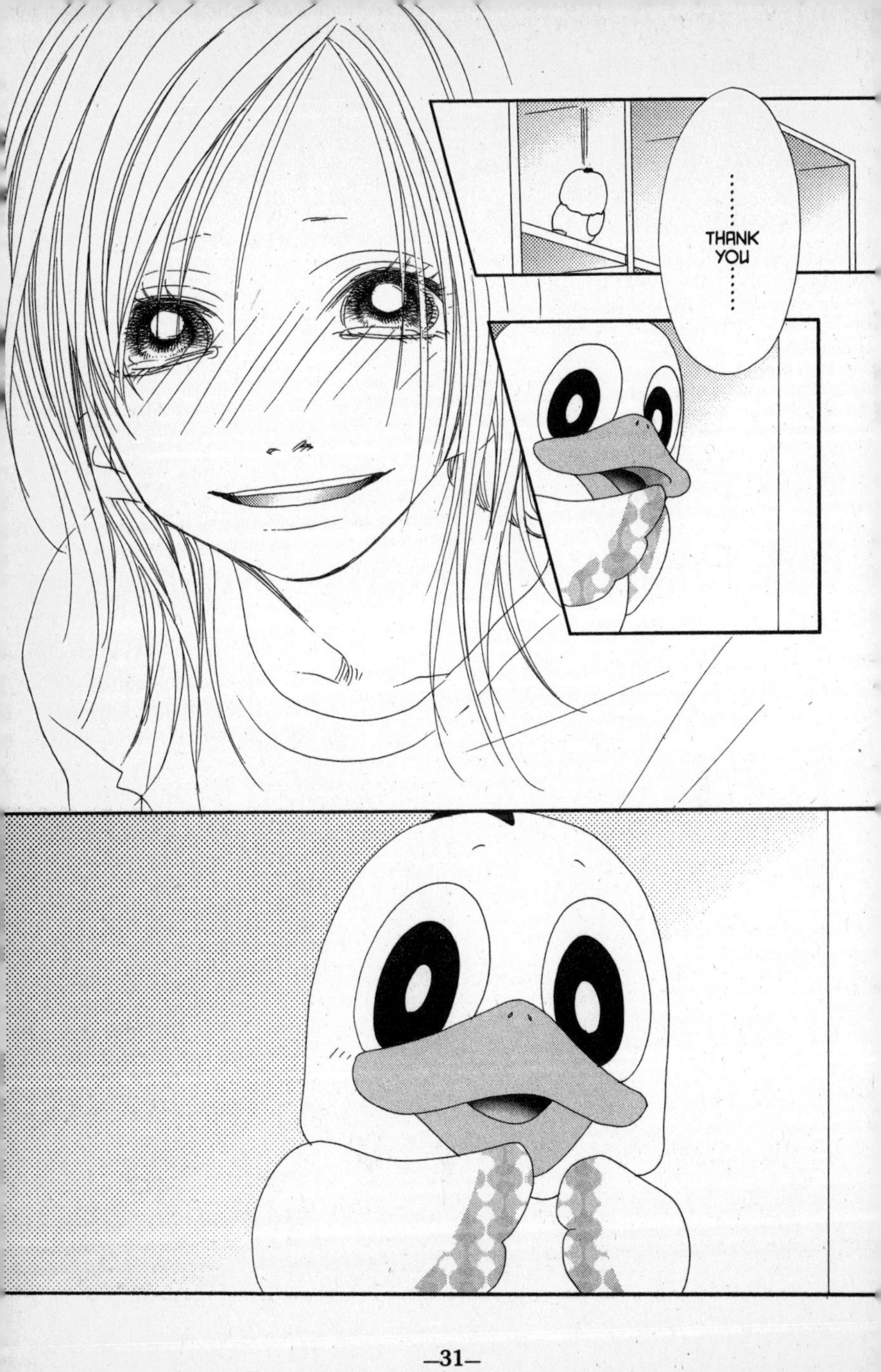
......THANK YOU......

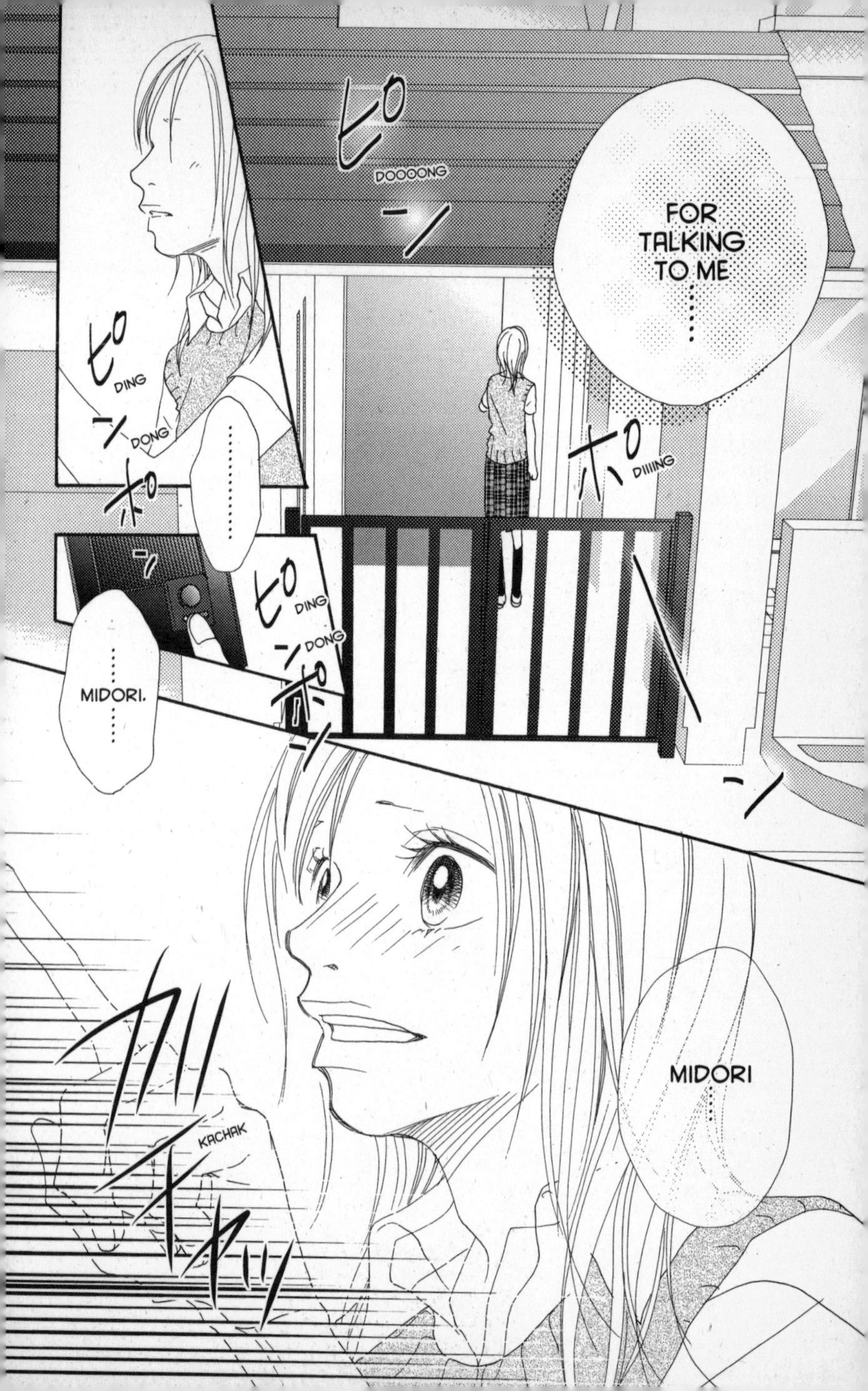
DOOOONG
FOR TALKING TO ME......
DIIING
DING
DONG
......
DING
DONG
......MIDORI......
MIDORI......
KACHAK

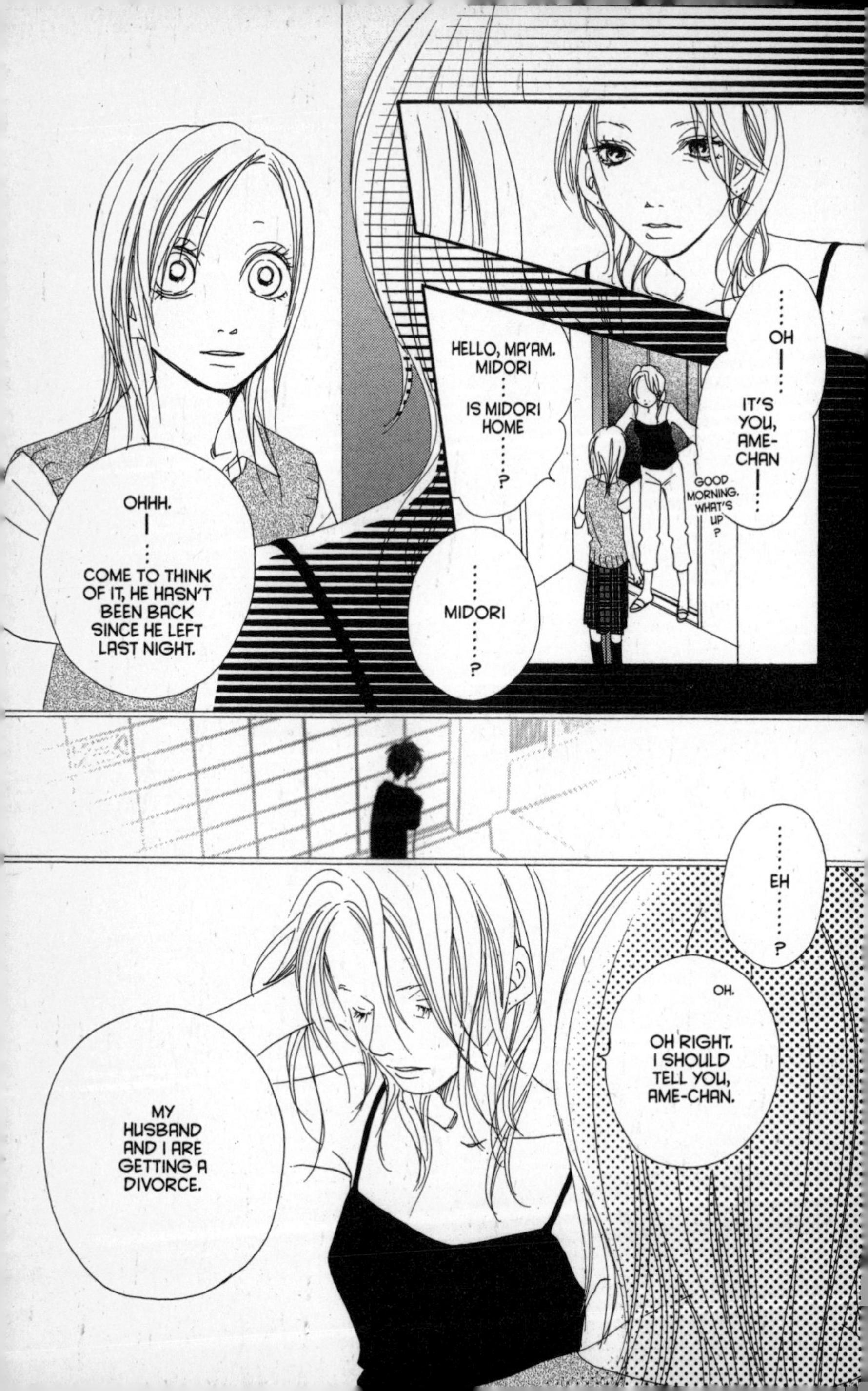
...OH ...IT'S YOU, AME-CHAN ...!
GOOD MORNING. WHAT'S UP?
HELLO, MA'AM. MIDORI ... IS MIDORI HOME ...?
...MIDORI ...?
OHHH. I ... COME TO THINK OF IT, HE HASN'T BEEN BACK SINCE HE LEFT LAST NIGHT.
...EH ...?
OH.
OH RIGHT. I SHOULD TELL YOU, AME-CHAN.
MY HUSBAND AND I ARE GETTING A DIVORCE.

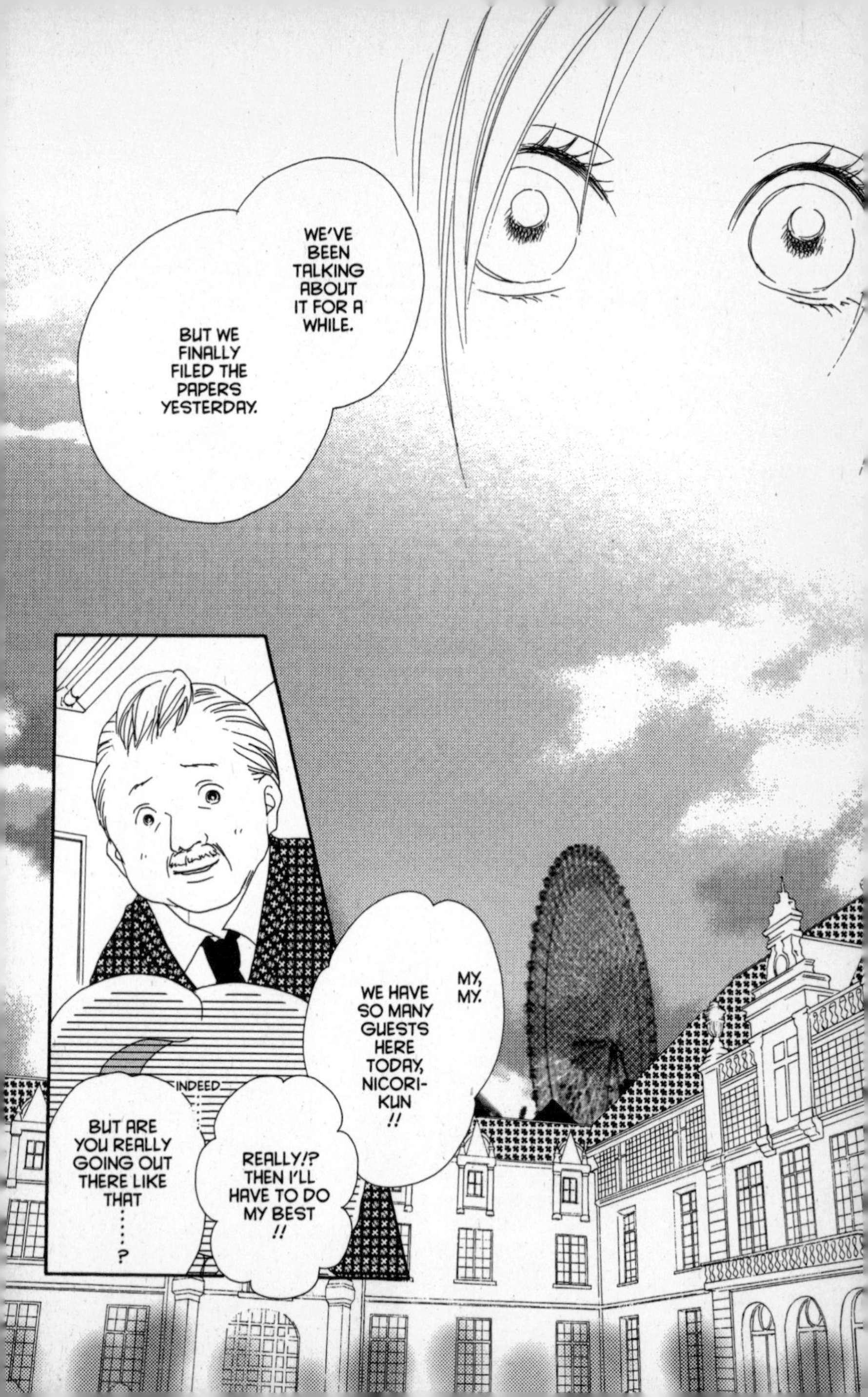
WE'VE BEEN TALKING ABOUT IT FOR A WHILE.
BUT WE FINALLY FILED THE PAPERS YESTERDAY.
MY, MY.
WE HAVE SO MANY GUESTS HERE TODAY, NICORI-KUN!!
REALLY!? THEN I'LL HAVE TO DO MY BEST!!
INDEED......
BUT ARE YOU REALLY GOING OUT THERE LIKE THAT.....?

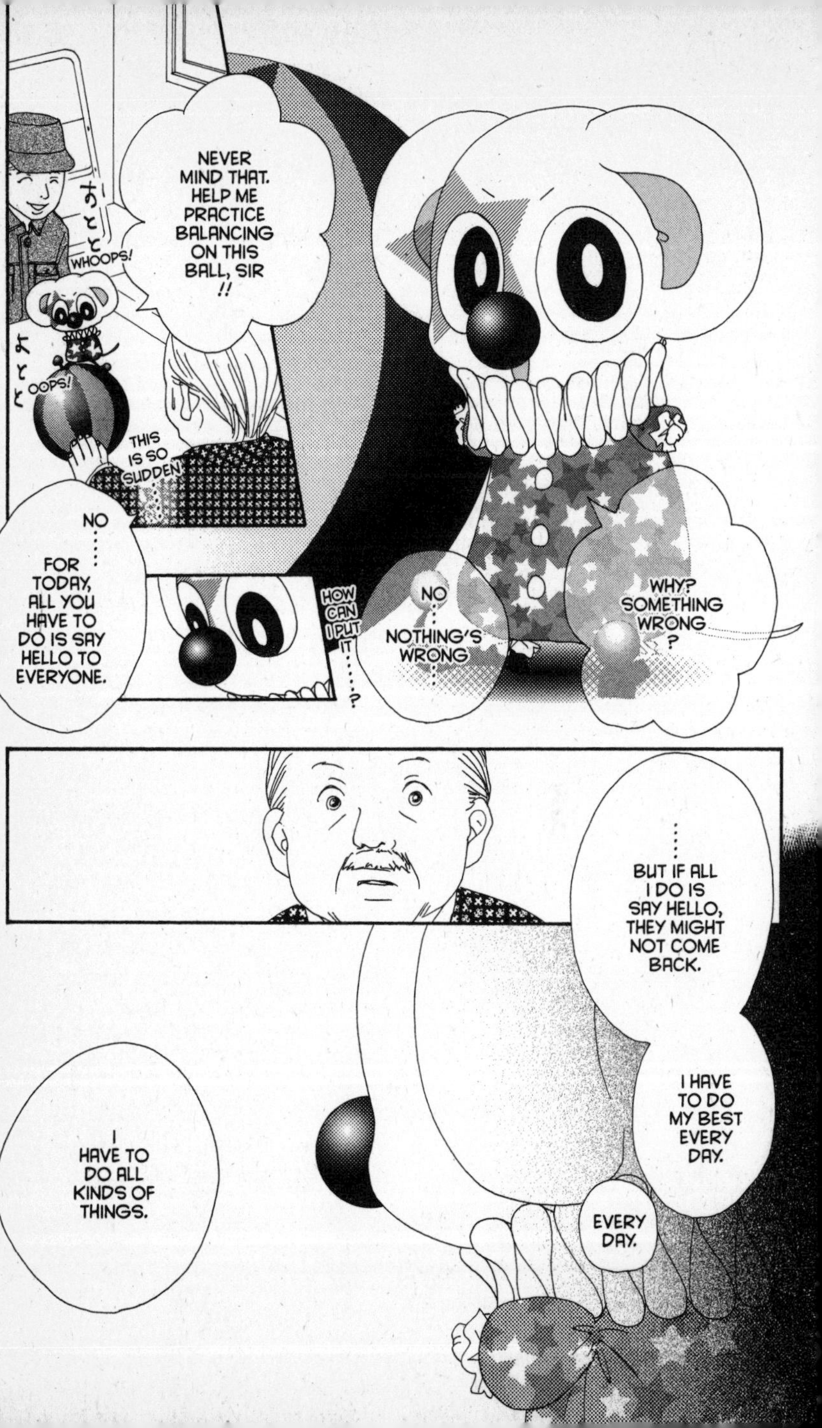
NEVER MIND THAT. HELP ME PRACTICE BALANCING ON THIS BALL, SIR!!
おとと
WHOOPS!
よとと
OOPS!
THIS IS SO SUDDEN
WHY? SOMETHING WRONG?
NO... NOTHING'S WRONG...
HOW CAN I PUT IT.....?
NO... FOR TODAY, ALL YOU HAVE TO DO IS SAY HELLO TO EVERYONE.
..... BUT IF ALL I DO IS SAY HELLO, THEY MIGHT NOT COME BACK.
I HAVE TO DO MY BEST EVERY DAY.
EVERY DAY.
I HAVE TO DO ALL KINDS OF THINGS.

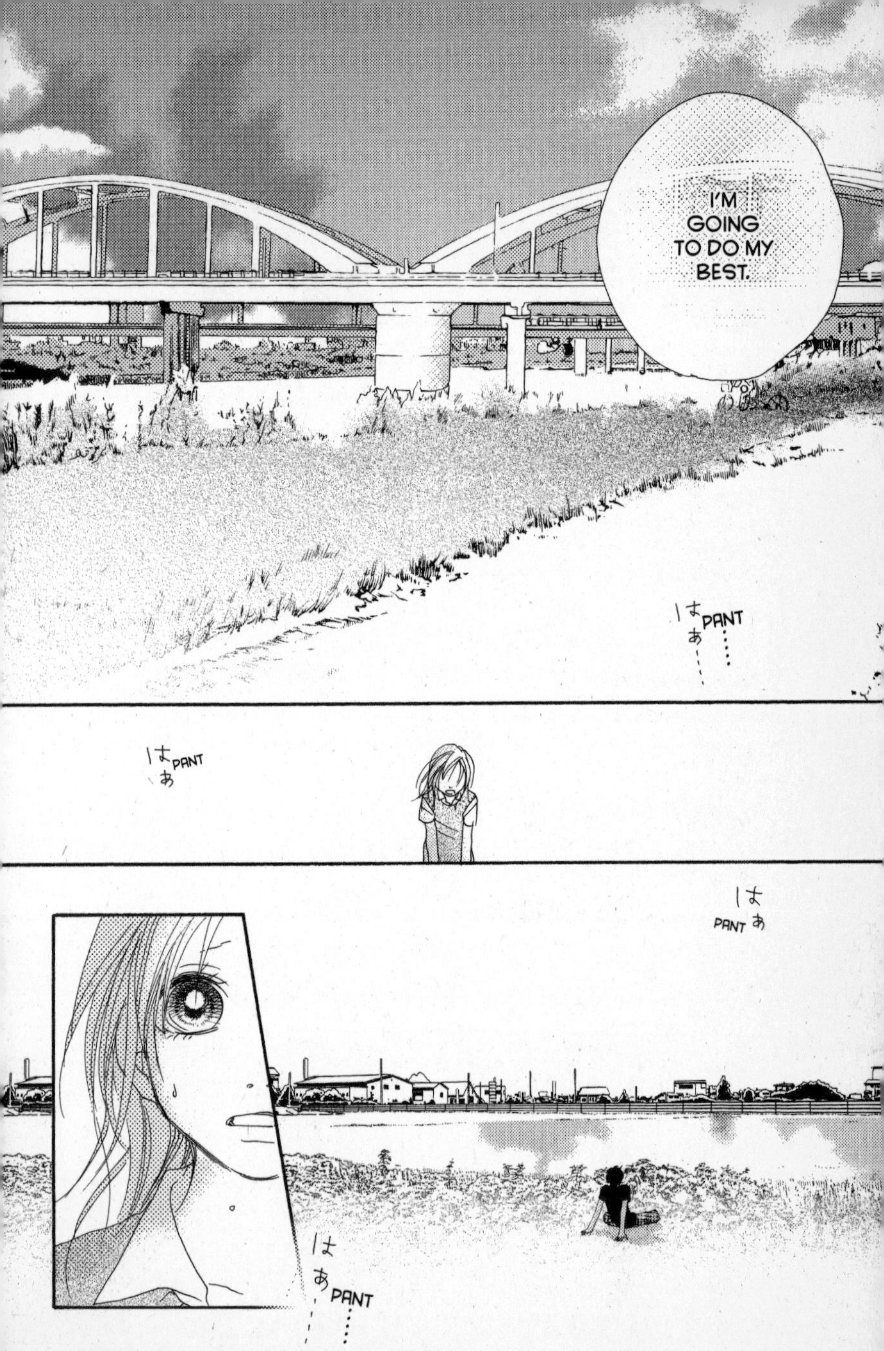
I'M GOING TO DO MY BEST.
はあ PANT……
はあ PANT
はあ PANT
はあ PANT……

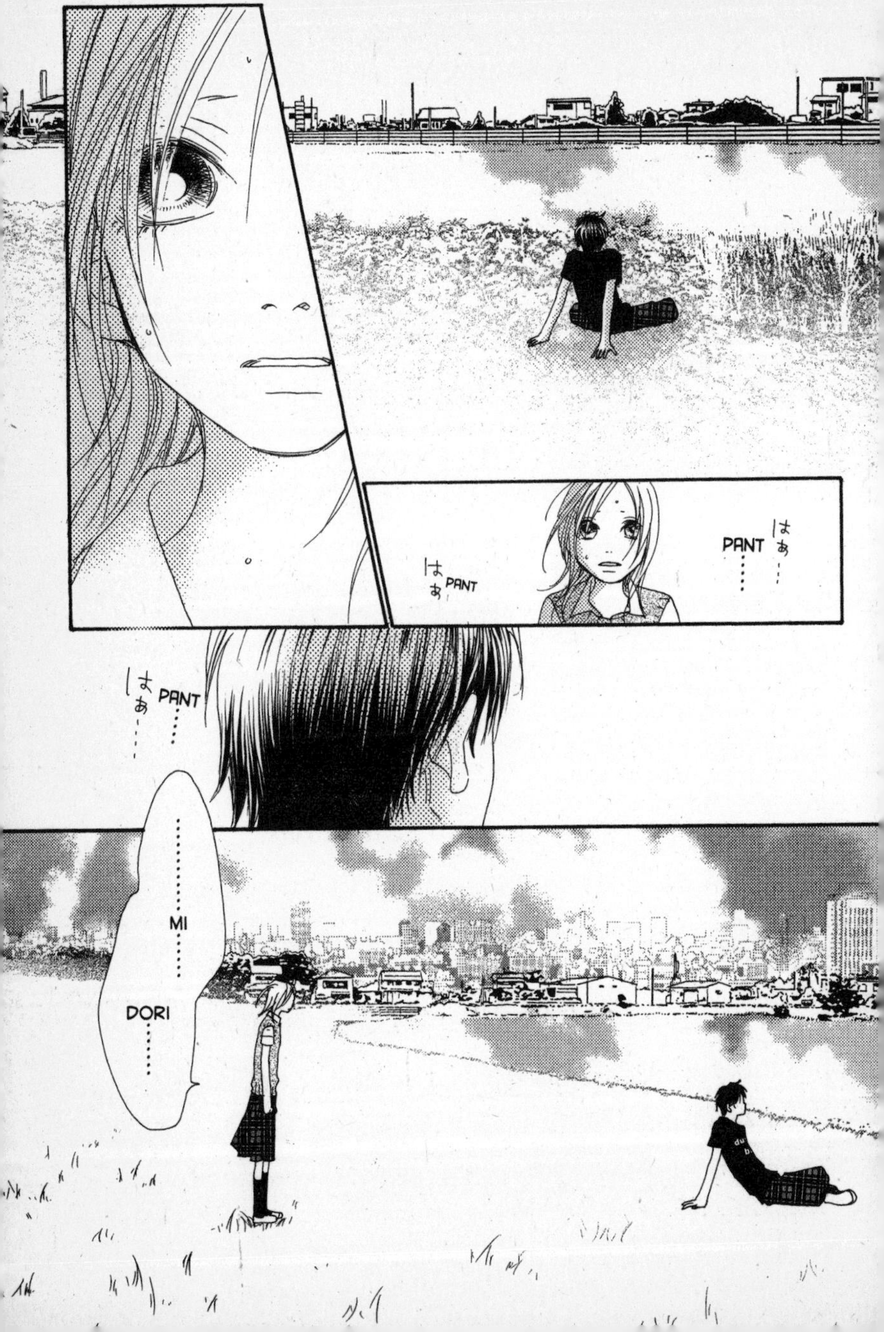
はぁ……
PANT……
はぁ
PANT
はぁ……
PANT……
……MI……DORI……

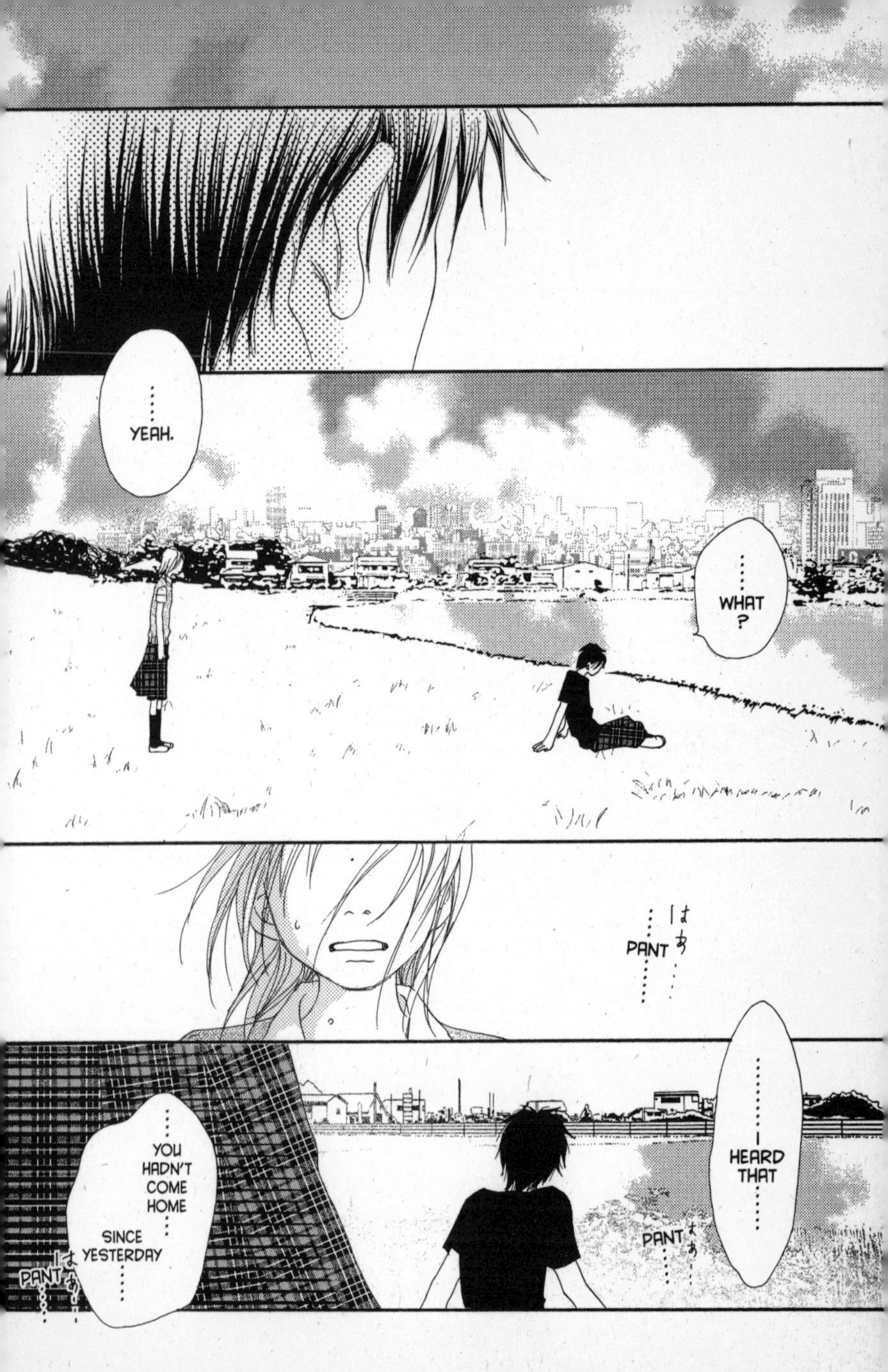
…YEAH.
…WHAT?
はあ… PANT…
…I HEARD THAT…
はあ… PANT…
…YOU HADN'T COME HOME… SINCE YESTERDAY…
はあ… PANT…

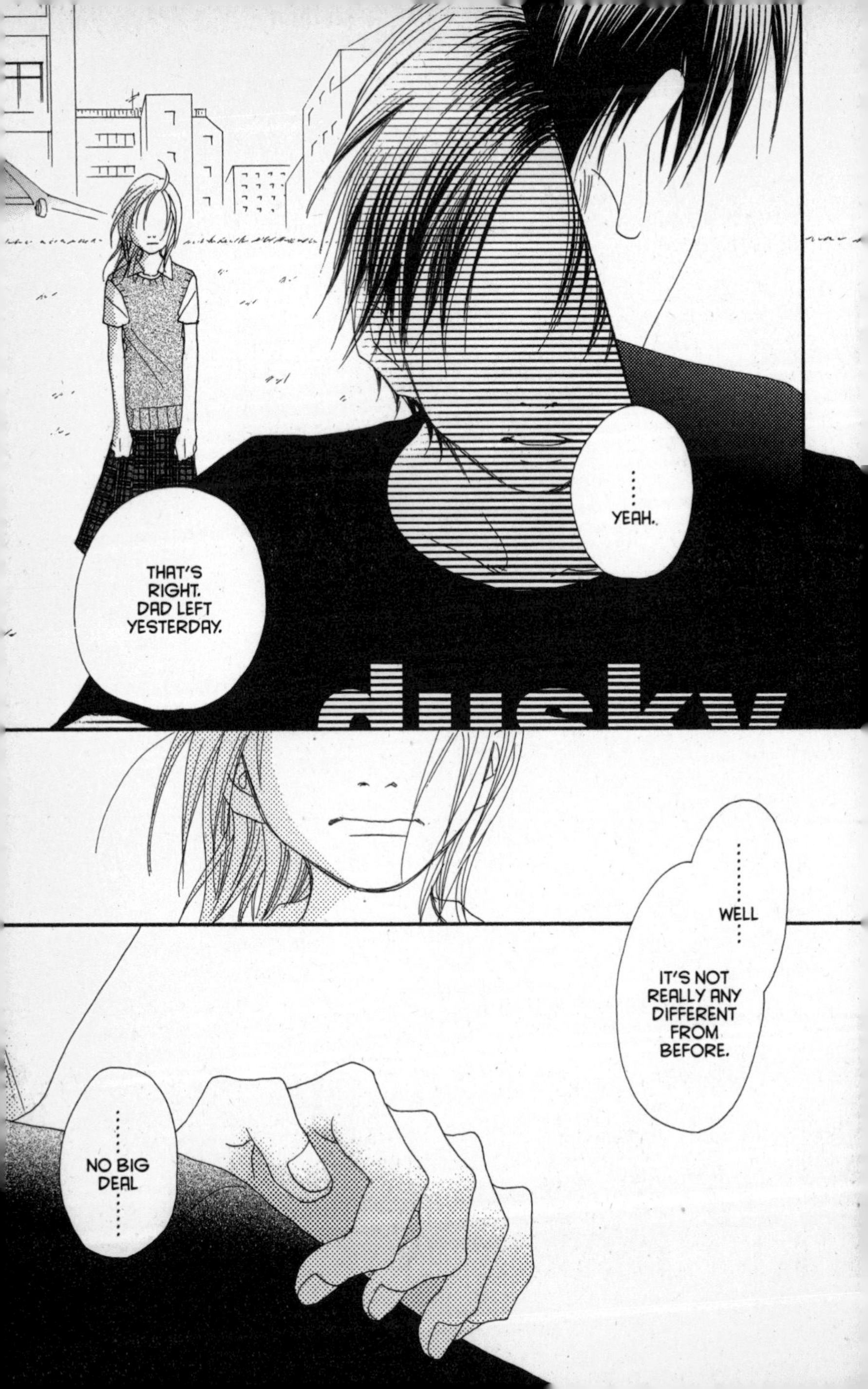
......YEAH.
THAT'S RIGHT. DAD LEFT YESTERDAY.
......WELL......
IT'S NOT REALLY ANY DIFFERENT FROM BEFORE.
......NO BIG DEAL......

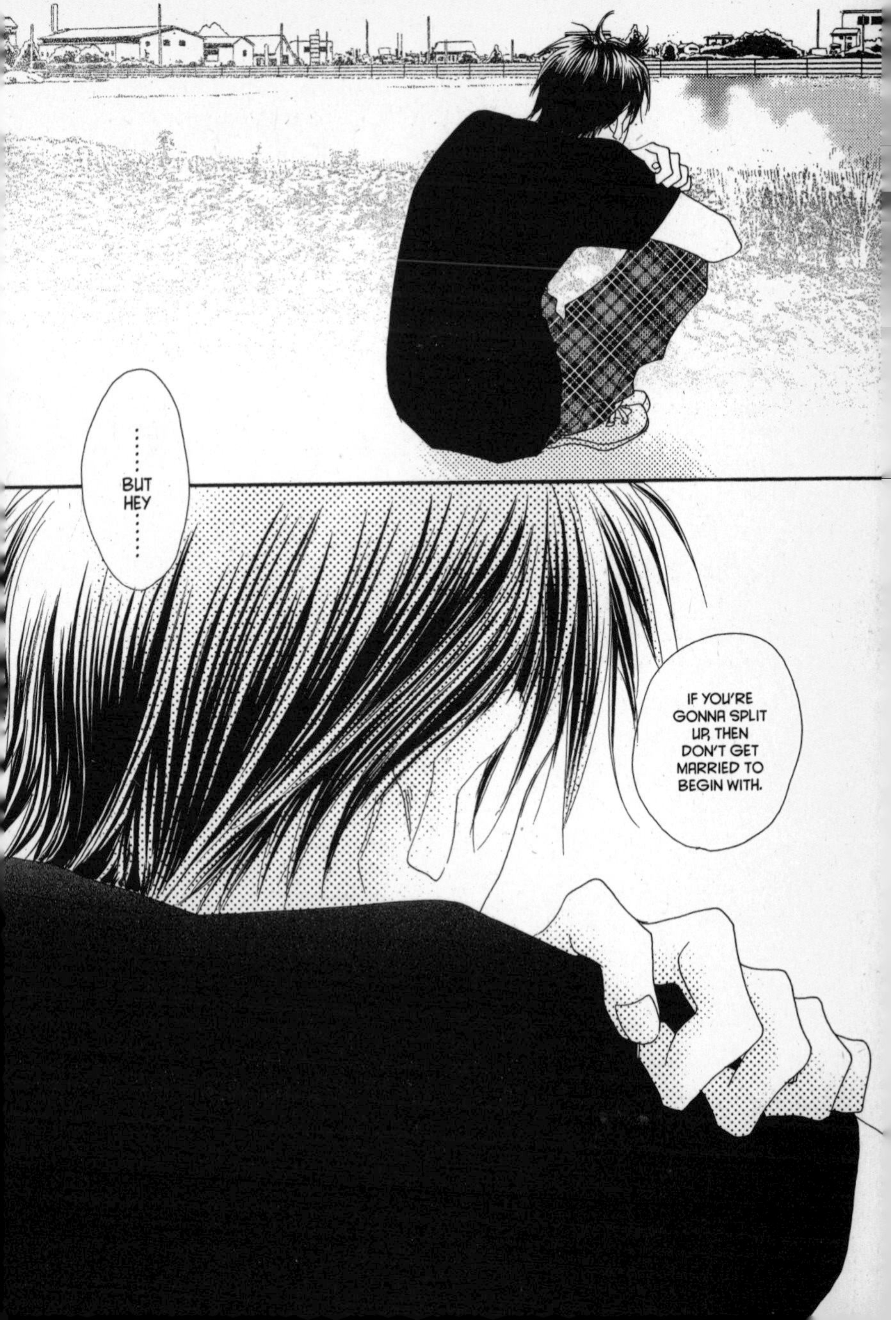
……BUT HEY……
IF YOU'RE GONNA SPLIT UP, THEN DON'T GET MARRIED TO BEGIN WITH.

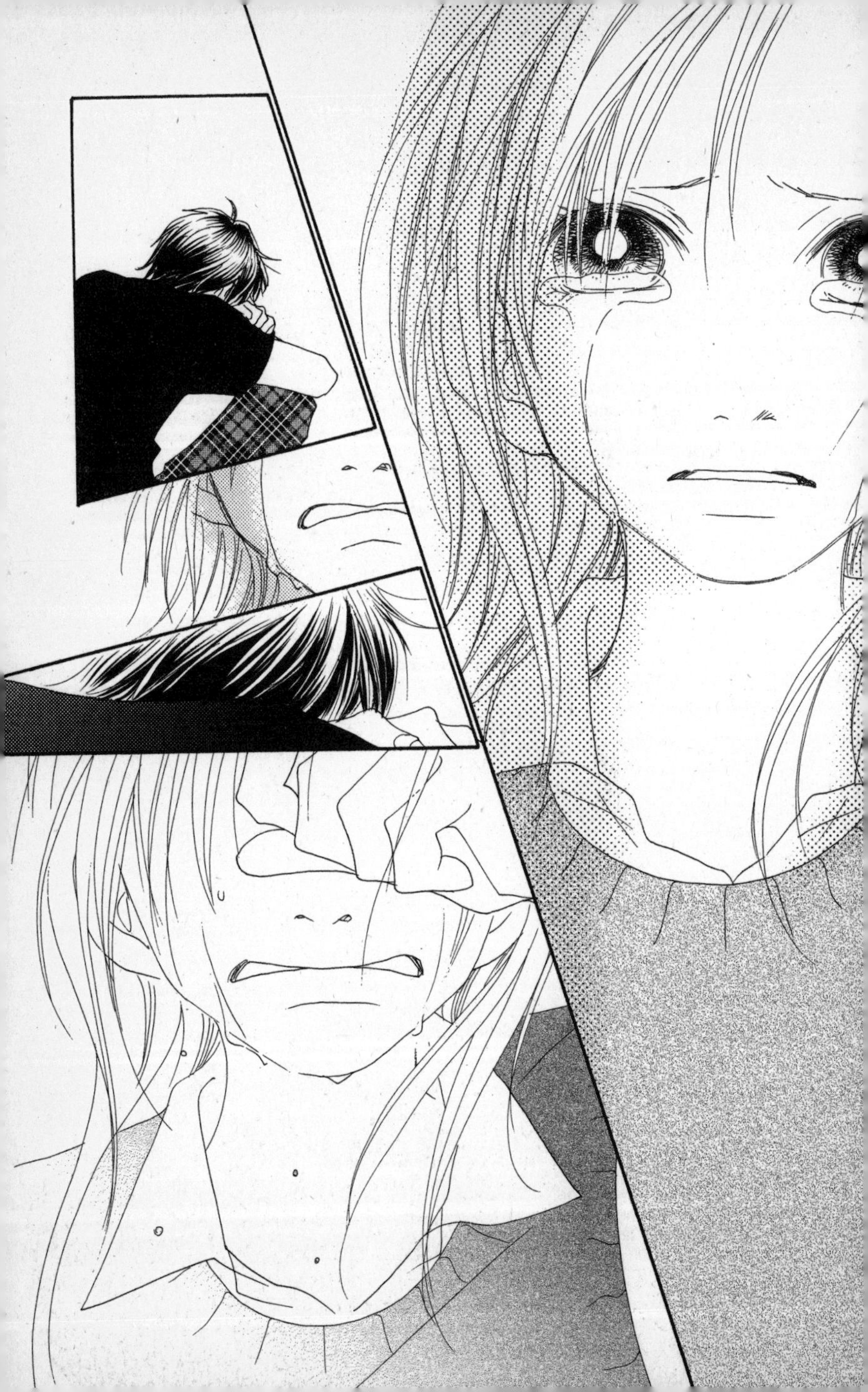

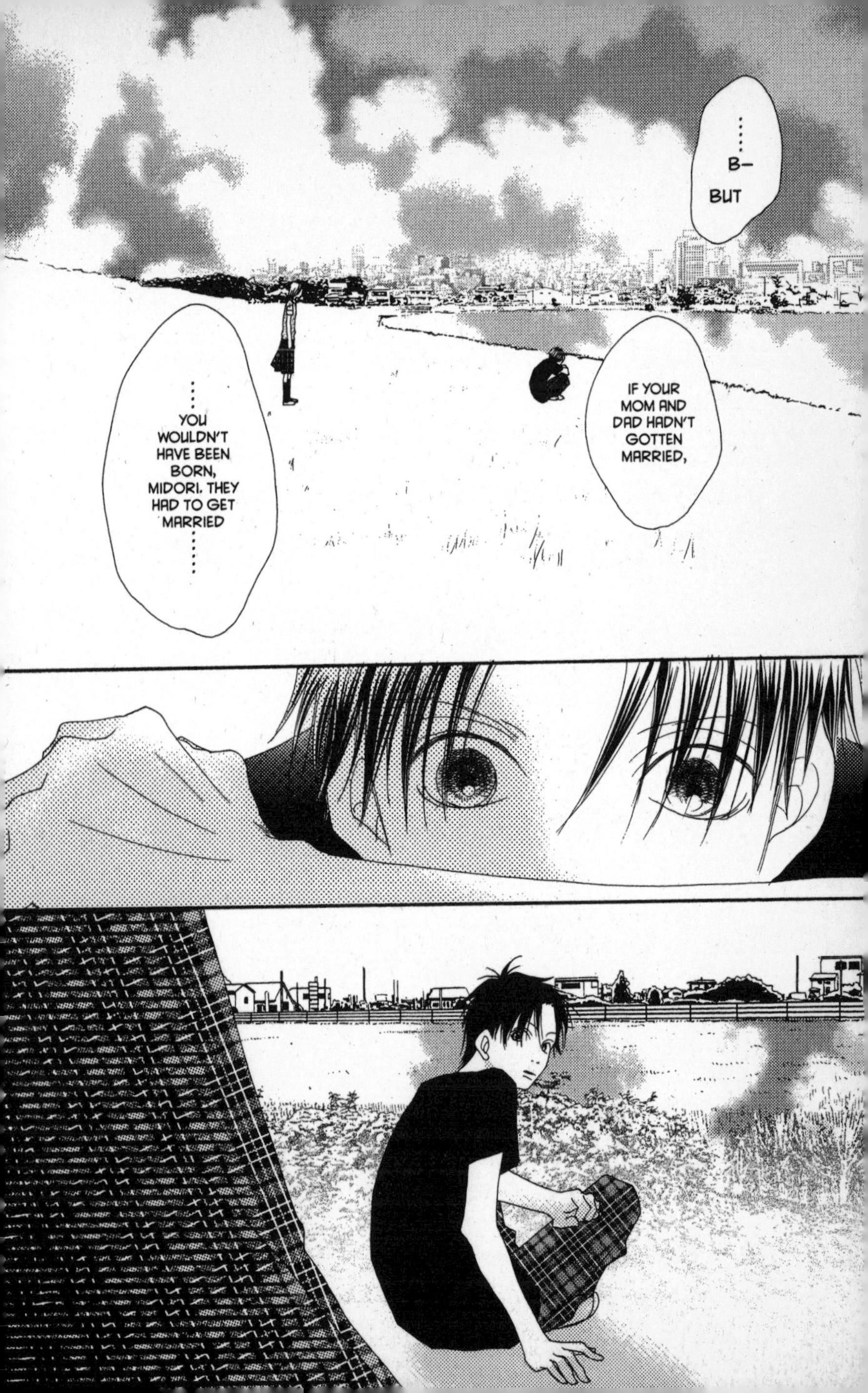
.....B– BUT
IF YOUR MOM AND DAD HADN'T GOTTEN MARRIED,
.....YOU WOULDN'T HAVE BEEN BORN, MIDORI. THEY HAD TO GET MARRIED.....

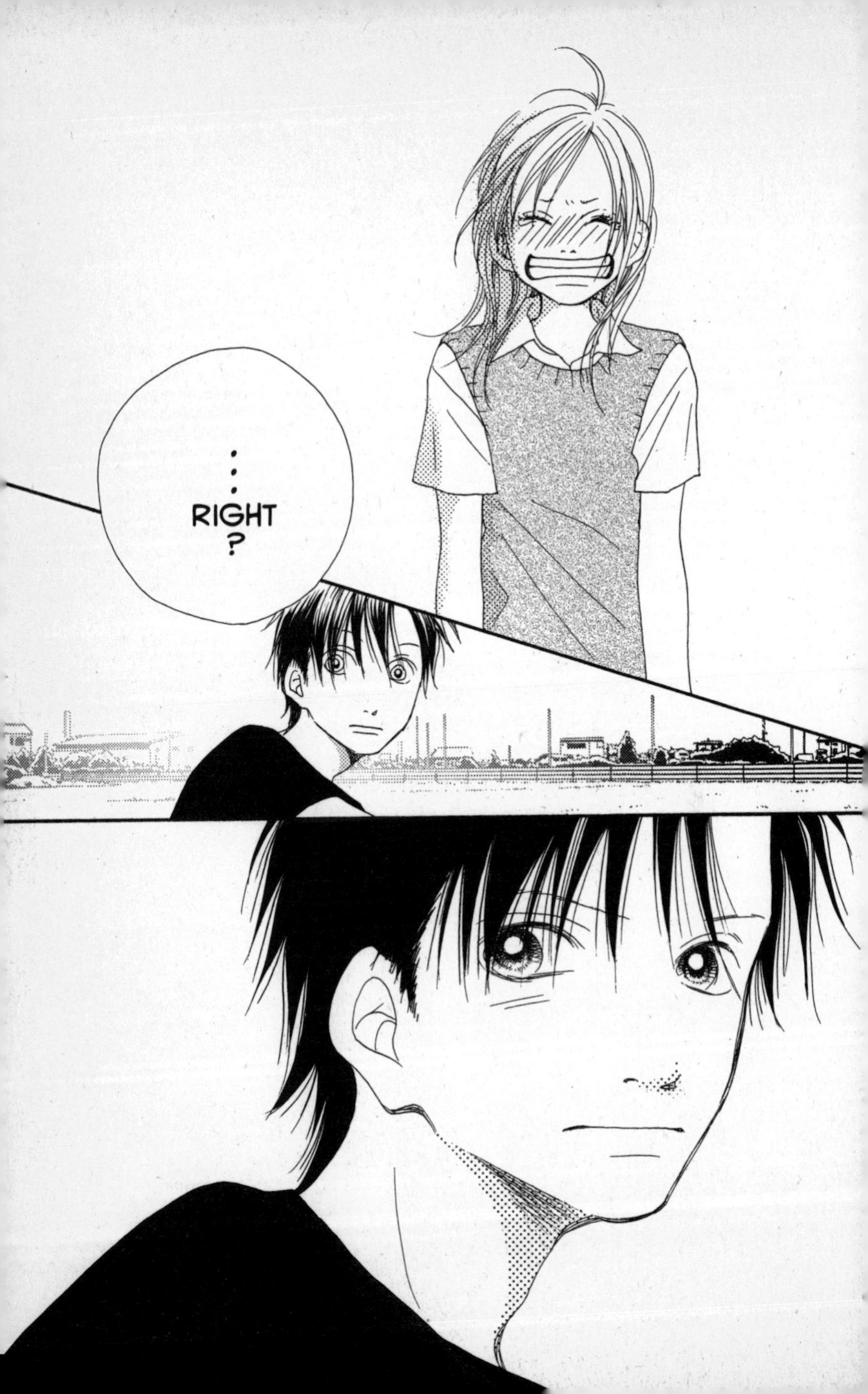
...RIGHT?

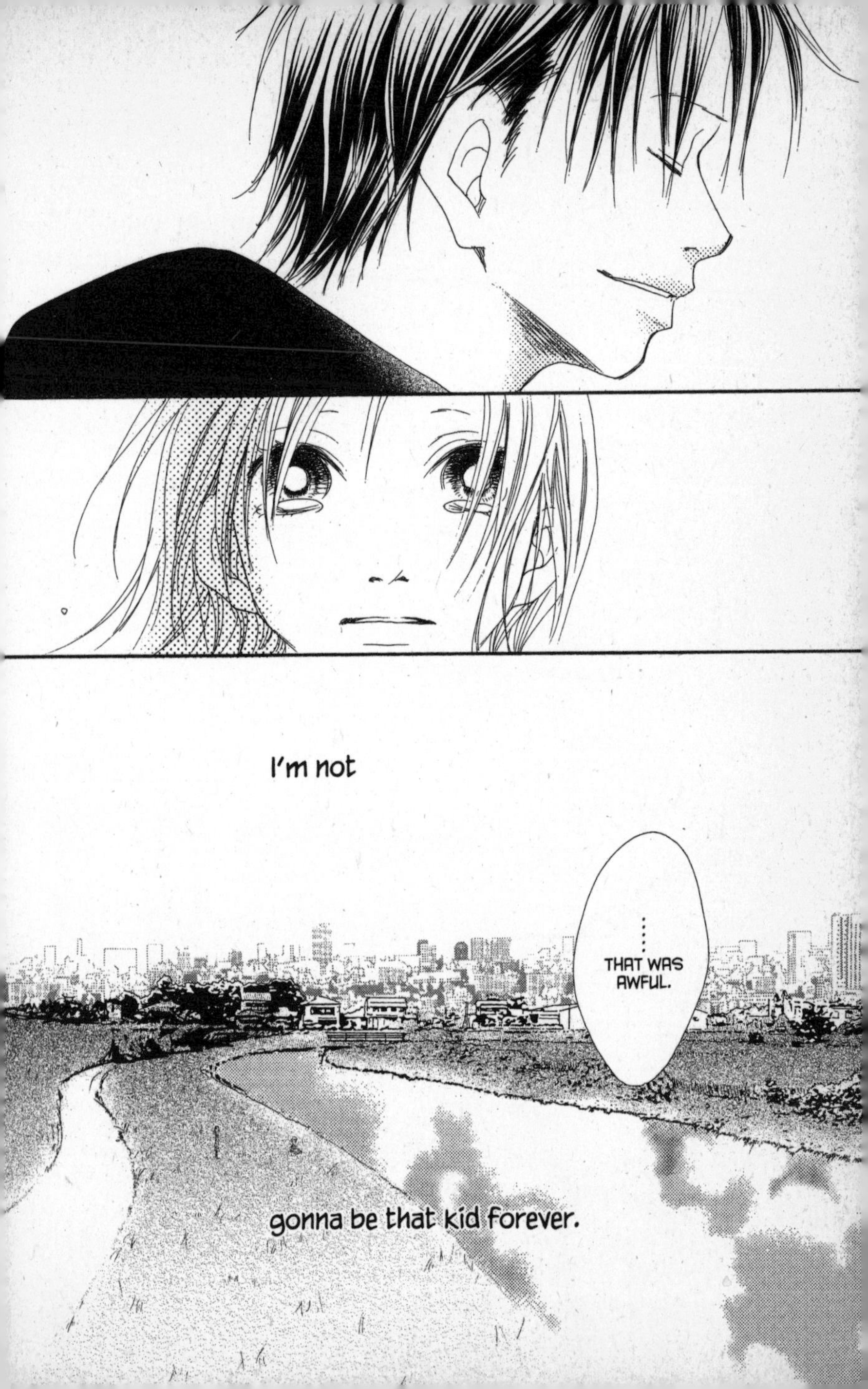
I'm not
...... THAT WAS AWFUL.
gonna be that kid forever.

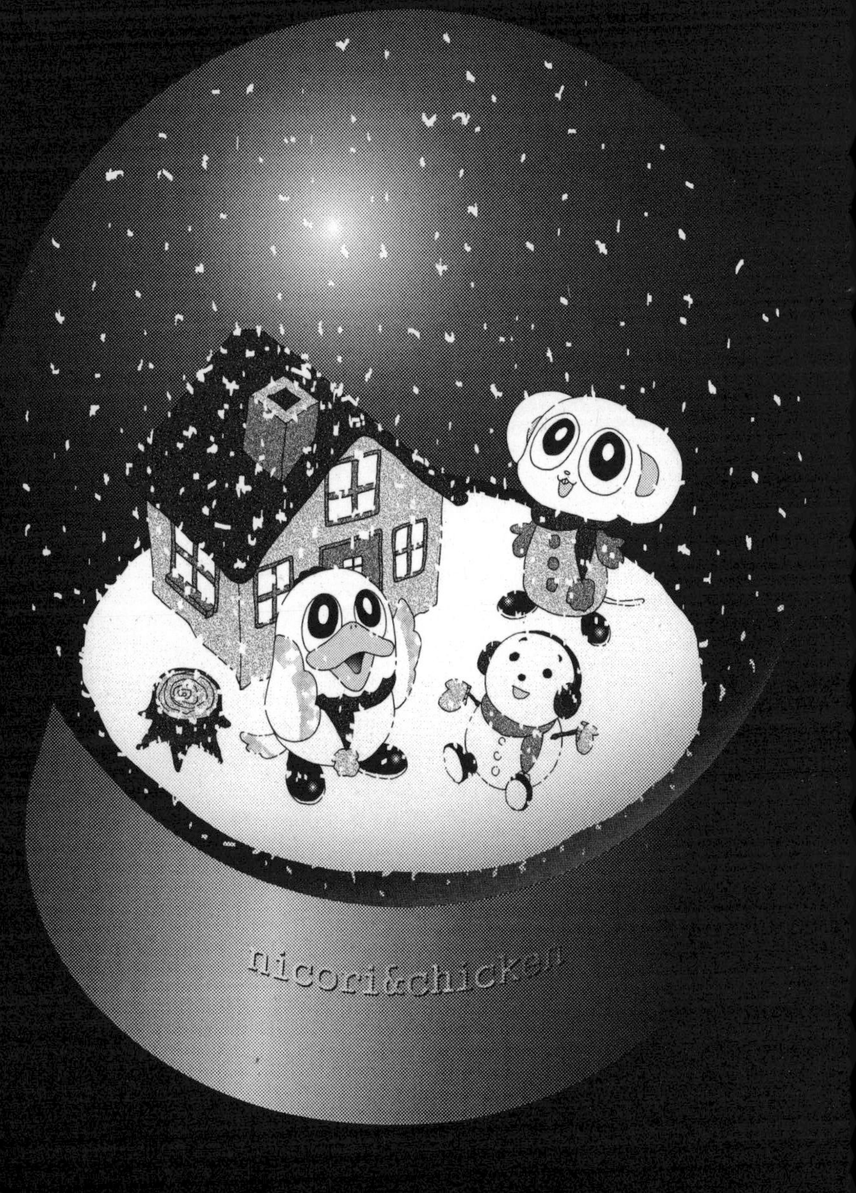
nicori&chicken

Stage: 14

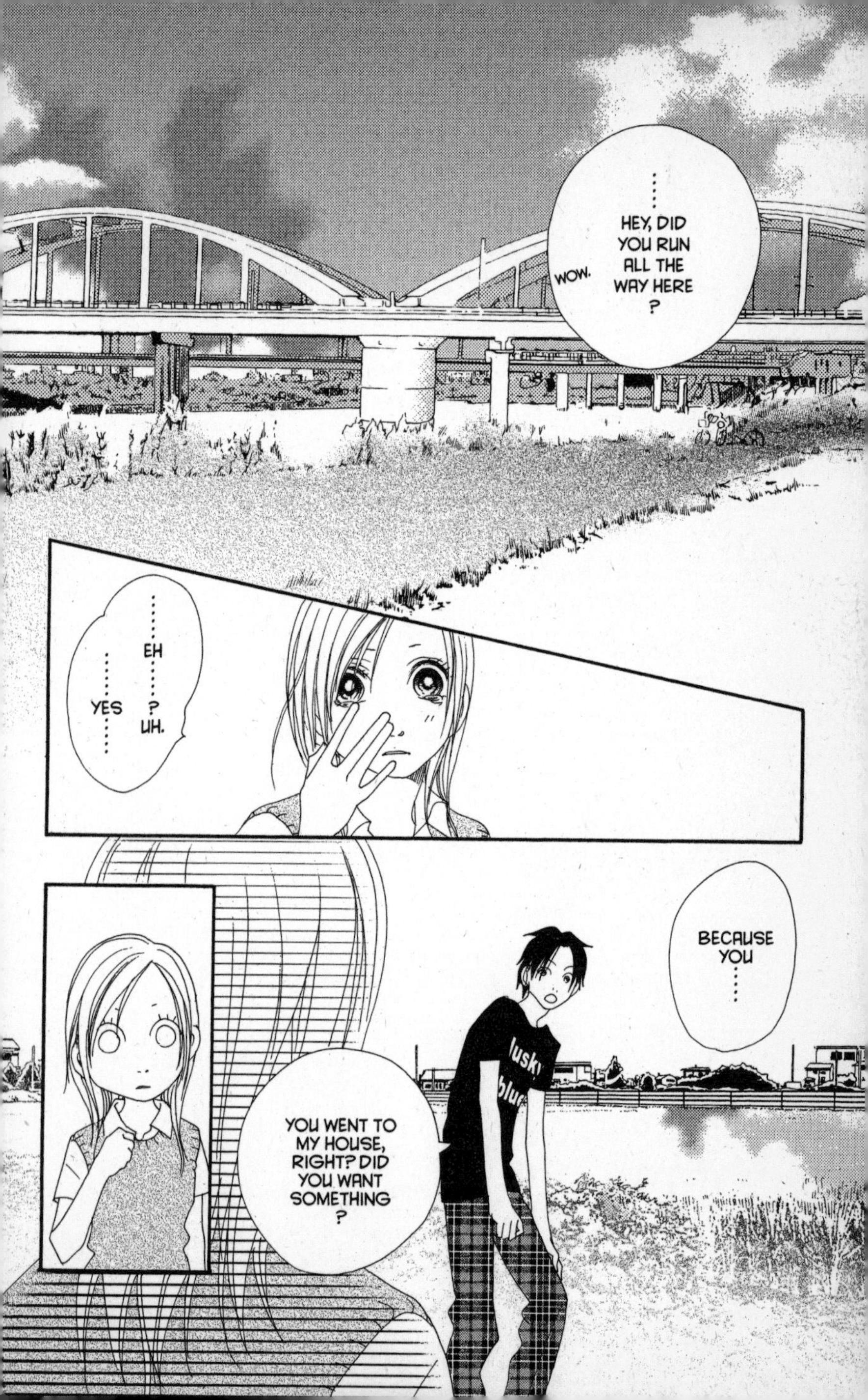

…… HEY, DID YOU RUN ALL THE WAY HERE?
WOW.
…… EH…… ? UH.
…… YES ……
BECAUSE YOU ……
YOU WENT TO MY HOUSE, RIGHT? DID YOU WANT SOMETHING?

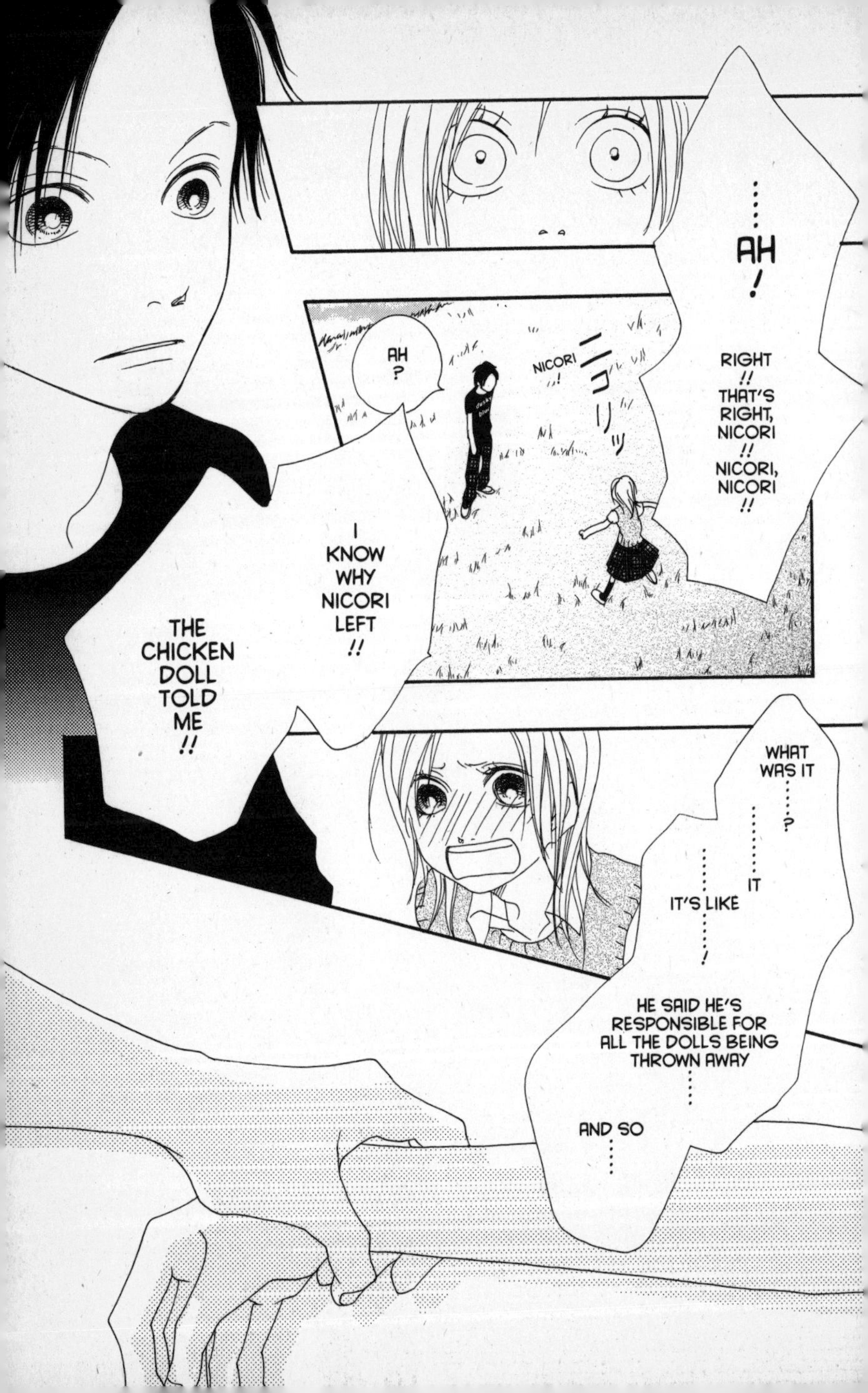

....AH!
RIGHT!! THAT'S RIGHT, NICORI!! NICORI, NICORI!!
ニコリッ
NICORI!!
AH?
I KNOW WHY NICORI LEFT!!
THE CHICKEN DOLL TOLD ME!!
WHAT WAS IT.....?
......IT
IT'S LIKE......!
HE SAID HE'S RESPONSIBLE FOR ALL THE DOLLS BEING THROWN AWAY......
AND SO.....

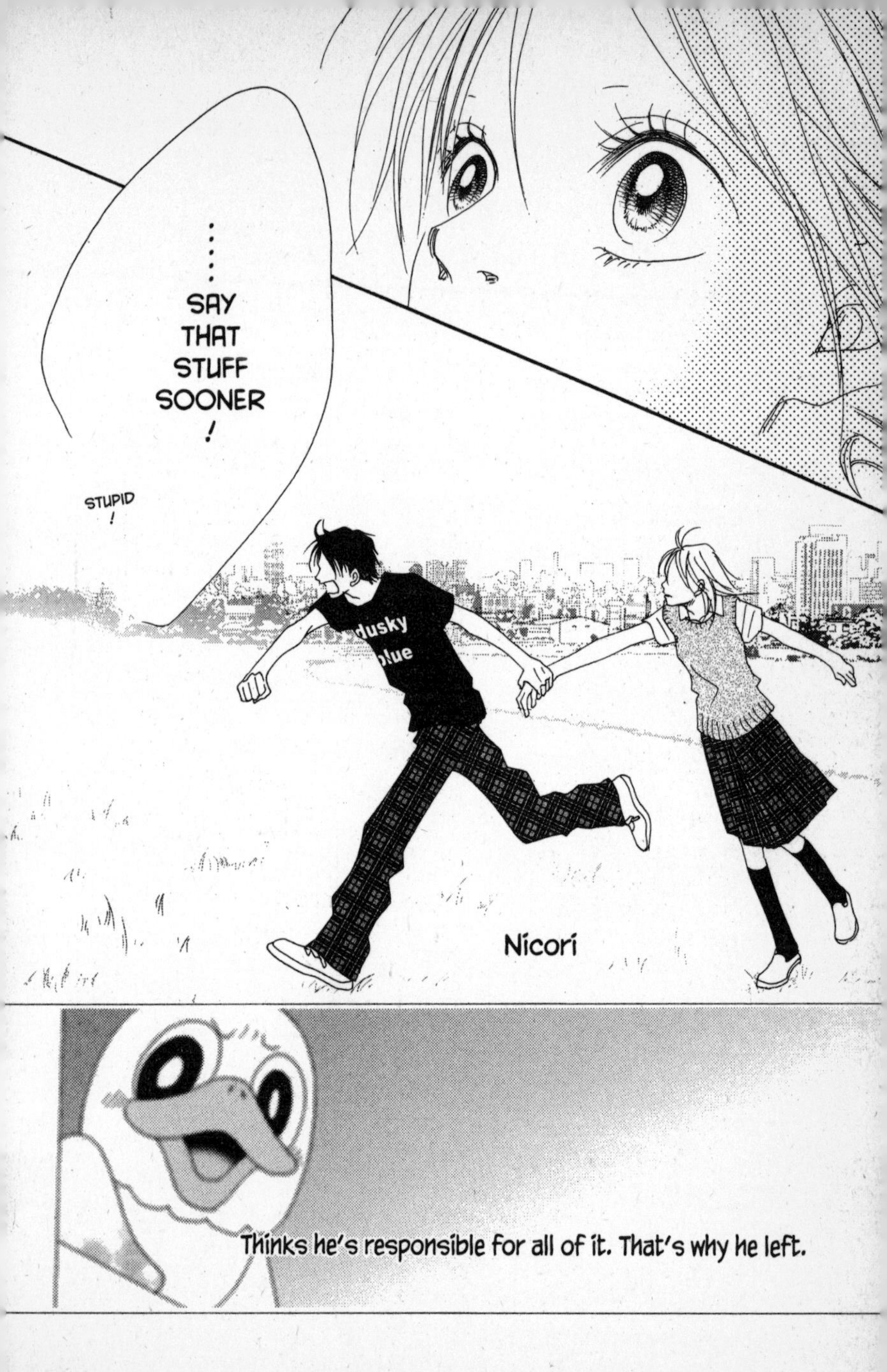
.... SAY THAT STUFF SOONER !
STUPID !
dusky blue
Nicori
Thinks he's responsible for all of it. That's why he left.

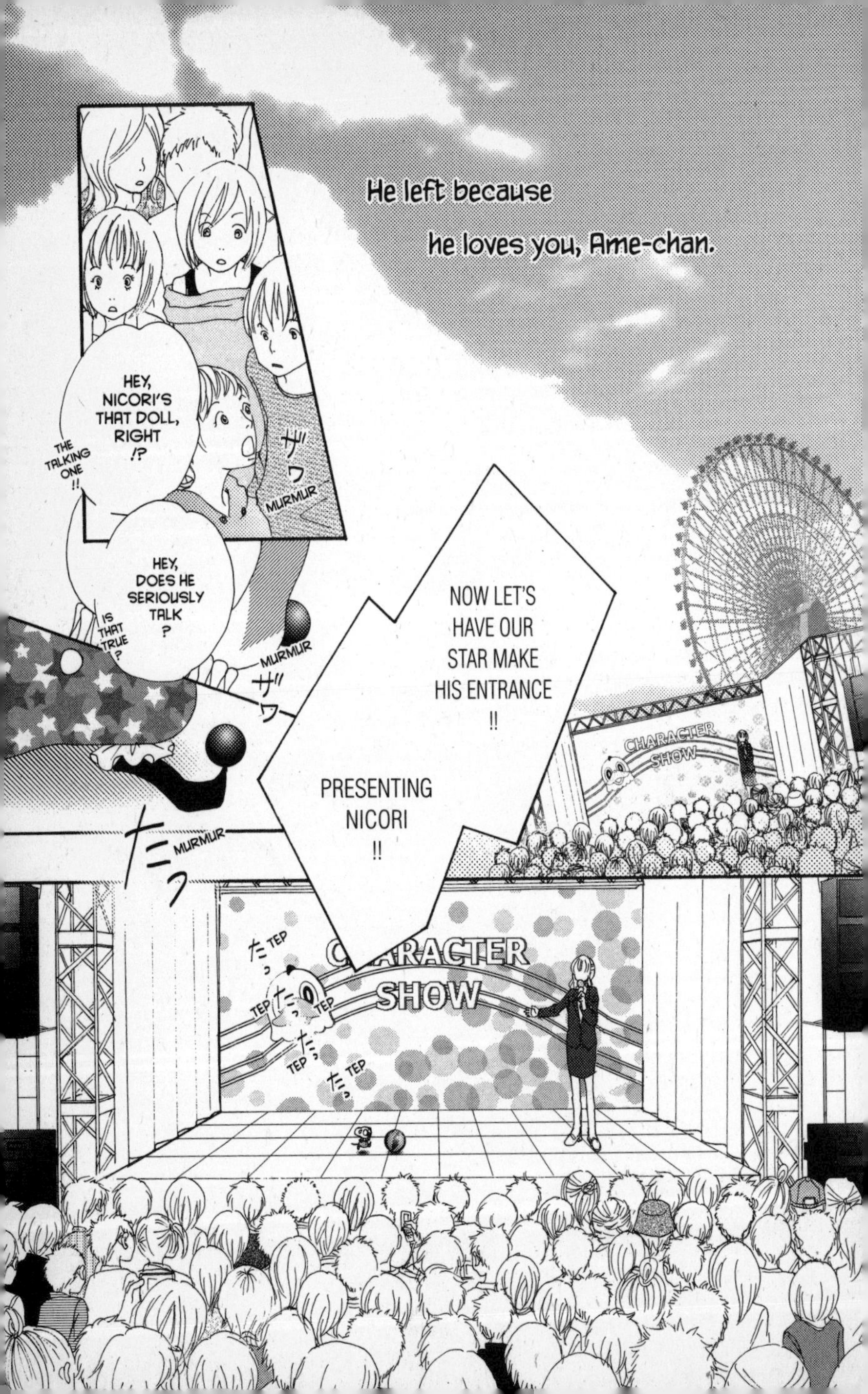
He left because
he loves you, Ame-chan.
HEY, NICORI'S THAT DOLL, RIGHT !?
THE TALKING ONE !!
MURMUR
HEY, DOES HE SERIOUSLY TALK ?
IS THAT TRUE ?
MURMUR
NOW LET'S HAVE OUR STAR MAKE HIS ENTRANCE !!
PRESENTING NICORI !!
MURMUR
CHARACTER SHOW
TEP TEP TEP TEP TEP
CHARACTER SHOW

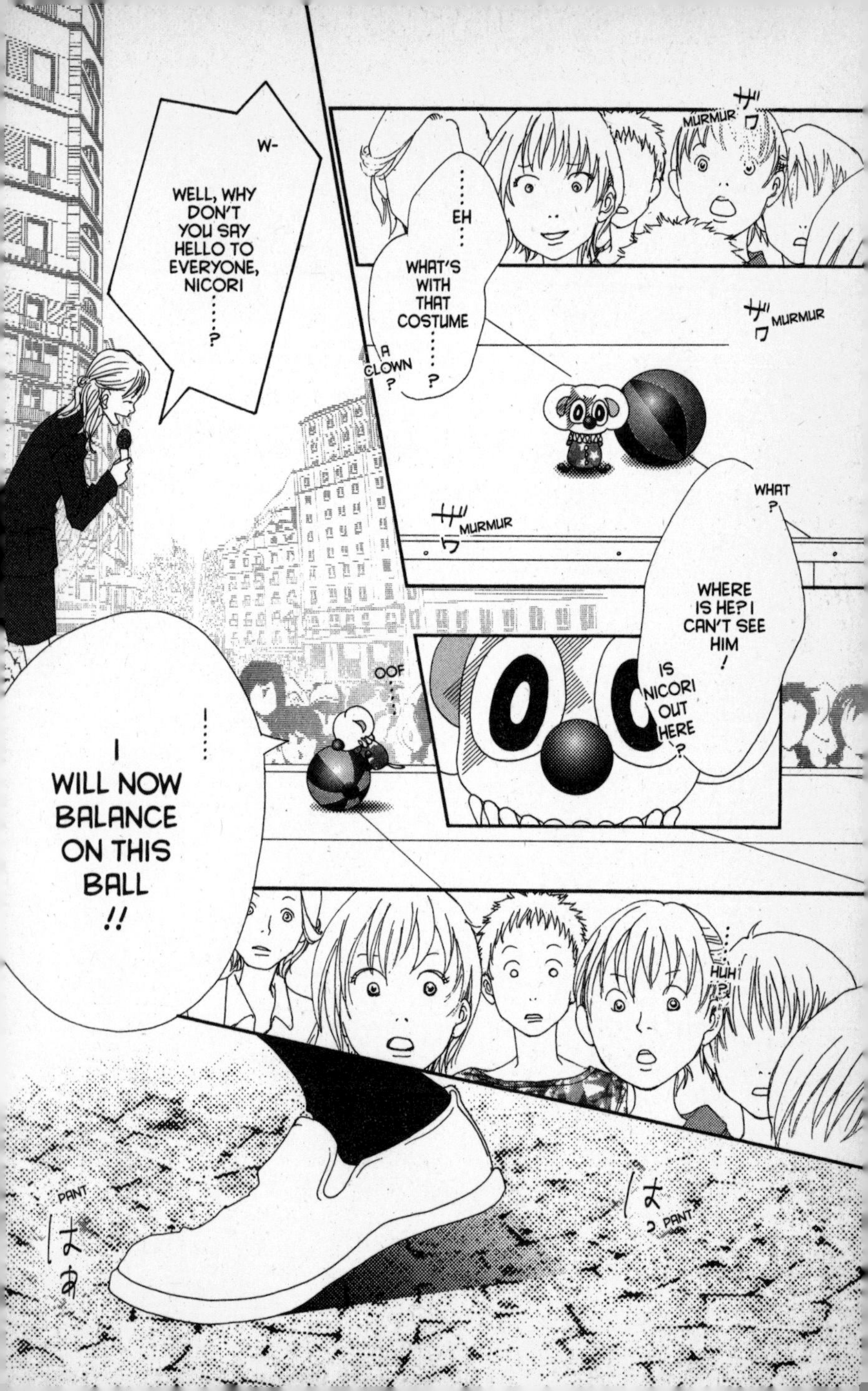

W-
WELL, WHY DON'T YOU SAY HELLO TO EVERYONE, NICORI......?
MURMUR
EH...... WHAT'S WITH THAT COSTUME......?
A CLOWN?
MURMUR
MURMUR
WHAT?
WHERE IS HE? I CAN'T SEE HIM!
IS NICORI OUT HERE?
OOF......
I...... I WILL NOW BALANCE ON THIS BALL!!
......HUH?
PANT
PANT

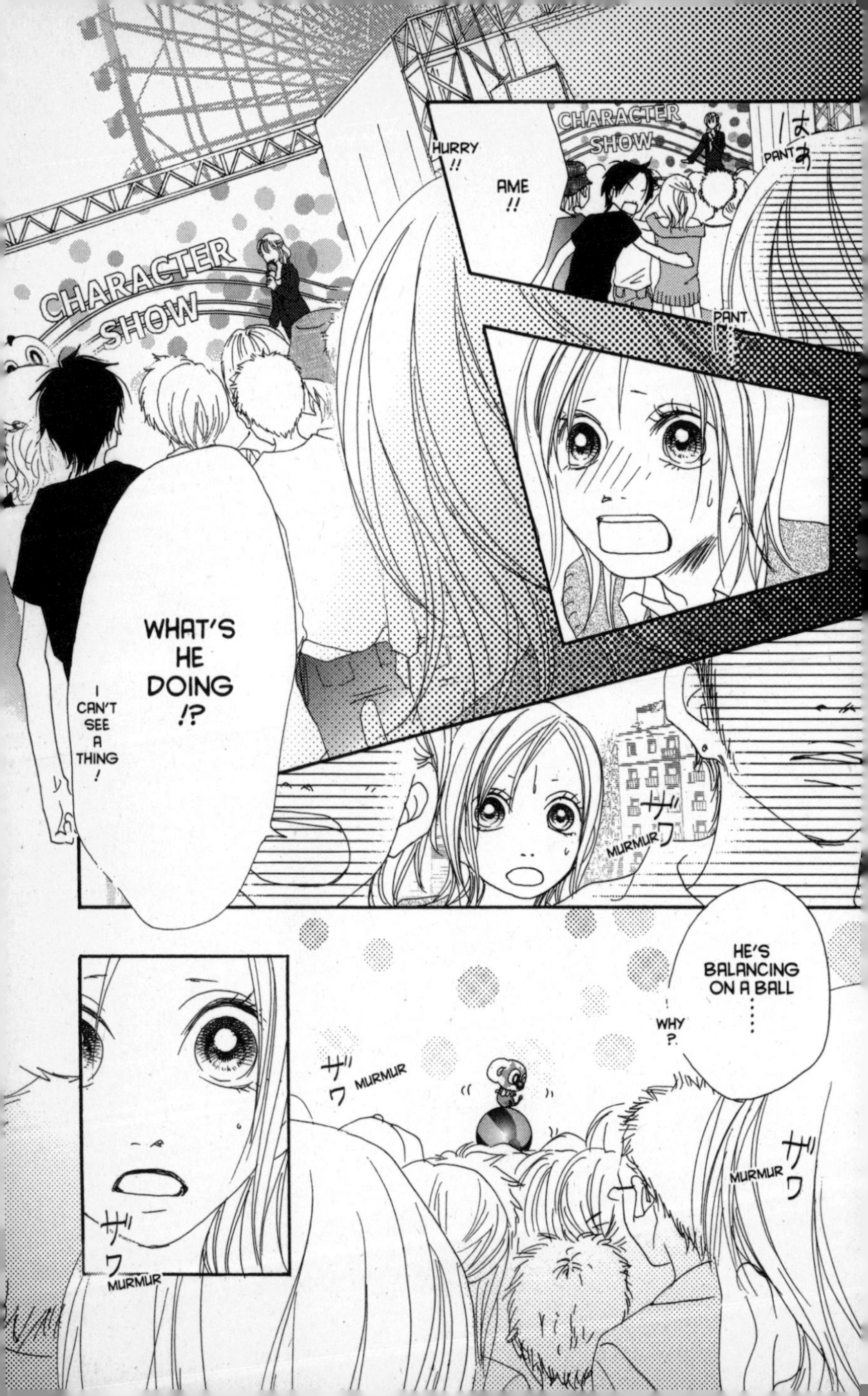
CHARACTER SHOW
HURRY !!
AME !!
はあ PANT
PANT
CHARACTER SHOW
WHAT'S HE DOING !?
I CAN'T SEE A THING !
ザワ MURMUR
HE'S BALANCING ON A BALL......
WHY ?
ザワ MURMUR
ザワ MURMUR
ザワ MURMUR

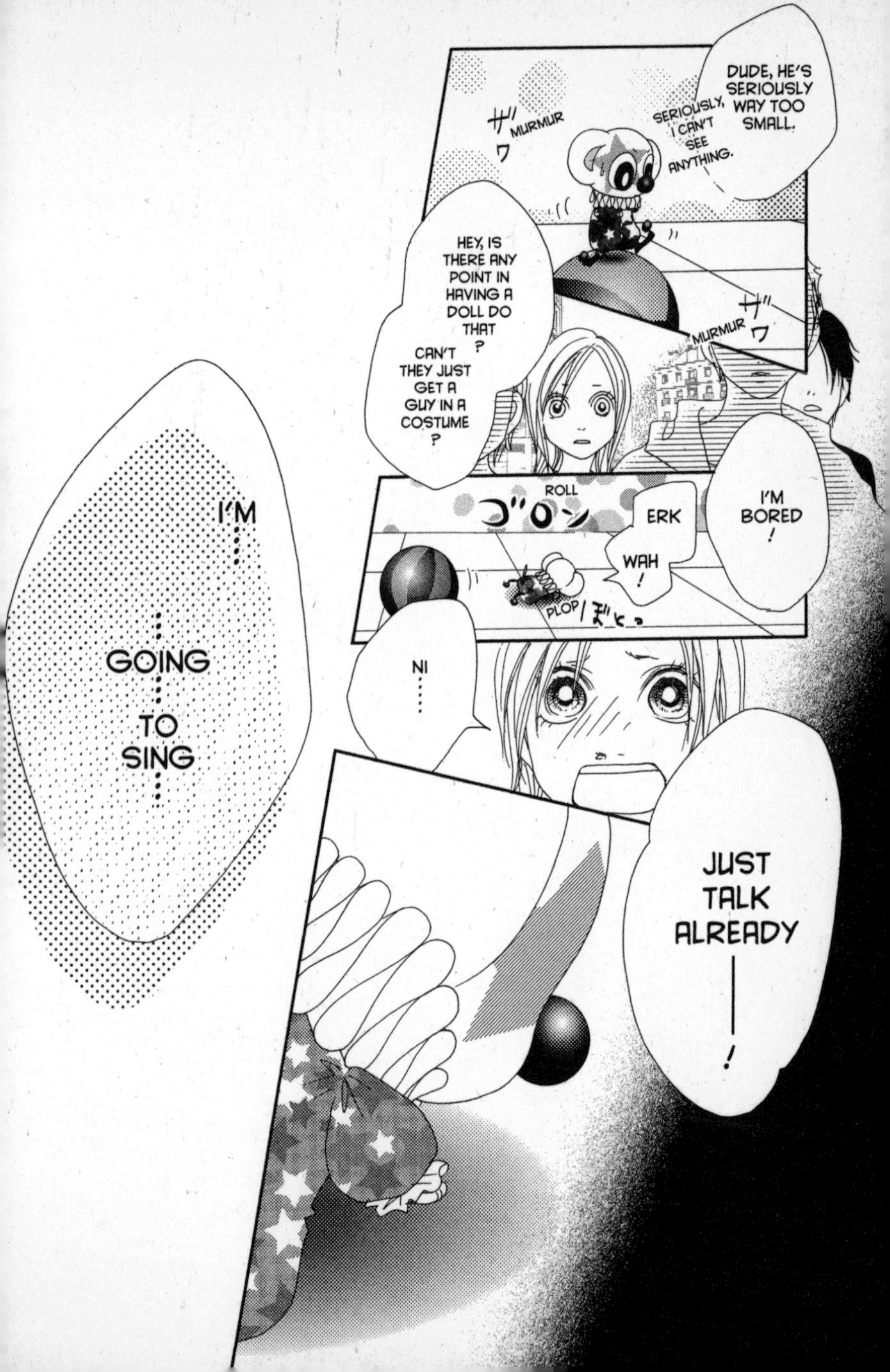
DUDE, HE'S SERIOUSLY WAY TOO SMALL.
SERIOUSLY, I CAN'T SEE ANYTHING.
ザワ MURMUR
HEY, IS THERE ANY POINT IN HAVING A DOLL DO THAT?
CAN'T THEY JUST GET A GUY IN A COSTUME?
ザワ MURMUR
I'M BORED!
ERK
WAH!
ゴロン ROLL
PLOP
NI.....
JUST TALK ALREADY—!
I'M... GOING... TO SING...

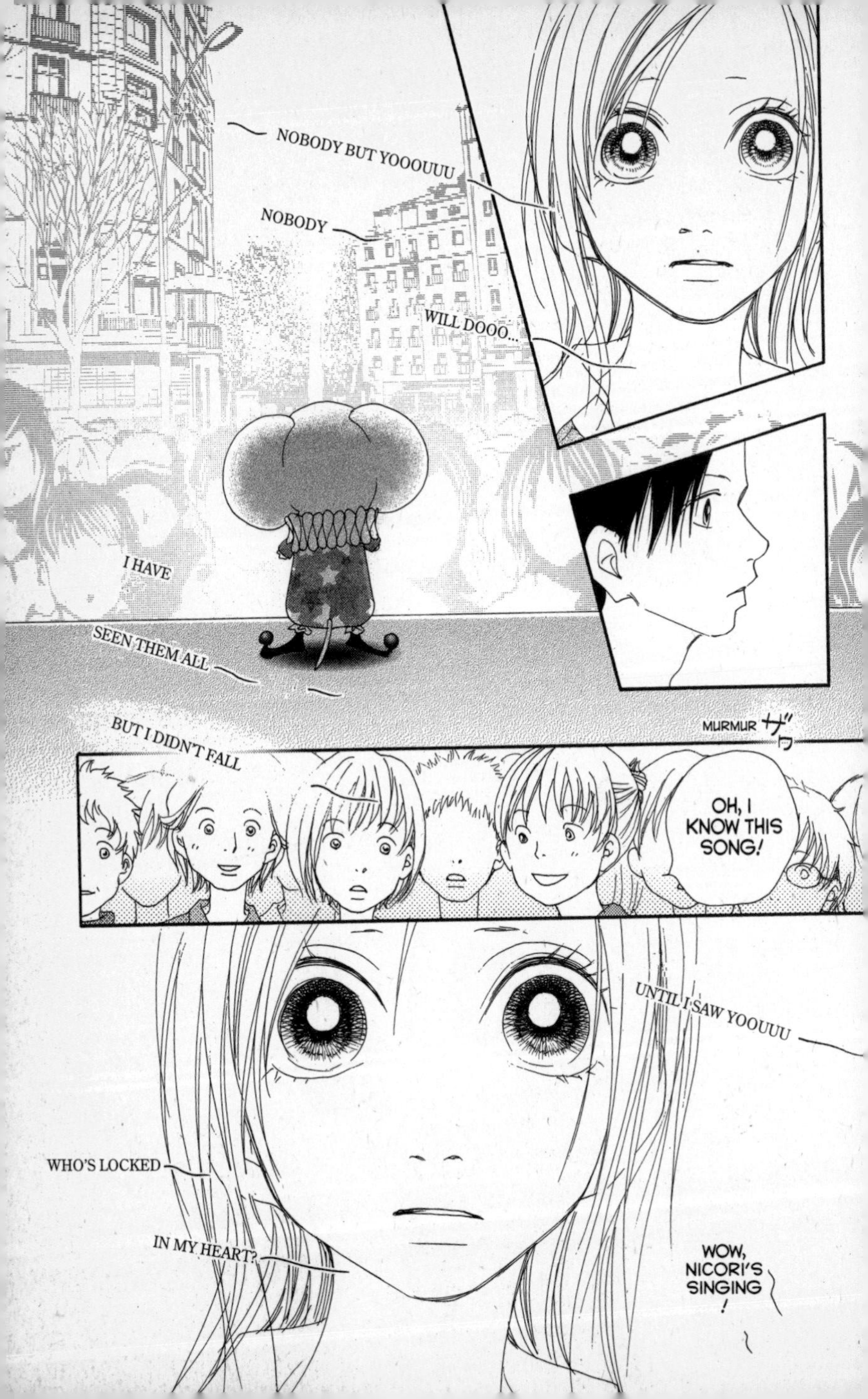
NOBODY BUT YOOOUUU
NOBODY
WILL DOOO...
I HAVE
SEEN THEM ALL
BUT I DIDN'T FALL
MURMUR ザワ
OH, I KNOW THIS SONG!
UNTIL I SAW YOOUUU
WHO'S LOCKED
IN MY HEART?
WOW, NICORI'S SINGING!

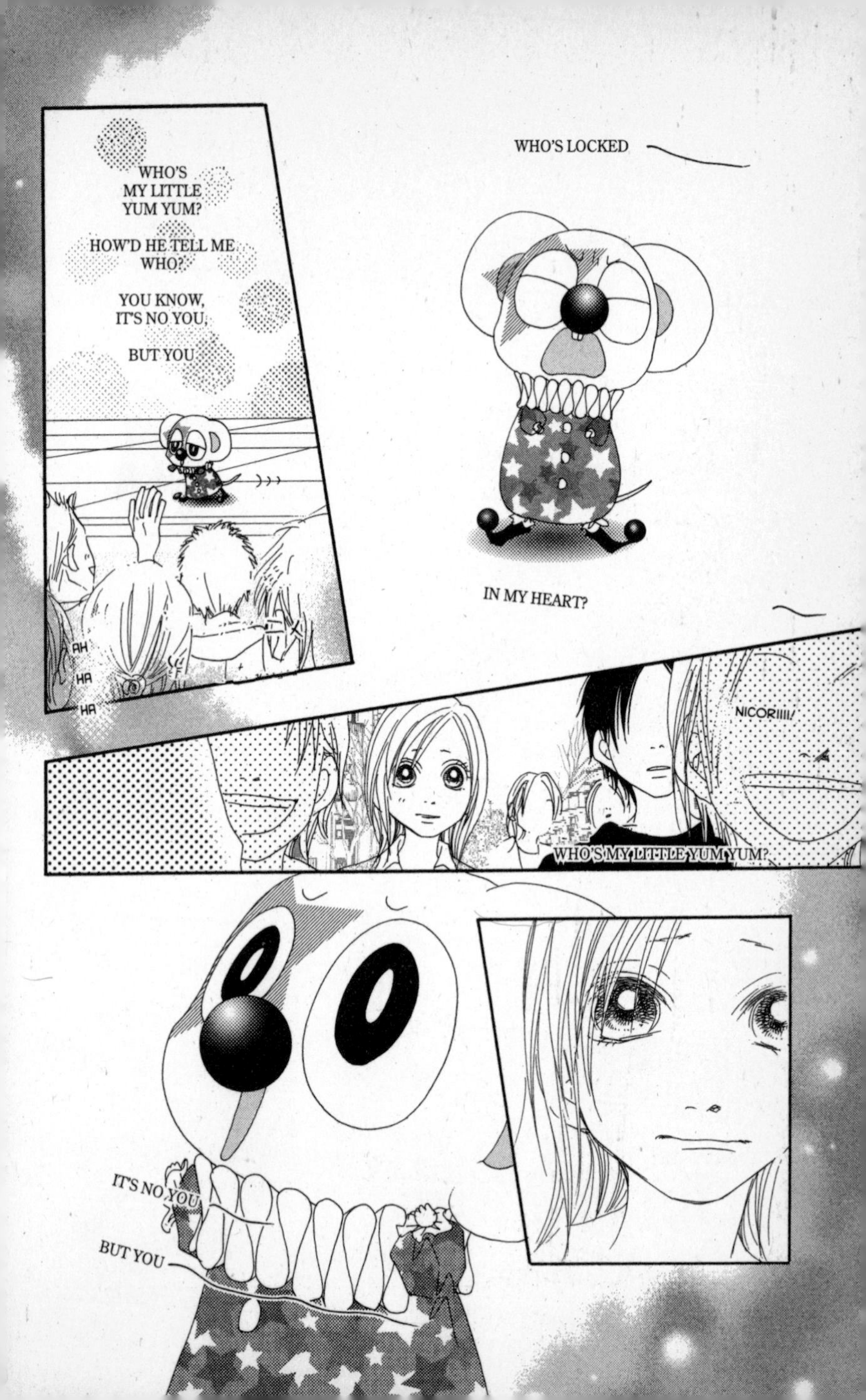
WHO'S LOCKED
IN MY HEART?
WHO'S MY LITTLE YUM YUM?
HOW'D HE TELL ME WHO?
YOU KNOW, IT'S NO YOU,
BUT YOU
AH HA HA
NICORIIII!
WHO'S MY LITTLE YUM YUM?
IT'S NO YOU
BUT YOU

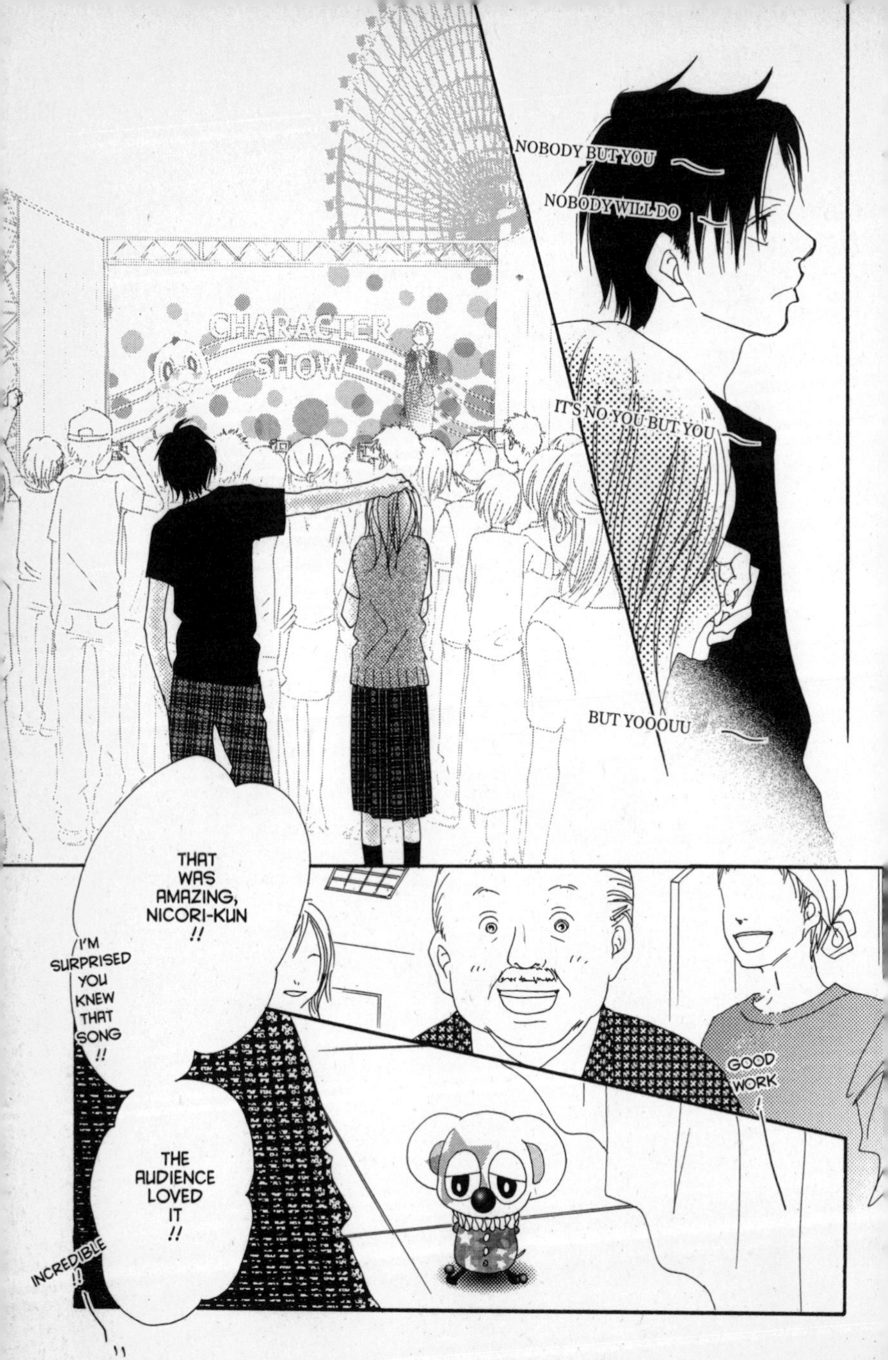
NOBODY BUT YOU
NOBODY WILL DO
IT'S NO YOU BUT YOU
BUT YOOOUU
CHARACTER SHOW
GOOD WORK !
THAT WAS AMAZING, NICORI-KUN !!
I'M SURPRISED YOU KNEW THAT SONG !!
THE AUDIENCE LOVED IT !!
INCREDIBLE !!
!!

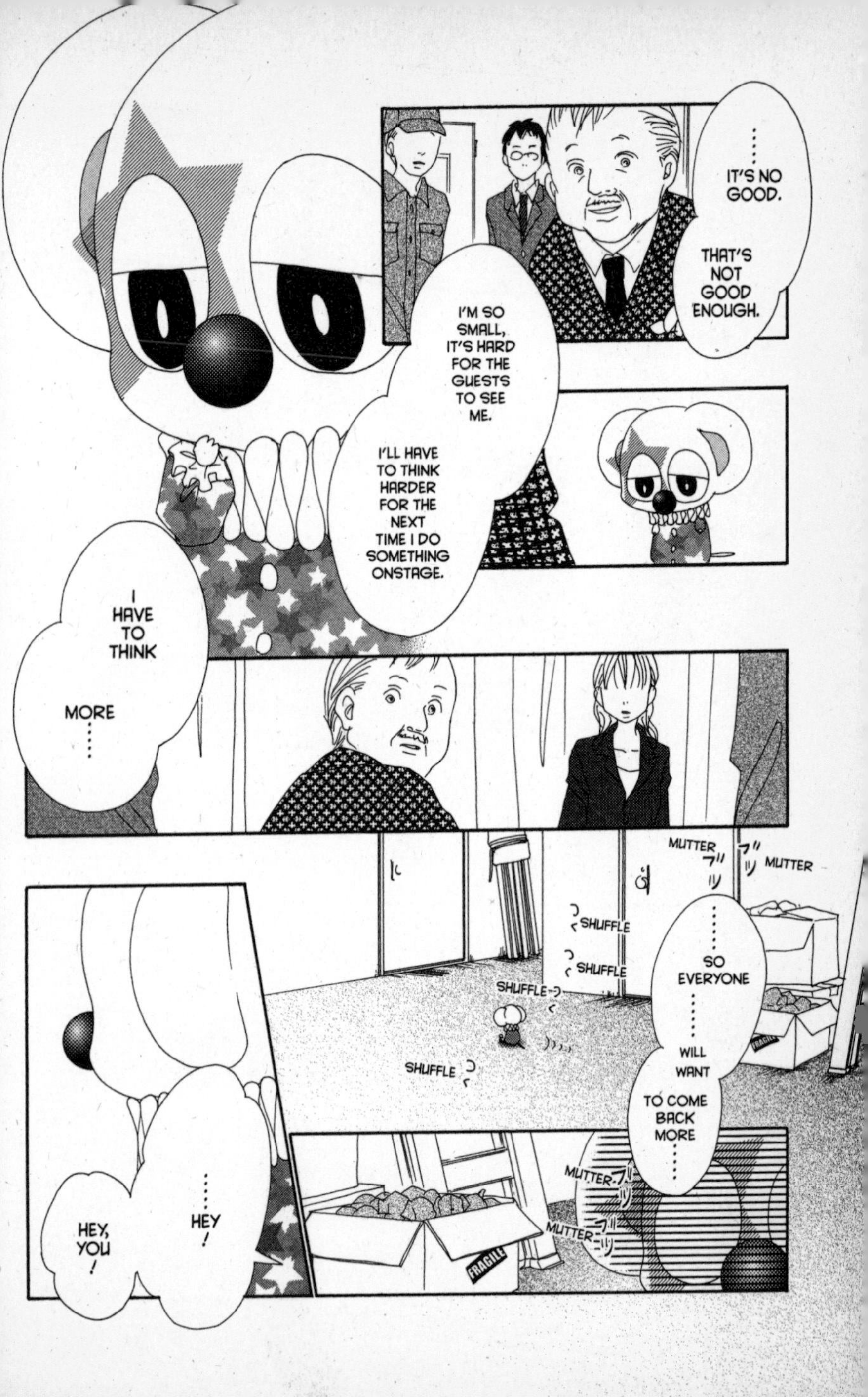
......IT'S NO GOOD.
THAT'S NOT GOOD ENOUGH.
I'M SO SMALL, IT'S HARD FOR THE GUESTS TO SEE ME.
I'LL HAVE TO THINK HARDER FOR THE NEXT TIME I DO SOMETHING ONSTAGE.
I HAVE TO THINK
MORE......
MUTTER
MUTTER
......SO EVERYONE......
WILL WANT
TO COME BACK MORE......
SHUFFLE
SHUFFLE
SHUFFLE
SHUFFLE
MUTTER
MUTTER
......HEY!
HEY, YOU!
FRAGILE

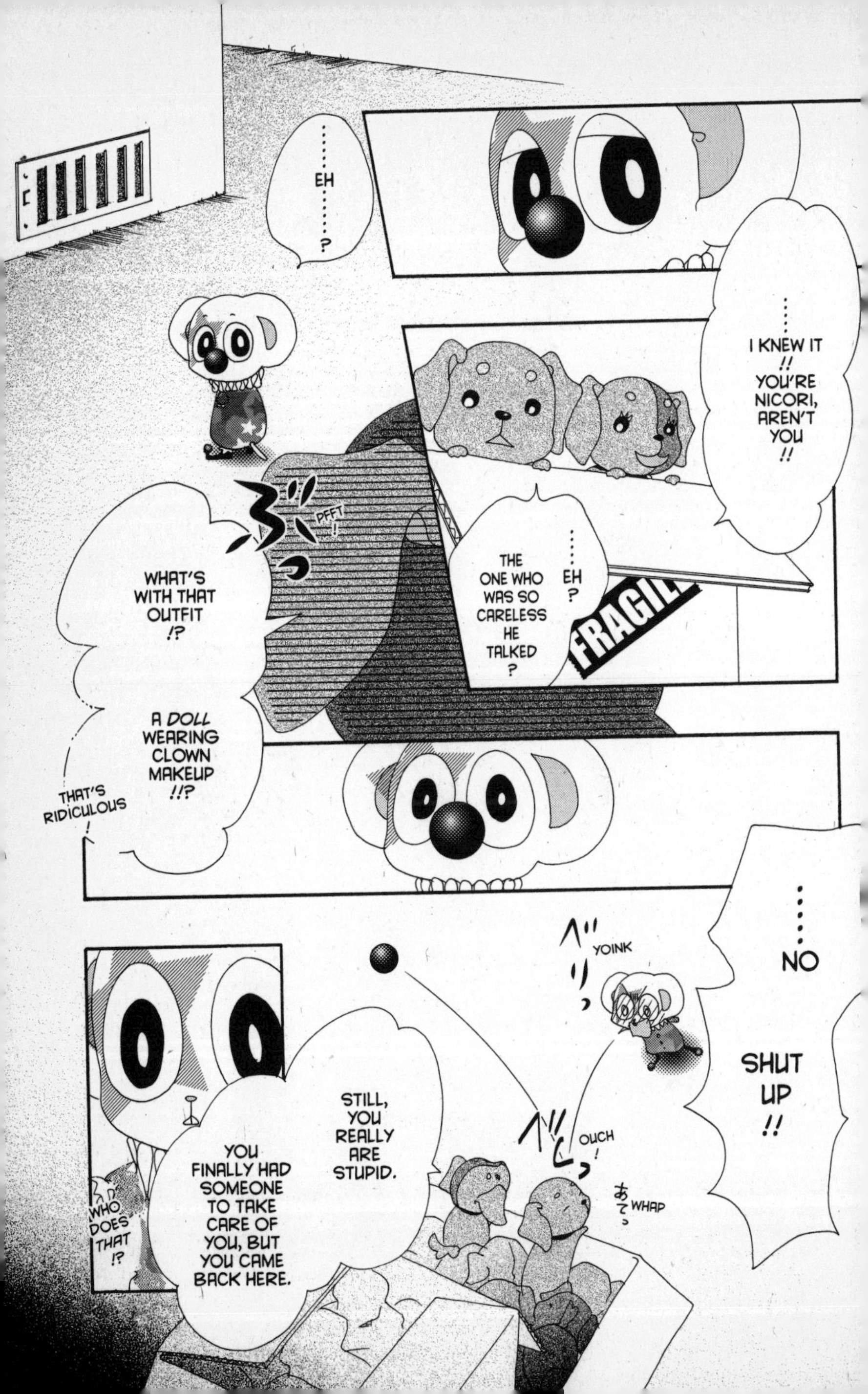
......EH......?
......I KNEW IT!! YOU'RE NICORI, AREN'T YOU!!
......EH? THE ONE WHO WAS SO CARELESS HE TALKED?
FRAGILE
ぶっ PFFT!
WHAT'S WITH THAT OUTFIT!?
A DOLL WEARING CLOWN MAKEUP!!?
THAT'S RIDICULOUS!
......NO
SHUT UP!!
YOINK
OUCH!
WHAP
STILL, YOU REALLY ARE STUPID.
YOU FINALLY HAD SOMEONE TO TAKE CARE OF YOU, BUT YOU CAME BACK HERE.
WHO DOES THAT!?

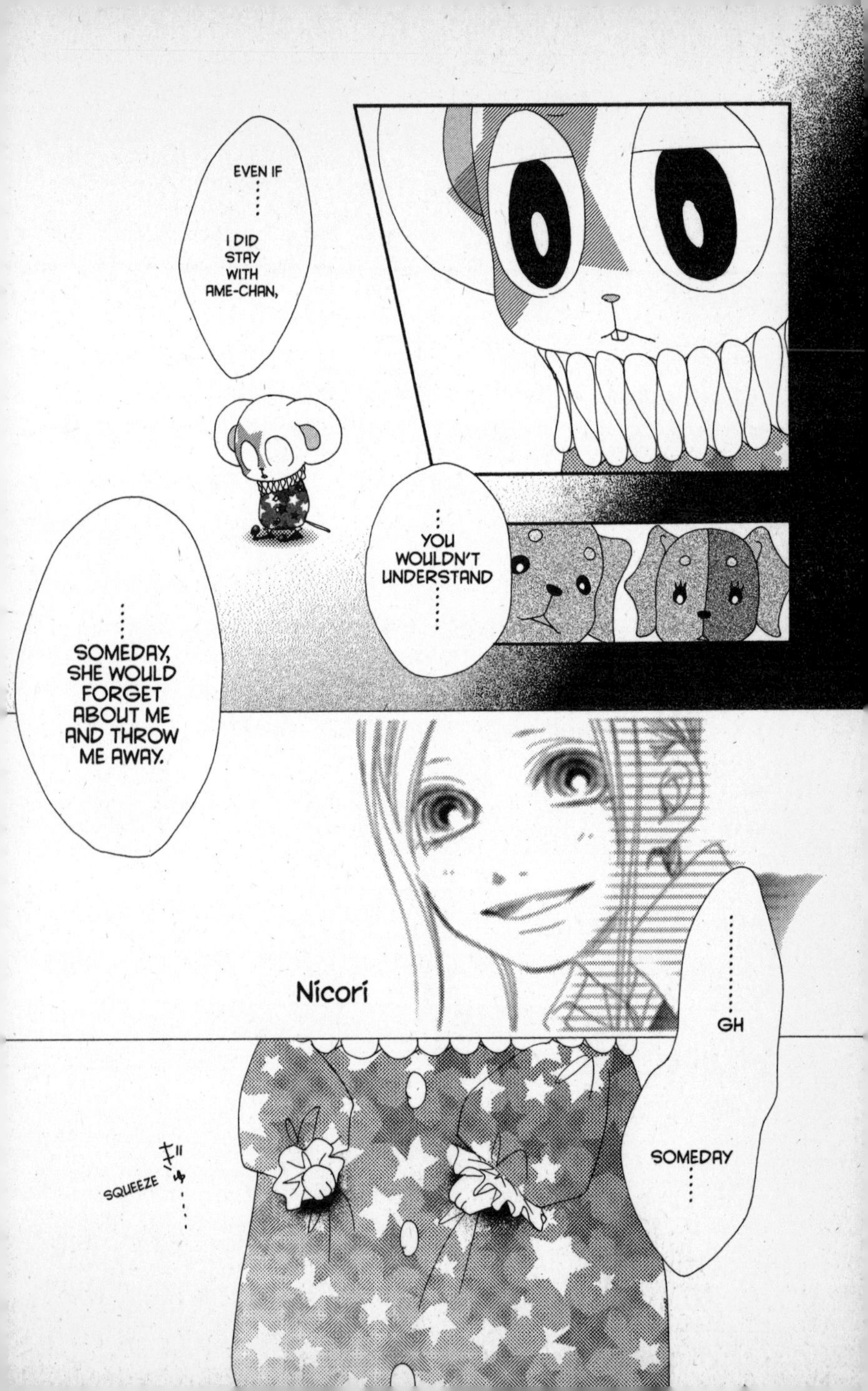
EVEN IF ... I DID STAY WITH AME-CHAN,
...YOU WOULDN'T UNDERSTAND...
...SOMEDAY, SHE WOULD FORGET ABOUT ME AND THROW ME AWAY.
......GH
Nicori
SOMEDAY...
SQUEEZE

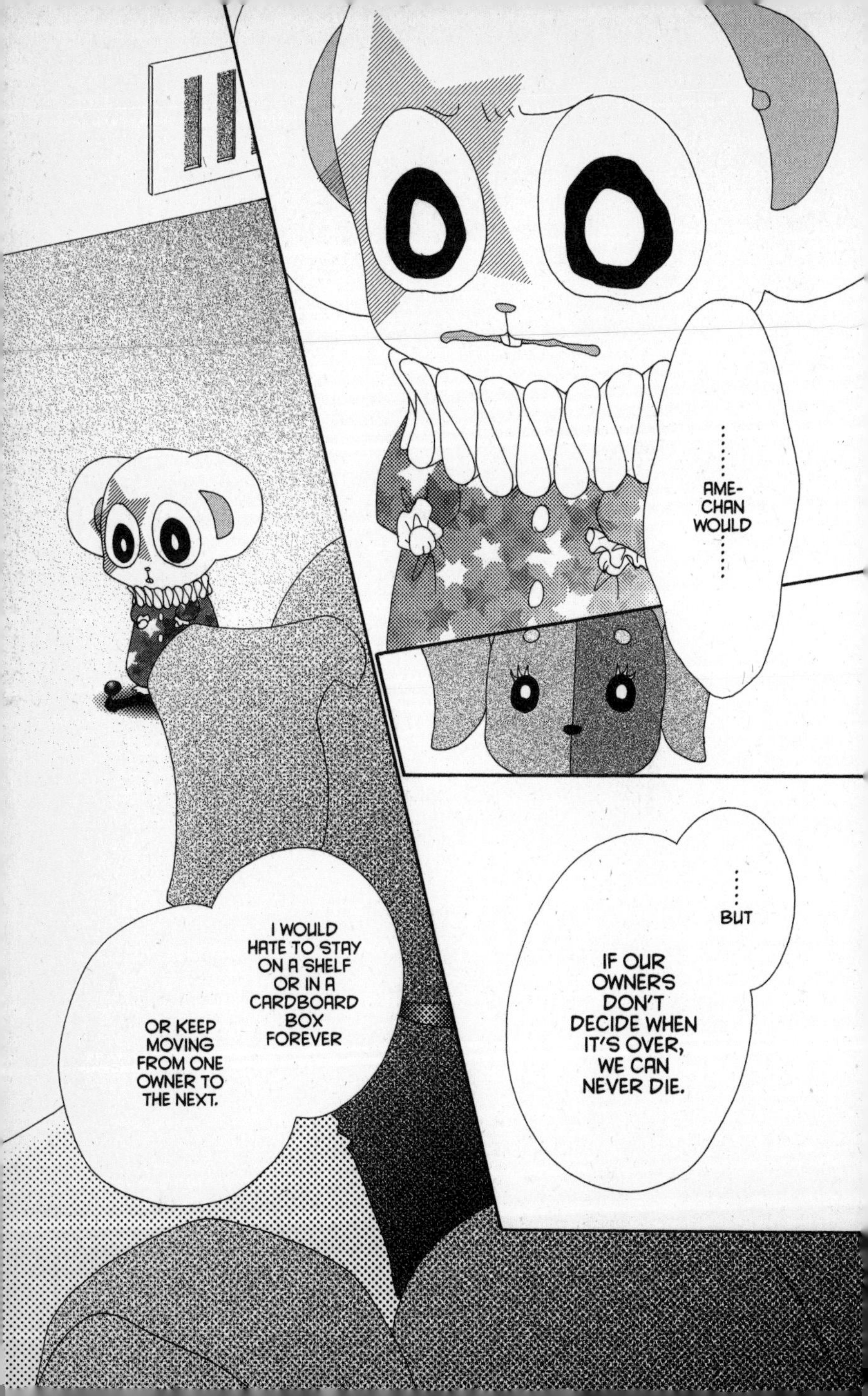

...AME-CHAN WOULD...
...BUT
IF OUR OWNERS DON'T DECIDE WHEN IT'S OVER, WE CAN NEVER DIE.
I WOULD HATE TO STAY ON A SHELF OR IN A CARDBOARD BOX FOREVER
OR KEEP MOVING FROM ONE OWNER TO THE NEXT.

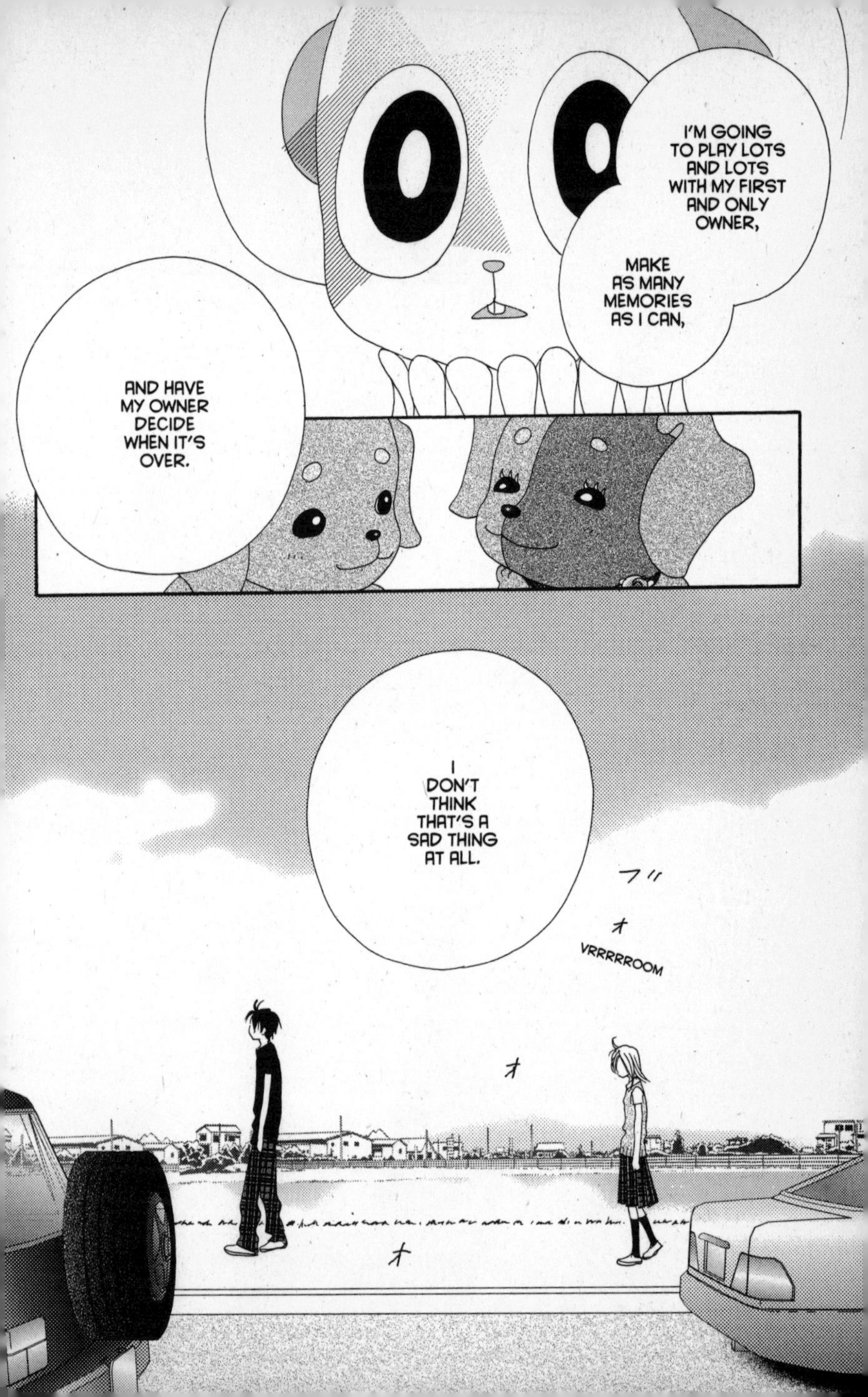
I'M GOING TO PLAY LOTS AND LOTS WITH MY FIRST AND ONLY OWNER,
MAKE AS MANY MEMORIES AS I CAN,
AND HAVE MY OWNER DECIDE WHEN IT'S OVER.
I DON'T THINK THAT'S A SAD THING AT ALL.
ブ
オ
VRRRRROOM
オ
オ

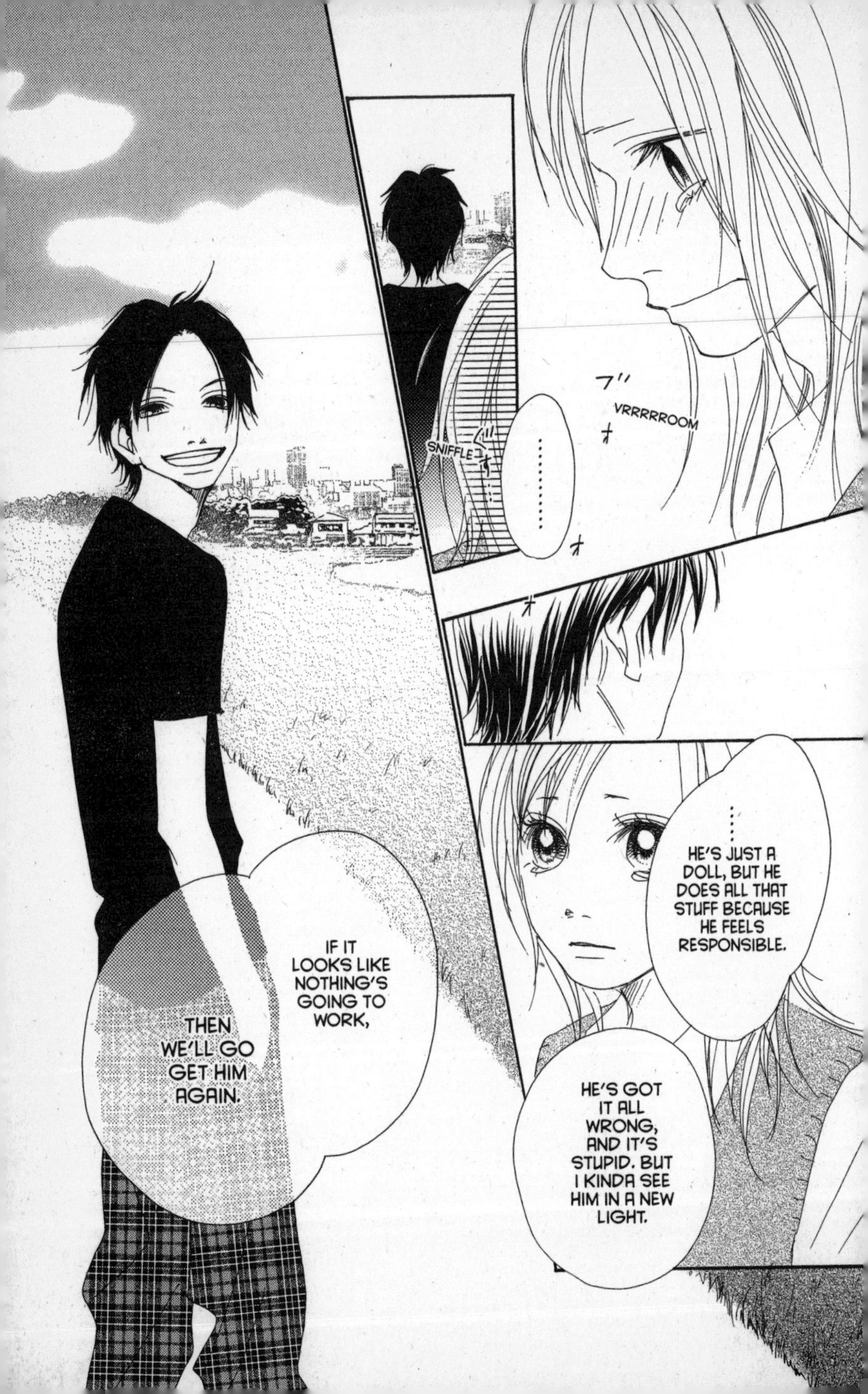
VRRRRROOM
......
SNIFFLE
......
HE'S JUST A DOLL, BUT HE DOES ALL THAT STUFF BECAUSE HE FEELS RESPONSIBLE.
HE'S GOT IT ALL WRONG, AND IT'S STUPID. BUT I KINDA SEE HIM IN A NEW LIGHT.
IF IT LOOKS LIKE NOTHING'S GOING TO WORK,
THEN WE'LL GO GET HIM AGAIN.

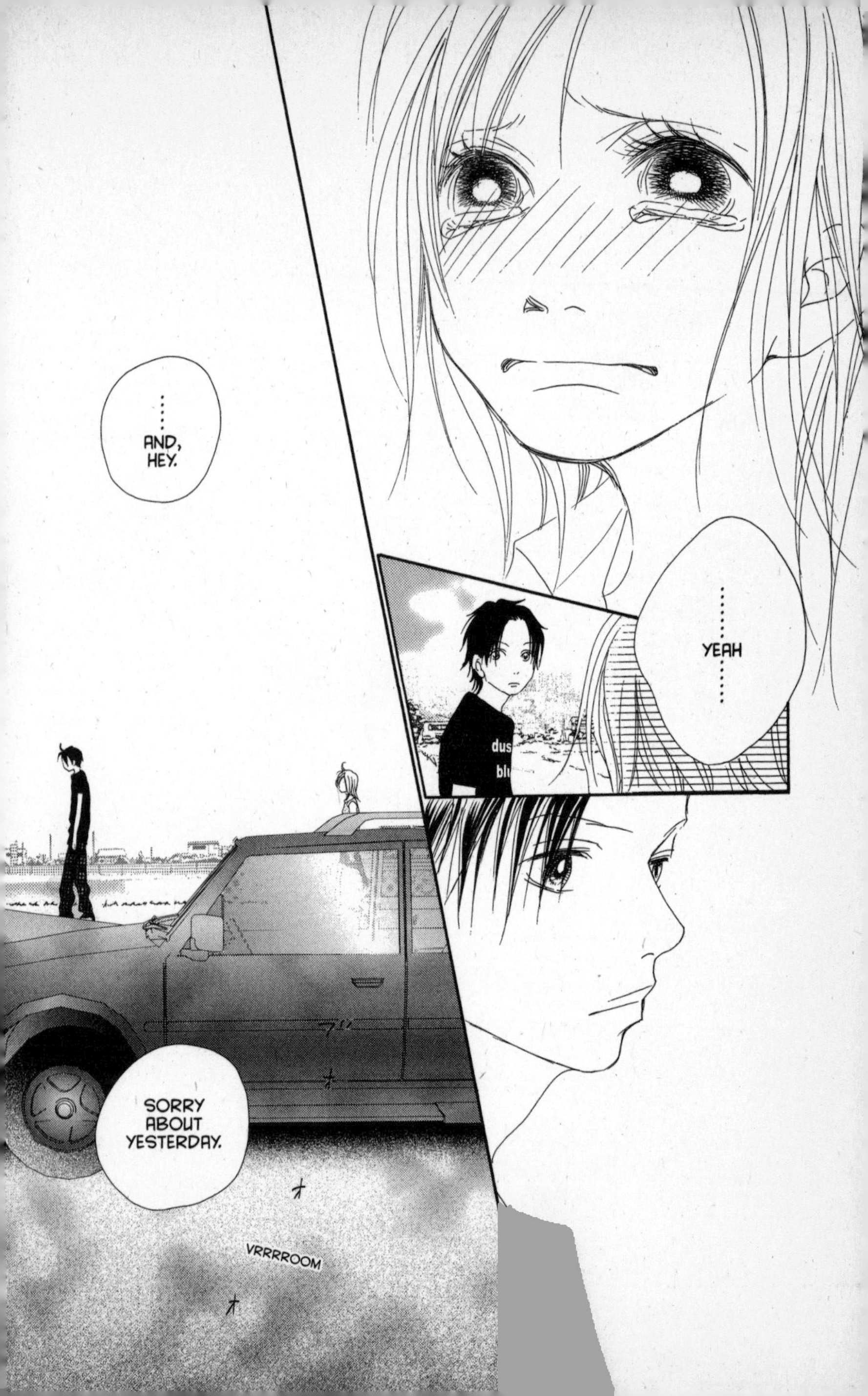

......YEAH......
......AND, HEY.
SORRY ABOUT YESTERDAY.
VRRRROOM

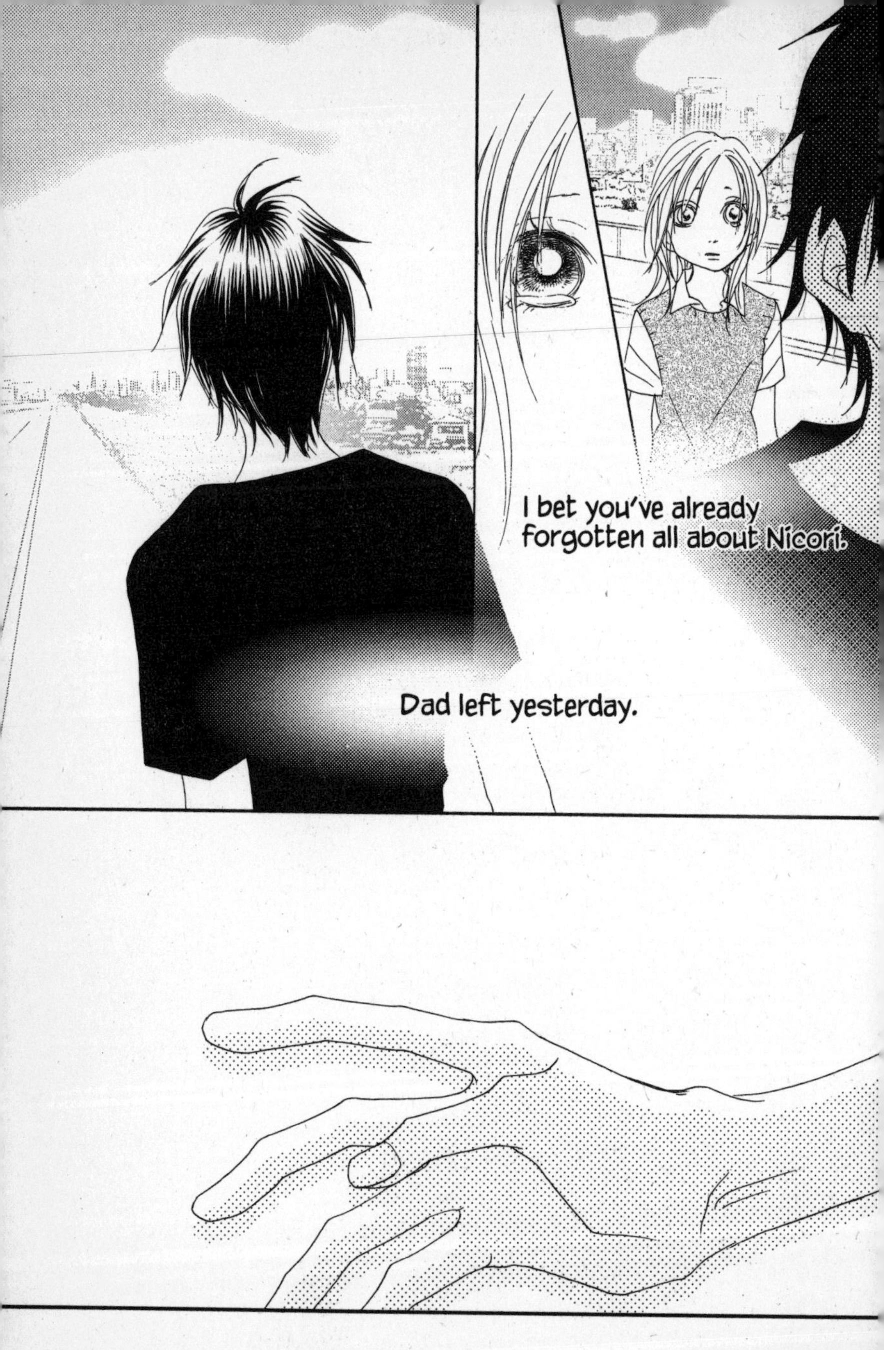
I bet you've already forgotten all about Nicori.
Dad left yesterday.

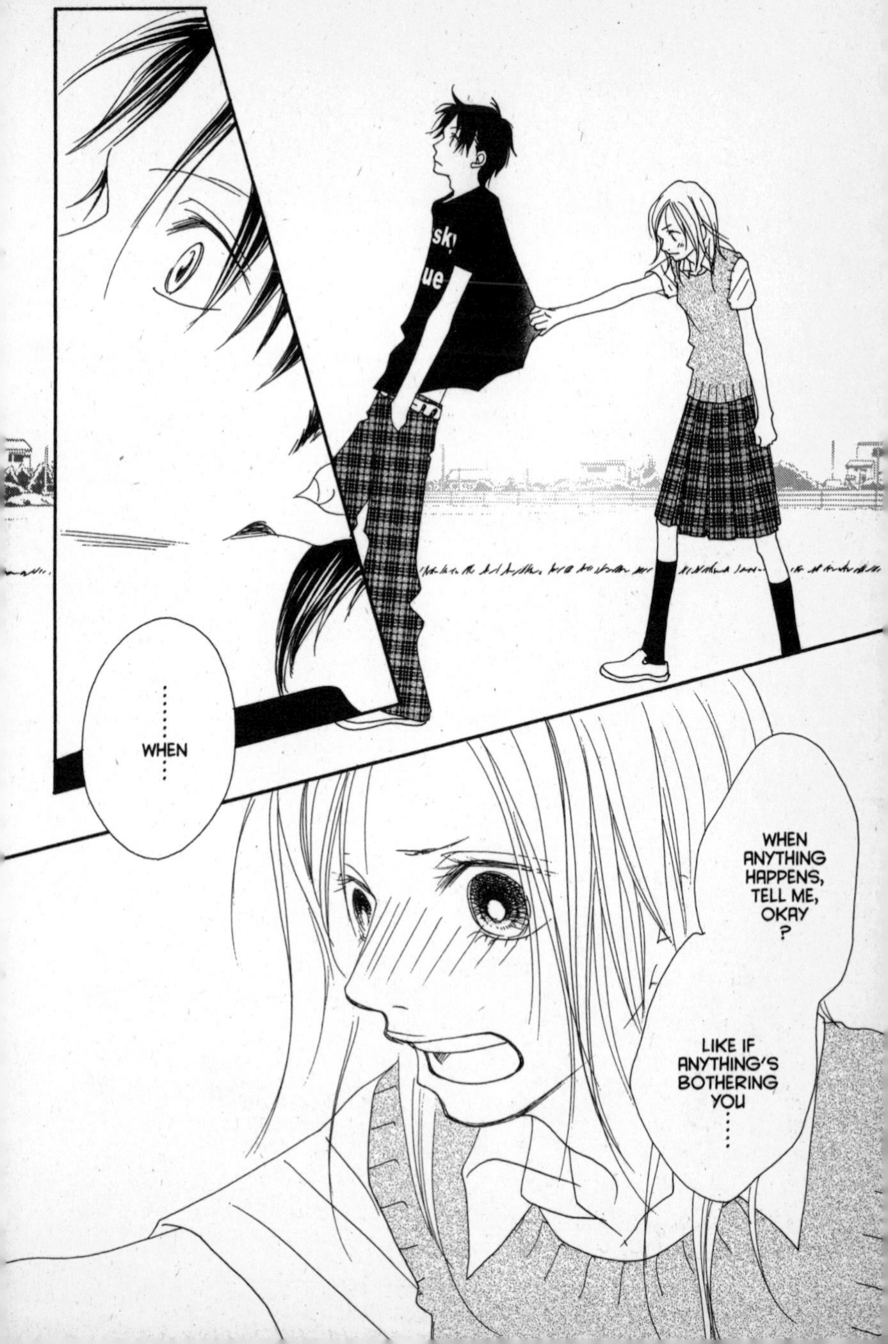
......WHEN......
WHEN ANYTHING HAPPENS, TELL ME, OKAY?
LIKE IF ANYTHING'S BOTHERING YOU......

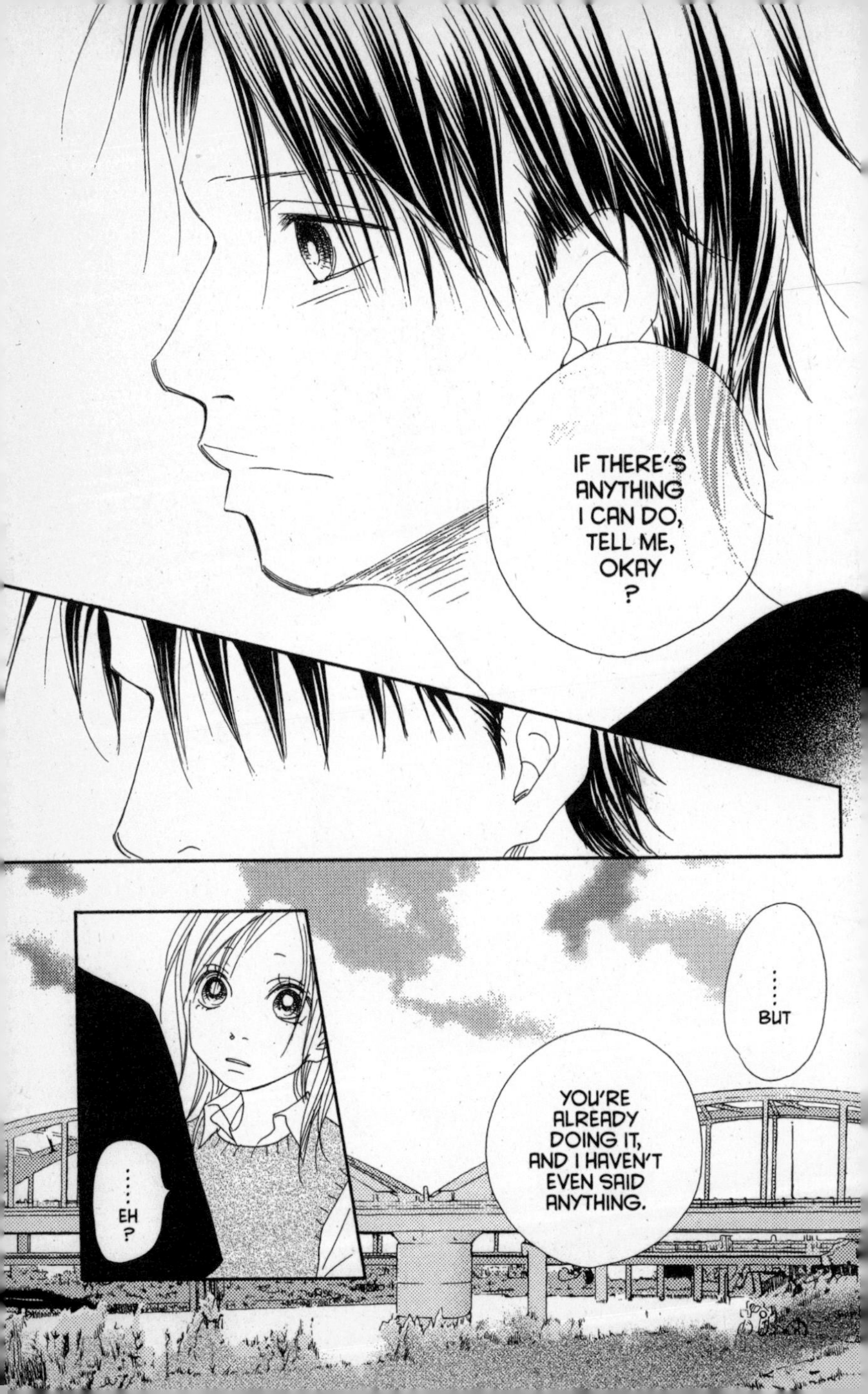
IF THERE'S ANYTHING I CAN DO, TELL ME, OKAY?
.....BUT
YOU'RE ALREADY DOING IT, AND I HAVEN'T EVEN SAID ANYTHING.
.....EH?

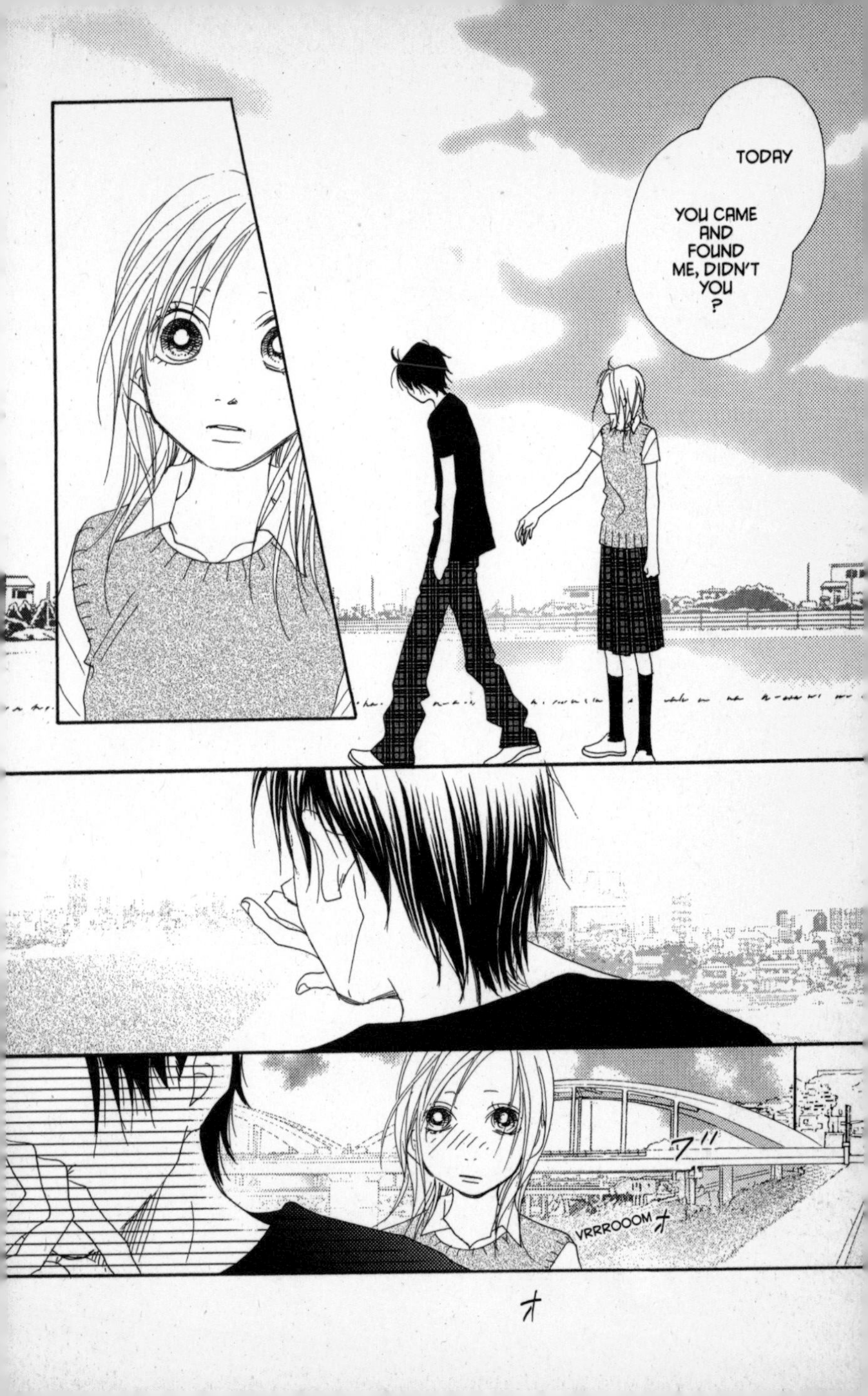
TODAY
YOU CAME AND FOUND ME, DIDN'T YOU ?
VRRROOOM

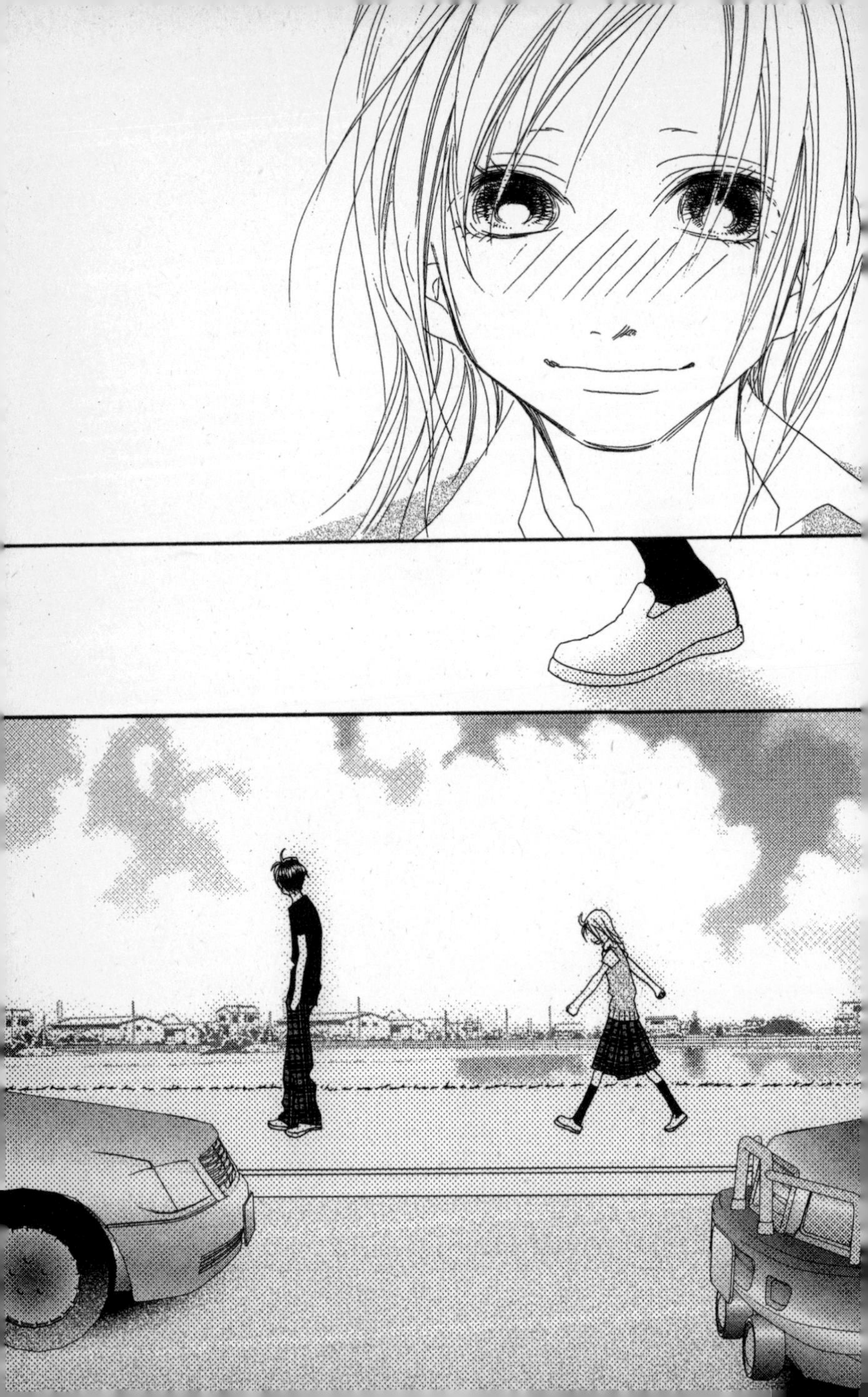

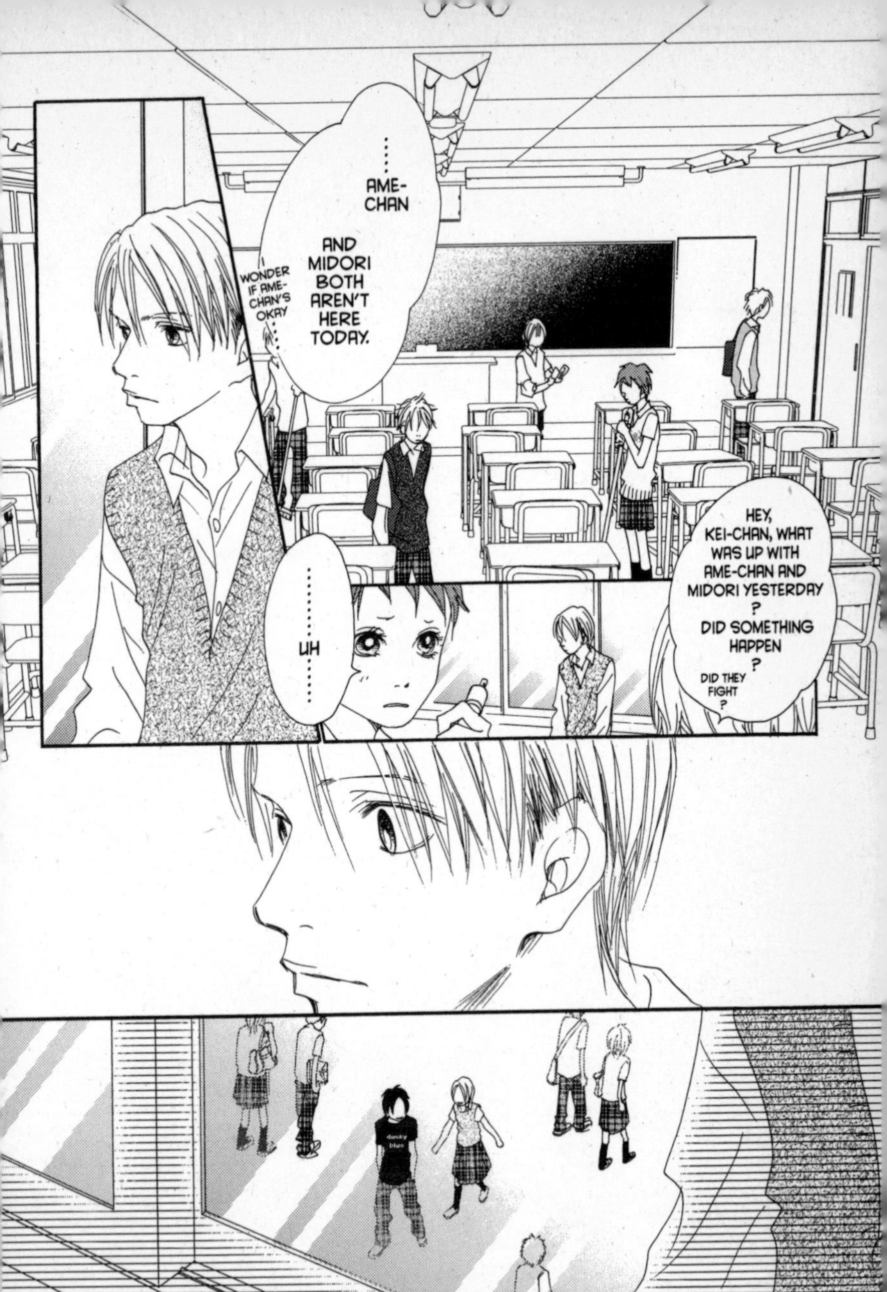

...AME-CHAN AND MIDORI BOTH AREN'T HERE TODAY.
I WONDER IF AME-CHAN'S OKAY...
HEY, KEI-CHAN, WHAT WAS UP WITH AME-CHAN AND MIDORI YESTERDAY? DID SOMETHING HAPPEN?
DID THEY FIGHT?
......UH......

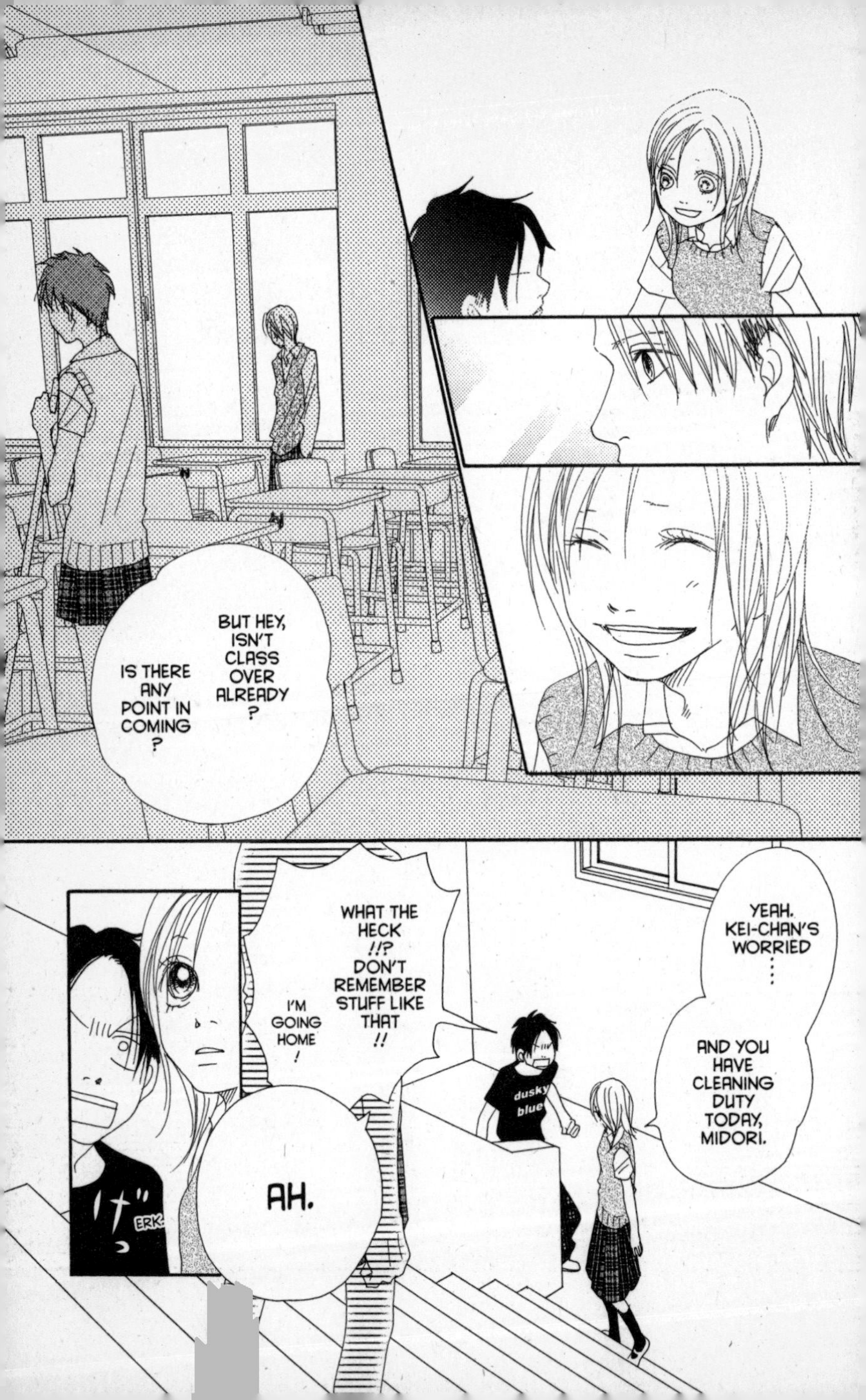
BUT HEY, ISN'T CLASS OVER ALREADY?
IS THERE ANY POINT IN COMING?
YEAH. KEI-CHAN'S WORRIED....
AND YOU HAVE CLEANING DUTY TODAY, MIDORI.
WHAT THE HECK!!? DON'T REMEMBER STUFF LIKE THAT!!
I'M GOING HOME!
AH.
ERK
dusky blue

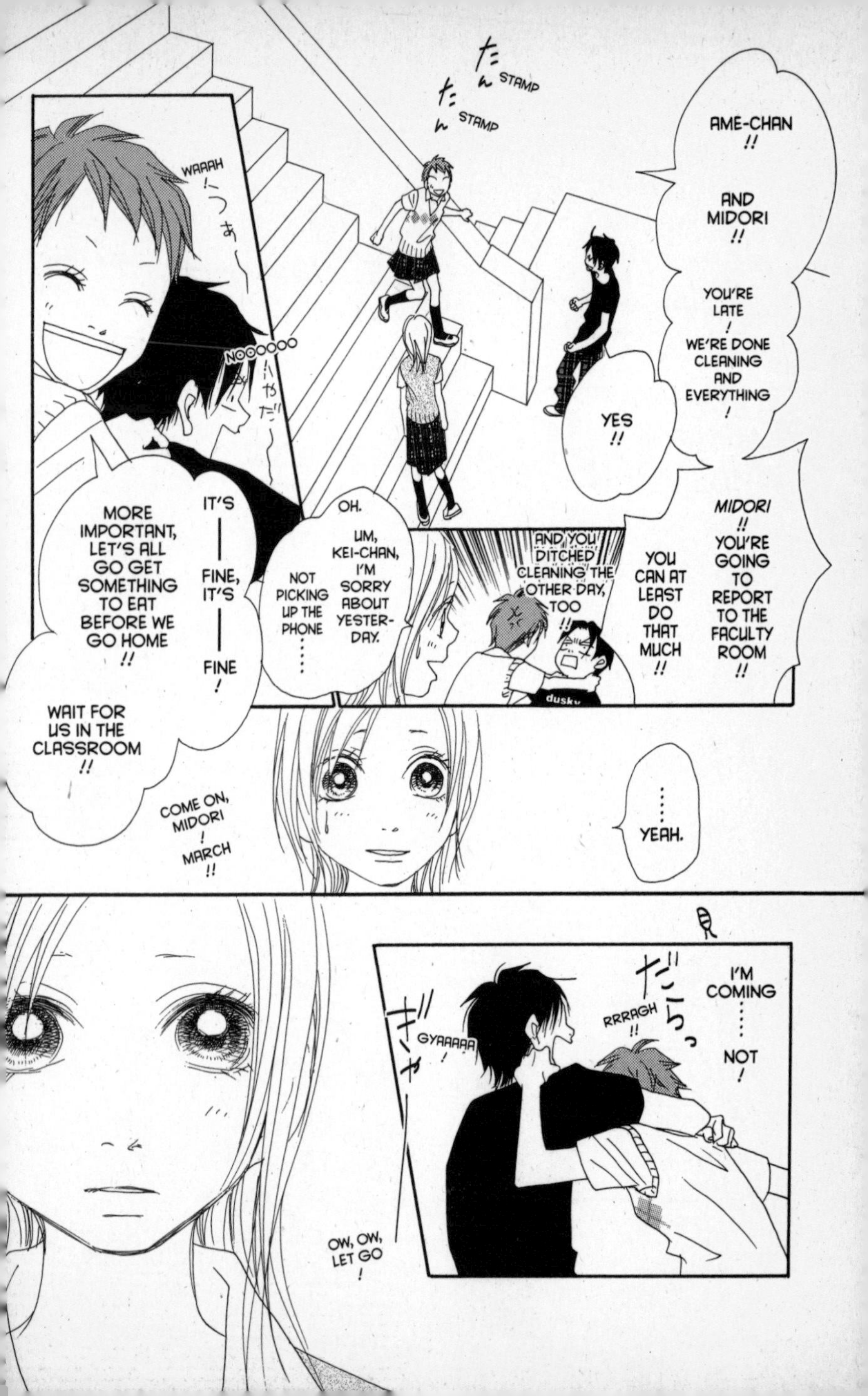

STAMP
STAMP
AME-CHAN!!
AND MIDORI!!
YOU'RE LATE! WE'RE DONE CLEANING AND EVERYTHING!
YES!!
WAAAH!
NOOOOOO
IT'S—FINE, IT'S—FINE!
MORE IMPORTANT, LET'S ALL GO GET SOMETHING TO EAT BEFORE WE GO HOME!!
WAIT FOR US IN THE CLASSROOM!!
COME ON, MIDORI! MARCH!!
MIDORI!! YOU'RE GOING TO REPORT TO THE FACULTY ROOM!!
YOU CAN AT LEAST DO THAT MUCH!!
AND YOU DITCHED CLEANING THE OTHER DAY, TOO!!
dusky
OH.
UM, KEI-CHAN, I'M SORRY ABOUT YESTERDAY.
NOT PICKING UP THE PHONE......
......YEAH.
I'M COMING...... NOT!
RRRAGH!!
GYAAAAA!
OW, OW, LET GO!

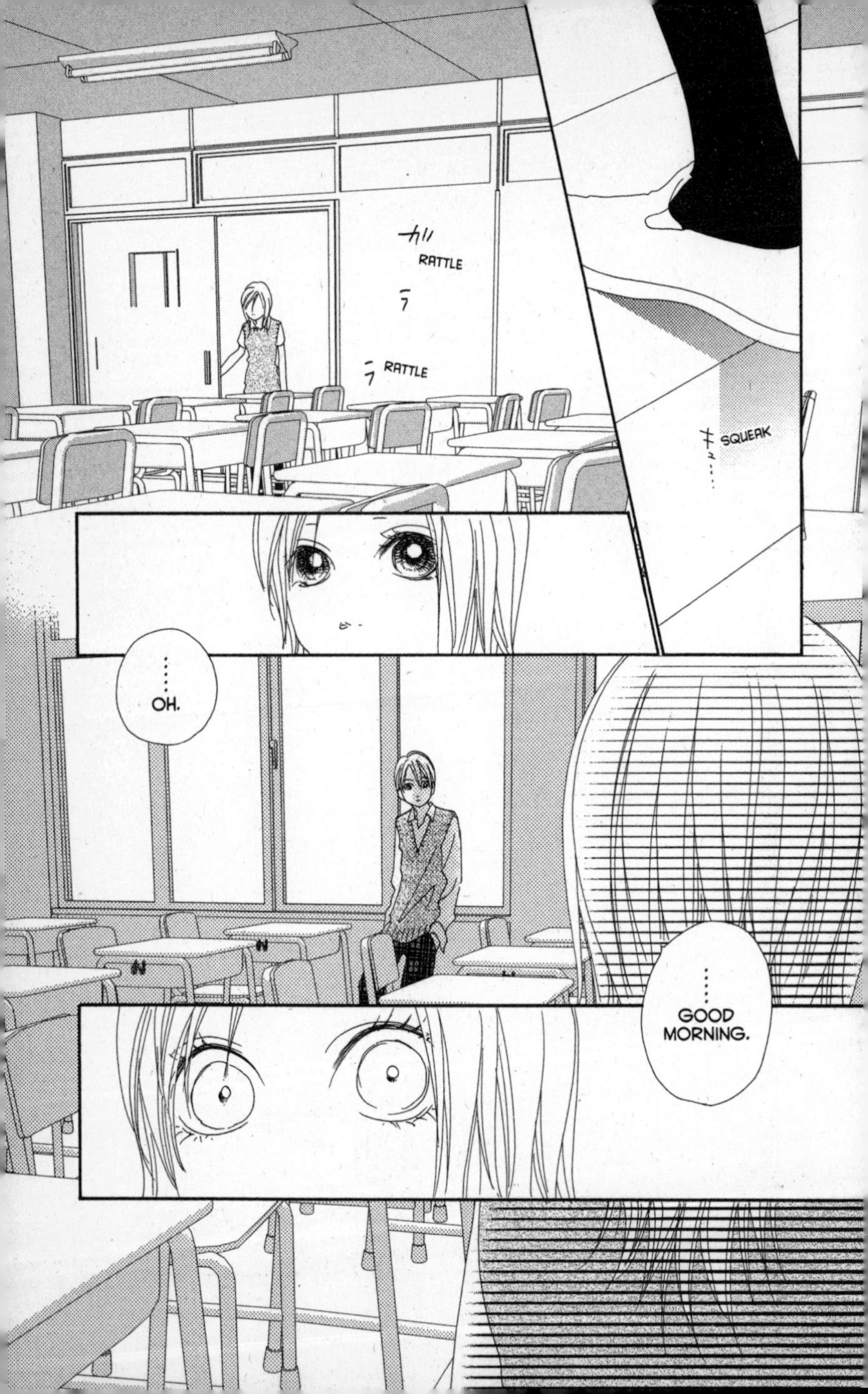
ガ
RATTLE
ラ
ラ
RATTLE
キ
SQUEAK
…OH.
…GOOD MORNING.

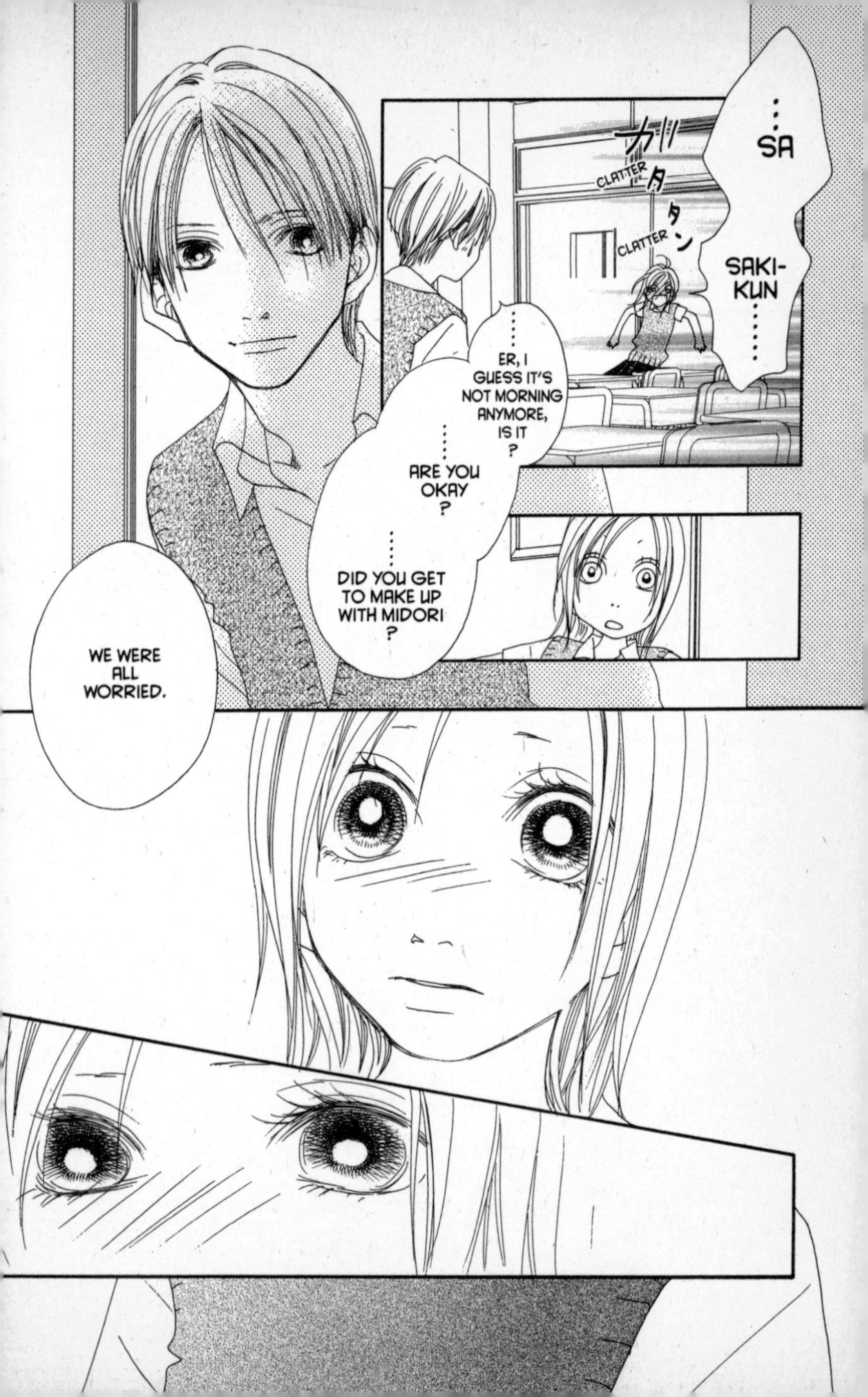

...SA
SAKI-KUN......
ガタ
CLATTER
ン
CLATTER
...ER, I GUESS IT'S NOT MORNING ANYMORE, IS IT?
...ARE YOU OKAY?
...DID YOU GET TO MAKE UP WITH MIDORI?
WE WERE ALL WORRIED.

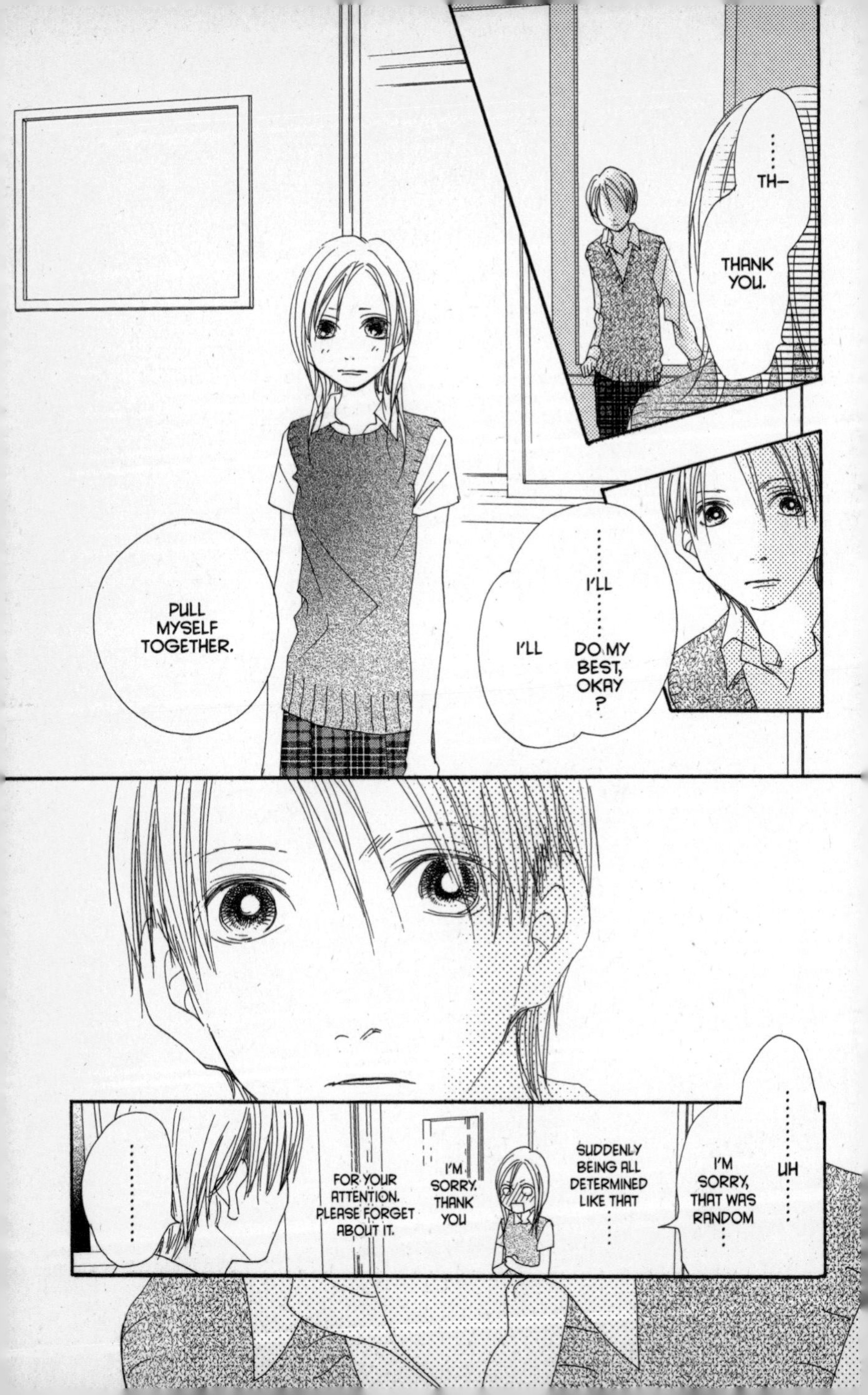
......TH—
THANK YOU.
......I'LL......
DO MY BEST, OKAY?
I'LL
PULL MYSELF TOGETHER.
UH......
I'M SORRY, THAT WAS RANDOM...
SUDDENLY BEING ALL DETERMINED LIKE THAT...
I'M SORRY. THANK YOU
FOR YOUR ATTENTION. PLEASE FORGET ABOUT IT.
......

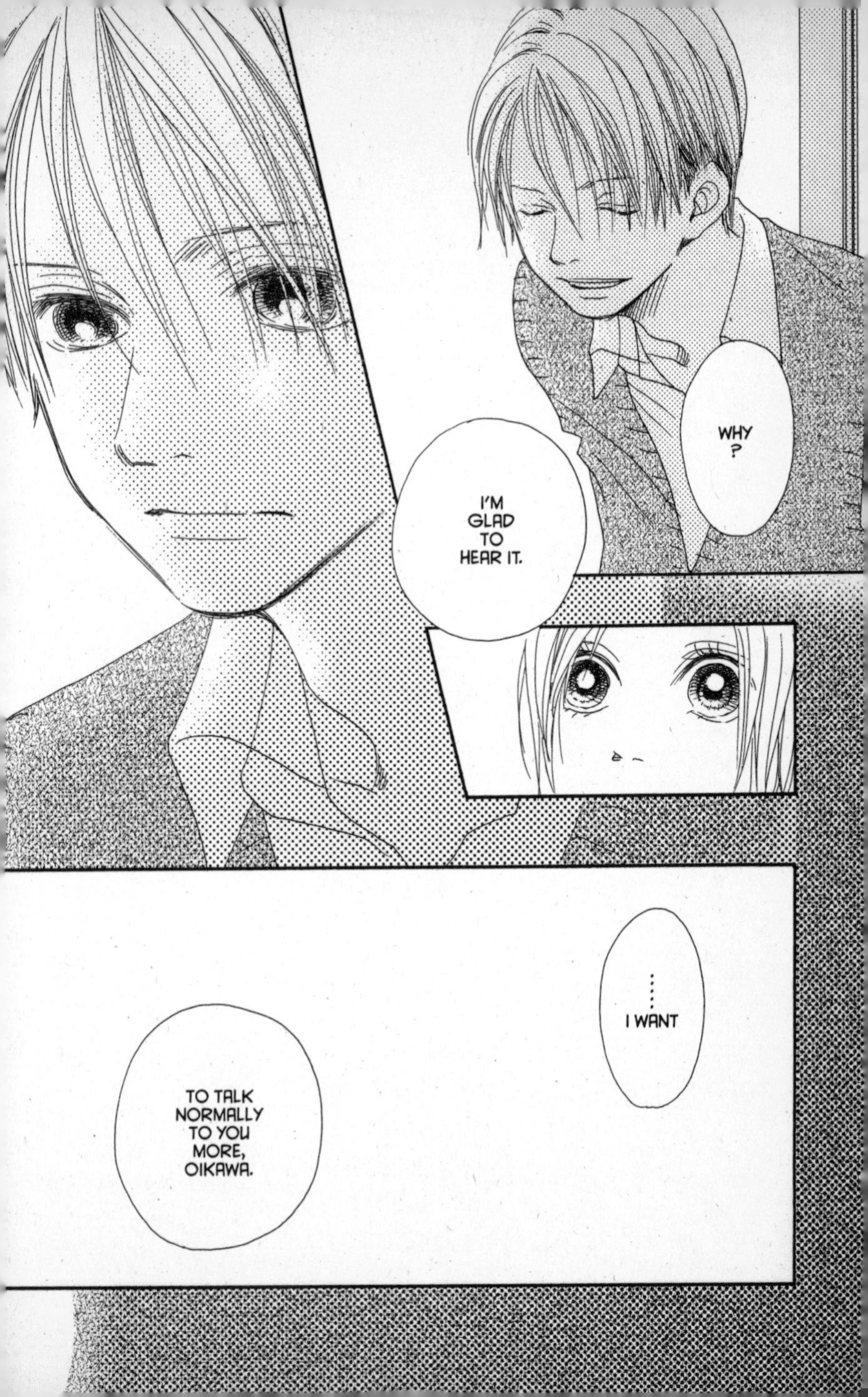
WHY?
I'M GLAD TO HEAR IT.
... I WANT
TO TALK NORMALLY TO YOU MORE, OIKAWA.

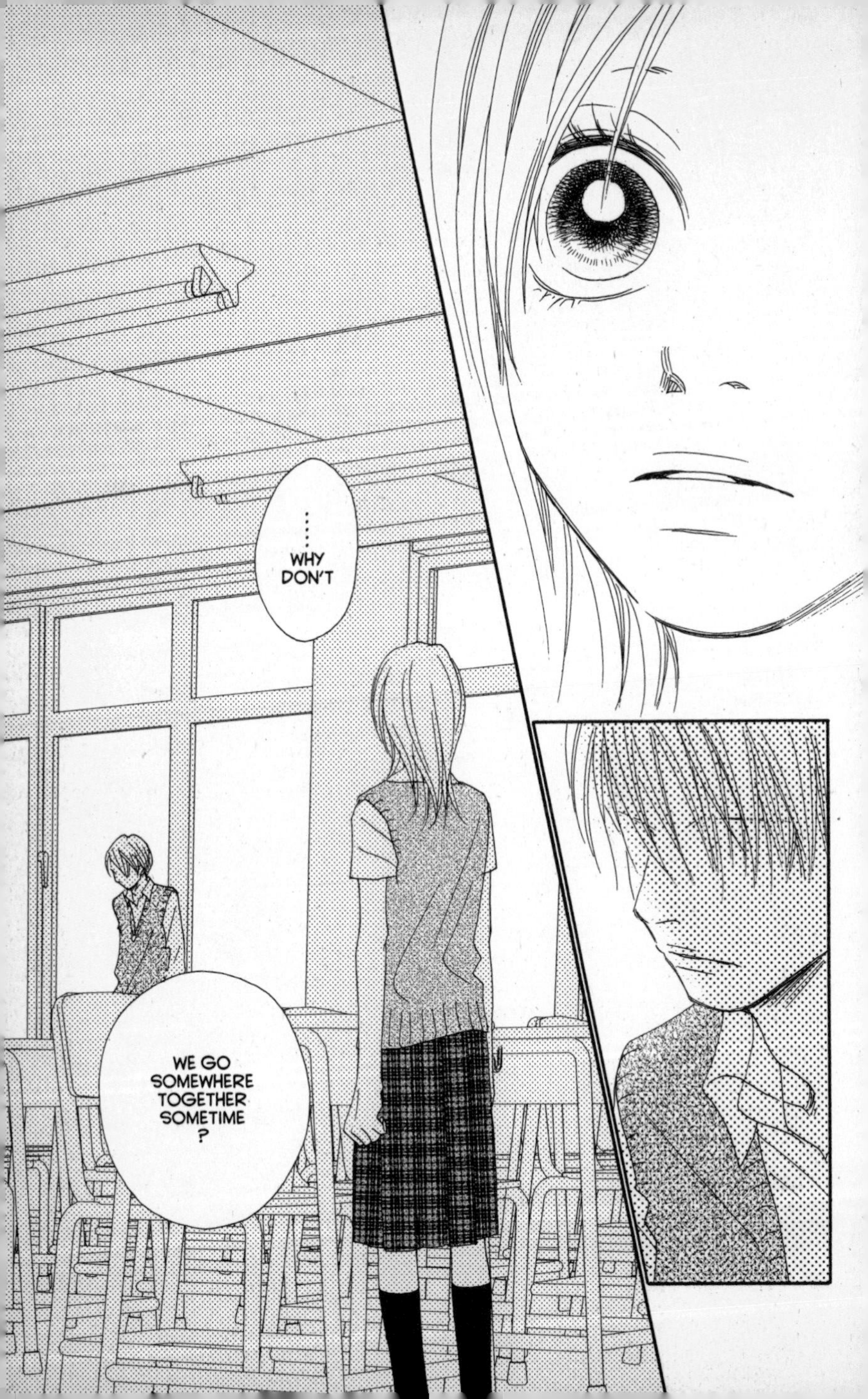
...WHY DON'T
WE GO SOMEWHERE TOGETHER SOMETIME?

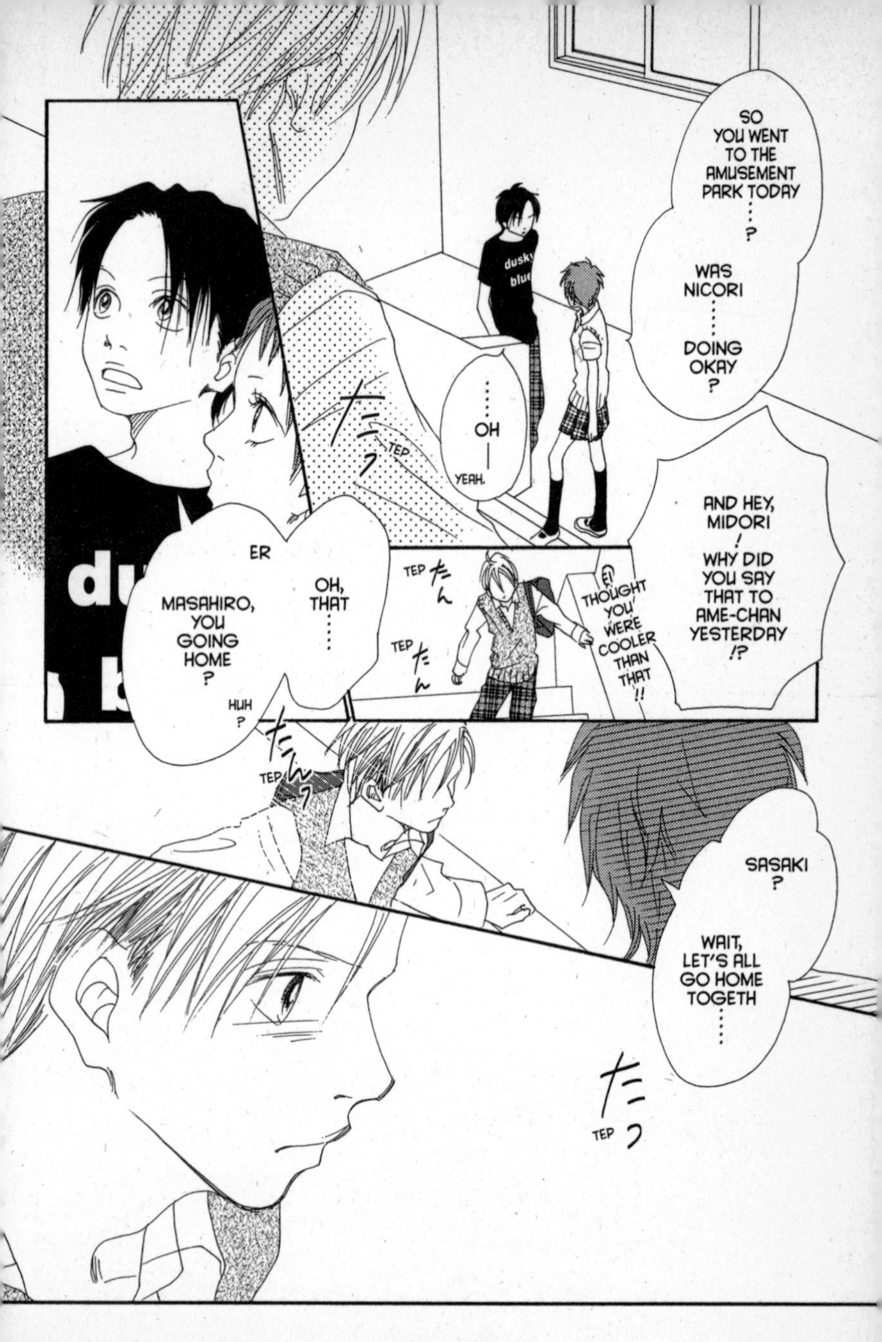
SO YOU WENT TO THE AMUSEMENT PARK TODAY...?
WAS NICORI ... DOING OKAY?
OH — YEAH.
TEP
AND HEY, MIDORI! WHY DID YOU SAY THAT TO AME-CHAN YESTERDAY!?
I THOUGHT YOU WERE COOLER THAN THAT!!
TEP
TEP
OH, THAT...
ER
MASAHIRO, YOU GOING HOME?
HUH?
TEP
SASAKI?
WAIT, LET'S ALL GO HOME TOGETH...
TEP

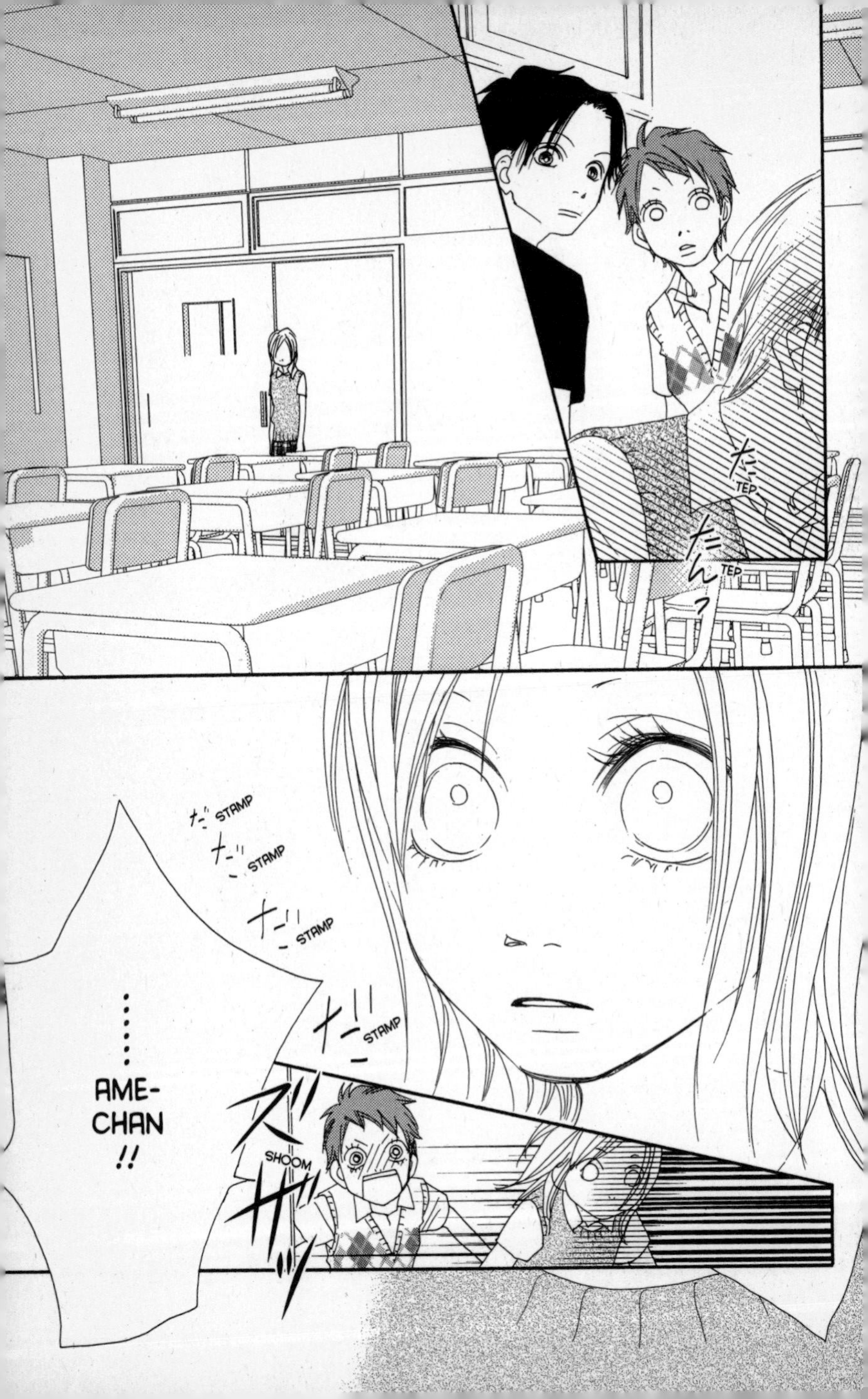
TEP
TEP
STAMP
STAMP
STAMP
STAMP
...... AME-CHAN!!
SHOOM

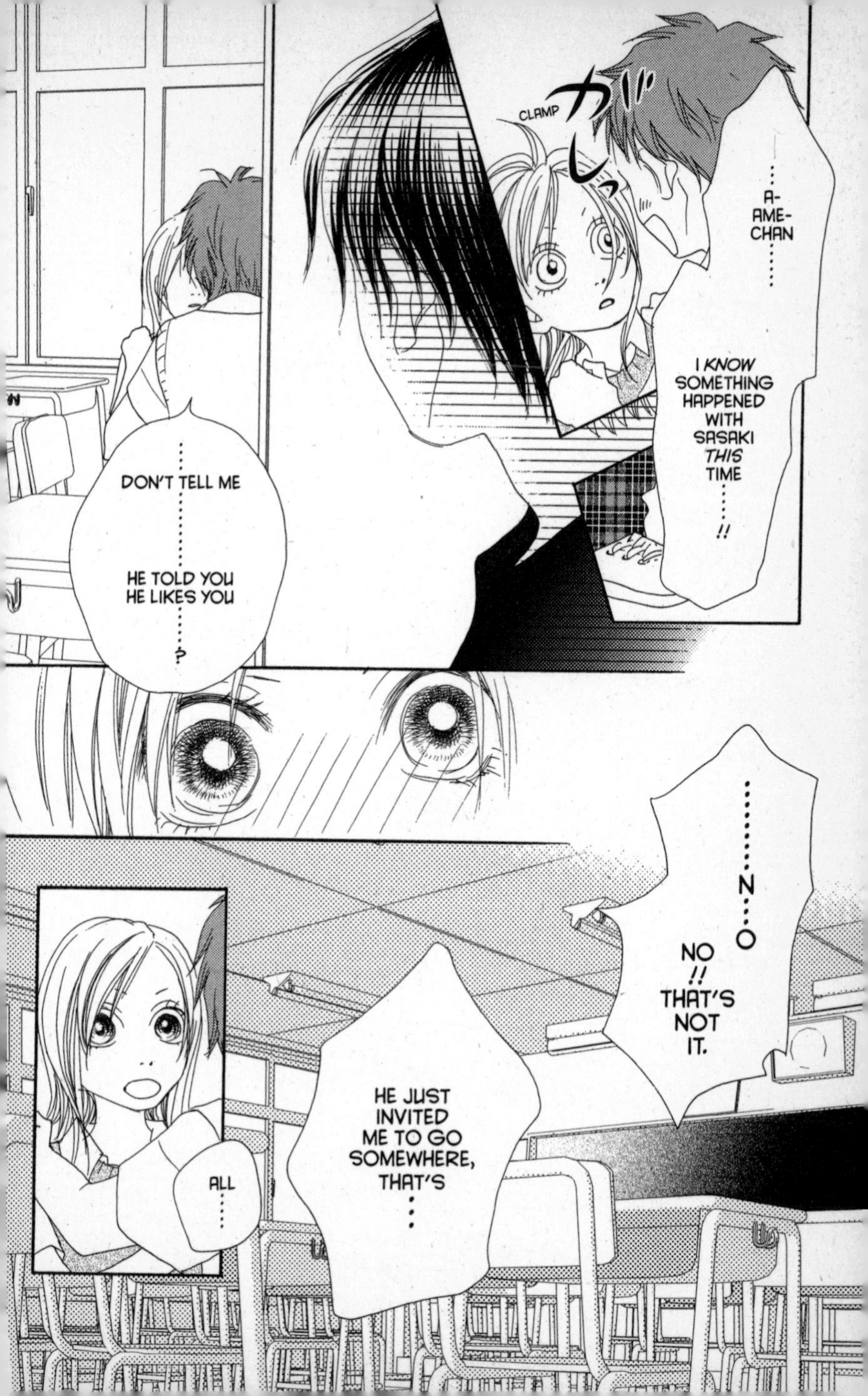

CLAMP
......A- AME-CHAN......
I KNOW SOMETHING HAPPENED WITH SASAKI THIS TIME......!!
......DON'T TELL ME ......HE TOLD YOU HE LIKES YOU......?
......N...O
NO!! THAT'S NOT IT.
HE JUST INVITED ME TO GO SOMEWHERE, THAT'S...
ALL...

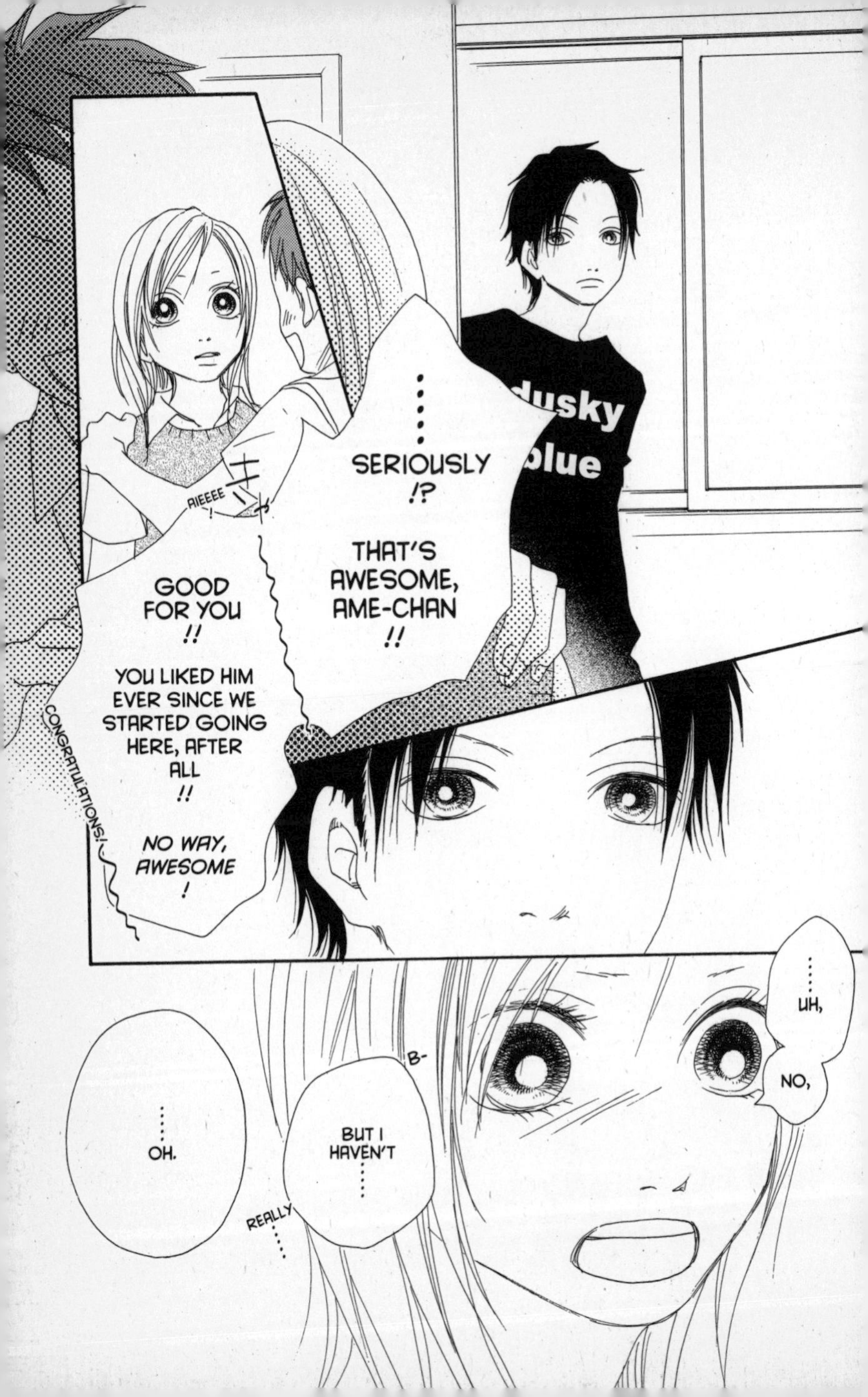

dusky blue
......SERIOUSLY !?
THAT'S AWESOME, AME-CHAN !!
GOOD FOR YOU !!
YOU LIKED HIM EVER SINCE WE STARTED GOING HERE, AFTER ALL !!
NO WAY, AWESOME !
AIEEEE !
CONGRATULATIONS!
......UH,
NO,
B-
BUT I HAVEN'T ......
REALLY ......
......OH.

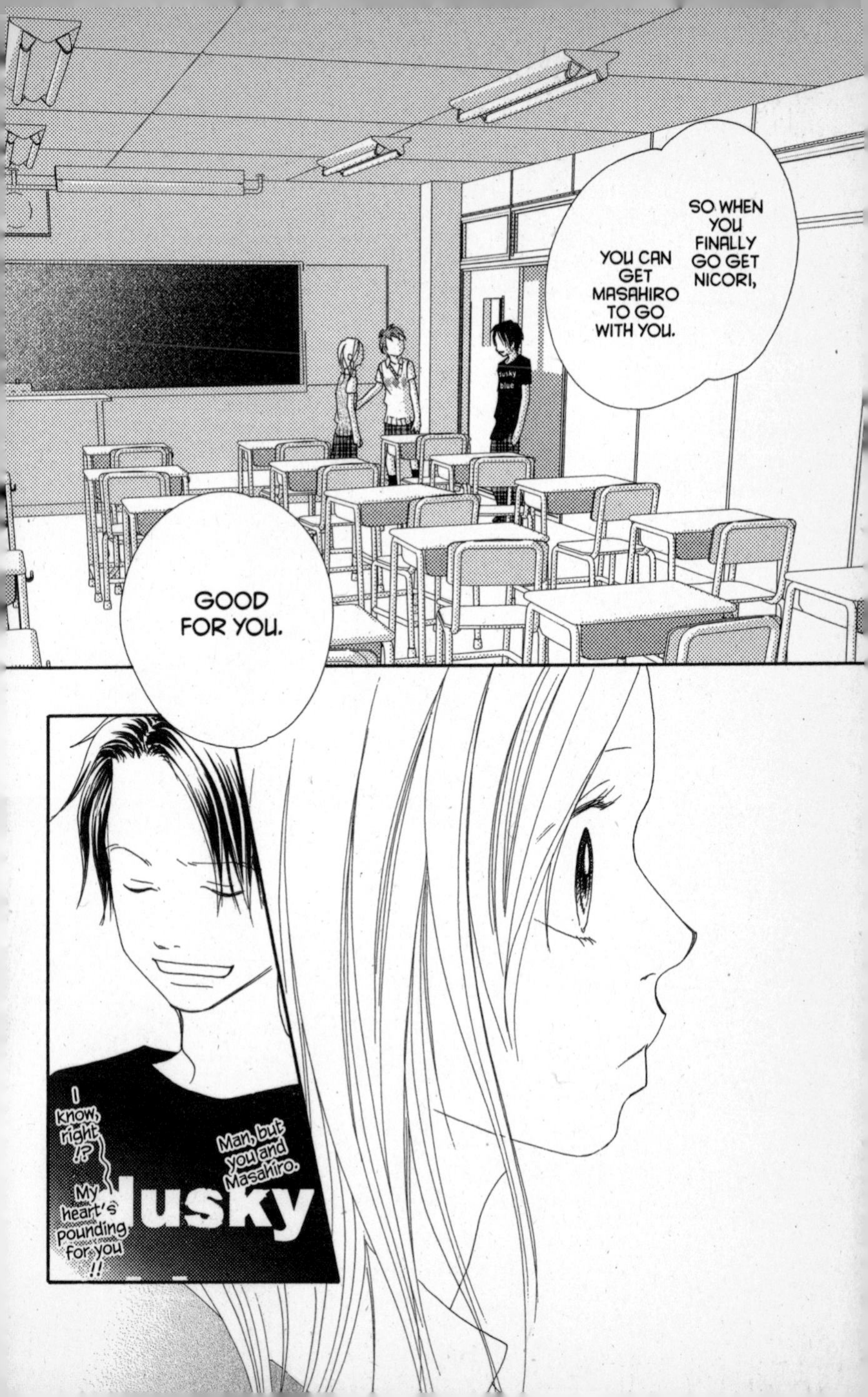
SO WHEN YOU FINALLY GO GET NICORI,
YOU CAN GET MASAHIRO TO GO WITH YOU.
GOOD FOR YOU.
Man, but you and Masahiro.
I know, right!? My heart's pounding for you!!

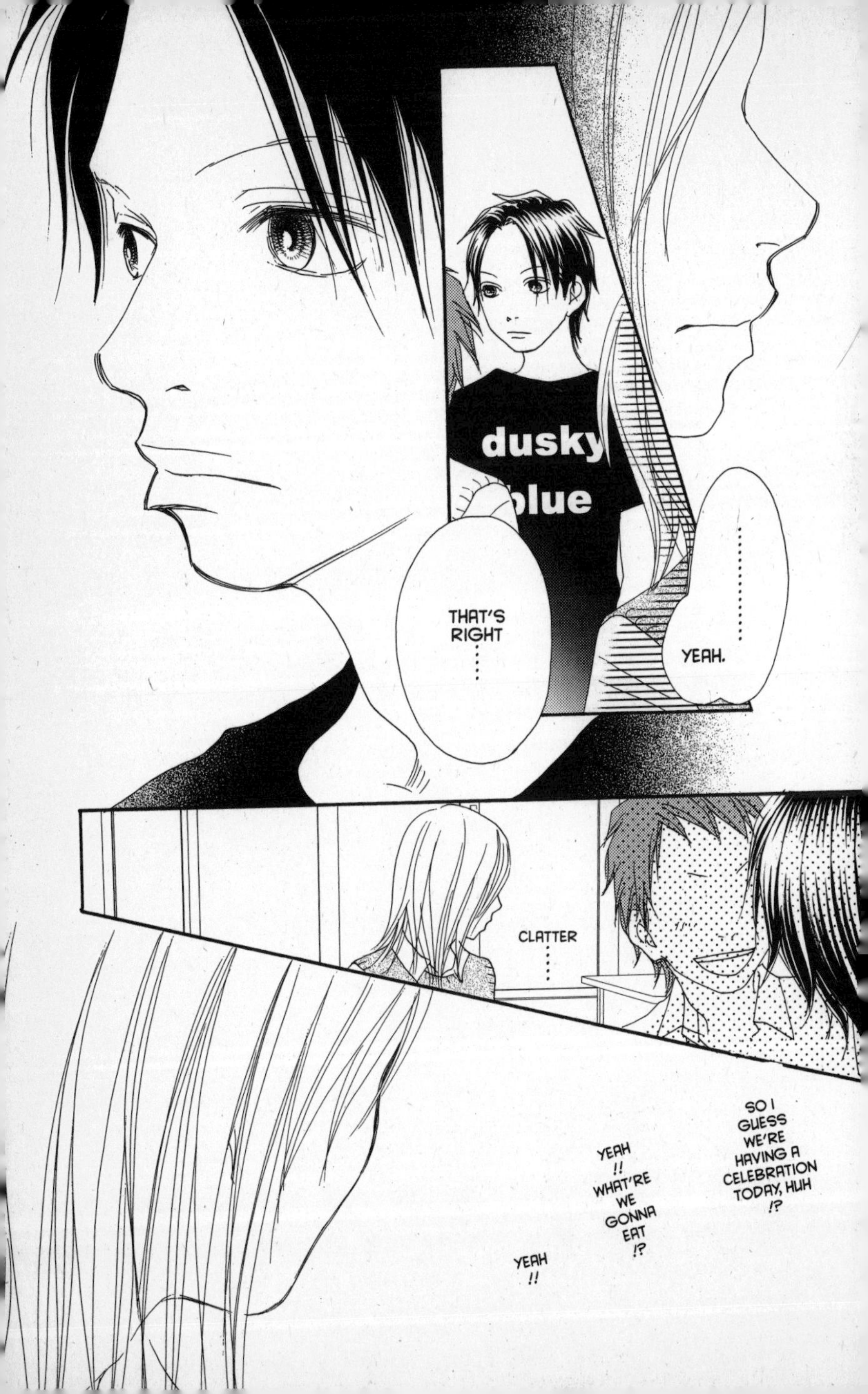
......YEAH.
dusky
THAT'S RIGHT......
CLATTER......
SO I GUESS WE'RE HAVING A CELEBRATION TODAY, HUH!?
YEAH!! WHAT'RE WE GONNA EAT!?
YEAH!!

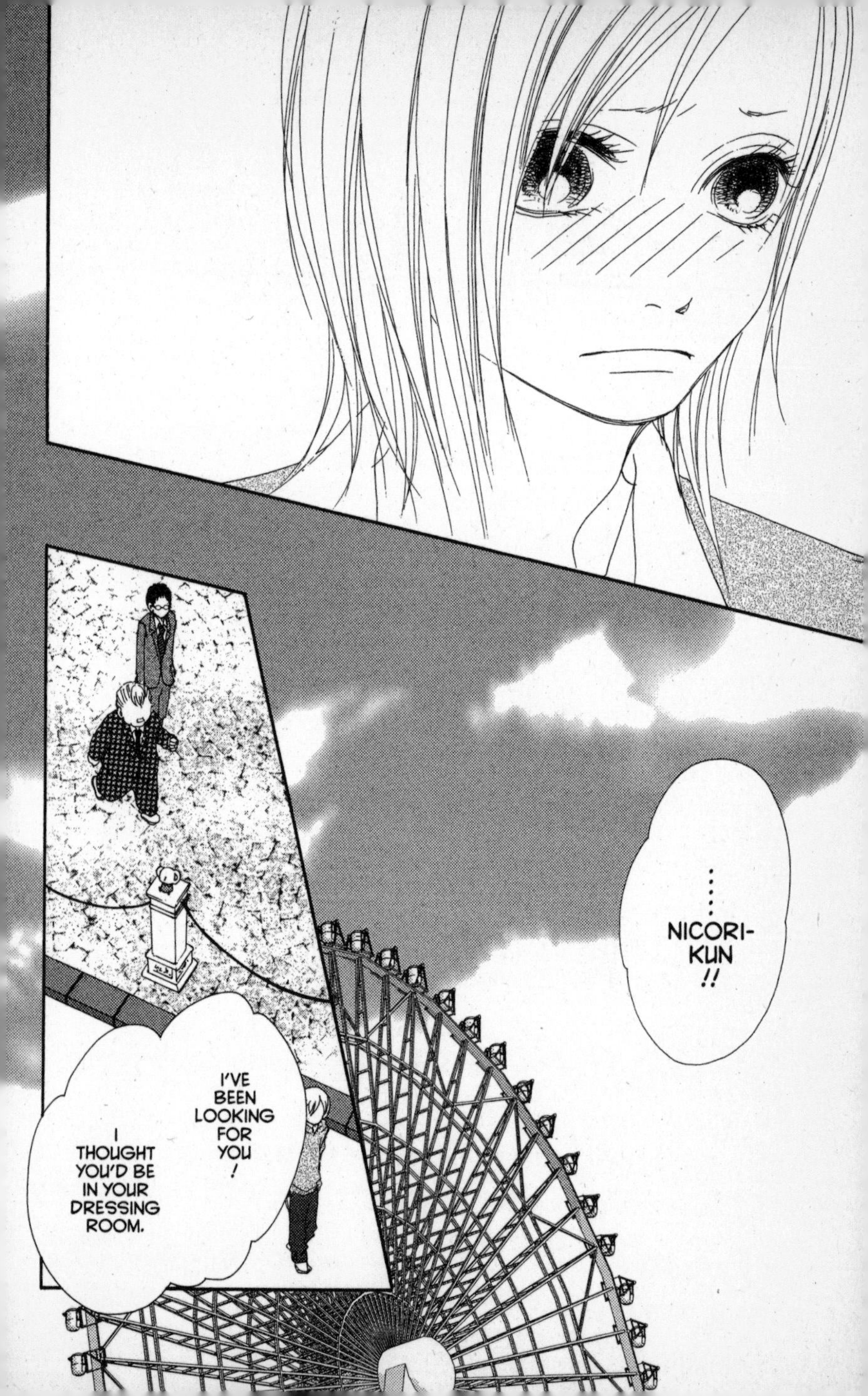
.....NICORI-KUN!!
I'VE BEEN LOOKING FOR YOU!
I THOUGHT YOU'D BE IN YOUR DRESSING ROOM.

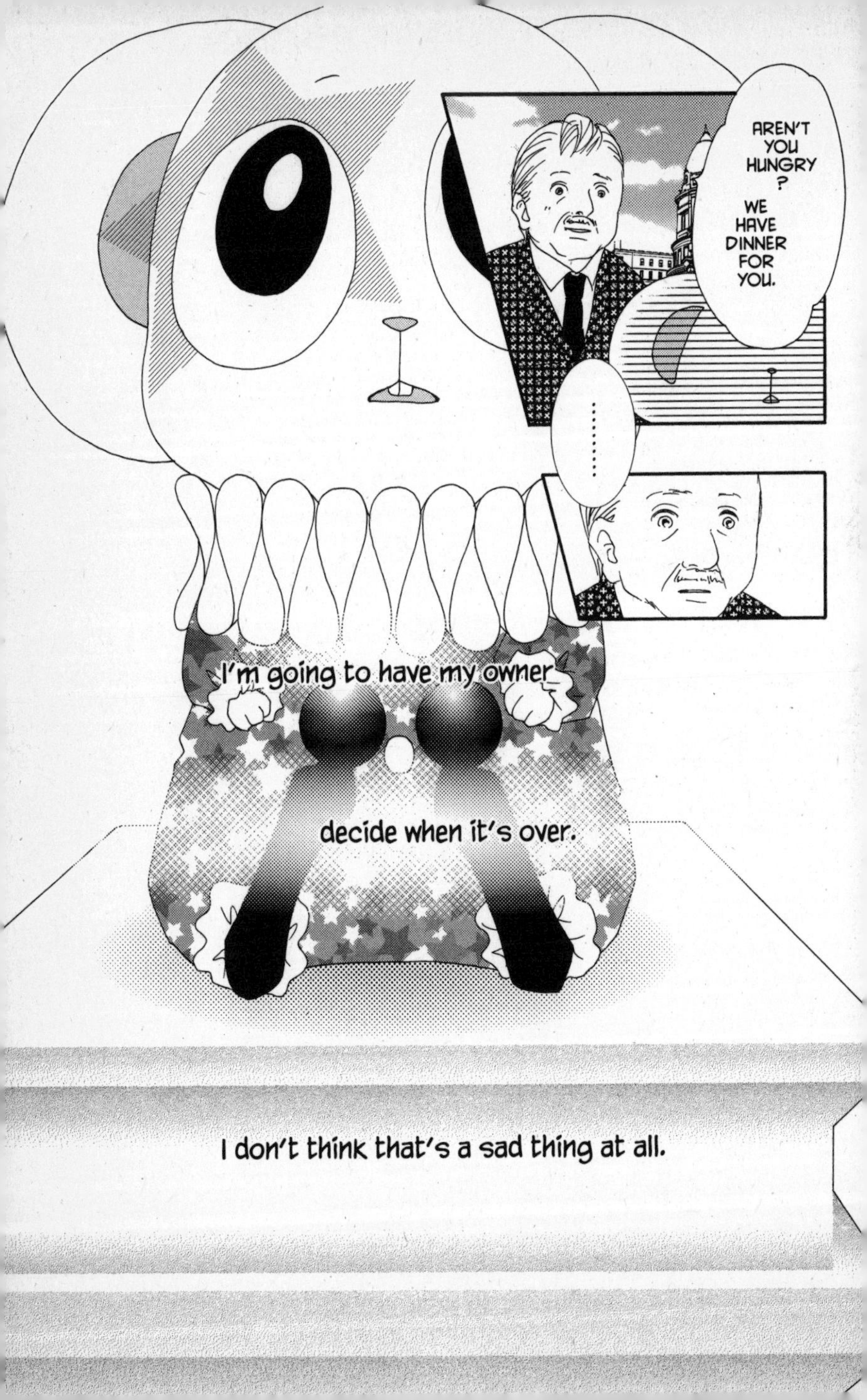
AREN'T YOU HUNGRY? WE HAVE DINNER FOR YOU.
......
I'm going to have my owner
decide when it's over.
I don't think that's a sad thing at all.

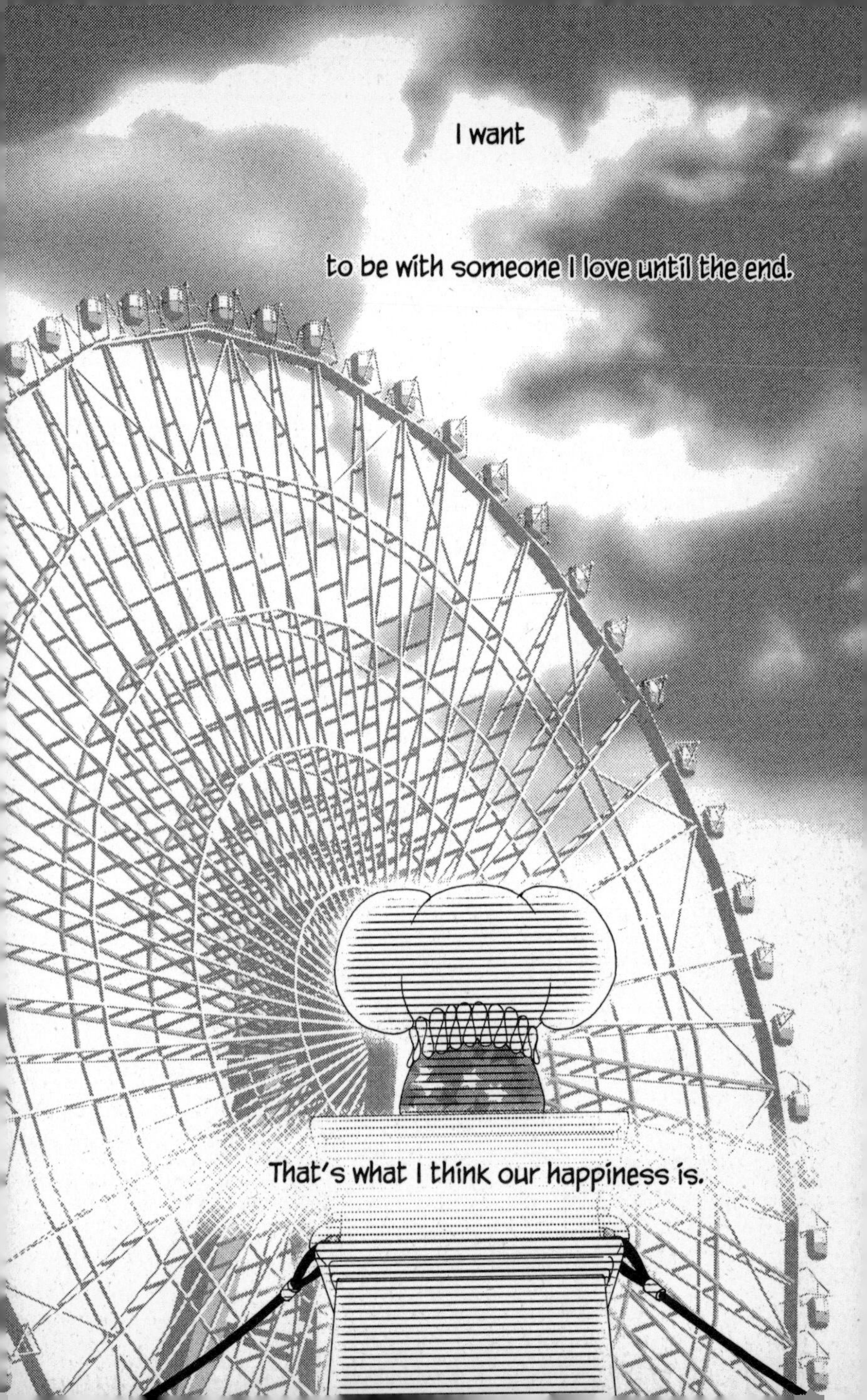
I want
to be with someone I love until the end.
That's what I think our happiness is.

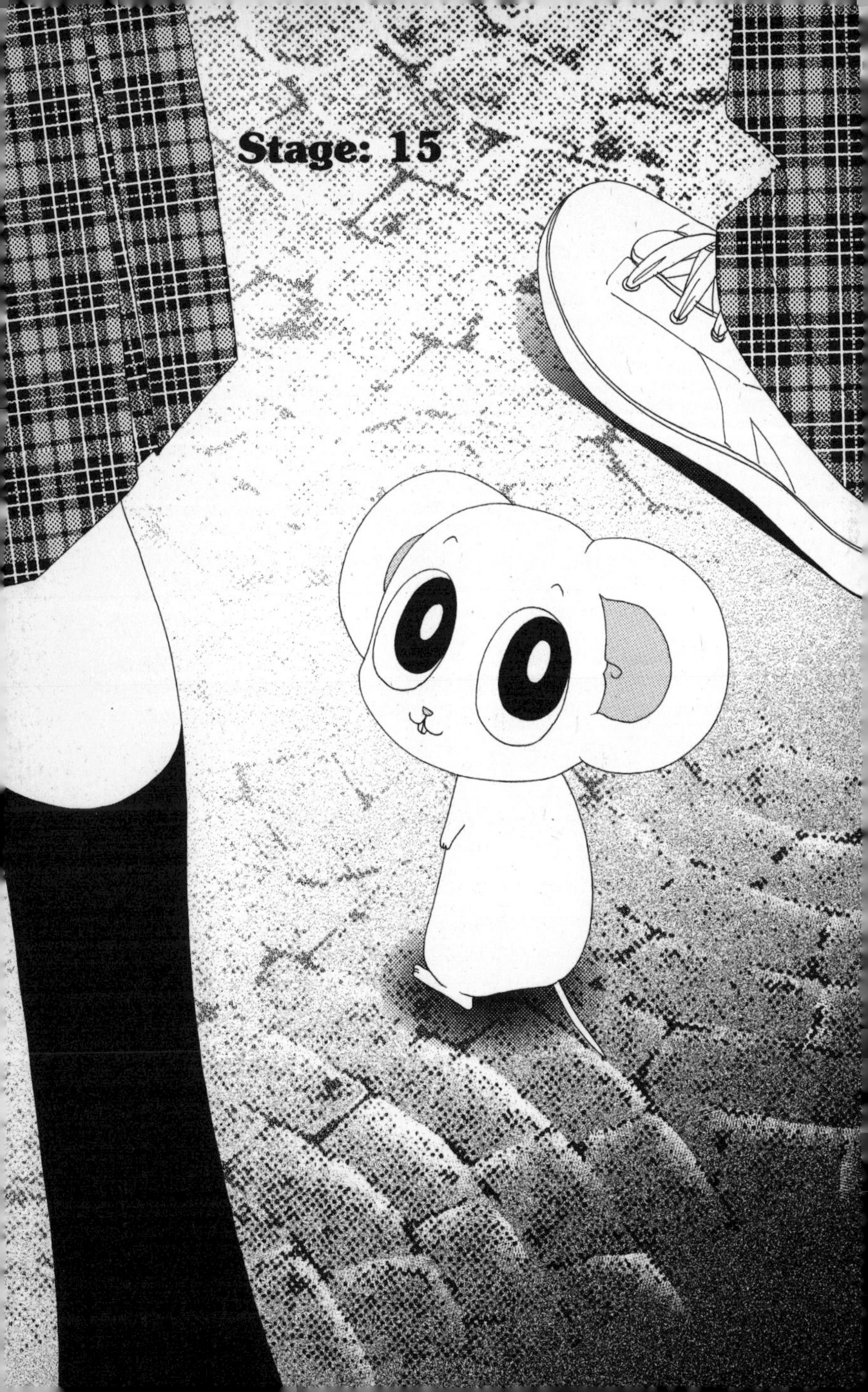
Stage: 15

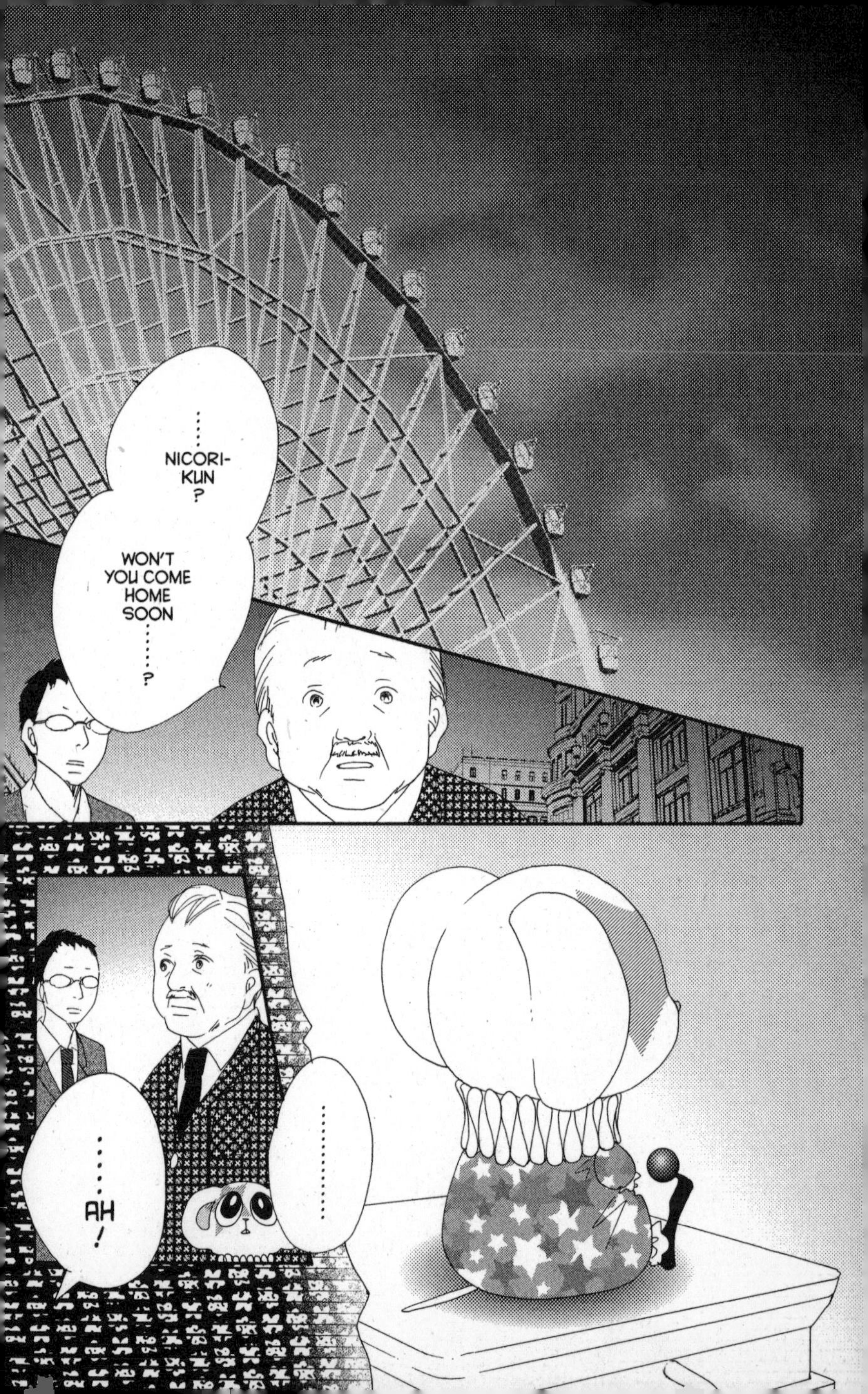
......NICORI-KUN?
WON'T YOU COME HOME SOON......?
....
......AH!

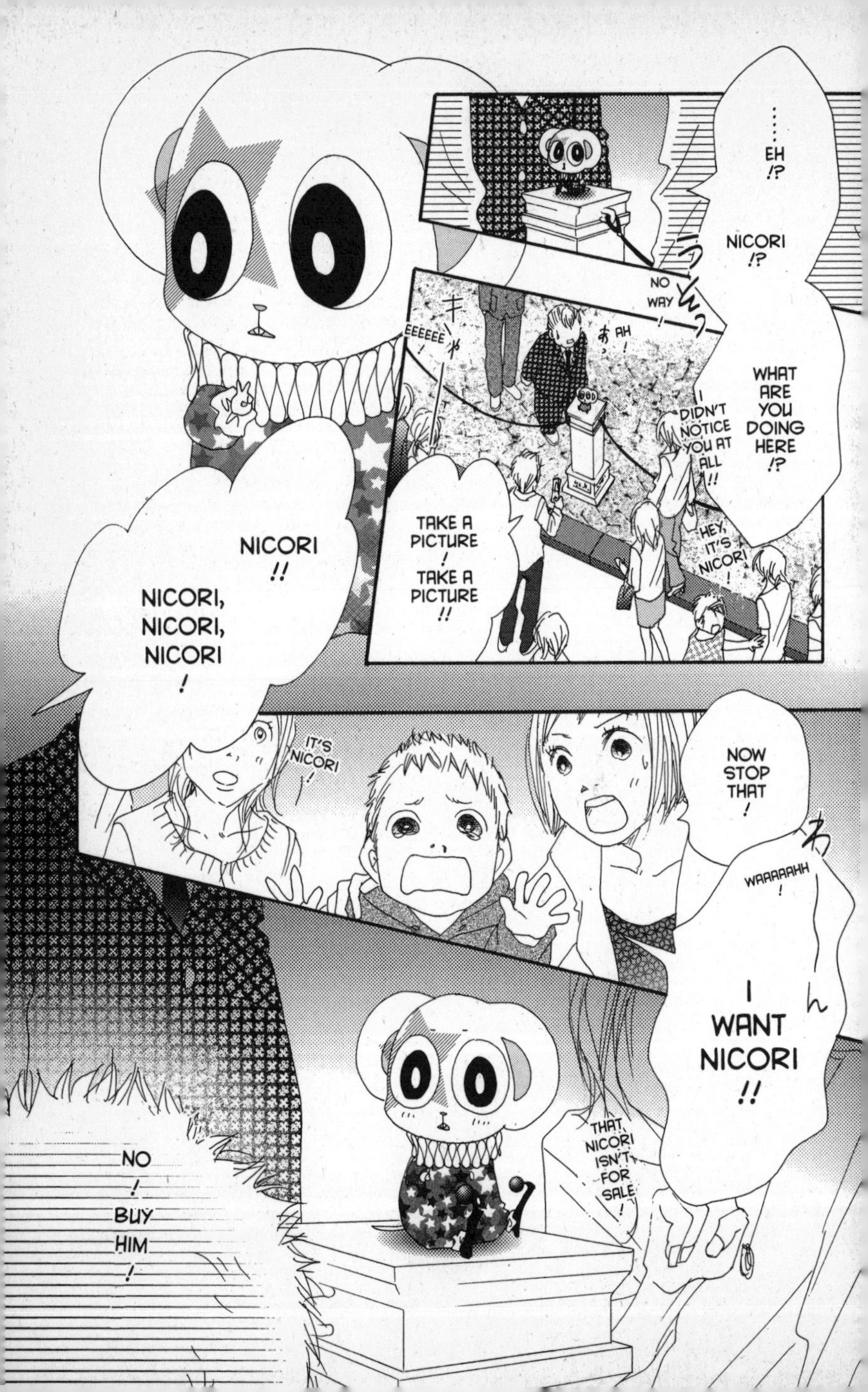
......EH!?
NICORI!?
NO WAY!
WHAT ARE YOU DOING HERE!?
I DIDN'T NOTICE YOU AT ALL!!
AH!
EEEEEE!
HEY, IT'S NICORI!
TAKE A PICTURE! TAKE A PICTURE!!
NICORI!!
NICORI, NICORI, NICORI!
NOW STOP THAT!
IT'S NICORI!
WAAAAAHH!
I WANT NICORI!!
THAT NICORI ISN'T FOR SALE!
NO! BUY HIM!

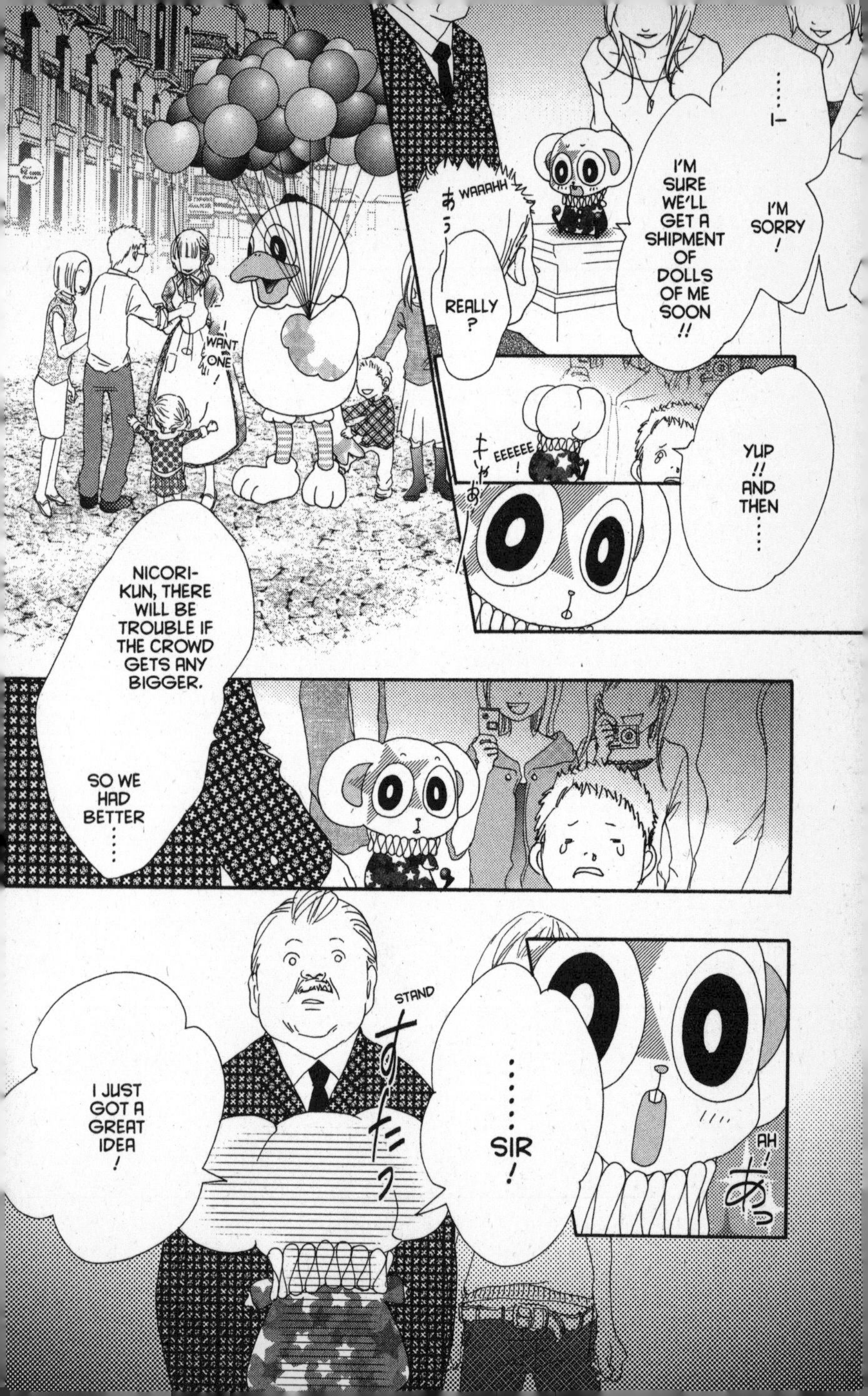
......I—
I'M SORRY!
I'M SURE WE'LL GET A SHIPMENT OF DOLLS OF ME SOON!!
あう WAAAHH
REALLY?
YUP!! AND THEN......
EEEEEE!
I WANT ONE!
NICORI-KUN, THERE WILL BE TROUBLE IF THE CROWD GETS ANY BIGGER.
SO WE HAD BETTER......
AH! あっ
......SIR!
STAND
I JUST GOT A GREAT IDEA!

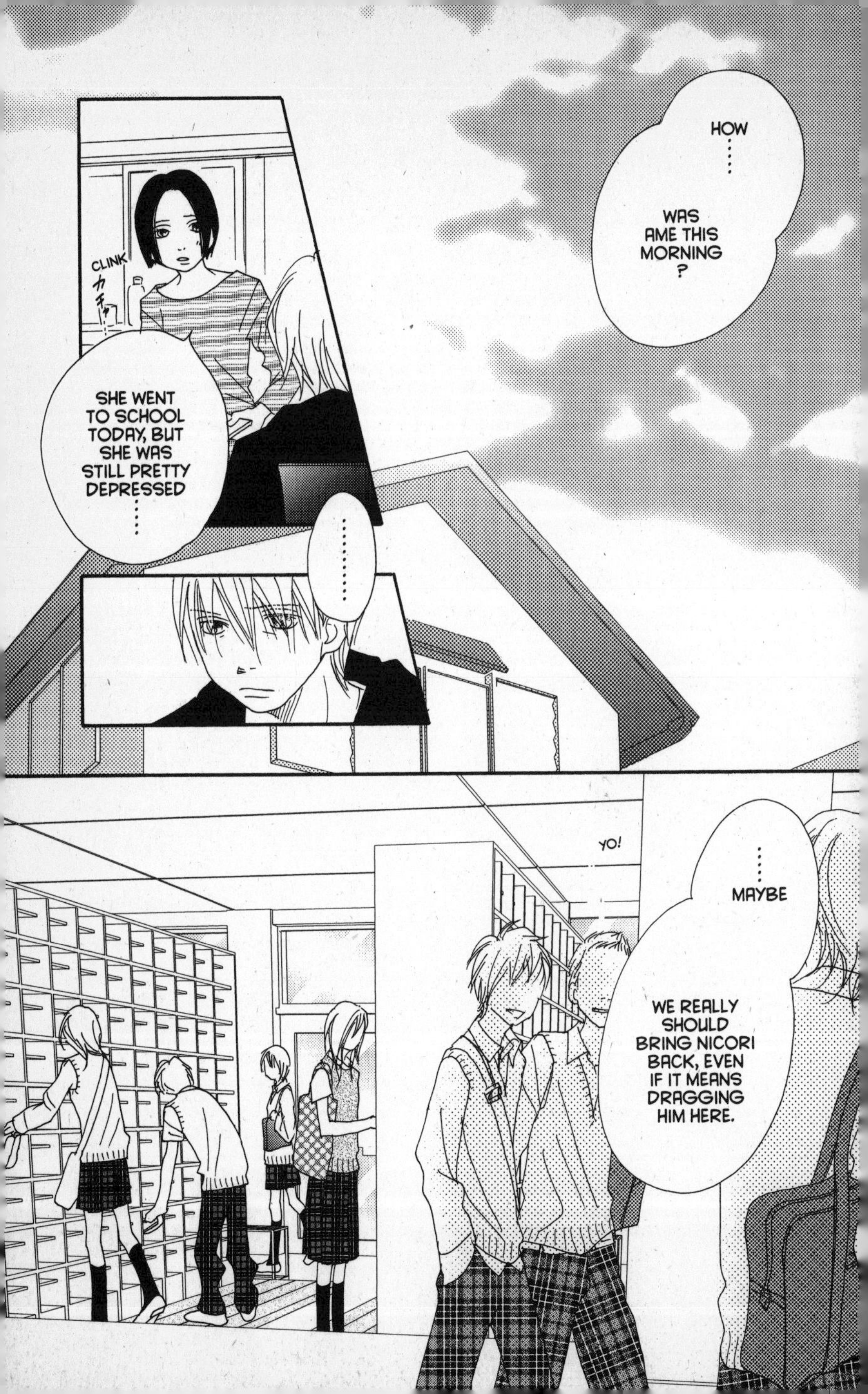
HOW......
WAS AME THIS MORNING?
CLINK
カチャ...
SHE WENT TO SCHOOL TODAY, BUT SHE WAS STILL PRETTY DEPRESSED......
......
YO!
......MAYBE
WE REALLY SHOULD BRING NICORI BACK, EVEN IF IT MEANS DRAGGING HIM HERE.

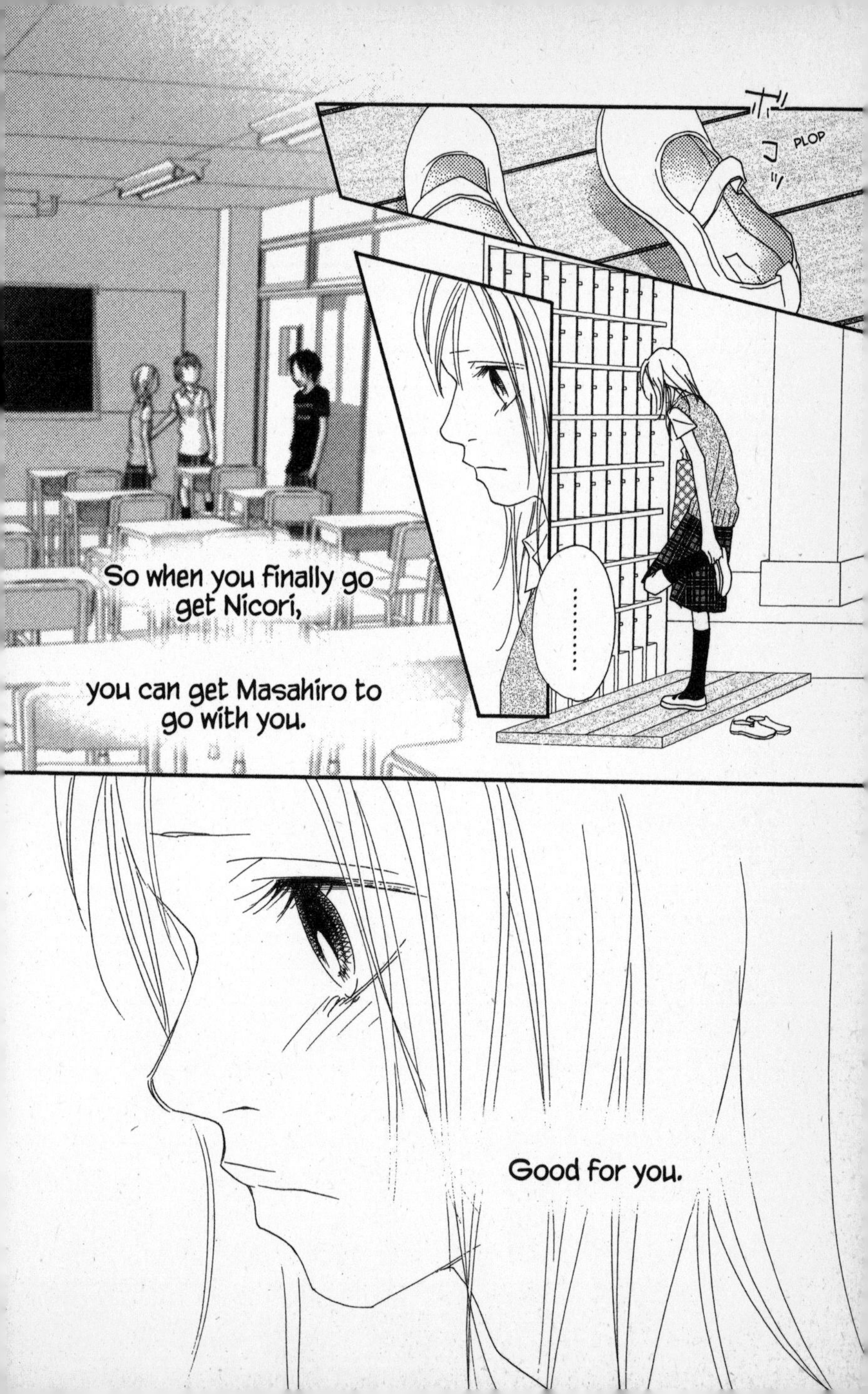
ボコッ
PLOP
......
So when you finally go get Nicori,
you can get Masahiro to go with you.
Good for you.

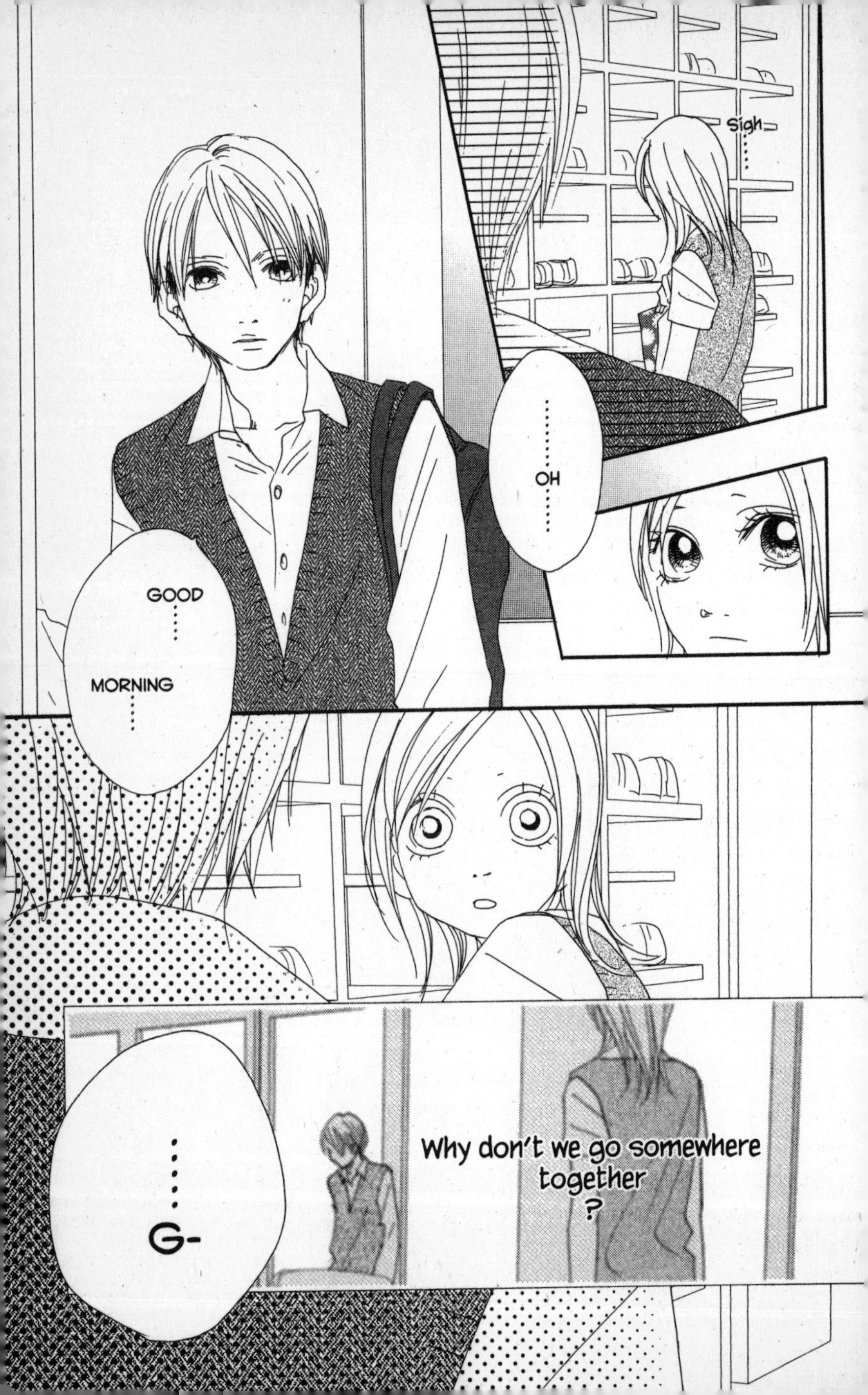
Sigh......
......OH......
GOOD... MORNING...
Why don't we go somewhere together?
....G-

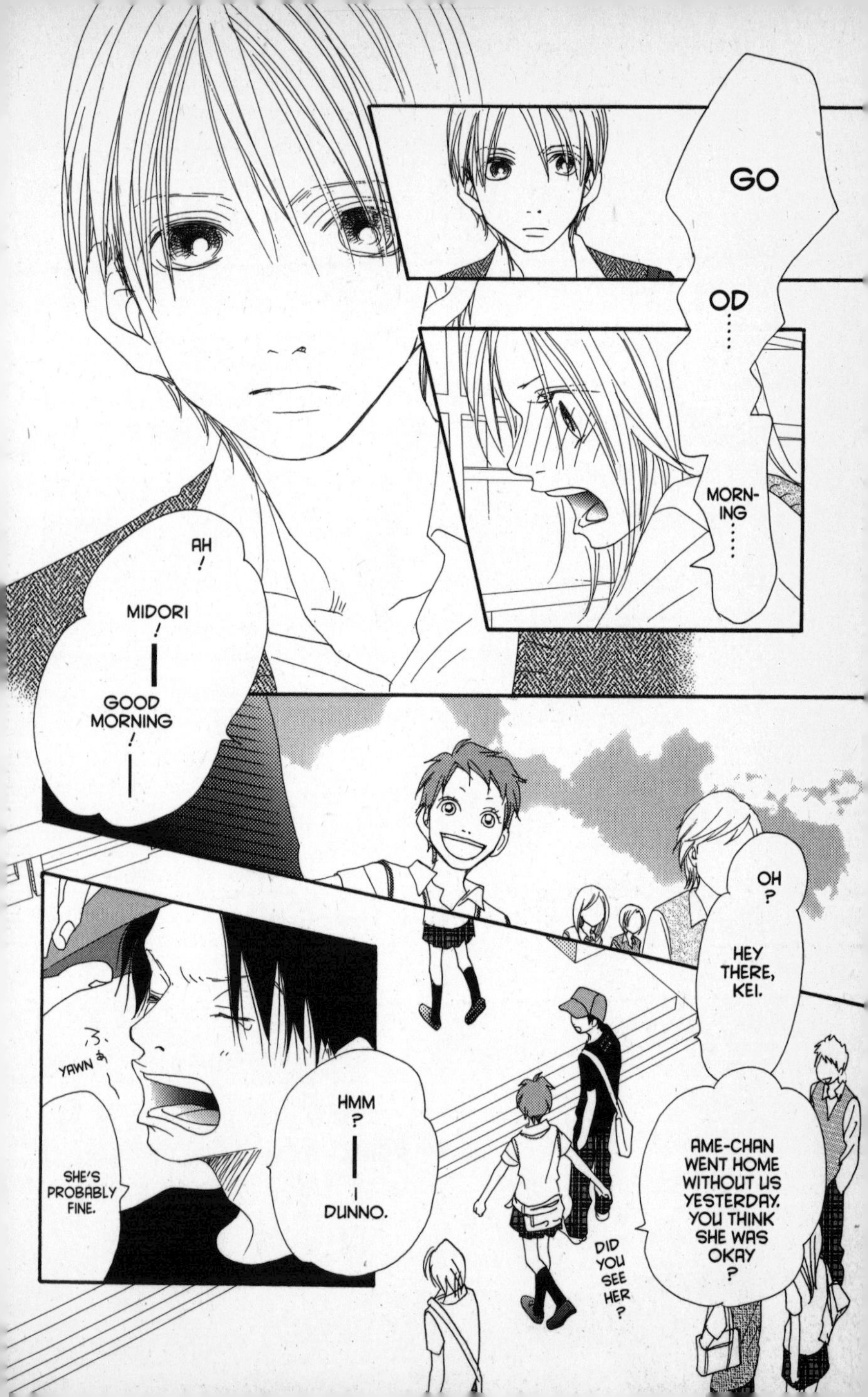
GO OD..... MORNING-ING.....
AH! MIDORI! GOOD MORNING!
OH? HEY THERE, KEI.
AME-CHAN WENT HOME WITHOUT US YESTERDAY. YOU THINK SHE WAS OKAY?
DID YOU SEE HER?
ふぁ
YAWN
HMM? DUNNO.
SHE'S PROBABLY FINE.

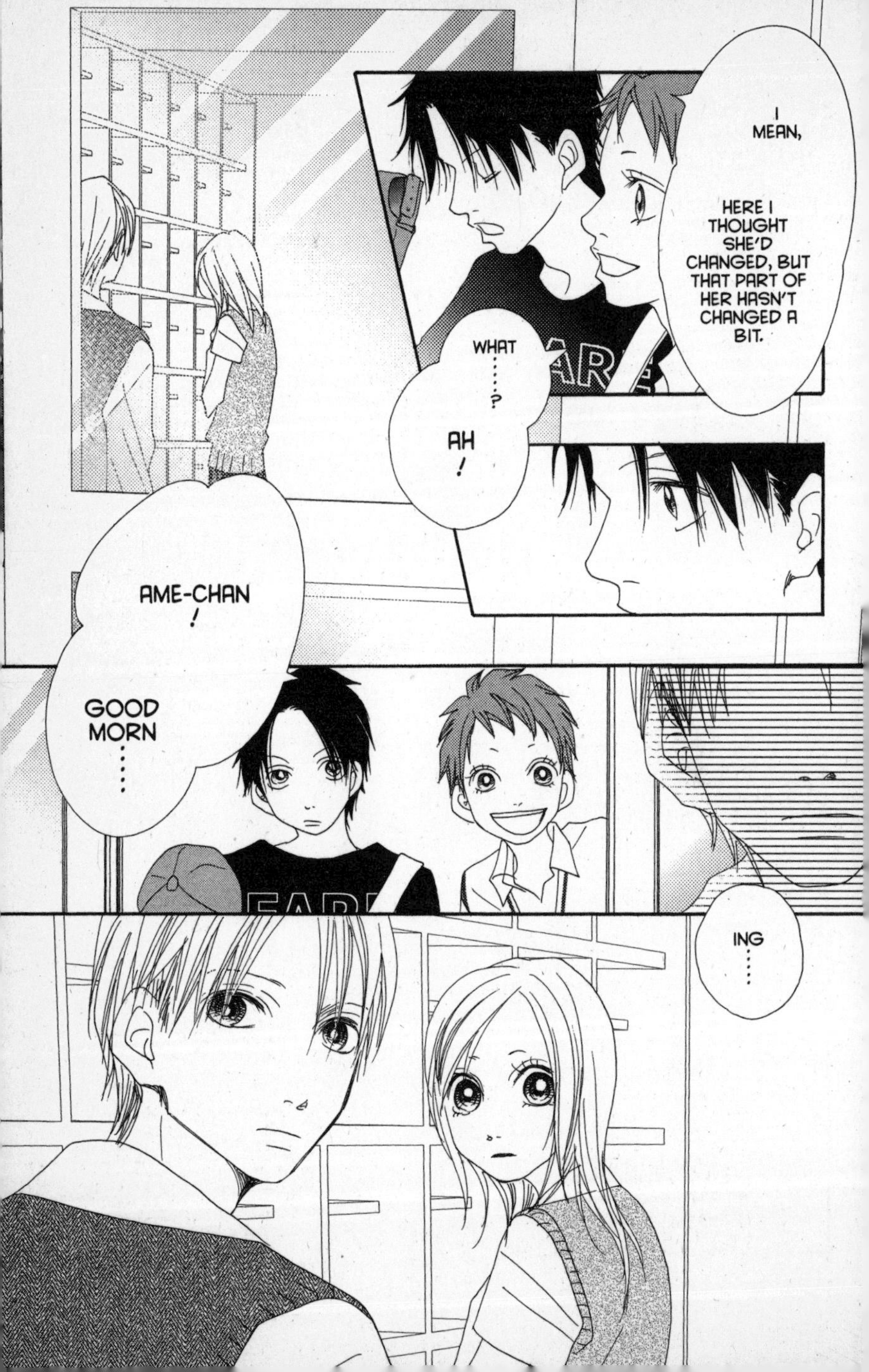
I MEAN,
HERE I THOUGHT SHE'D CHANGED, BUT THAT PART OF HER HASN'T CHANGED A BIT.
WHAT.....?
AH!
AME-CHAN!
GOOD MORN.....
ING.....

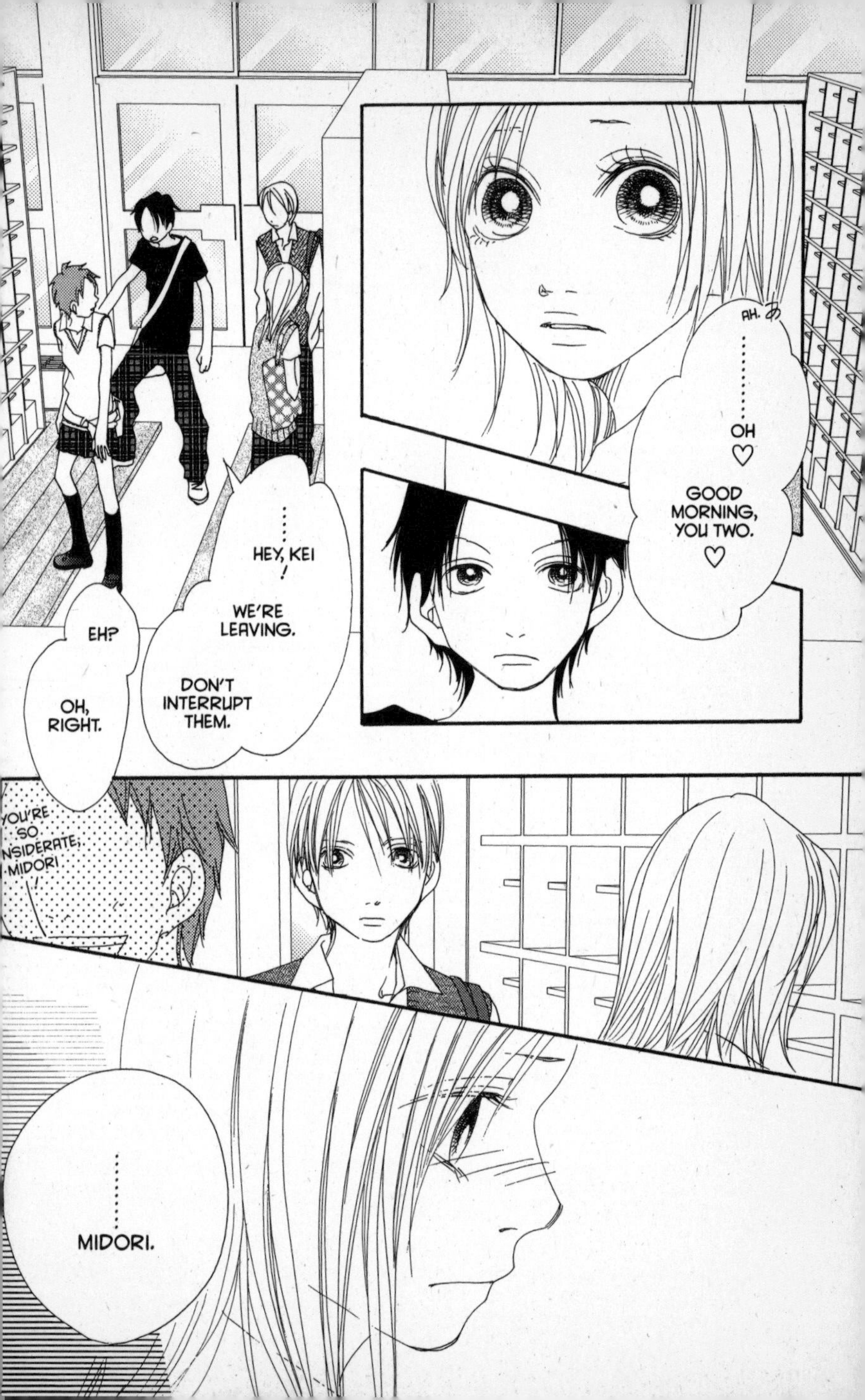
AH. あ ...... OH ♡ GOOD MORNING, YOU TWO. ♡
...... HEY, KEI! WE'RE LEAVING. DON'T INTERRUPT THEM.
EH? OH, RIGHT.
YOU'RE SO NSIDERATE, MIDORI!
...... MIDORI.

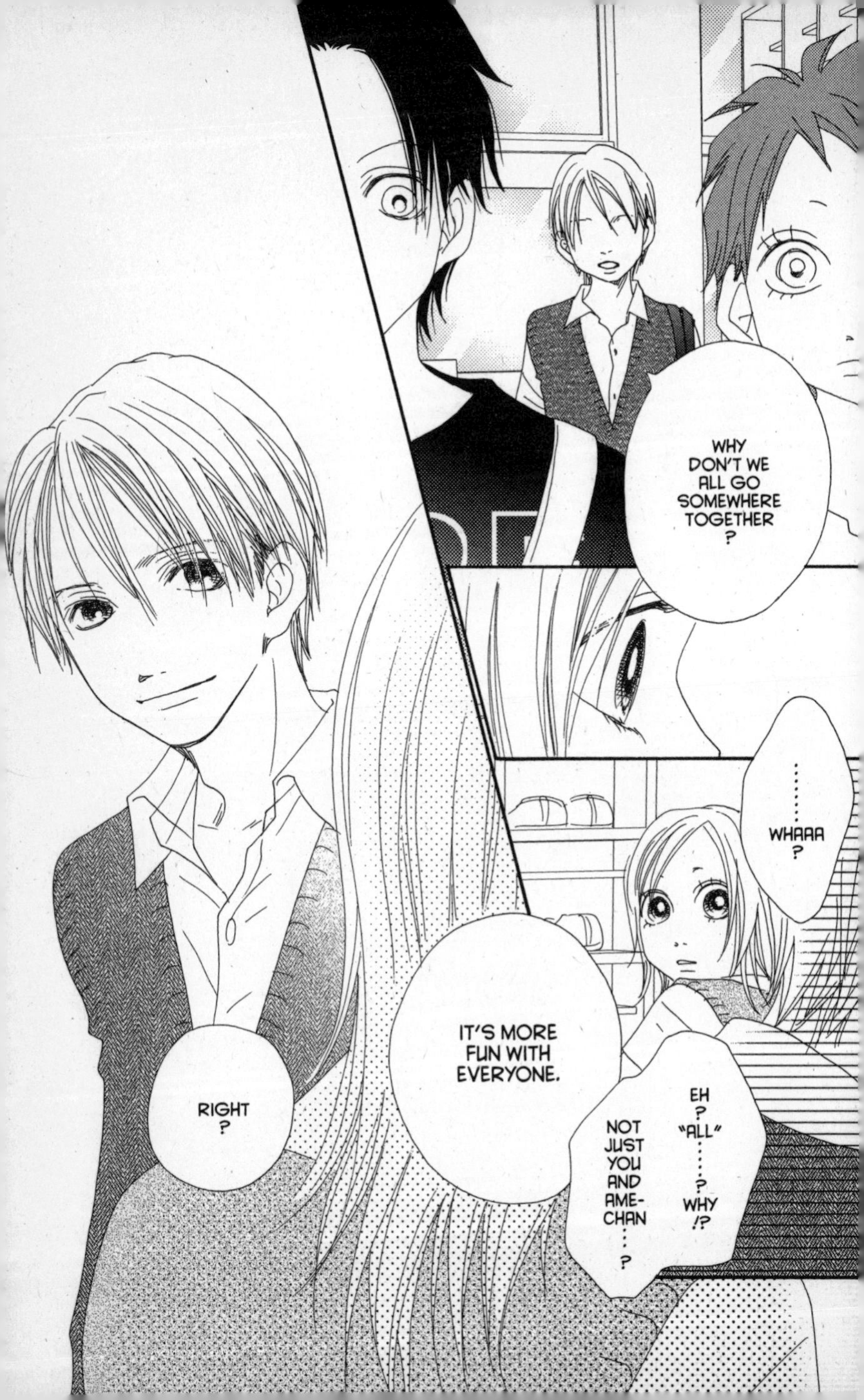
WHY DON'T WE ALL GO SOMEWHERE TOGETHER?
......WHAAA?
EH? "ALL"......? WHY!?
NOT JUST YOU AND AME-CHAN...?
IT'S MORE FUN WITH EVERYONE.
RIGHT?

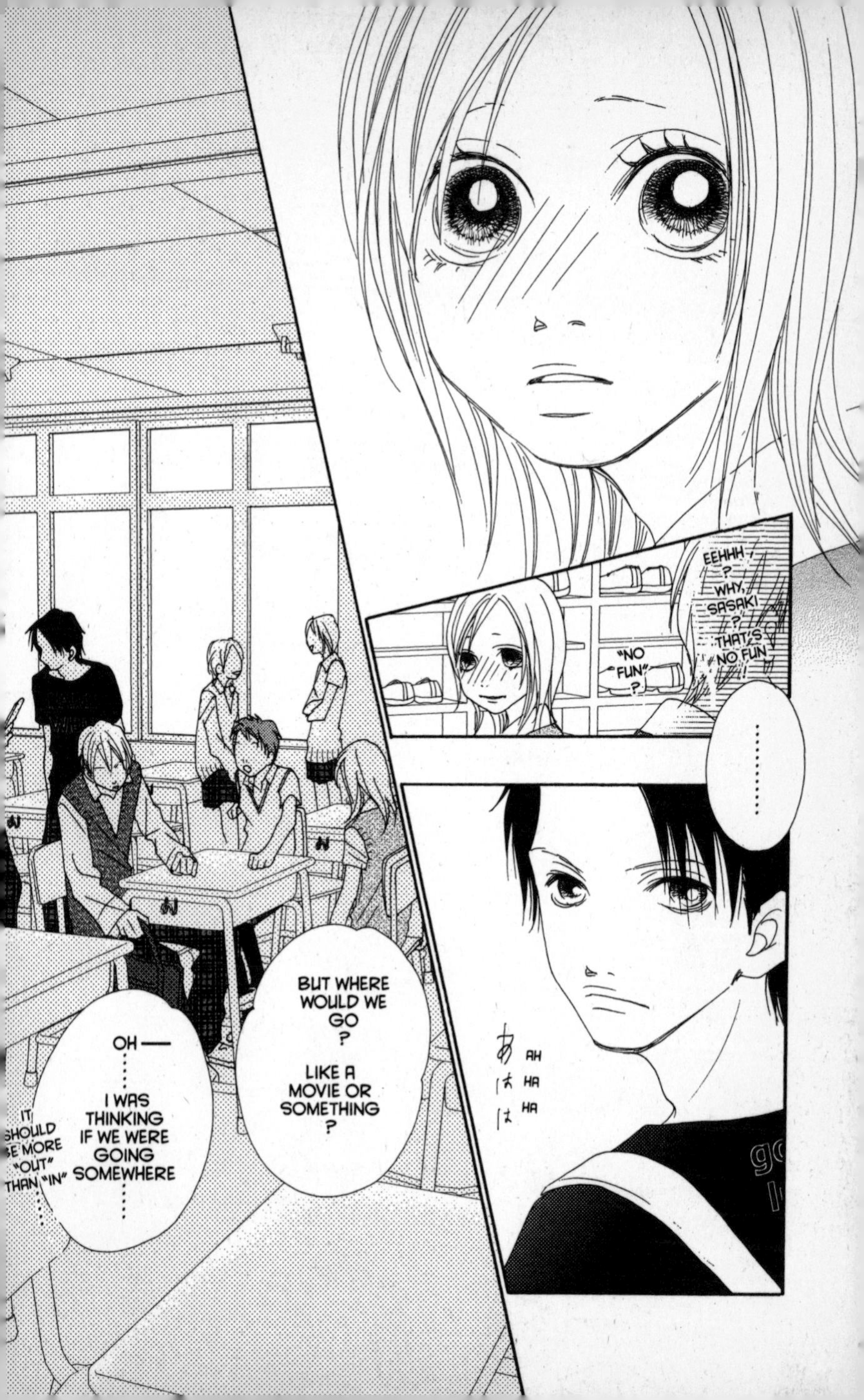
EEHHH? WHY, SASAKI? THAT'S NO FUN!
"NO FUN"?
......
あははは
AH HA HA
BUT WHERE WOULD WE GO? LIKE A MOVIE OR SOMETHING?
OH— ...... I WAS THINKING IF WE WERE GOING SOMEWHERE ......
IT SHOULD BE MORE "OUT" THAN "IN" ......

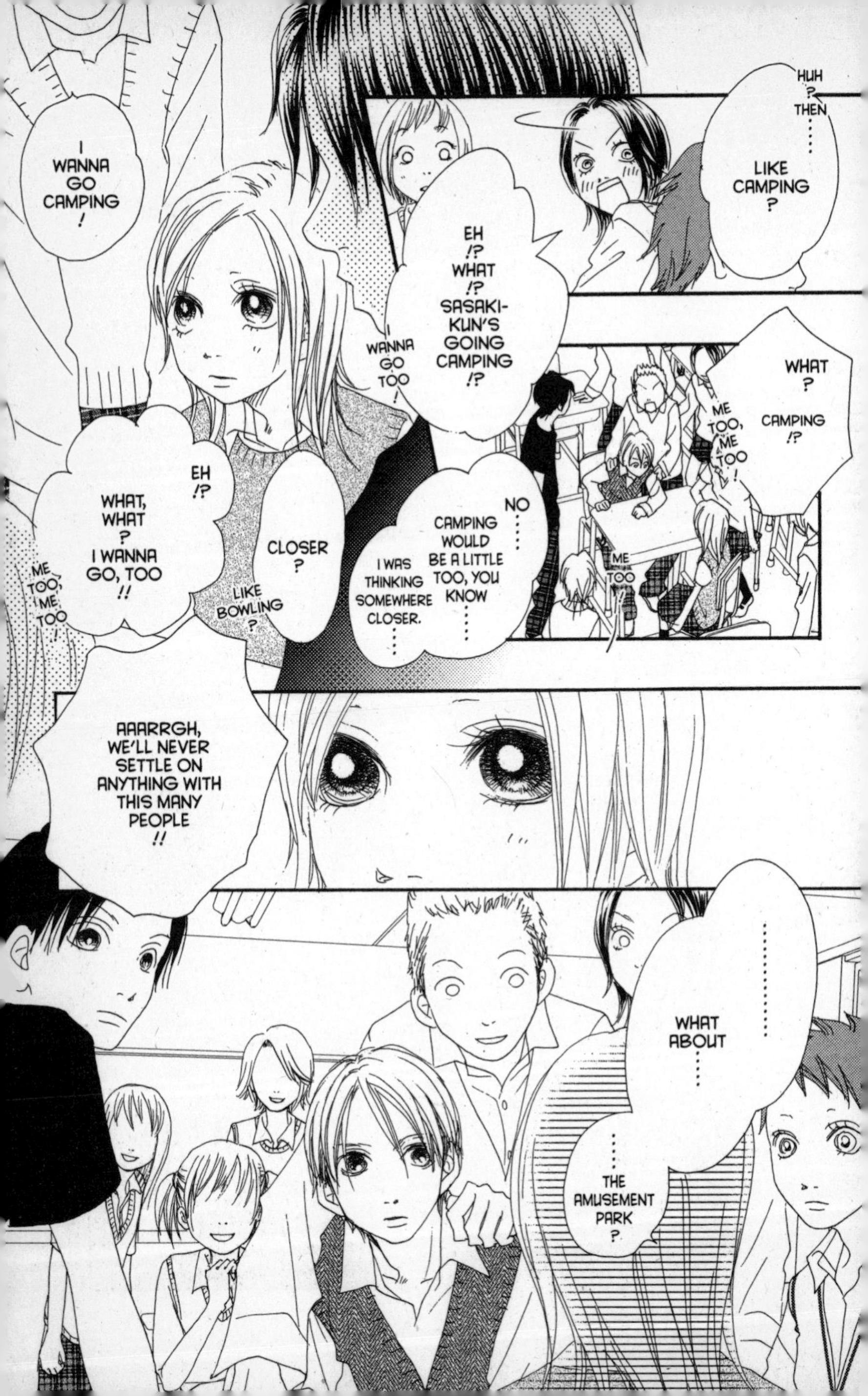
HUH? THEN......
LIKE CAMPING?
EH!? WHAT!? SASAKI-KUN'S GOING CAMPING!?
I WANNA GO CAMPING!
WHAT? CAMPING!?
ME TOO, ME TOO!
I WANNA GO TOO!
ME TOO!
NO...... CAMPING WOULD BE A LITTLE TOO, YOU KNOW......
I WAS THINKING SOMEWHERE CLOSER......
CLOSER?
LIKE BOWLING?
EH!? WHAT, WHAT? I WANNA GO, TOO!!
ME TOO, ME TOO!
AAARRGH, WE'LL NEVER SETTLE ON ANYTHING WITH THIS MANY PEOPLE!!
......
WHAT ABOUT......
......THE AMUSEMENT PARK?

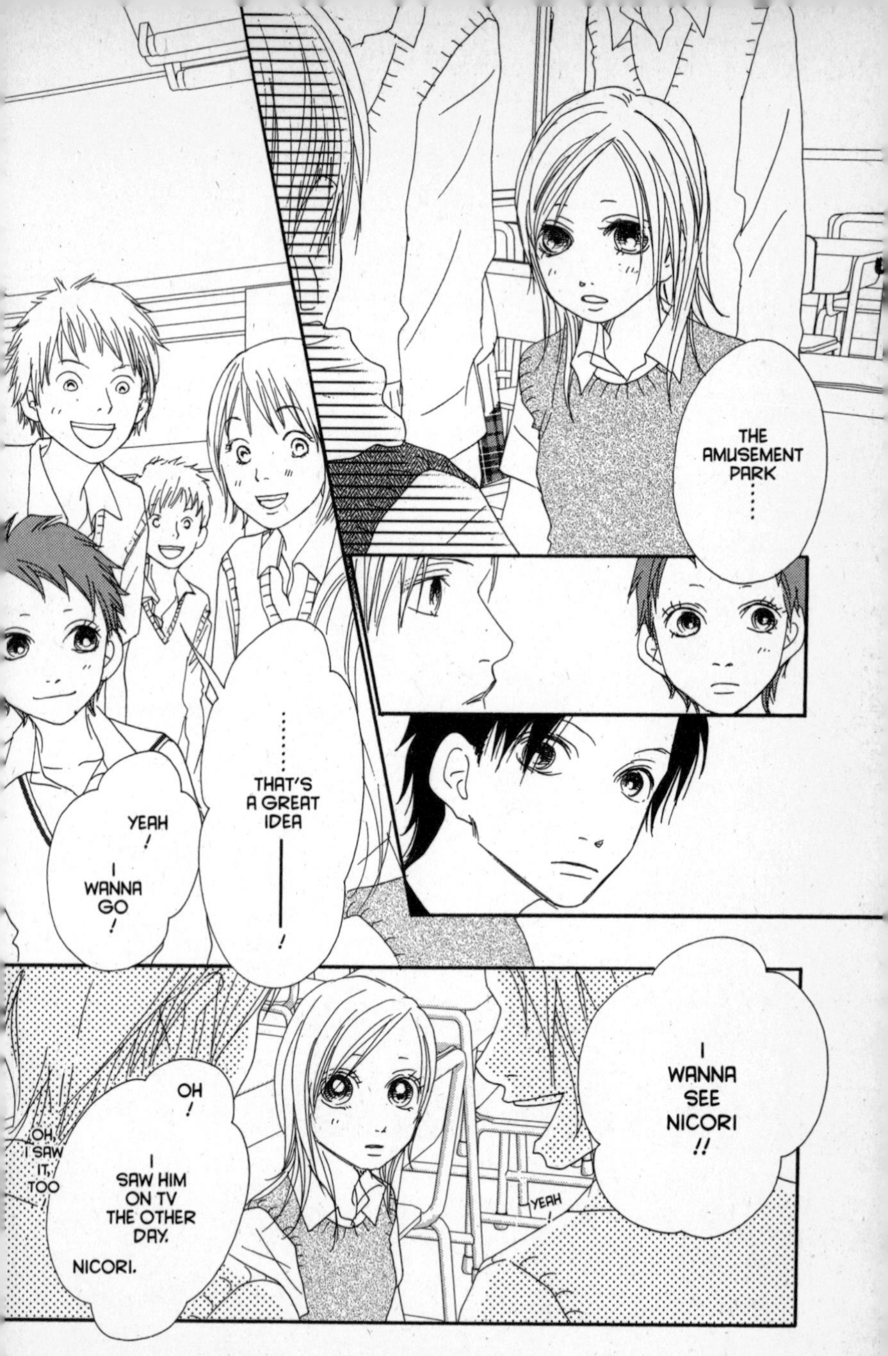
THE AMUSEMENT PARK……
……THAT'S A GREAT IDEA——!
YEAH! I WANNA GO!
I WANNA SEE NICORI!!
YEAH!
OH! I SAW HIM ON TV THE OTHER DAY. NICORI.
OH, I SAW IT, TOO!

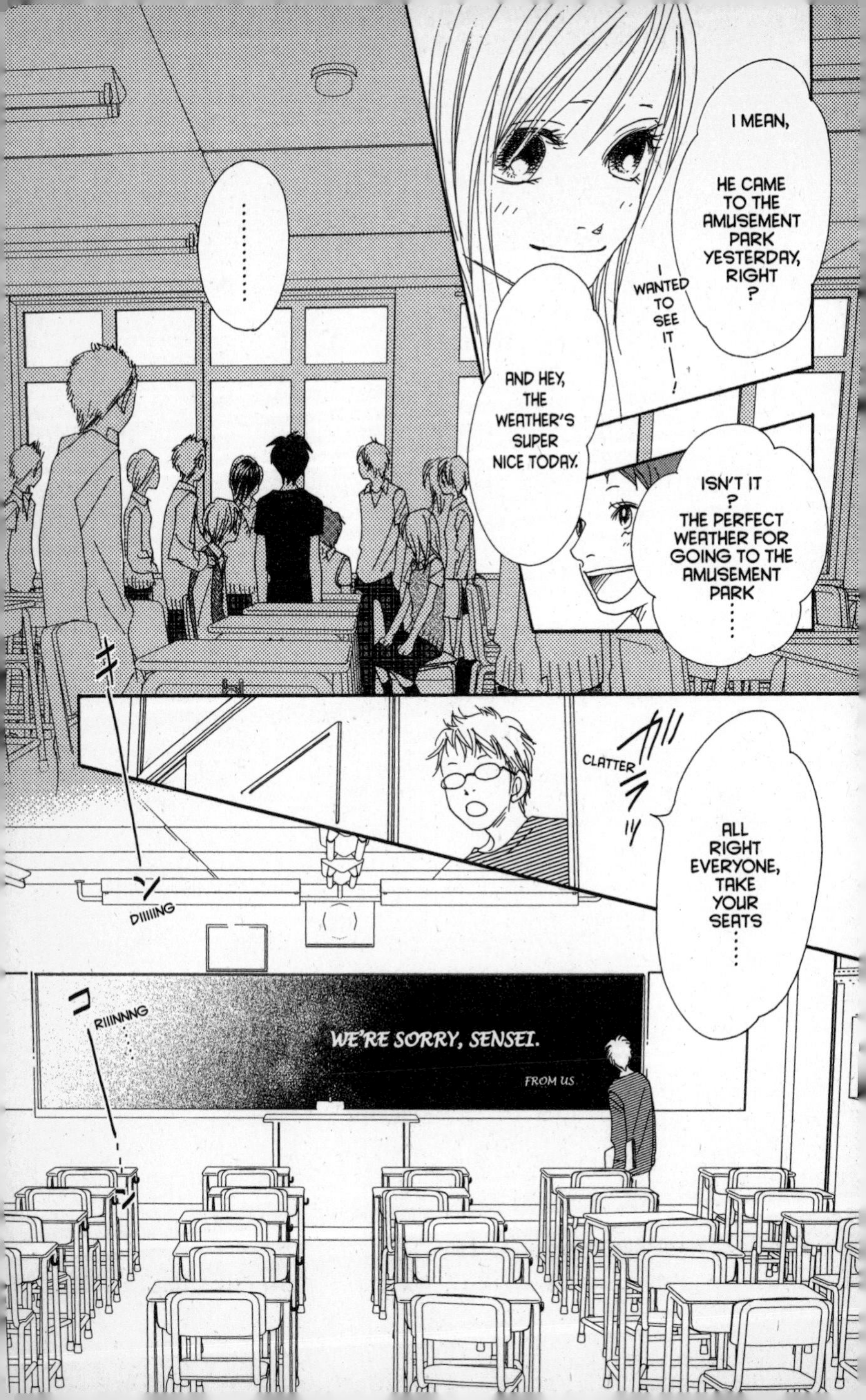
I MEAN,
HE CAME TO THE AMUSEMENT PARK YESTERDAY, RIGHT?
I WANTED TO SEE IT—!
AND HEY, THE WEATHER'S SUPER NICE TODAY.
ISN'T IT? THE PERFECT WEATHER FOR GOING TO THE AMUSEMENT PARK......
......
DIIIING
CLATTER
ALL RIGHT EVERYONE, TAKE YOUR SEATS......
RIIINNNG
WE'RE SORRY, SENSEI.
FROM US

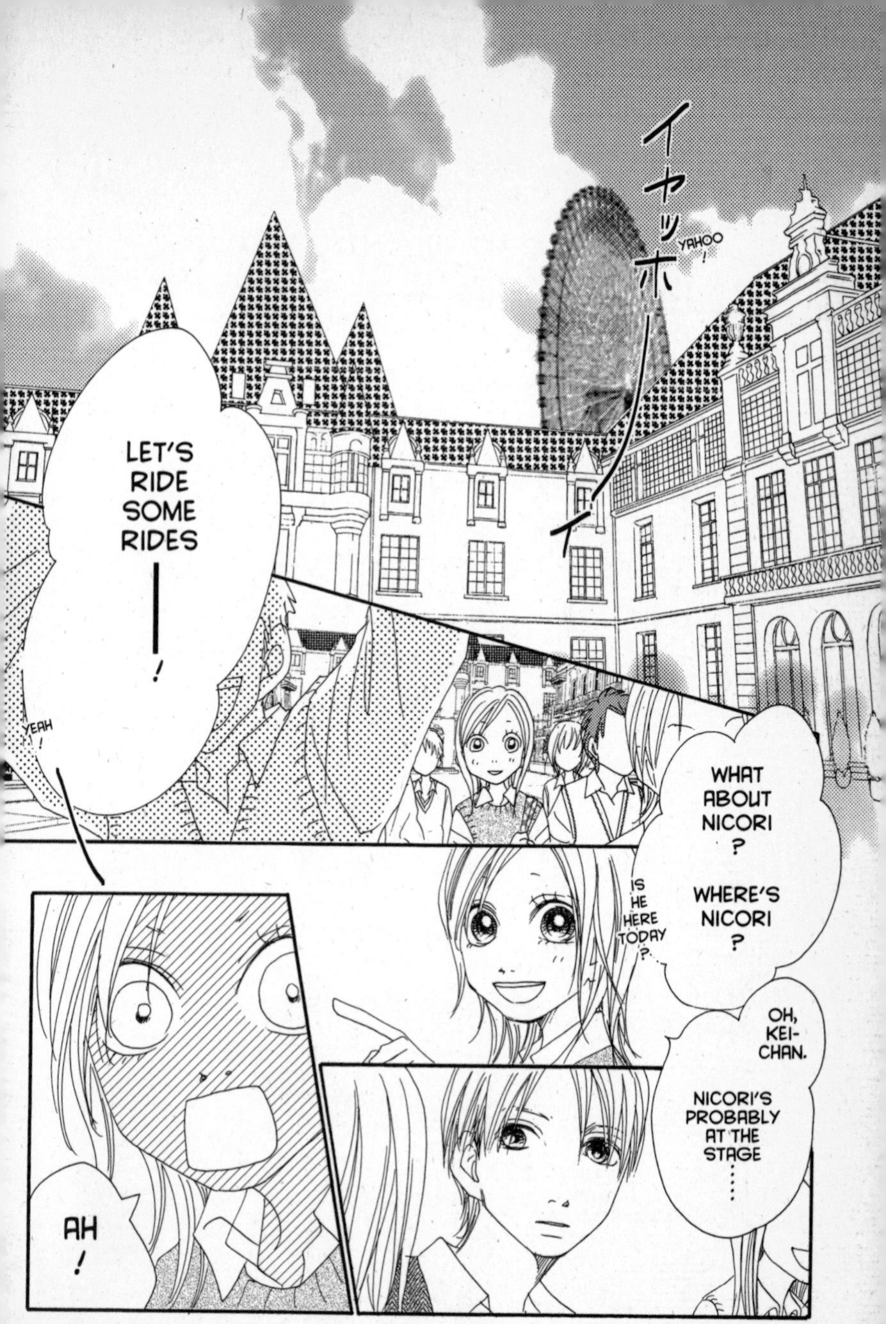

イヤッホーイ
YAHOO!
LET'S RIDE SOME RIDES—!
YEAH!
WHAT ABOUT NICORI?
WHERE'S NICORI?
IS HE HERE TODAY?...
OH, KEI-CHAN.
NICORI'S PROBABLY AT THE STAGE......
AH!

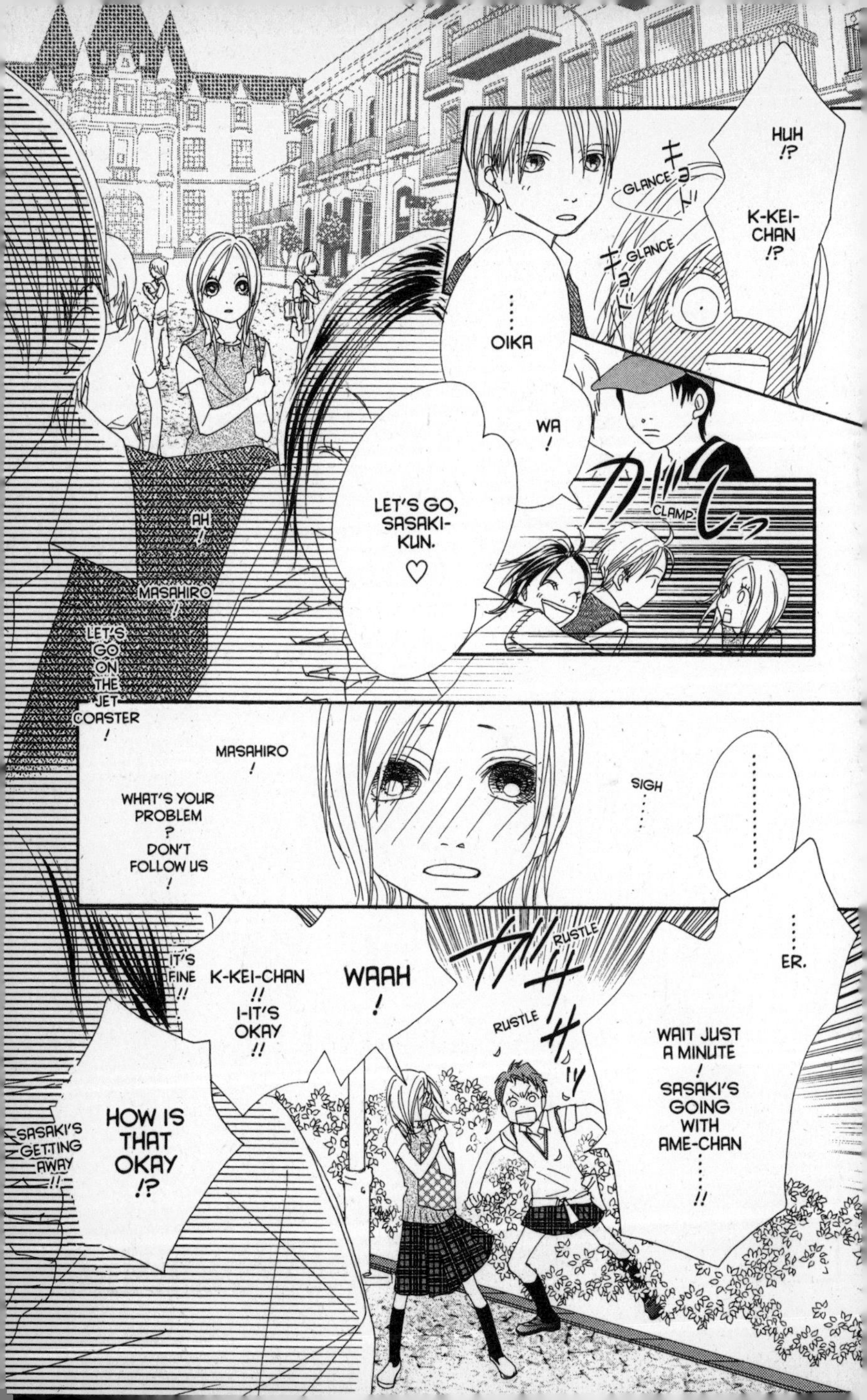
HUH!? K-KEI-CHAN!?
GLANCE
GLANCE
......OIKA WA!
CLAMP
LET'S GO, SASAKI-KUN. ♡
AH! MASAHIRO! LET'S GO ON THE JET COASTER!
......
SIGH......
MASAHIRO! WHAT'S YOUR PROBLEM? DON'T FOLLOW US!
......ER.
WAIT JUST A MINUTE! SASAKI'S GOING WITH AME-CHAN......!!
RUSTLE
RUSTLE
WAAH!
K-KEI-CHAN!! I-IT'S OKAY!!
IT'S FINE!!
HOW IS THAT OKAY!?
SASAKI'S GETTING AWAY!!

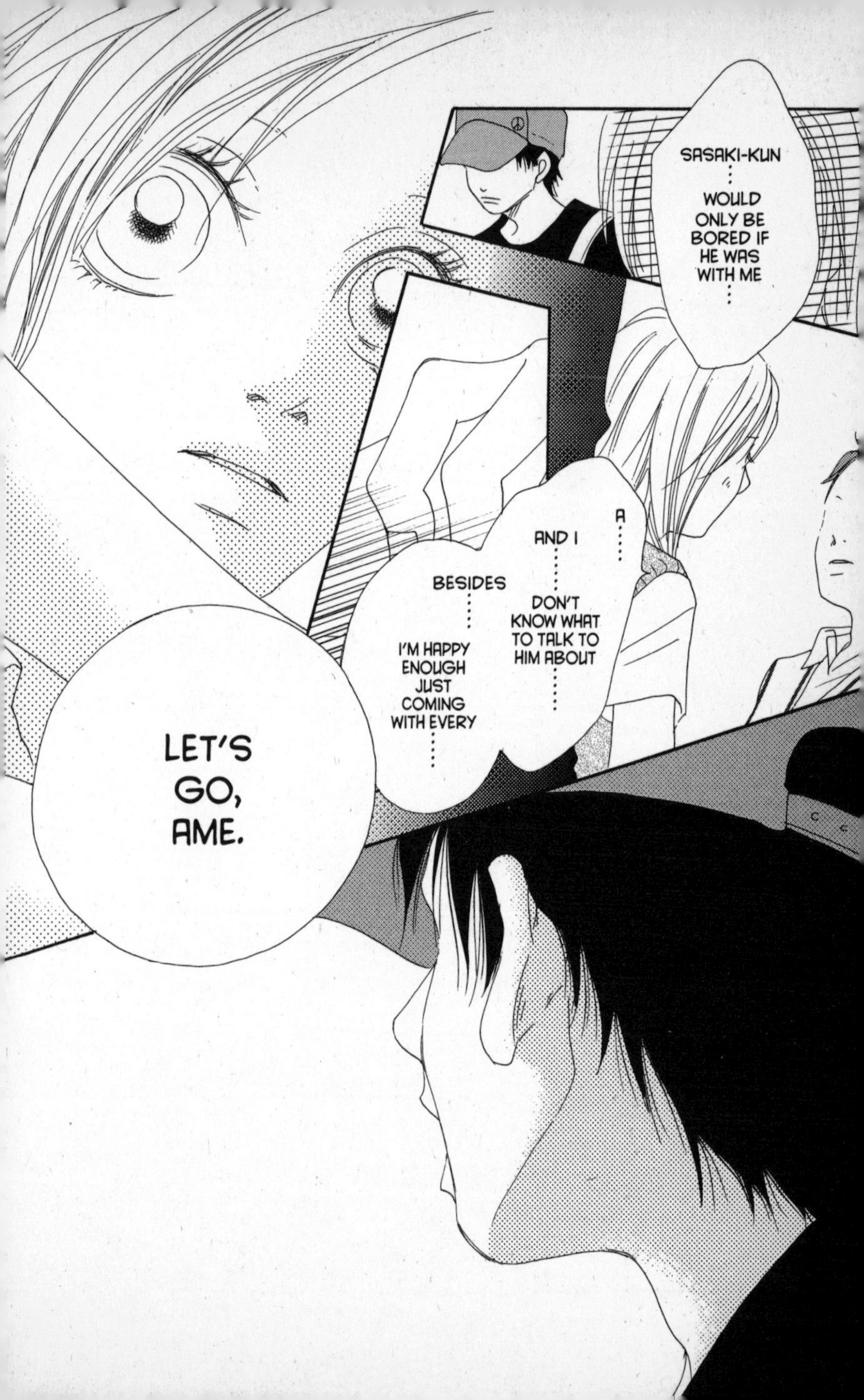
SASAKI-KUN … WOULD ONLY BE BORED IF HE WAS WITH ME …
BESIDES … I'M HAPPY ENOUGH JUST COMING WITH EVERY …
AND I … DON'T KNOW WHAT TO TALK TO HIM ABOUT …
A …
LET'S GO, AME.

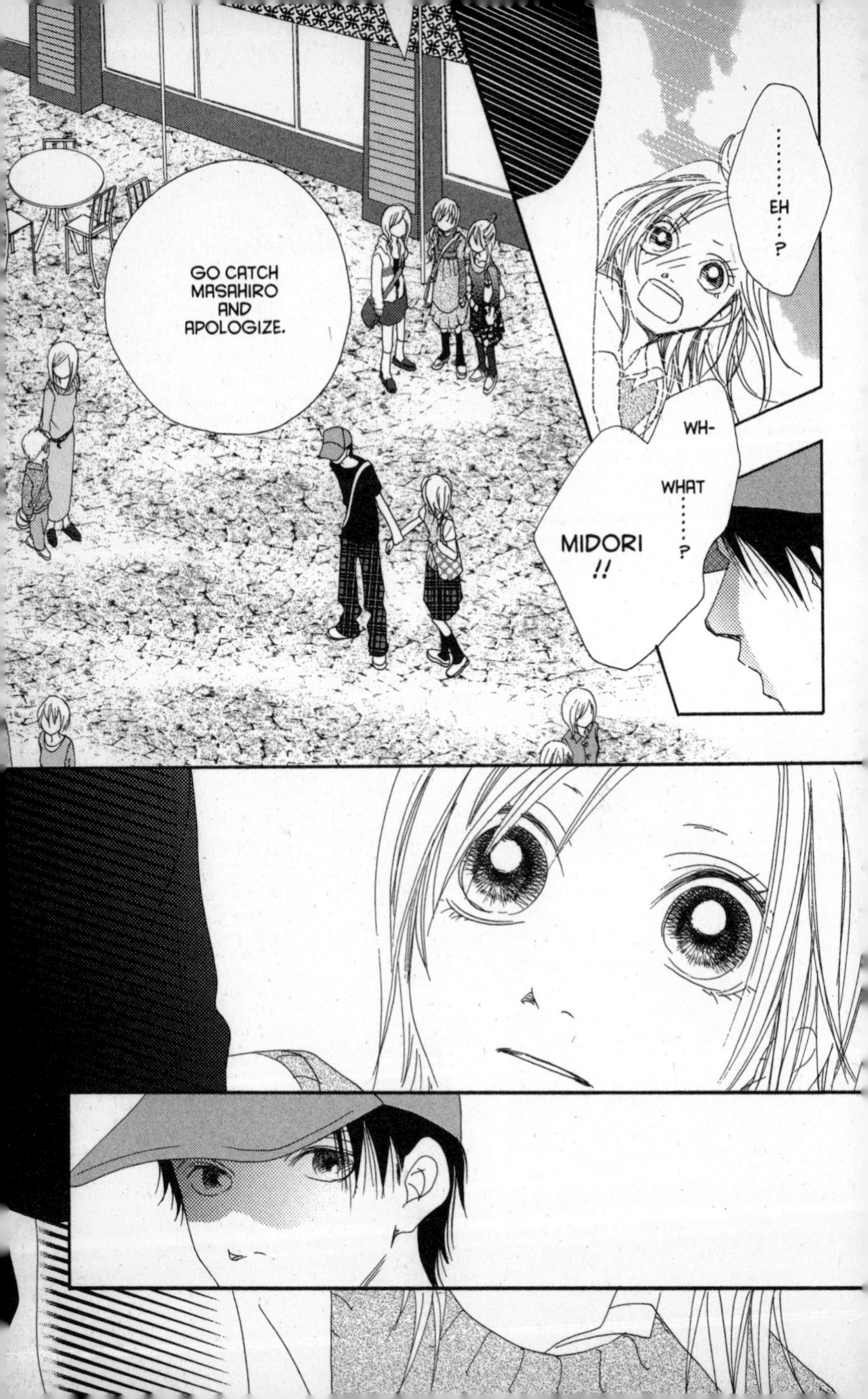
......EH......?
WH- WHAT......?
MIDORI!!
GO CATCH MASAHIRO AND APOLOGIZE.

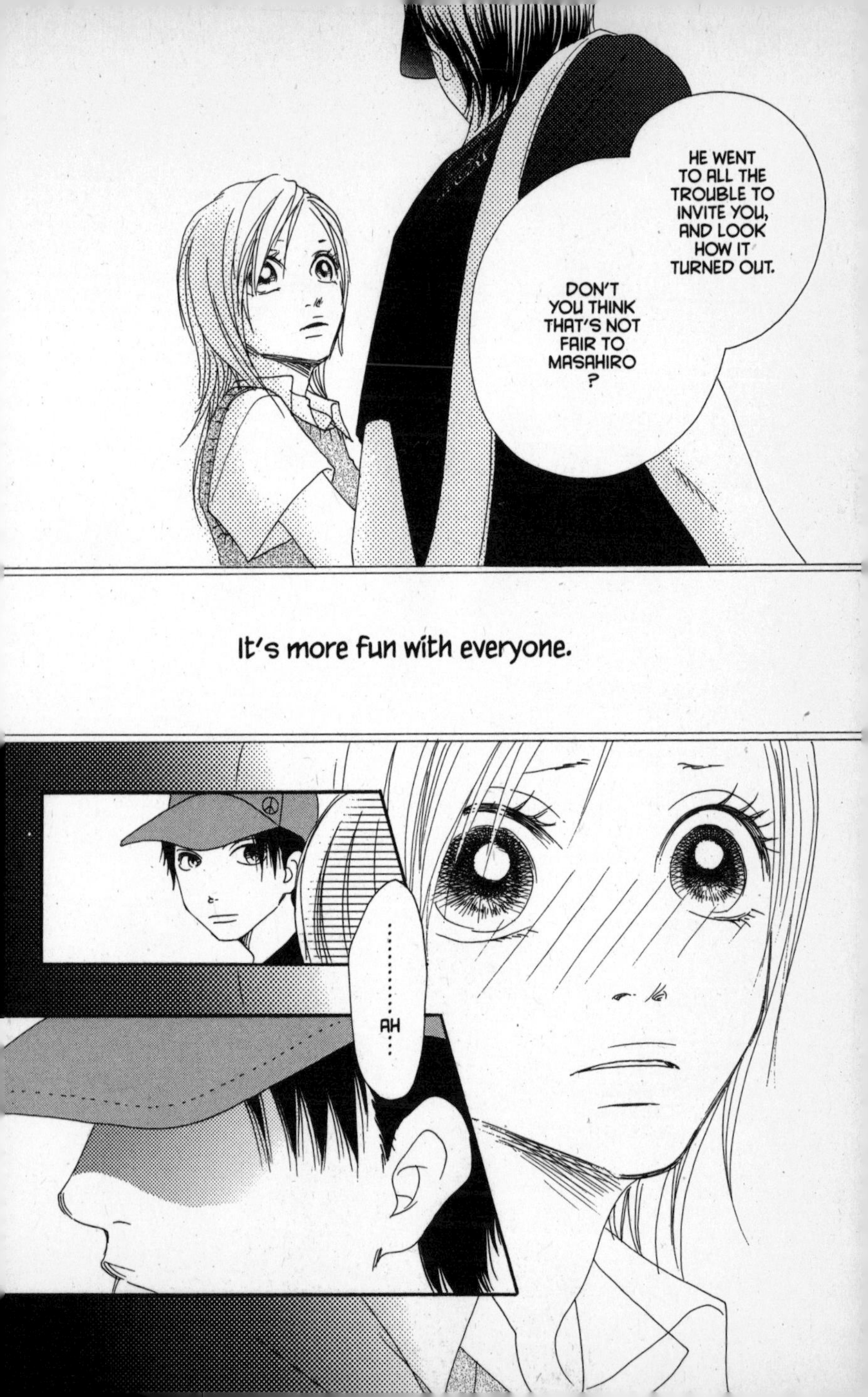
HE WENT TO ALL THE TROUBLE TO INVITE YOU, AND LOOK HOW IT TURNED OUT.
DON'T YOU THINK THAT'S NOT FAIR TO MASAHIRO?
It's more fun with everyone.
...AH...

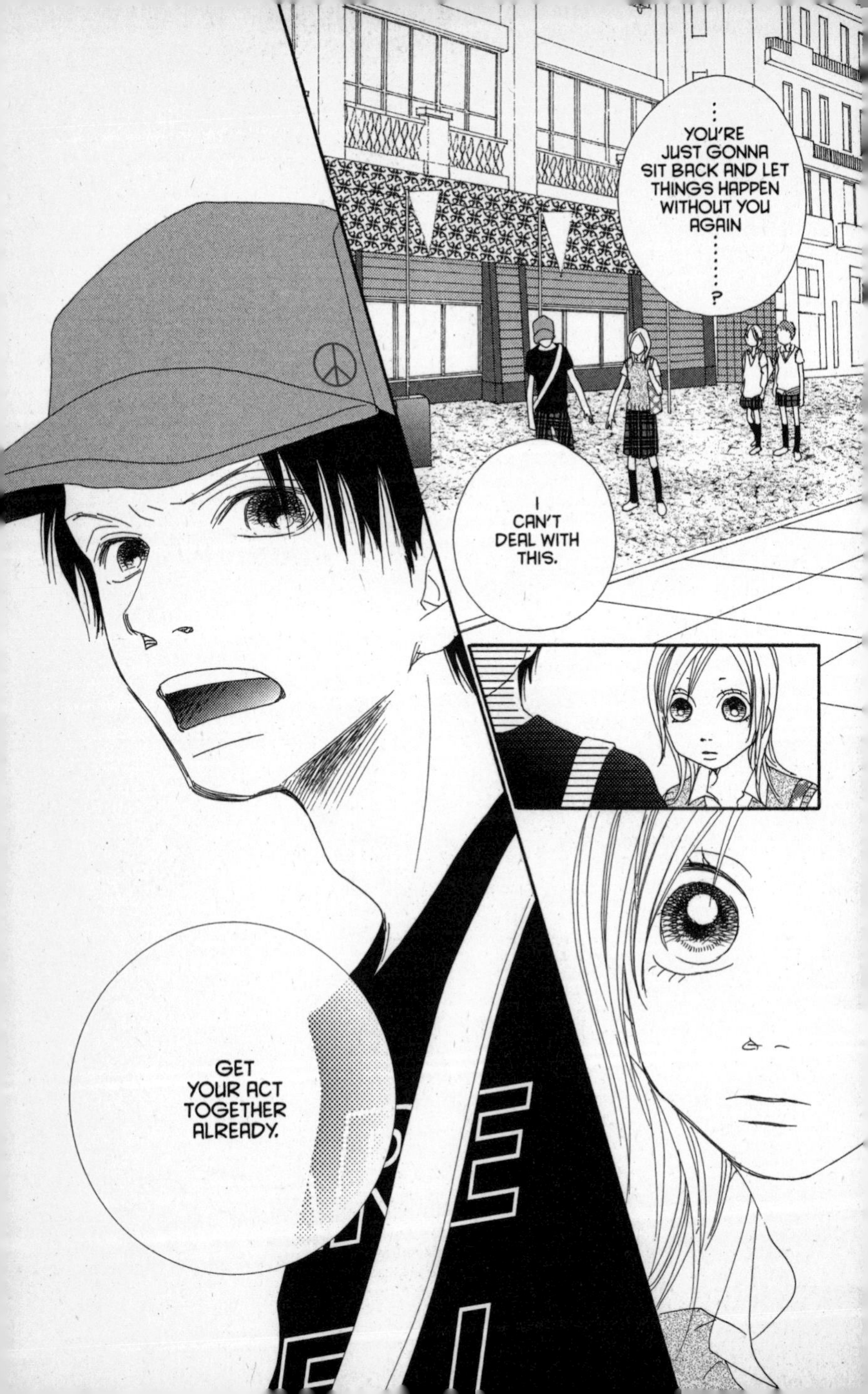
...YOU'RE JUST GONNA SIT BACK AND LET THINGS HAPPEN WITHOUT YOU AGAIN ......?
I CAN'T DEAL WITH THIS.
GET YOUR ACT TOGETHER ALREADY.

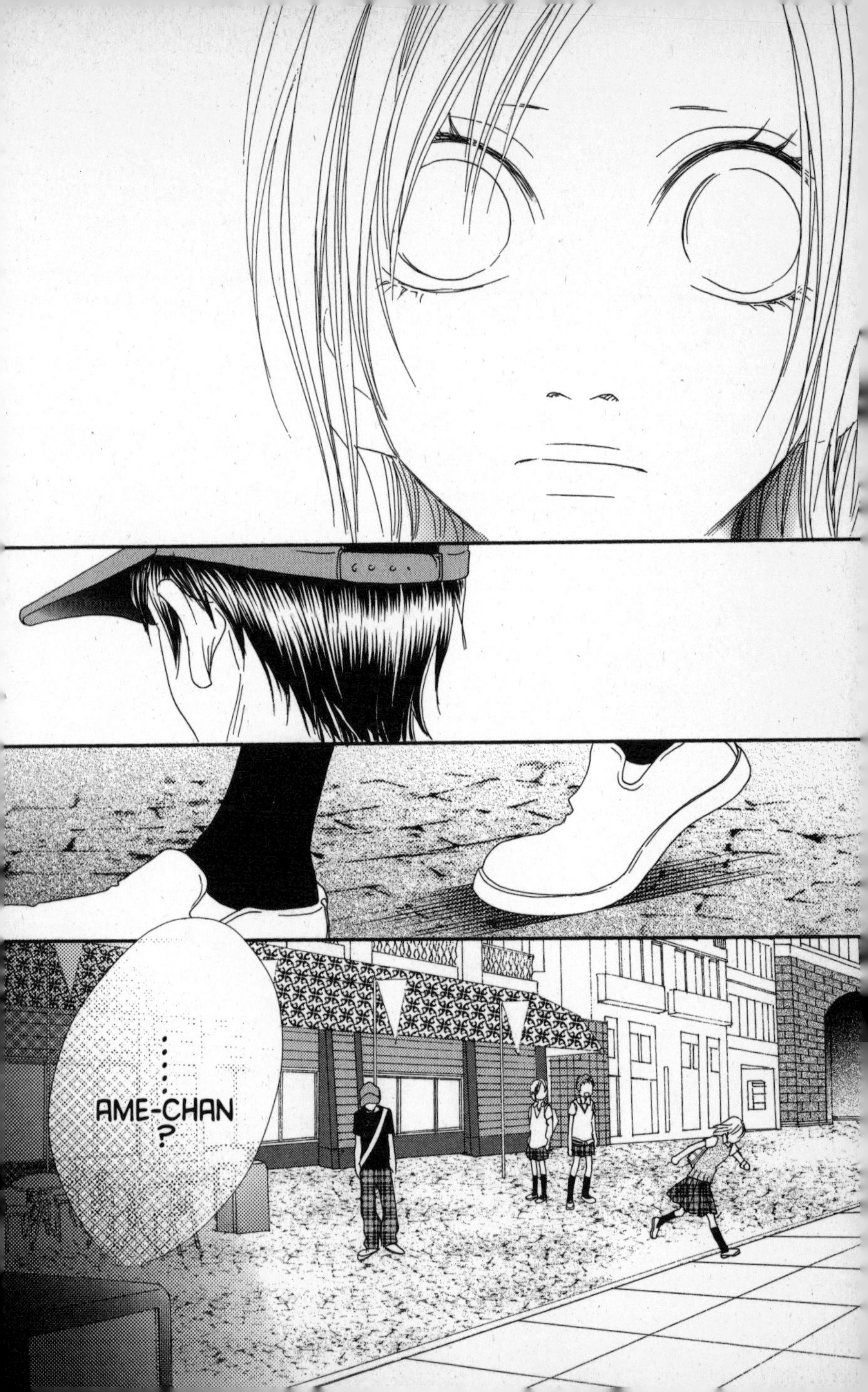
.....AME-CHAN?

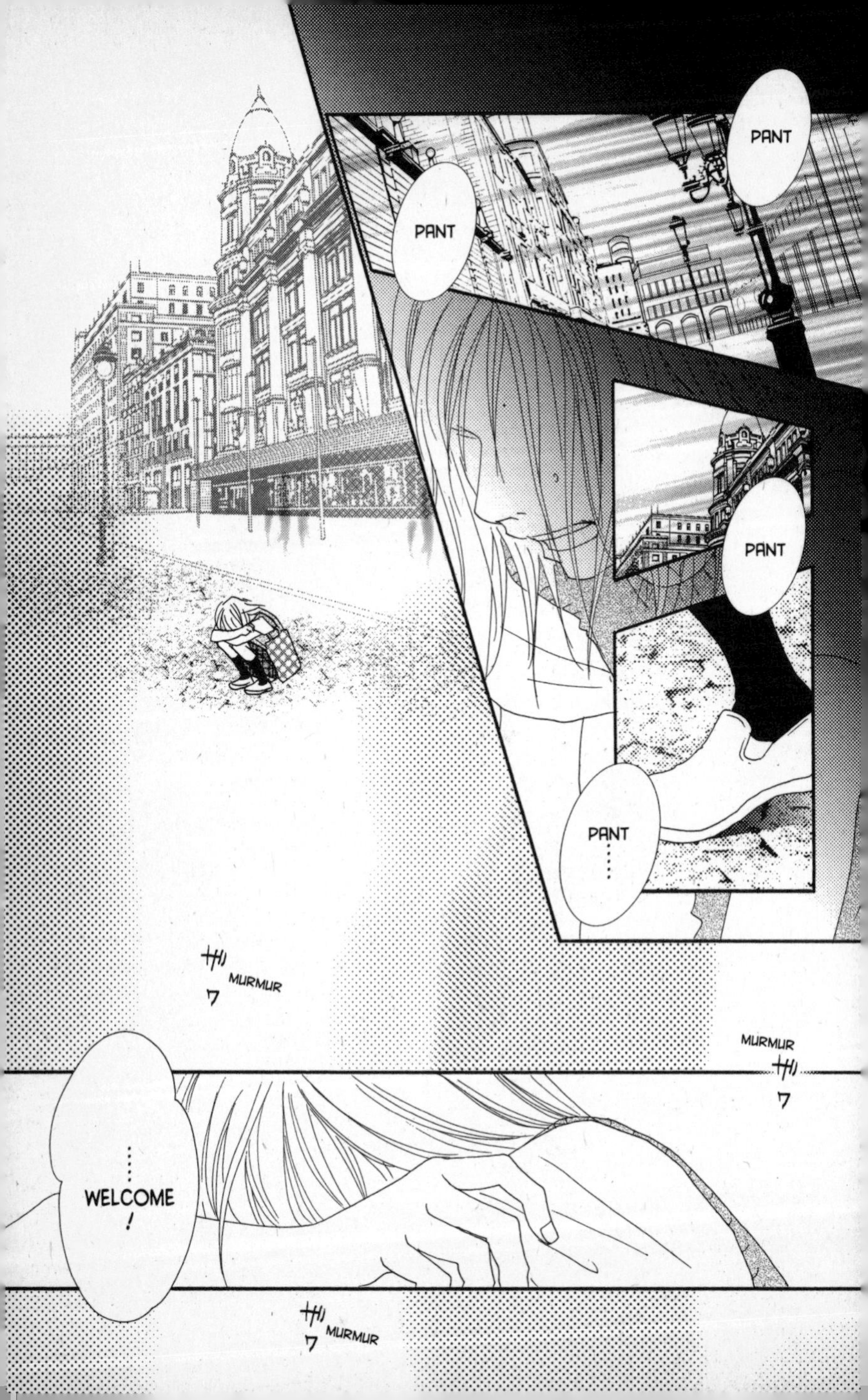
PANT
PANT
PANT
PANT......
MURMUR
MURMUR
......WELCOME!
MURMUR

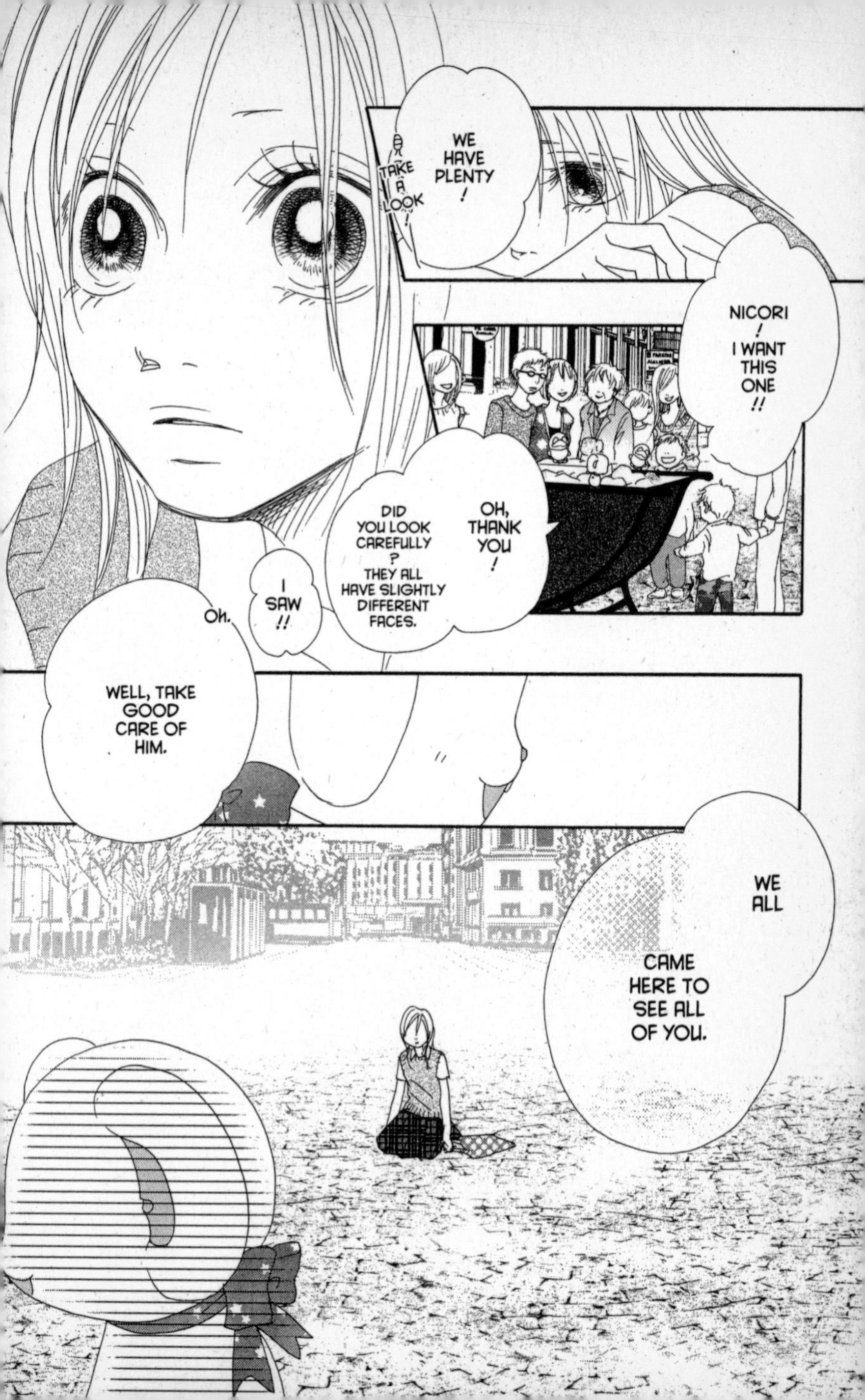
WE HAVE PLENTY!
TAKE A LOOK!
NICORI! I WANT THIS ONE!!
OH, THANK YOU!
DID YOU LOOK CAREFULLY? THEY ALL HAVE SLIGHTLY DIFFERENT FACES.
I SAW!!
Oh.
WELL, TAKE GOOD CARE OF HIM.
WE ALL
CAME HERE TO SEE ALL OF YOU.

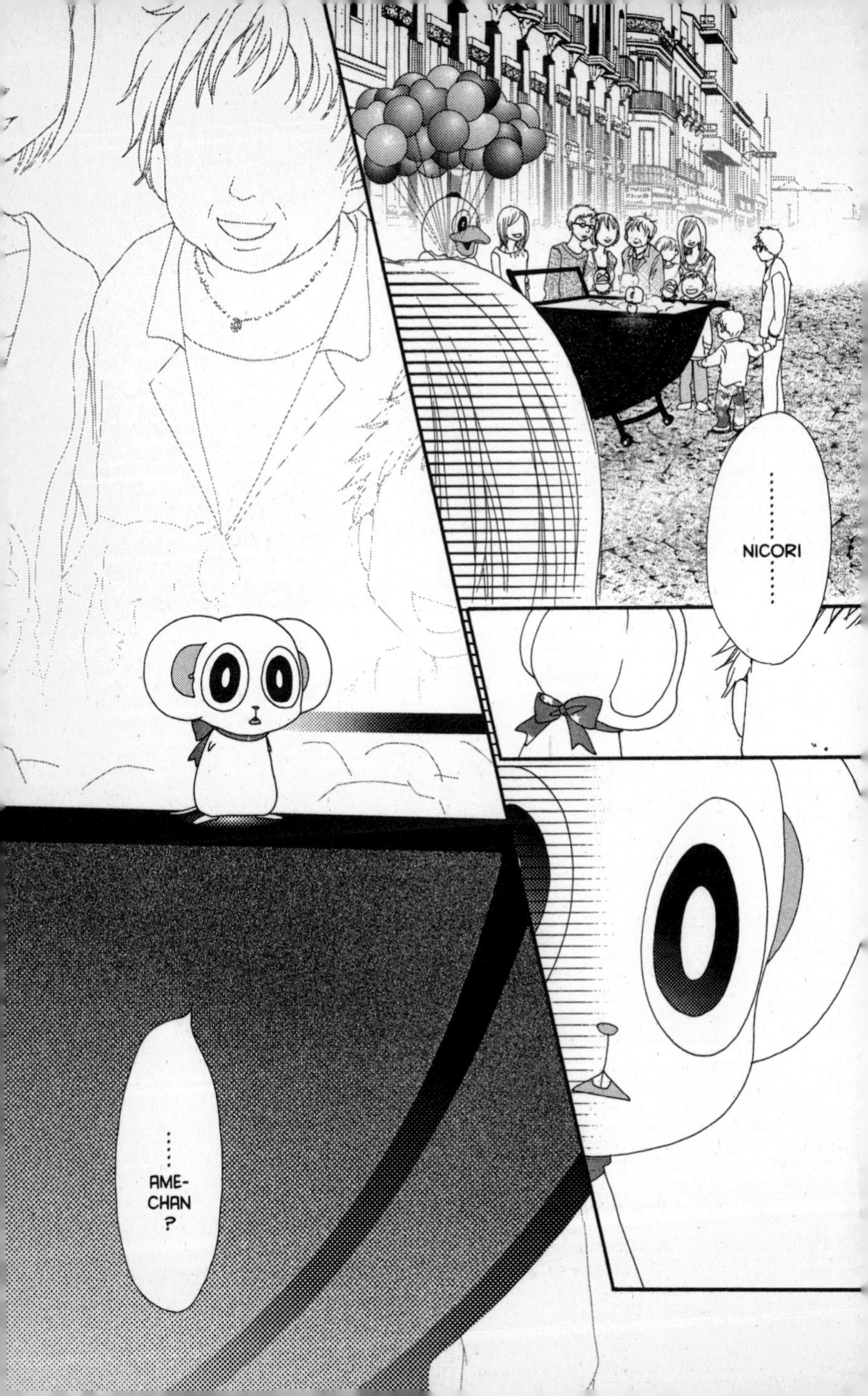

......NICORI......
......AME-CHAN?

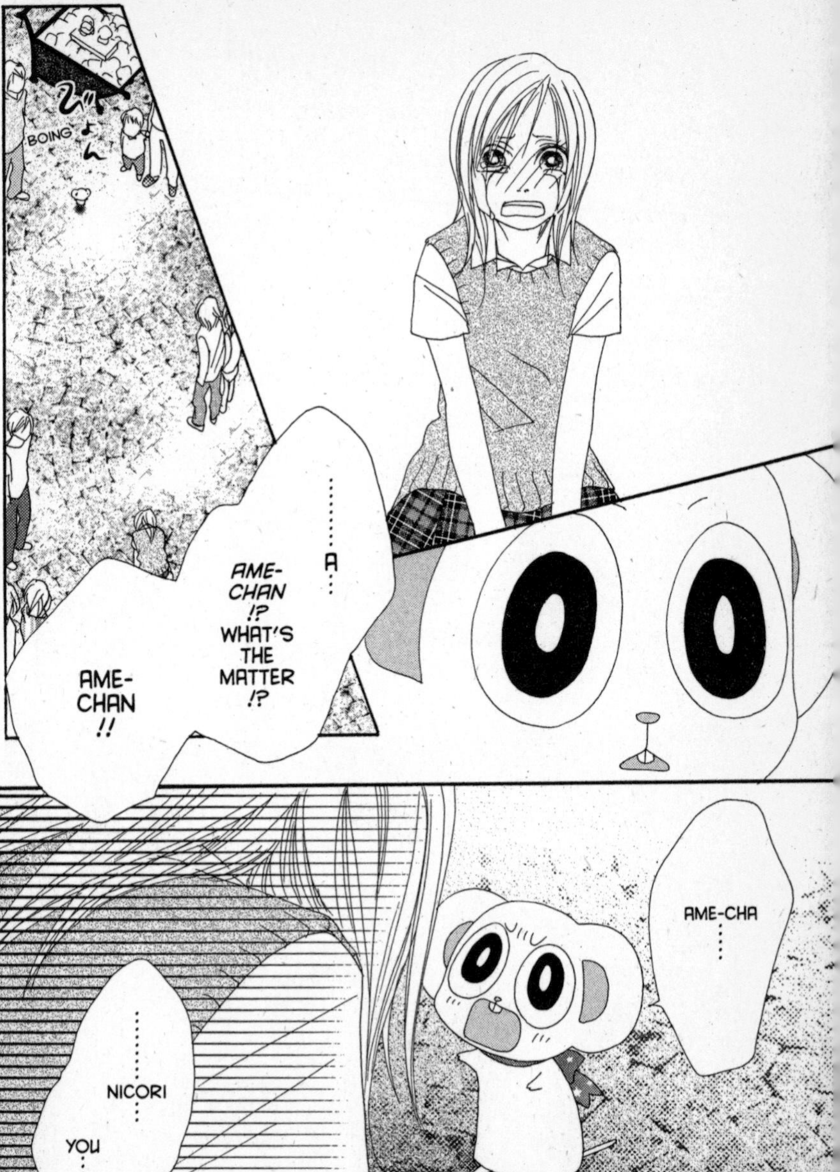
BOING
......A...
AME-CHAN!? WHAT'S THE MATTER!?
AME-CHAN!!
AME-CHA......
......NICORI... YOU...

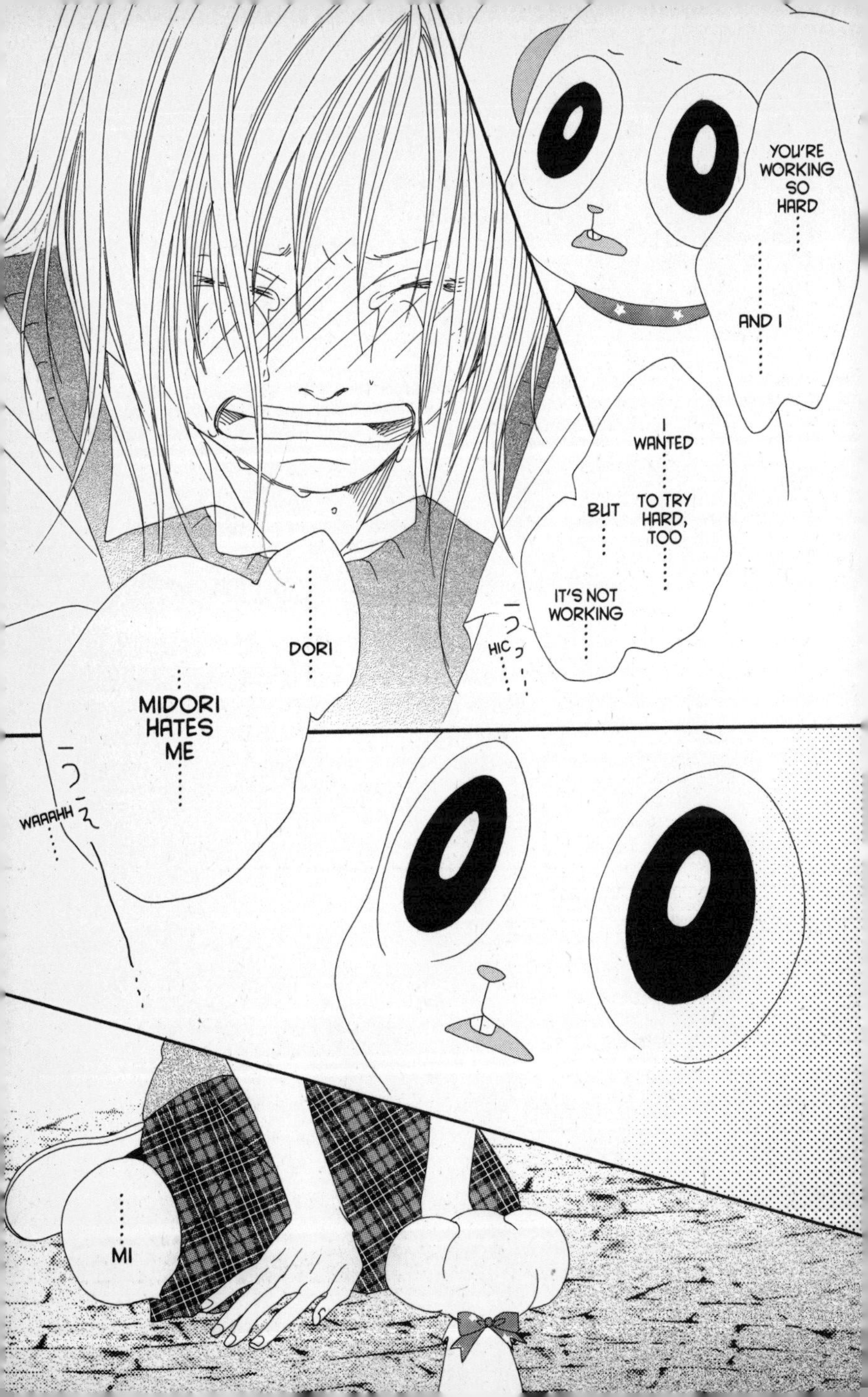

YOU'RE WORKING SO HARD……
……AND I……
I…… WANTED…… TO TRY HARD, TOO……
BUT……
IT'S NOT WORKING……
HIC……
……DORI……
……MIDORI HATES ME……
WAAAHH……
……MI

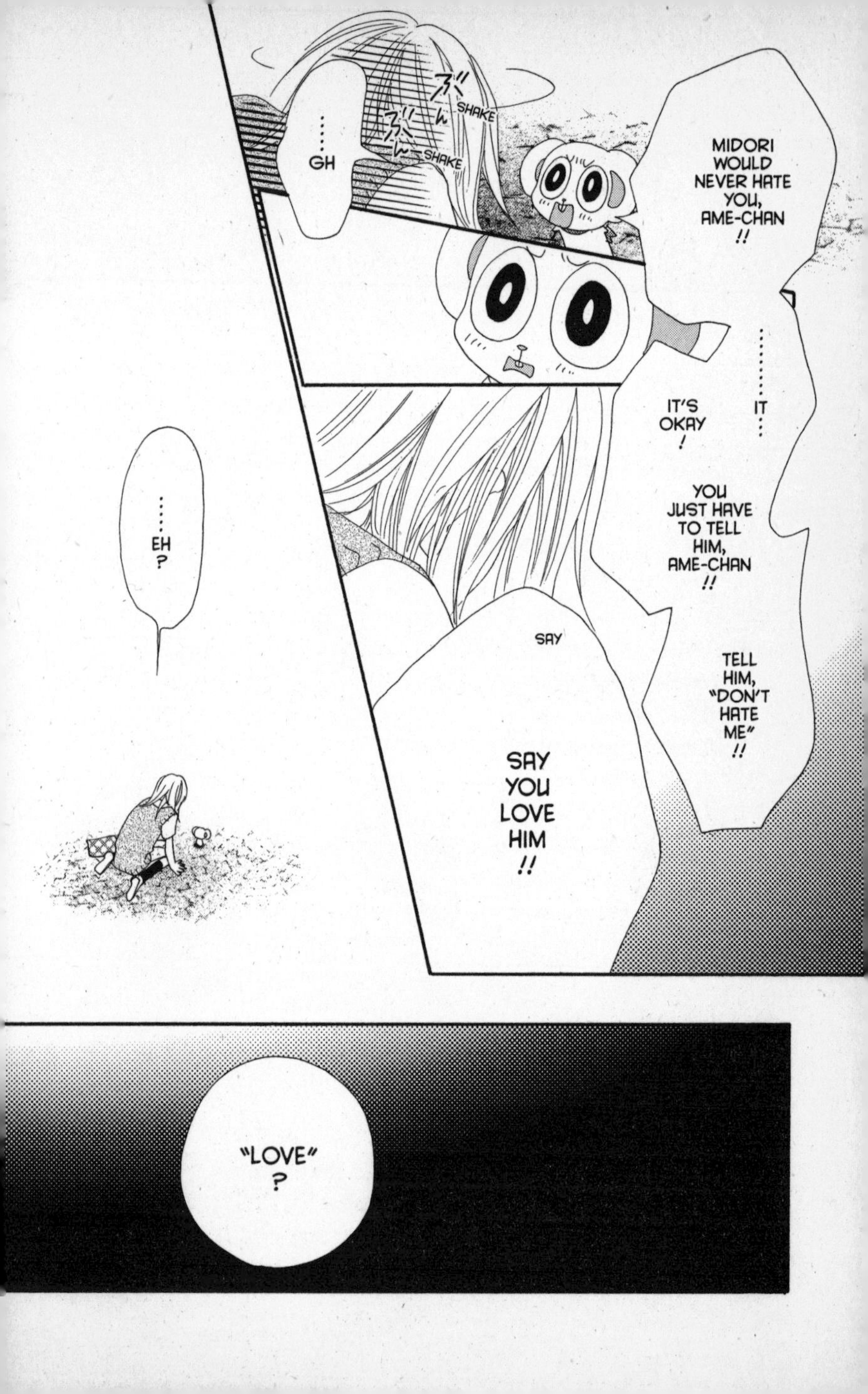
MIDORI WOULD NEVER HATE YOU, AME-CHAN!!
SHAKE
SHAKE
...GH
...IT...
IT'S OKAY!
YOU JUST HAVE TO TELL HIM, AME-CHAN!!
TELL HIM, "DON'T HATE ME"!!
SAY
SAY YOU LOVE HIM!!
...EH?
"LOVE"?

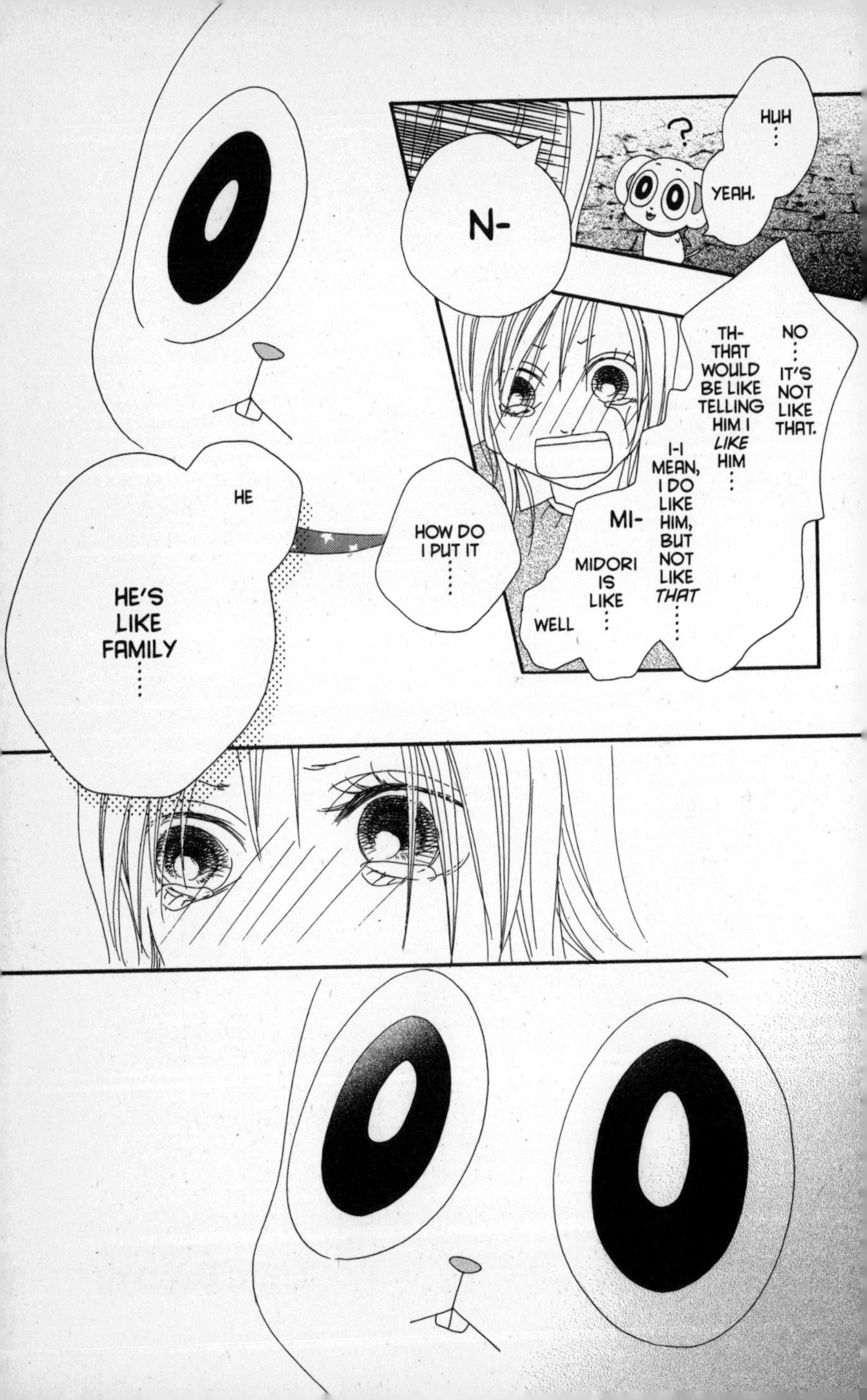
HUH...
YEAH.
?
N-
NO... IT'S NOT LIKE THAT.
TH- THAT WOULD BE LIKE TELLING HIM I LIKE HIM...
I-I MEAN, I DO LIKE HIM, BUT NOT LIKE THAT...
MI-
MIDORI IS LIKE...
WELL
HOW DO I PUT IT...
HE
HE'S LIKE FAMILY...

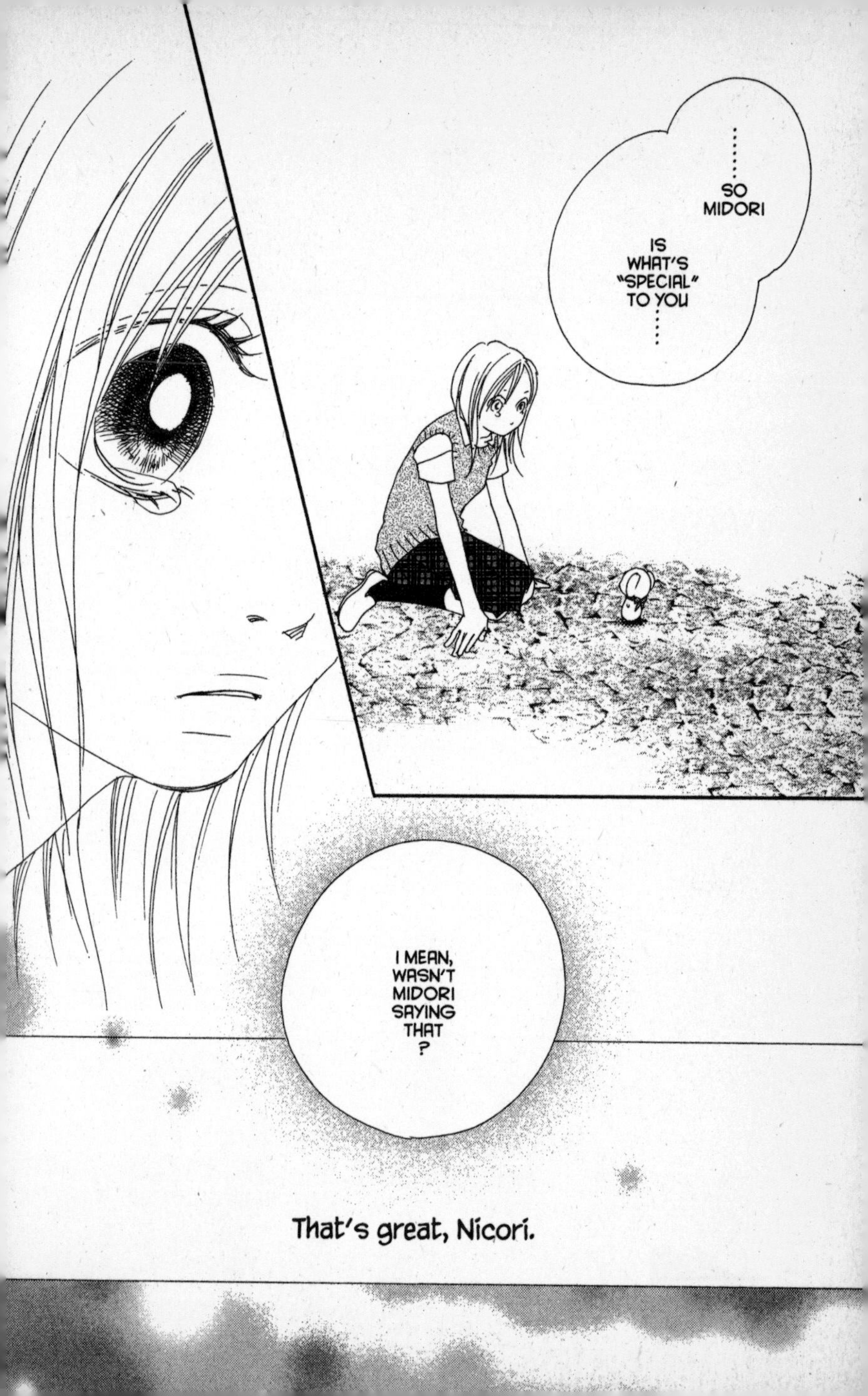
......SO MIDORI IS WHAT'S "SPECIAL" TO YOU......
I MEAN, WASN'T MIDORI SAYING THAT?
That's great, Nicori.

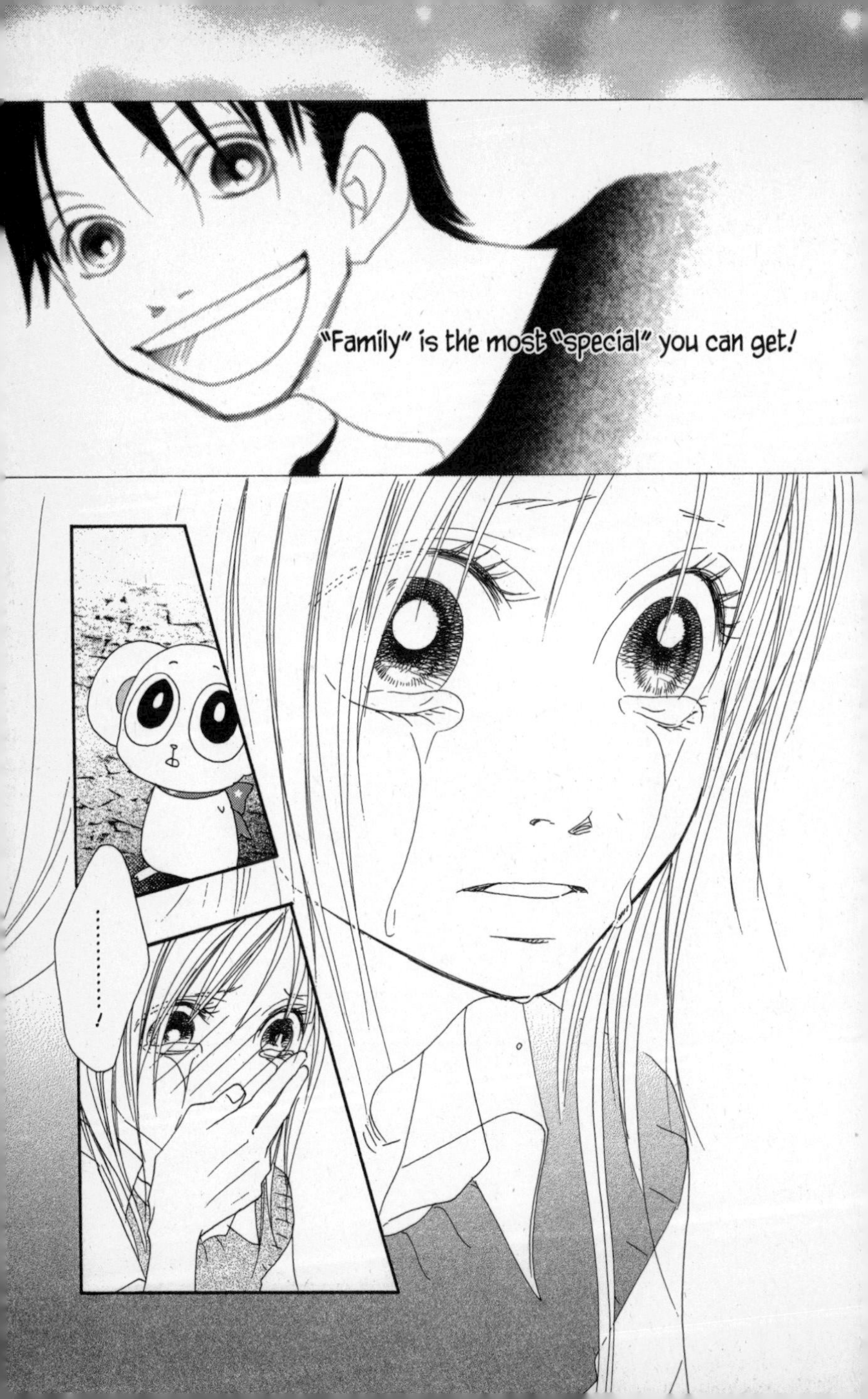
"Family" is the most "special" you can get!
......!

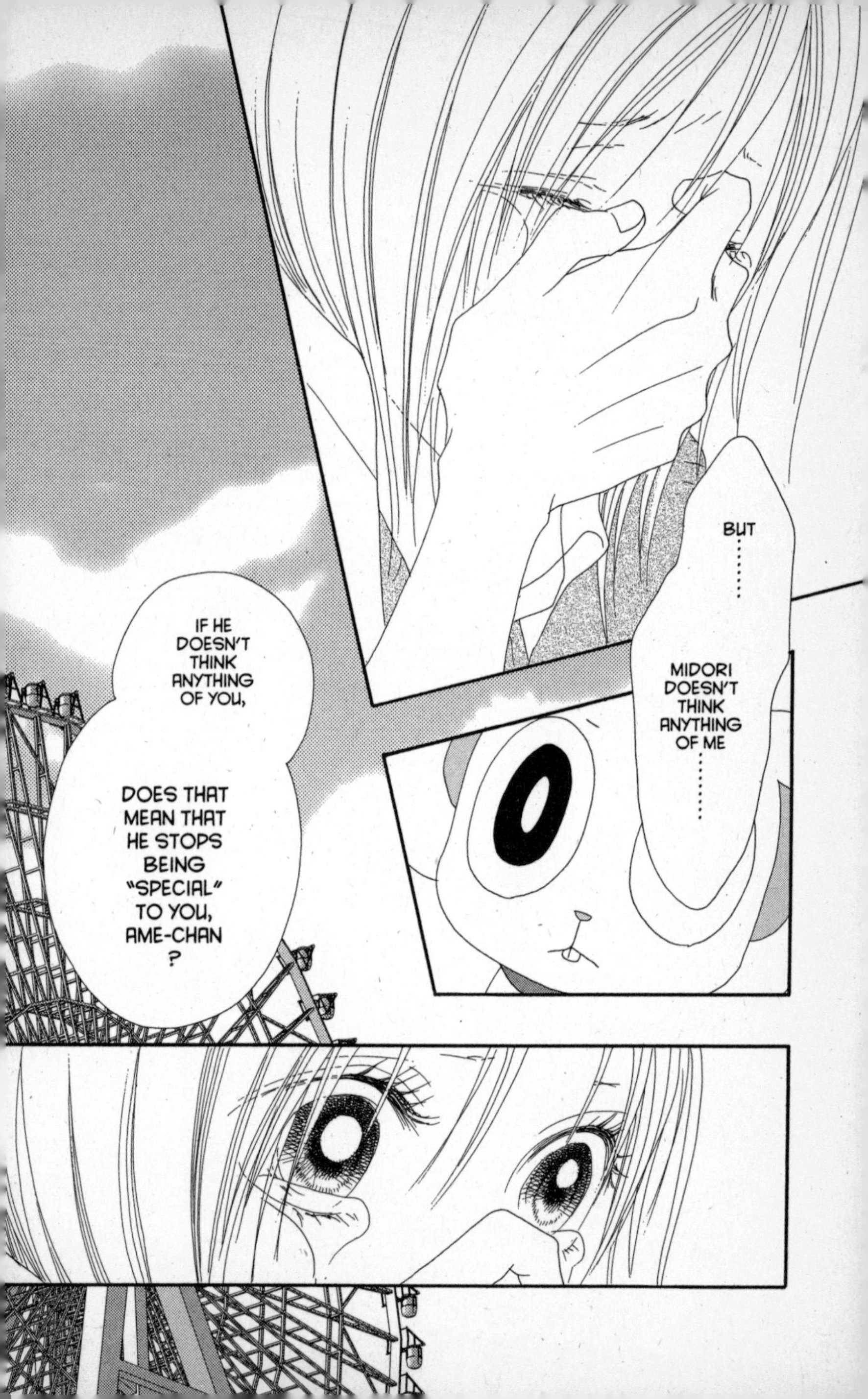

BUT ......
MIDORI DOESN'T THINK ANYTHING OF ME ......
IF HE DOESN'T THINK ANYTHING OF YOU,
DOES THAT MEAN THAT HE STOPS BEING "SPECIAL" TO YOU, AME-CHAN ?

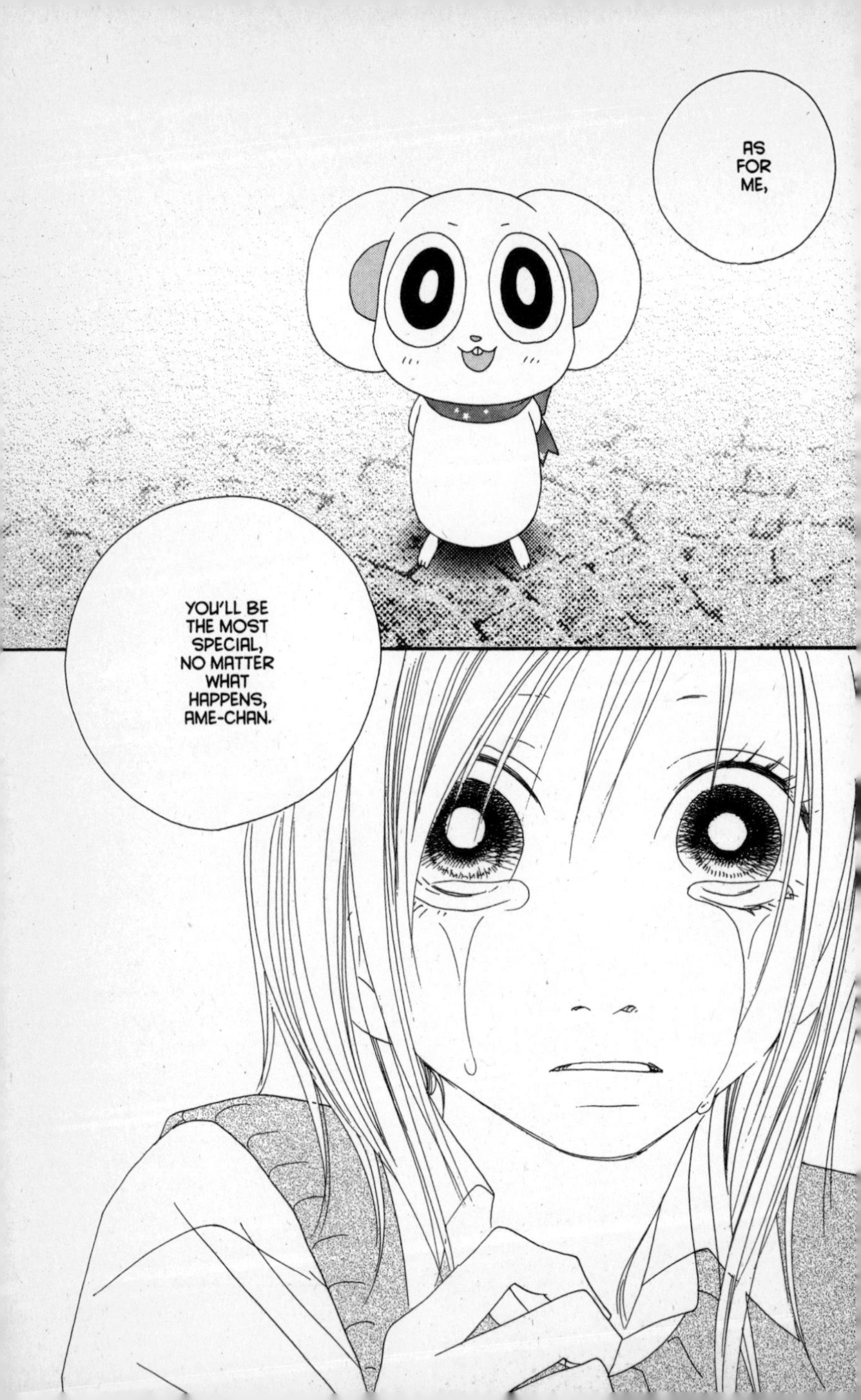
AS FOR ME,
YOU'LL BE THE MOST SPECIAL, NO MATTER WHAT HAPPENS, AME-CHAN.

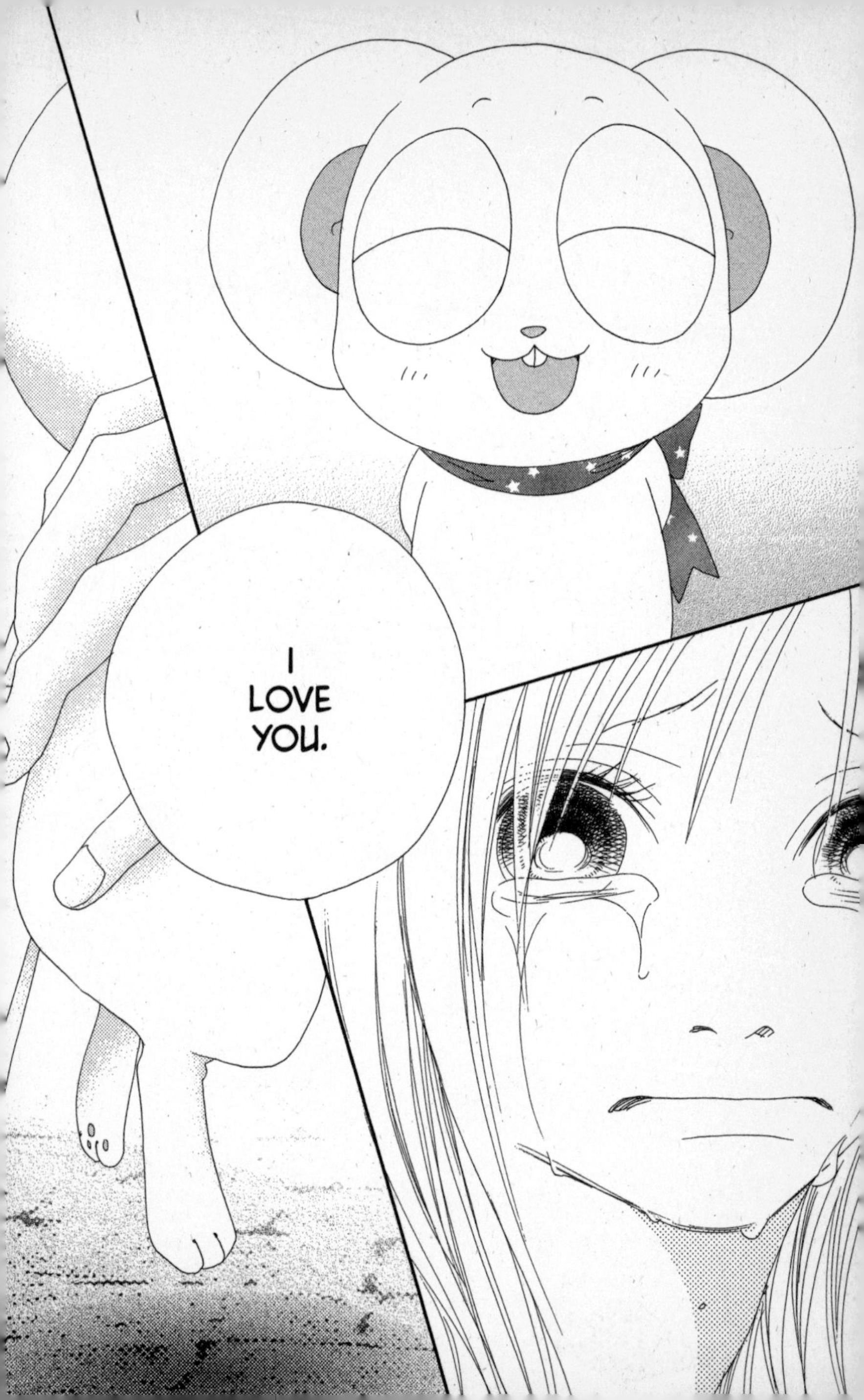
I LOVE YOU.

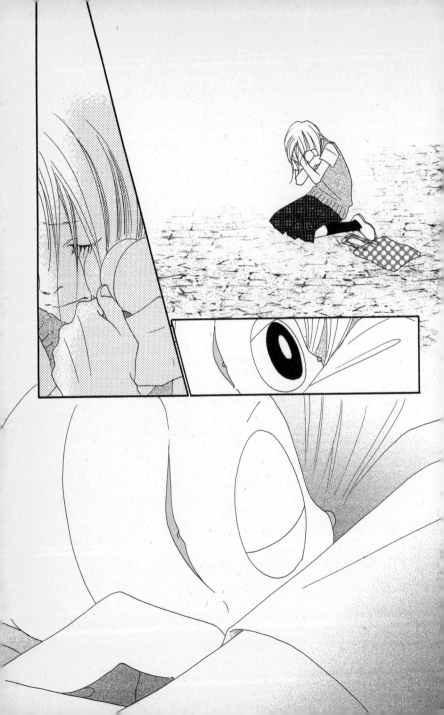

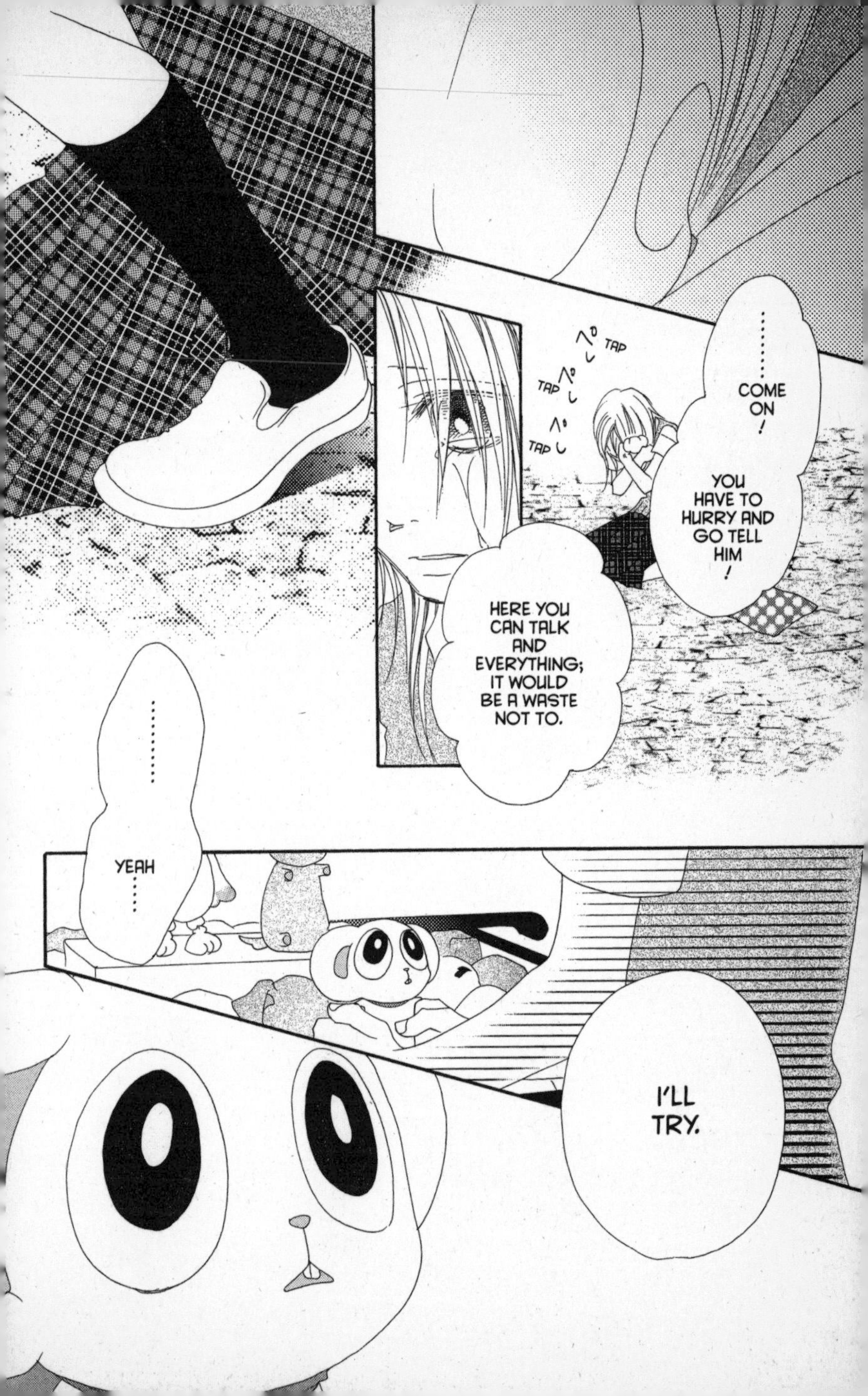

TAP
TAP
TAP
...... COME ON!
YOU HAVE TO HURRY AND GO TELL HIM!
HERE YOU CAN TALK AND EVERYTHING; IT WOULD BE A WASTE NOT TO.
...... YEAH ......
I'LL TRY.

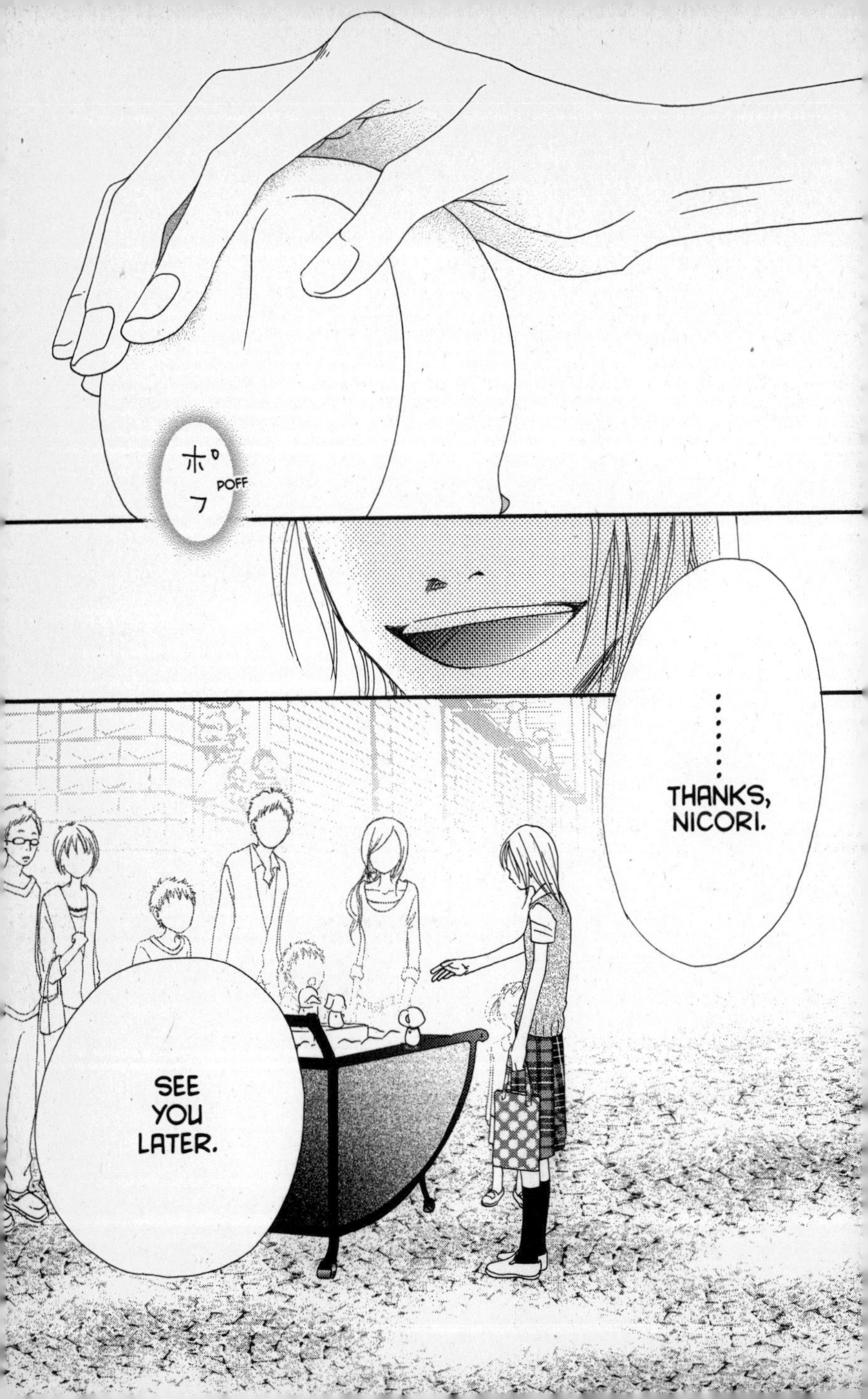
ポフ
POFF
...... THANKS, NICORI.
SEE YOU LATER.

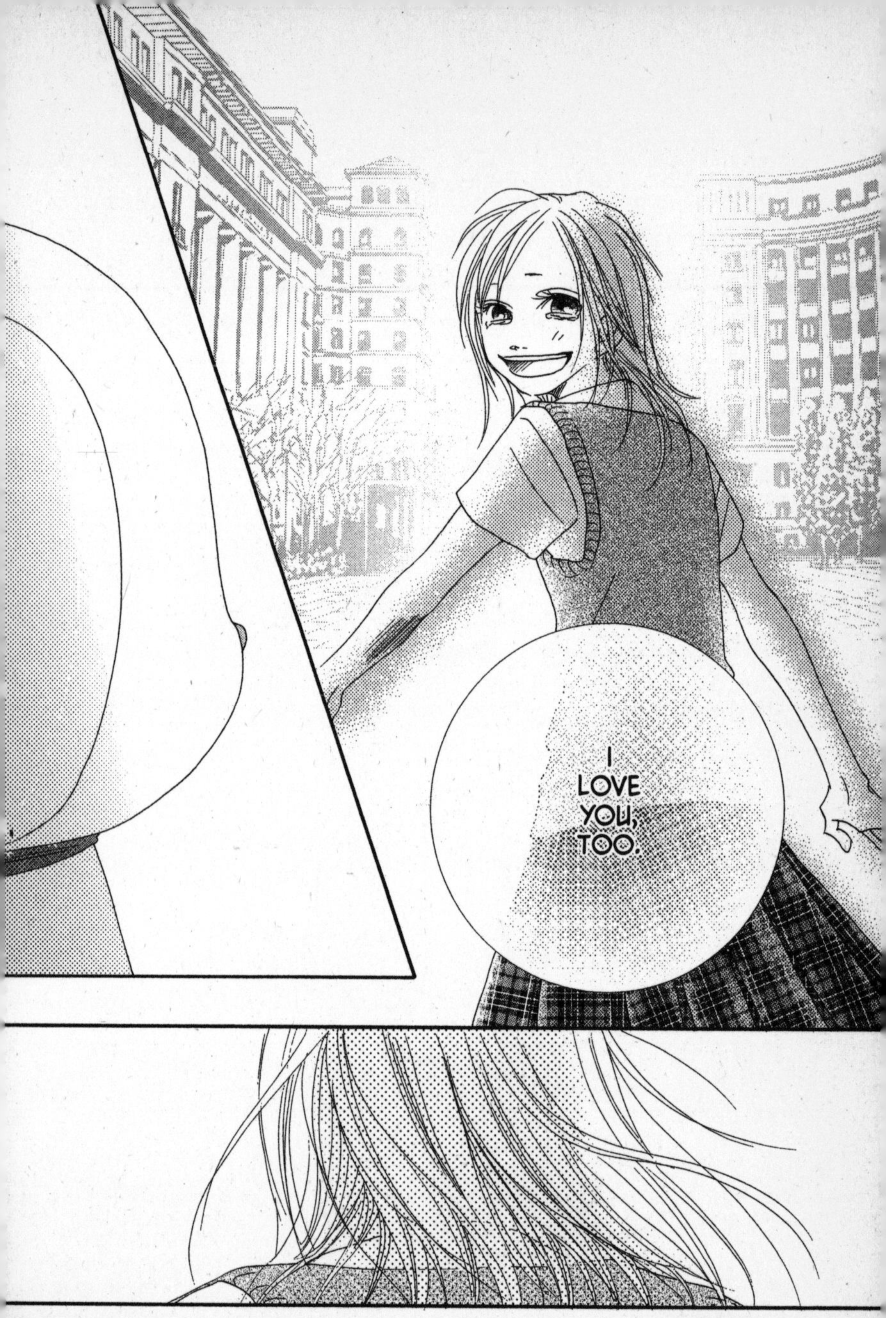
I LOVE YOU, TOO.

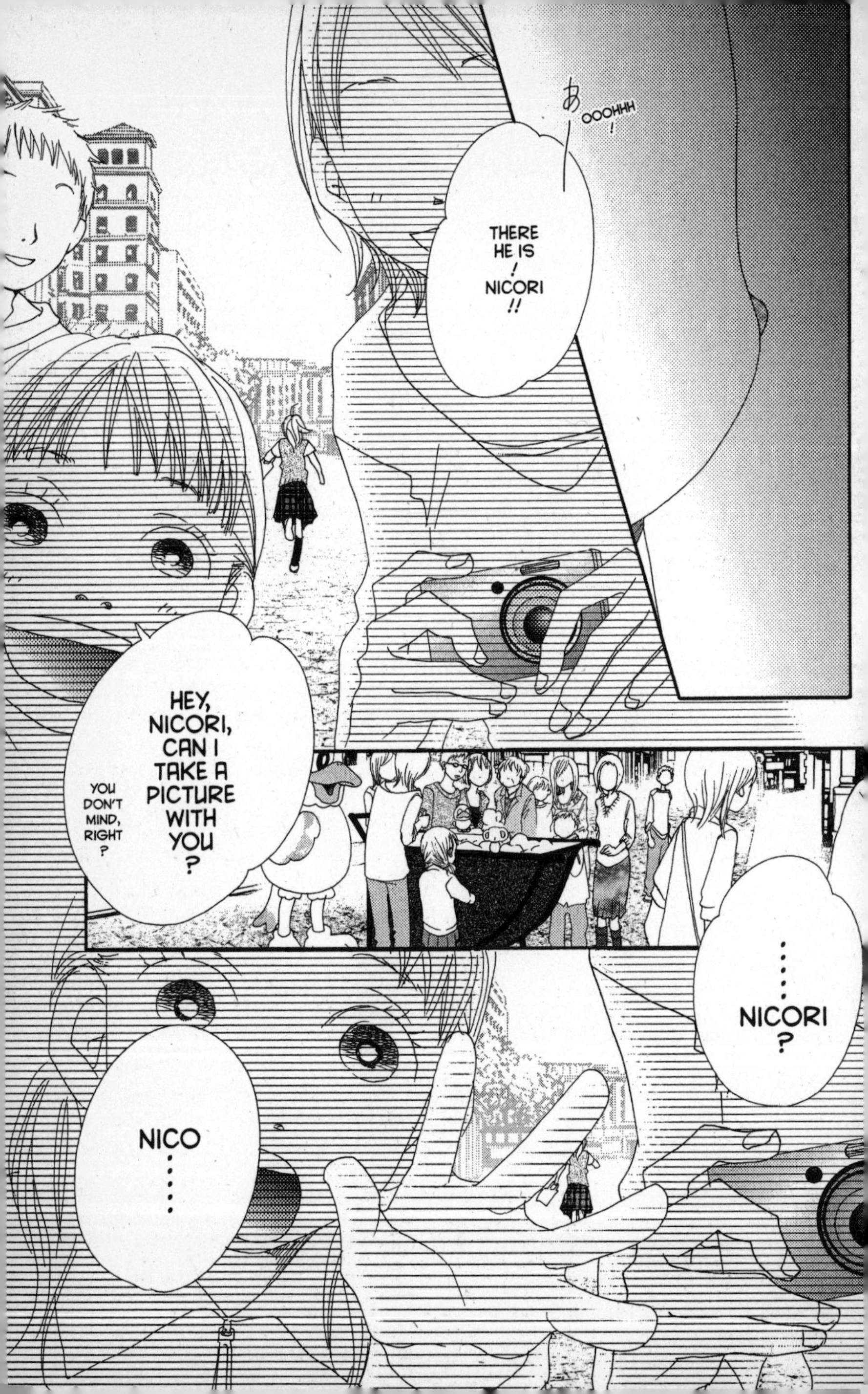
あ
OOOHHH!
THERE HE IS! NICORI!!
HEY, NICORI, CAN I TAKE A PICTURE WITH YOU?
YOU DON'T MIND, RIGHT?
......NICORI?
NICO......

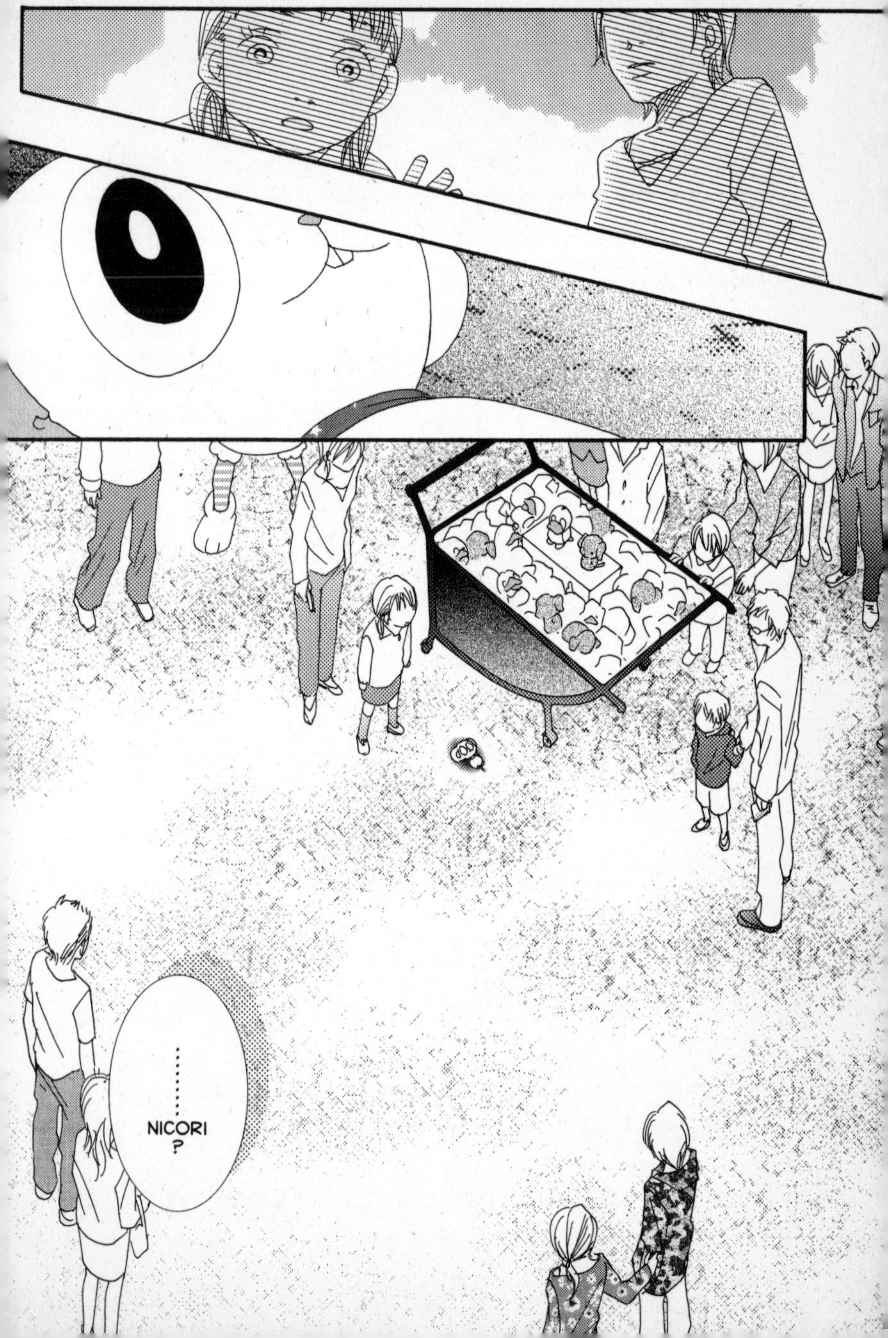

.... NICORI?

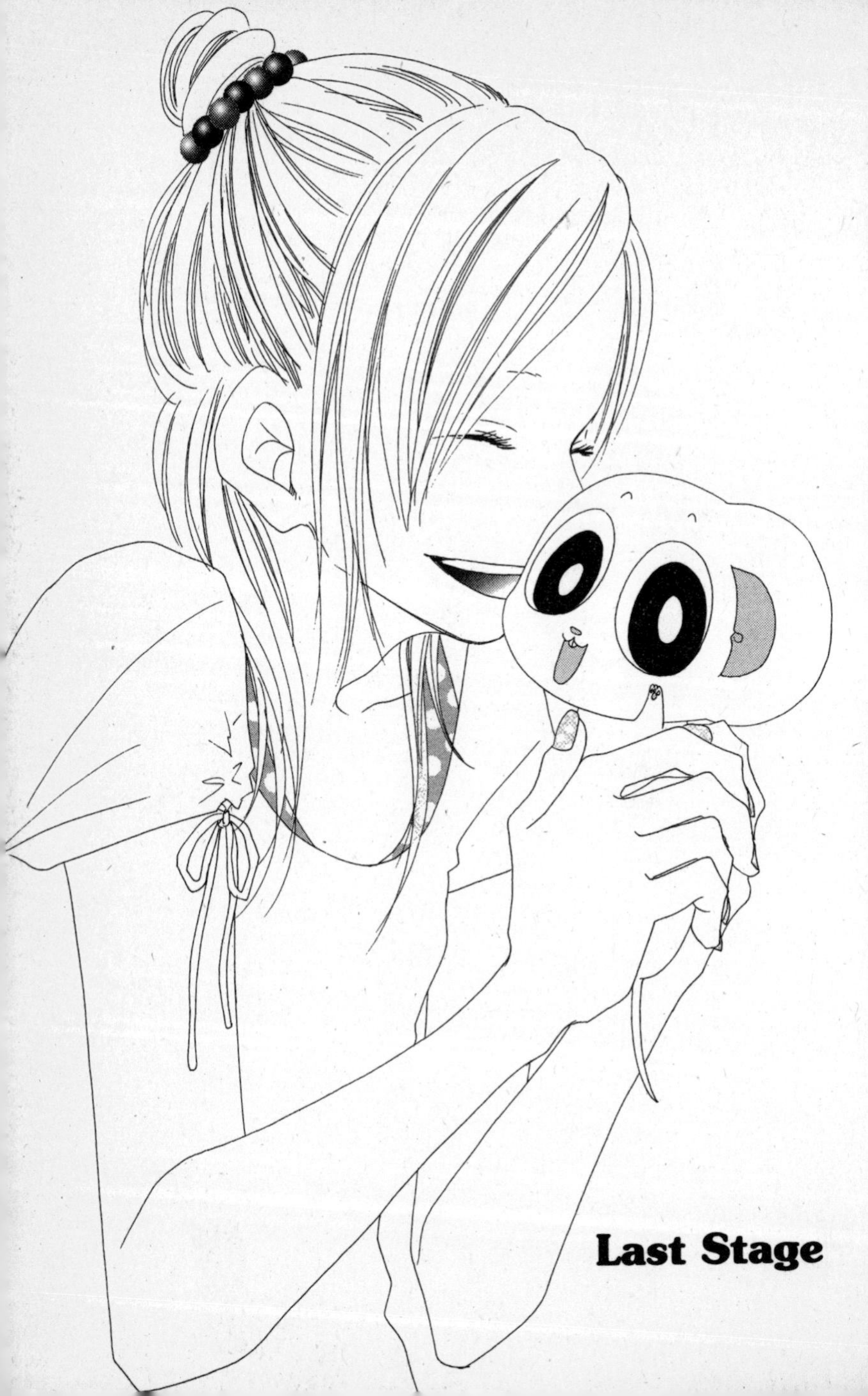

Last Stage

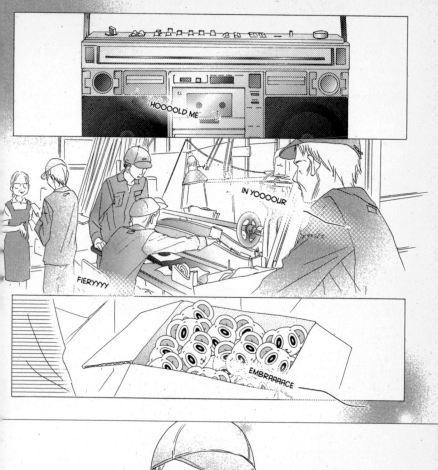

HOOOOLD ME

IN YOOOOUR

FIERYYYY

EMBRAAAACE

Hey.

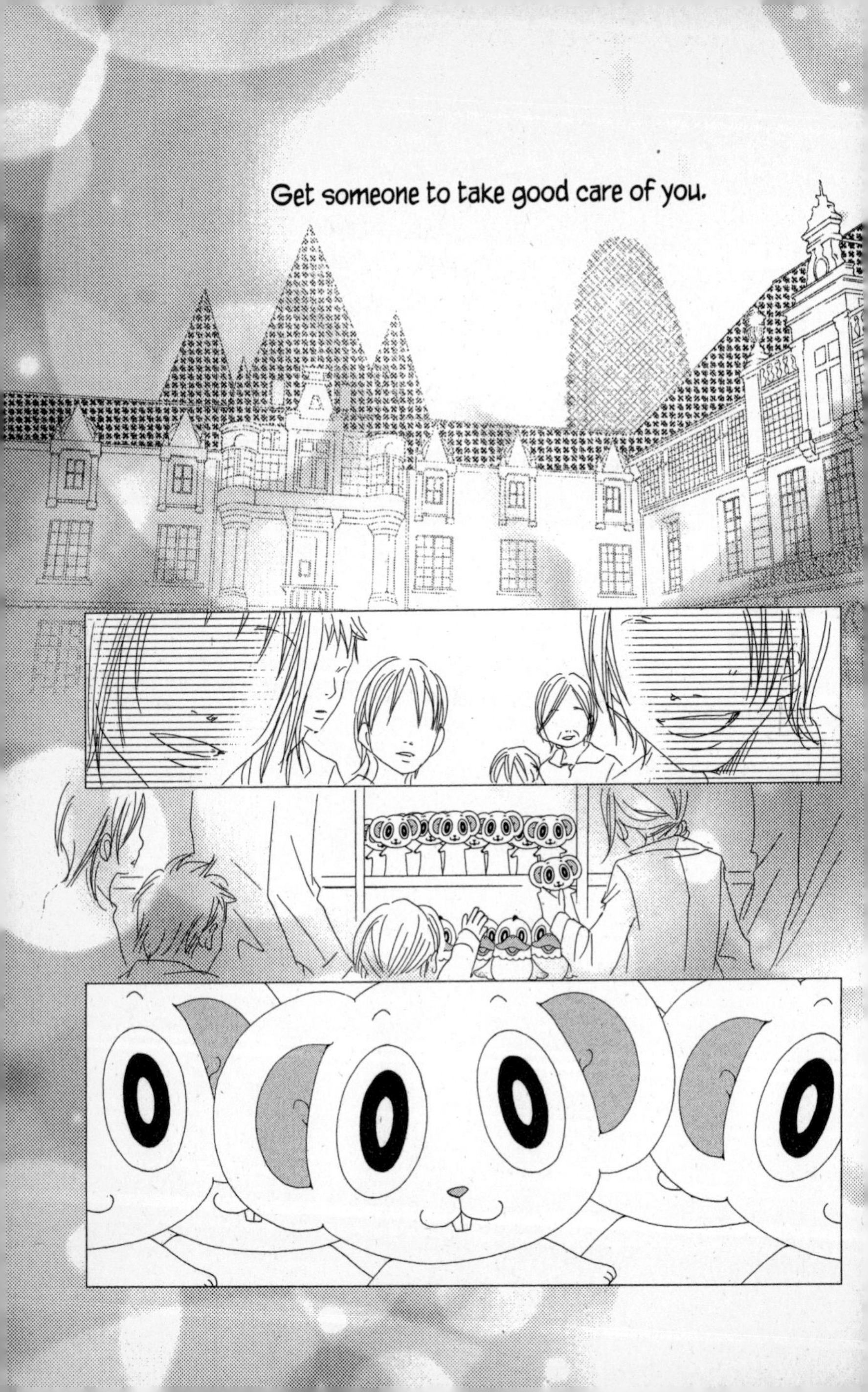
Get someone to take good care of you.

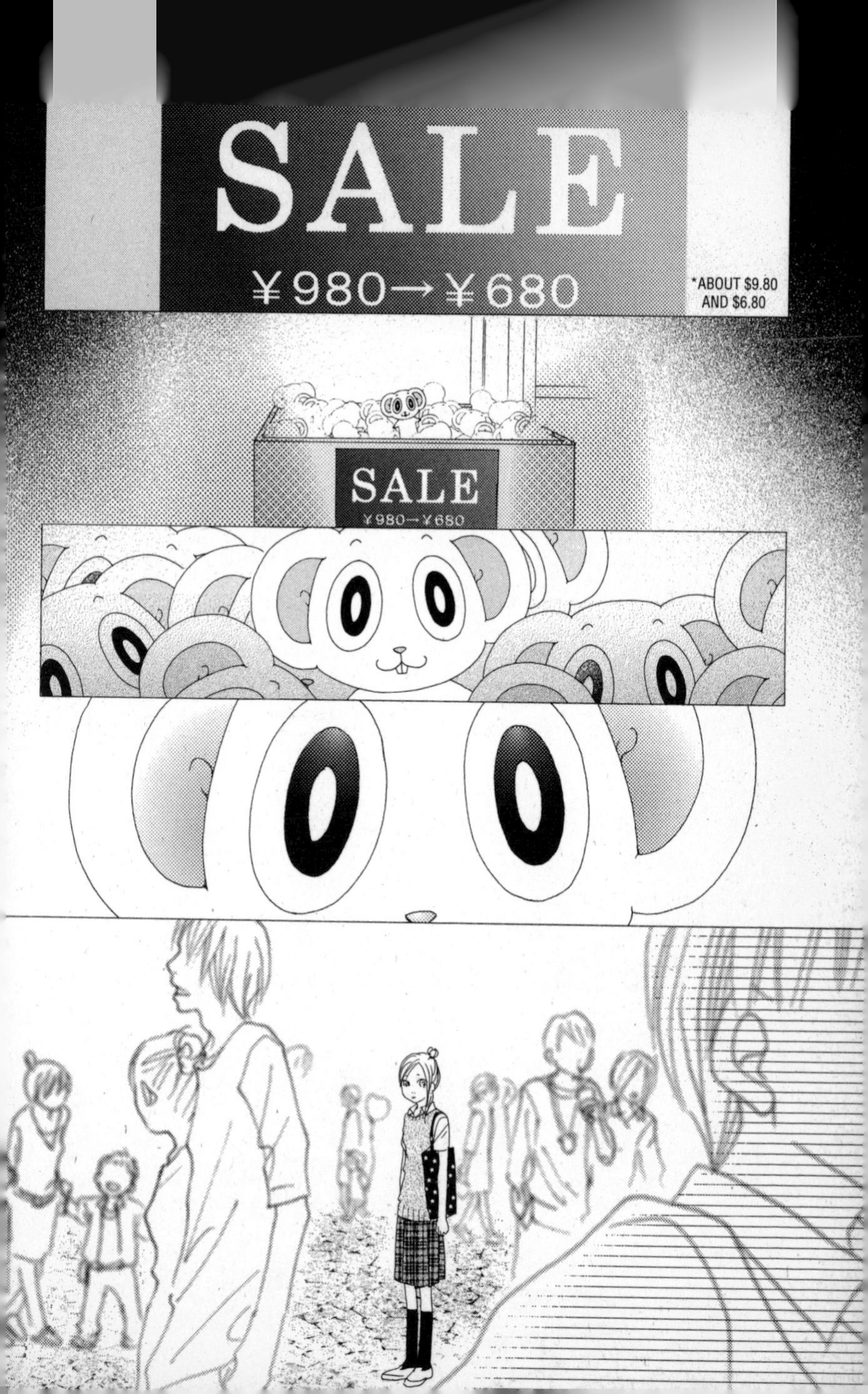
SALE
¥980→¥680
*ABOUT $9.80 AND $6.80
SALE
¥980→¥680

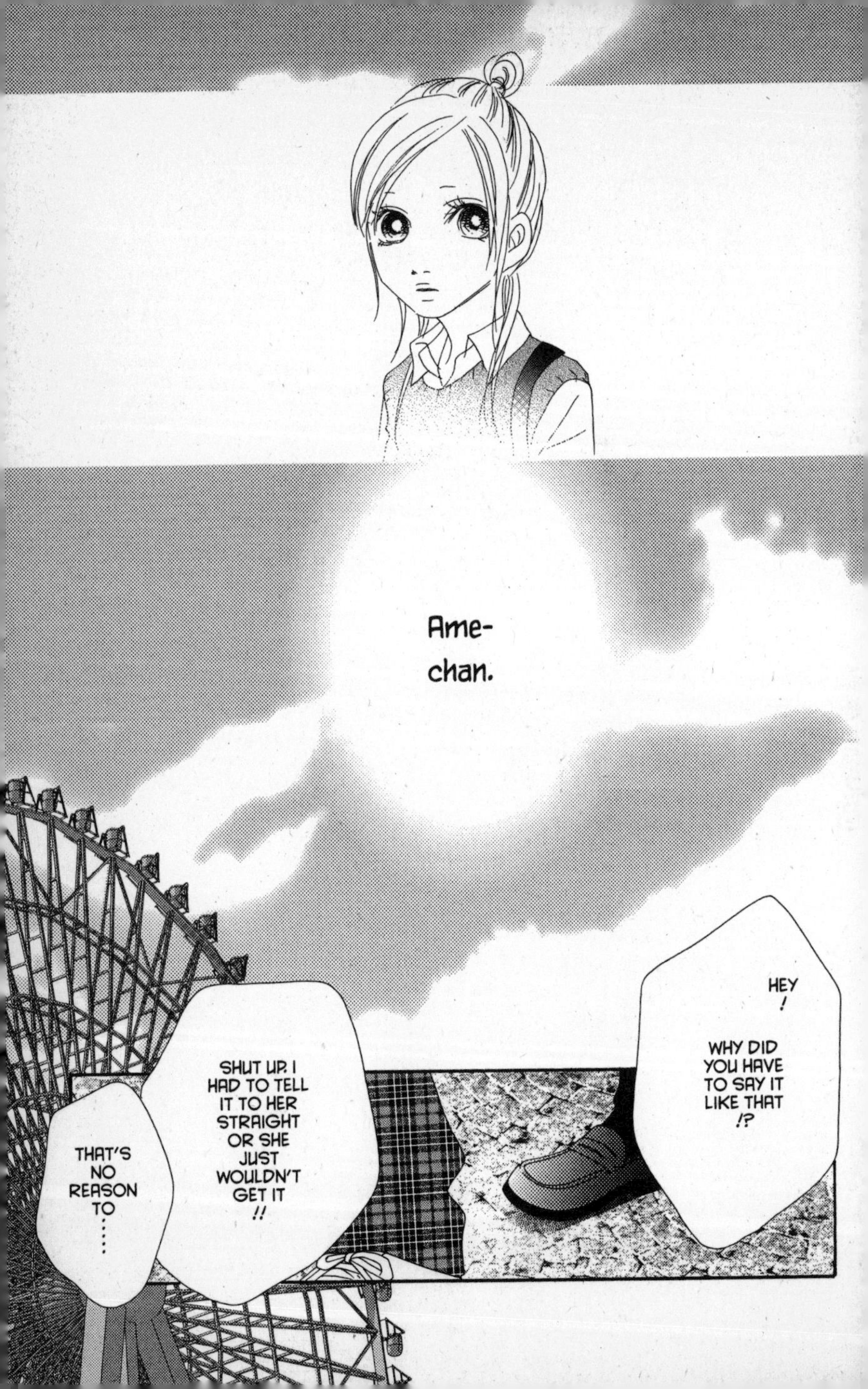
Ame-chan.
HEY!
WHY DID YOU HAVE TO SAY IT LIKE THAT!?
SHUT UP. I HAD TO TELL IT TO HER STRAIGHT OR SHE JUST WOULDN'T GET IT!!
THAT'S NO REASON TO.....

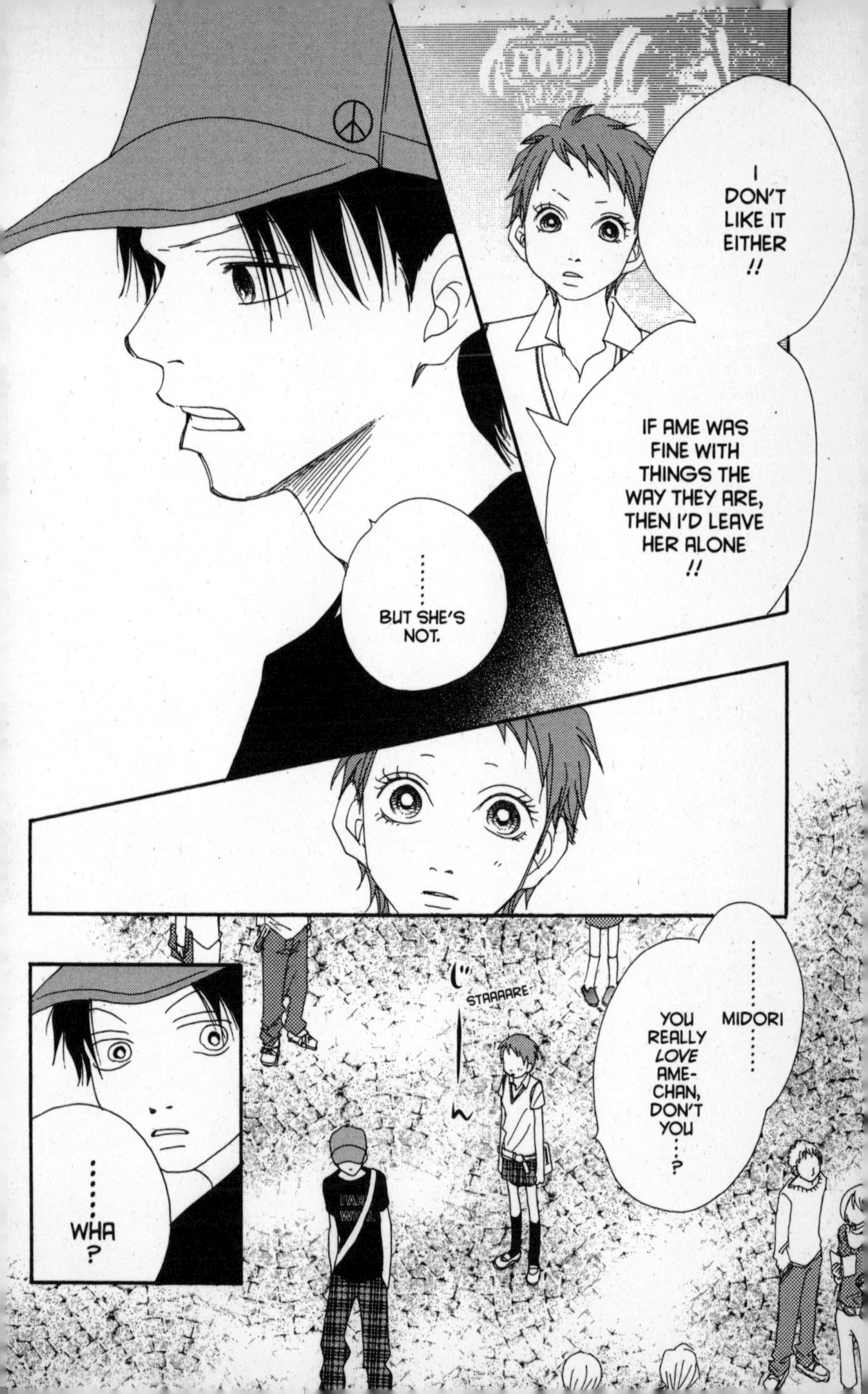
I DON'T LIKE IT EITHER !!
IF AME WAS FINE WITH THINGS THE WAY THEY ARE, THEN I'D LEAVE HER ALONE !!
......BUT SHE'S NOT.
MIDORI...... YOU REALLY *LOVE* AME-CHAN, DON'T YOU...?
STAAAARE
......WHA?

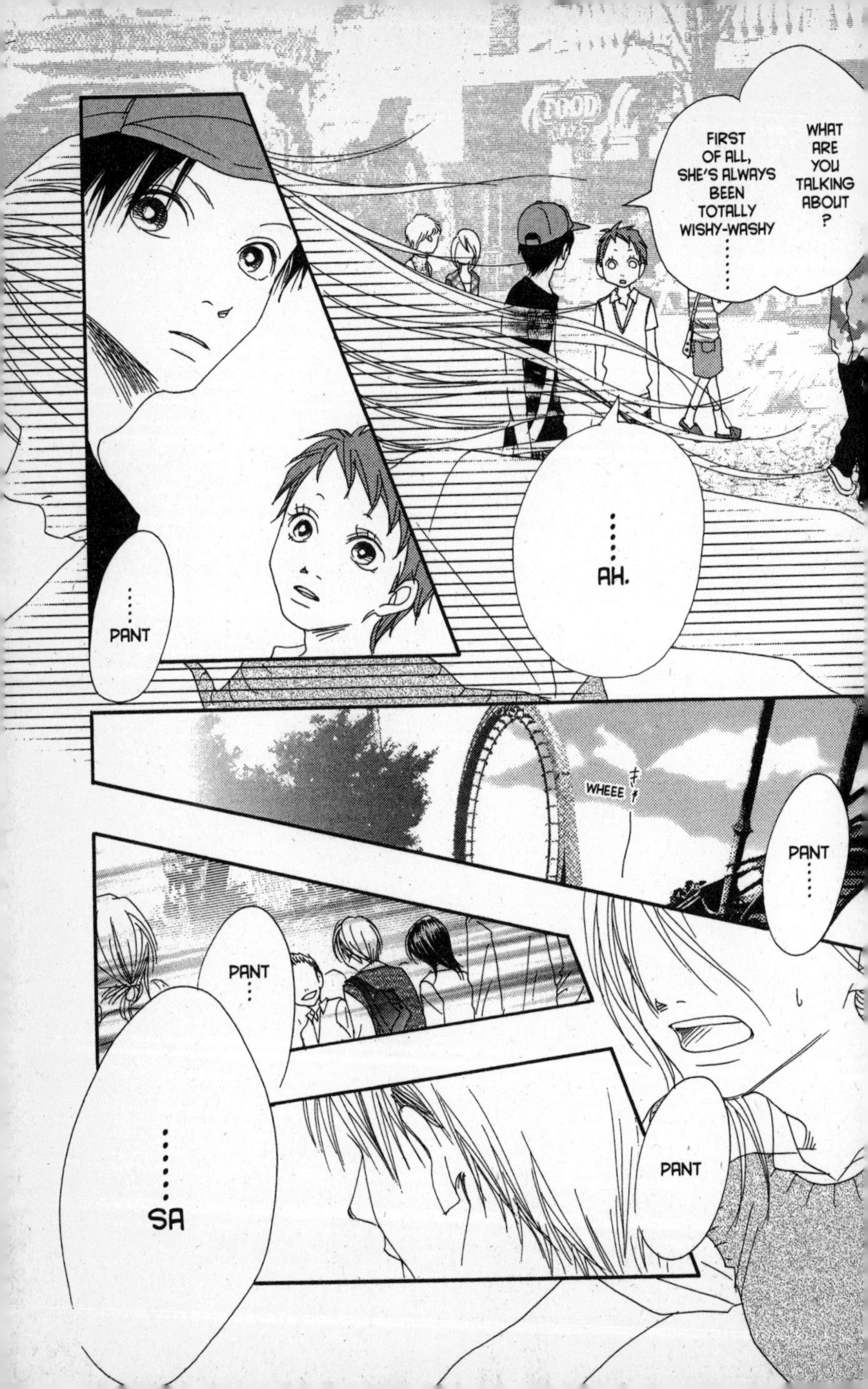
WHAT ARE YOU TALKING ABOUT ?
FIRST OF ALL, SHE'S ALWAYS BEEN TOTALLY WISHY-WASHY ......
...... AH.
...... PANT
PANT ......
WHEEE
PANT
PANT ...
...... SA

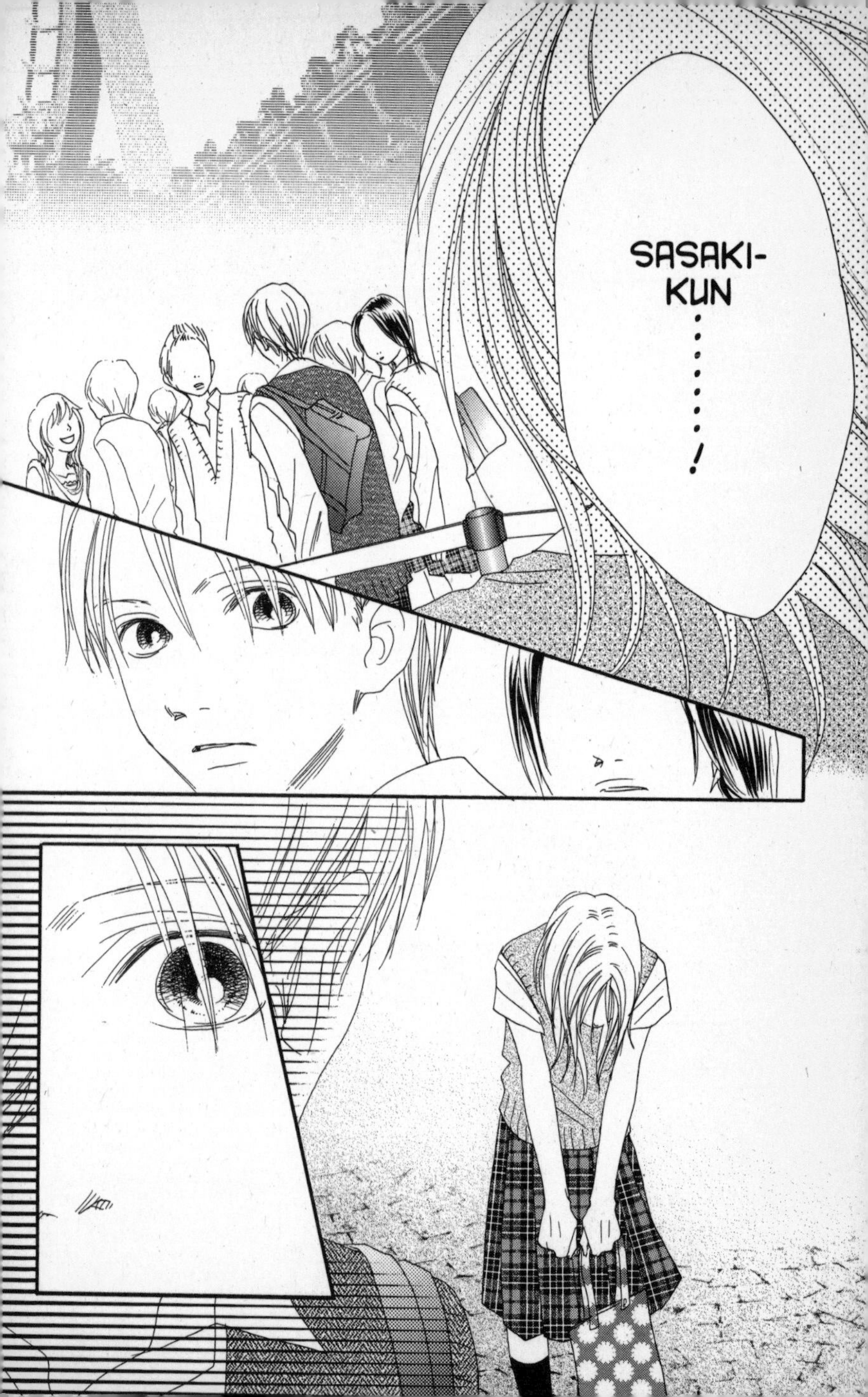
SASAKI-KUN ......!

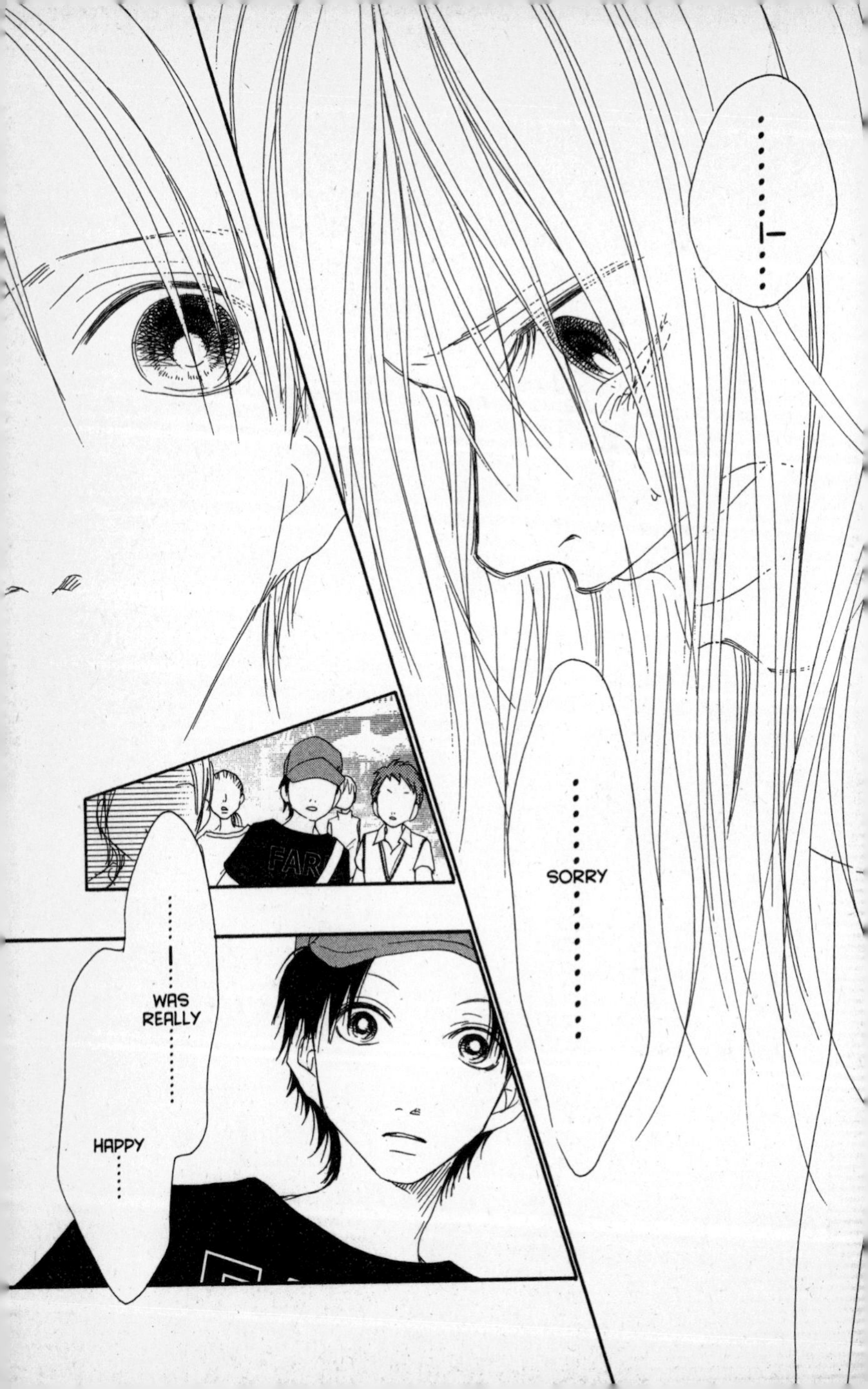
......I......
......SORRY......
......I WAS REALLY......HAPPY......

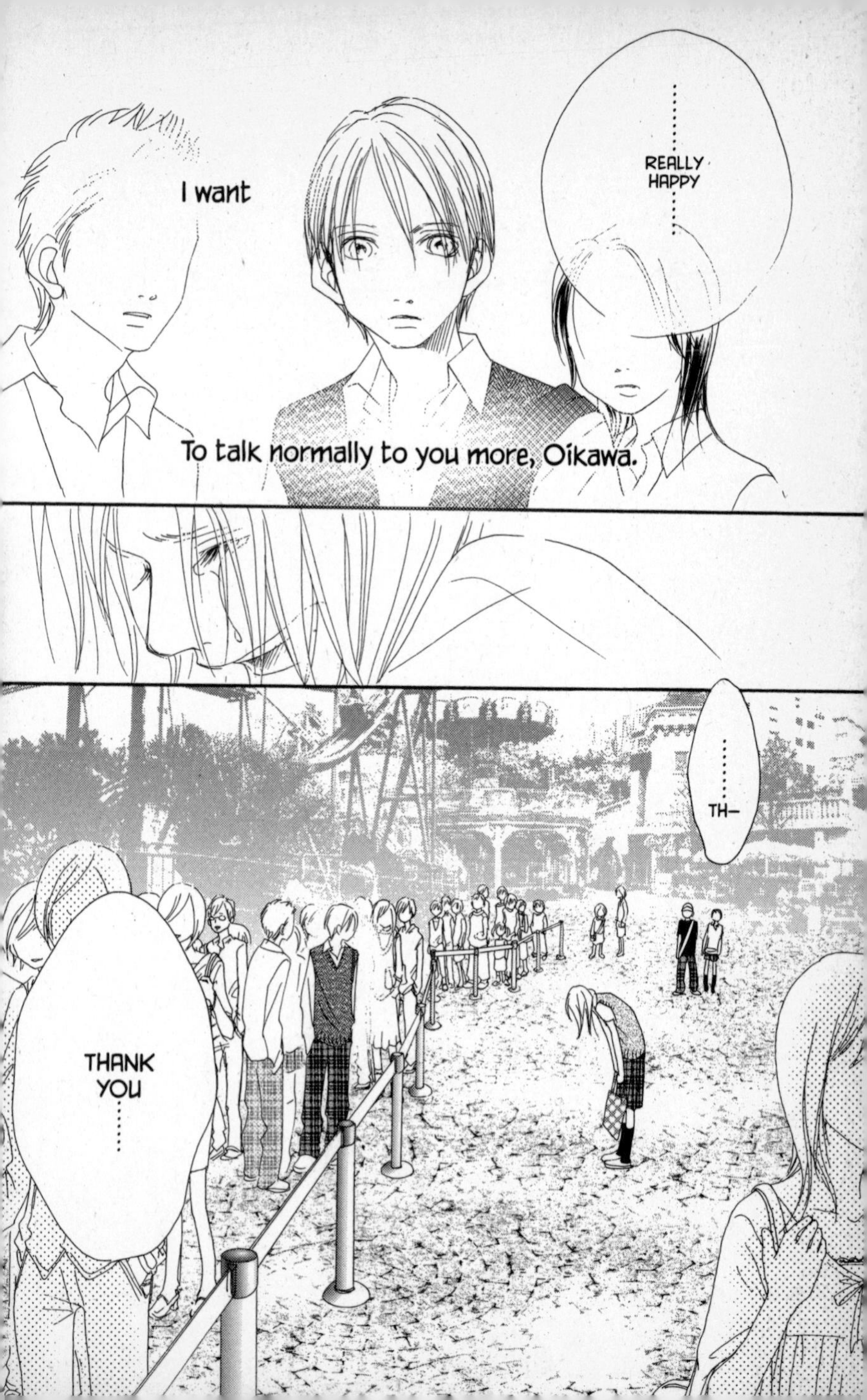

……REALLY HAPPY……
I want
To talk normally to you more, Oikawa.
……TH—
THANK YOU……

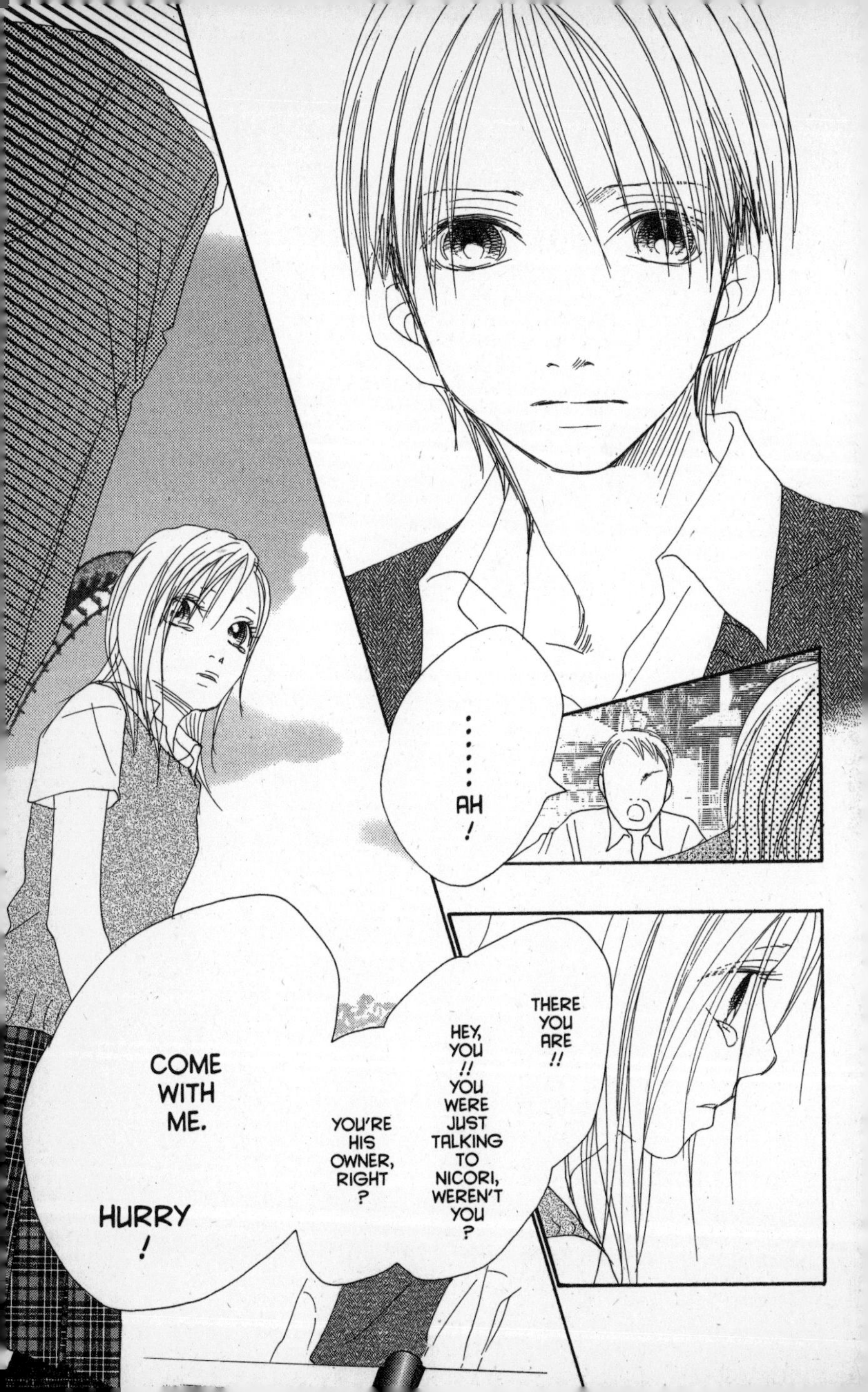
......AH!
THERE YOU ARE!!
HEY, YOU!! YOU WERE JUST TALKING TO NICORI, WEREN'T YOU?
YOU'RE HIS OWNER, RIGHT?
COME WITH ME.
HURRY!

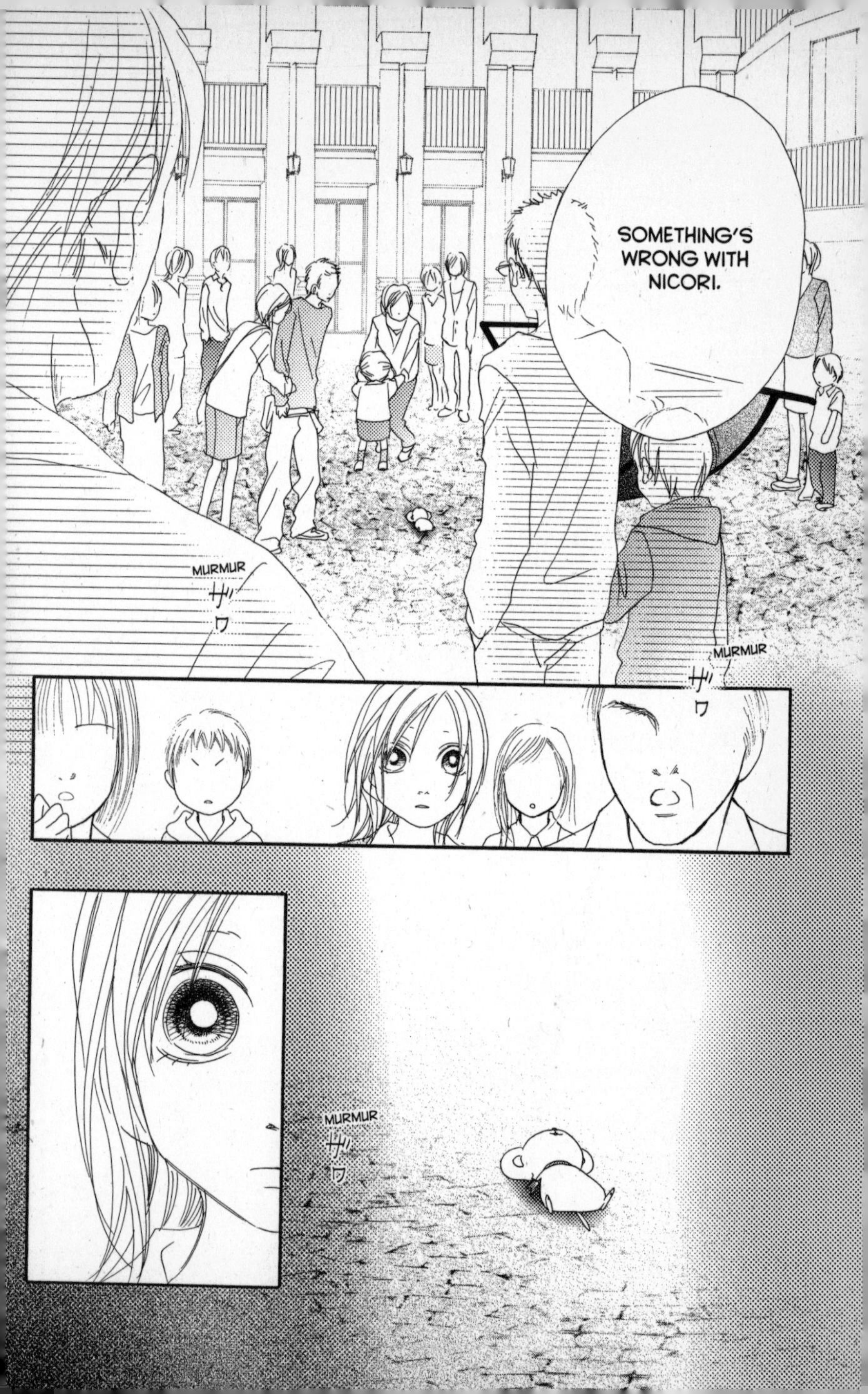
SOMETHING'S WRONG WITH NICORI.
MURMUR
ザワ
MURMUR
ザワ
MURMUR
ザワ

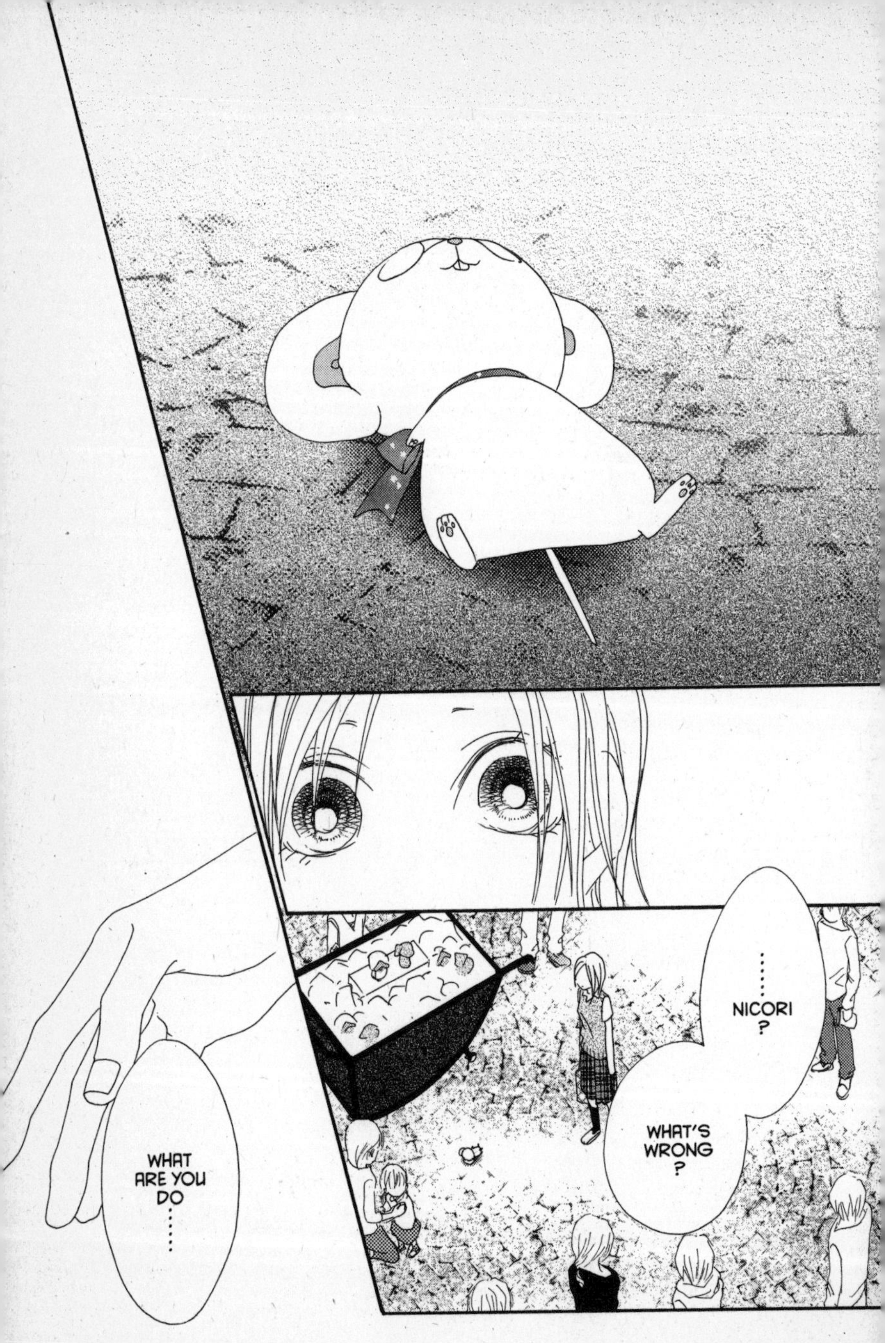

......NICORI?
WHAT'S WRONG?
WHAT ARE YOU DO......

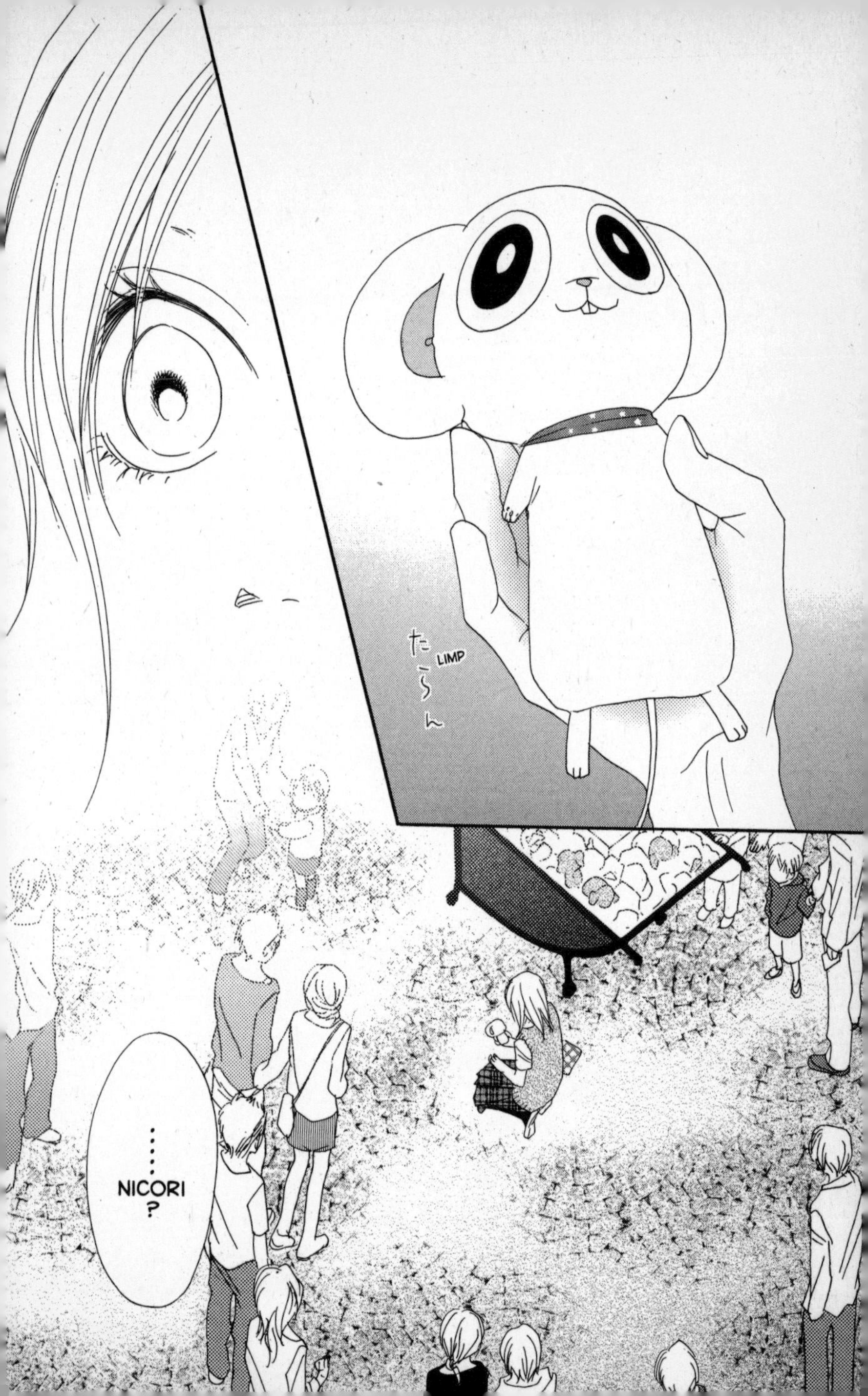
たらん
LIMP
……NICORI?

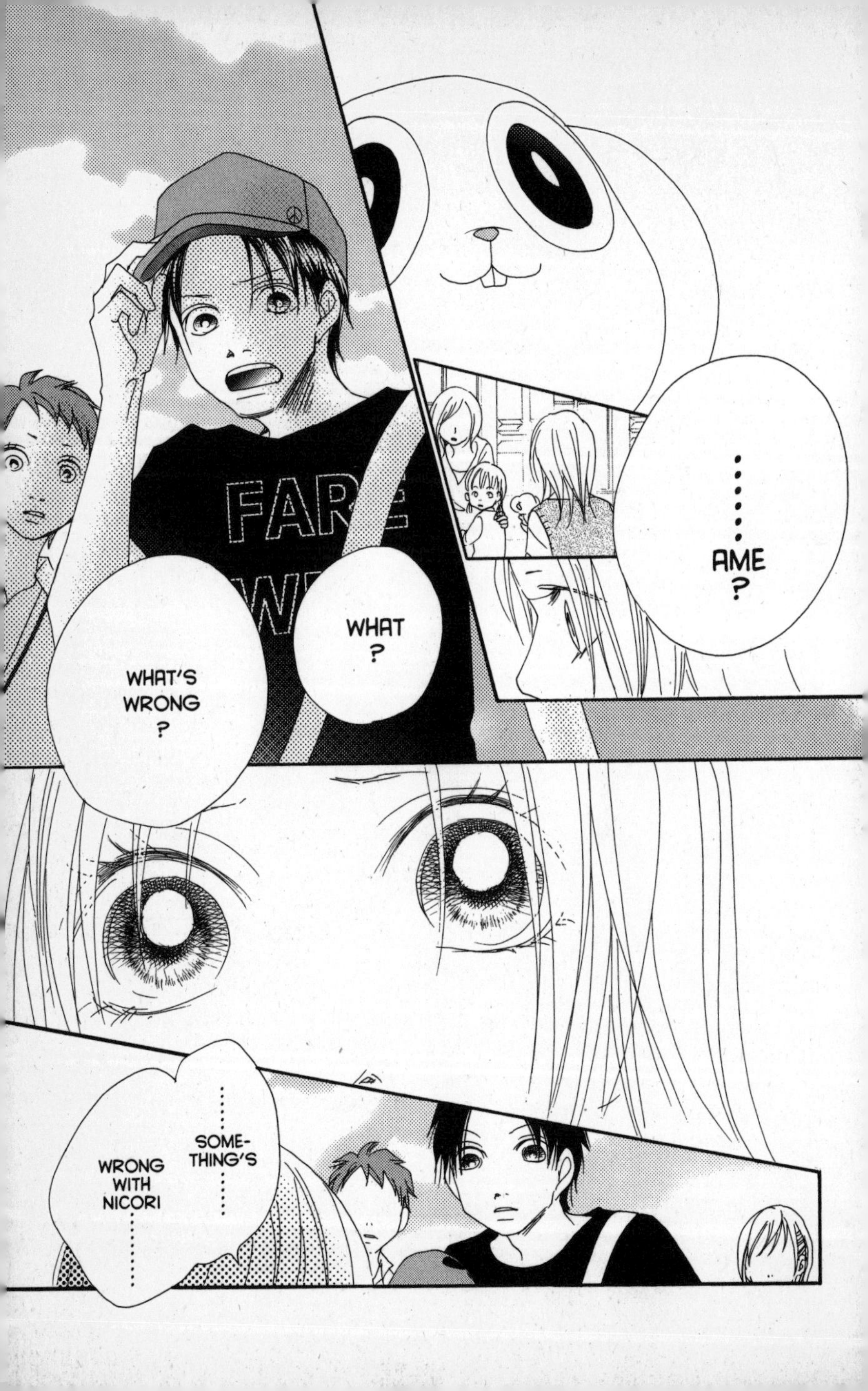

......AME?
WHAT?
WHAT'S WRONG?
......SOME-THING'S...... WRONG WITH NICORI......

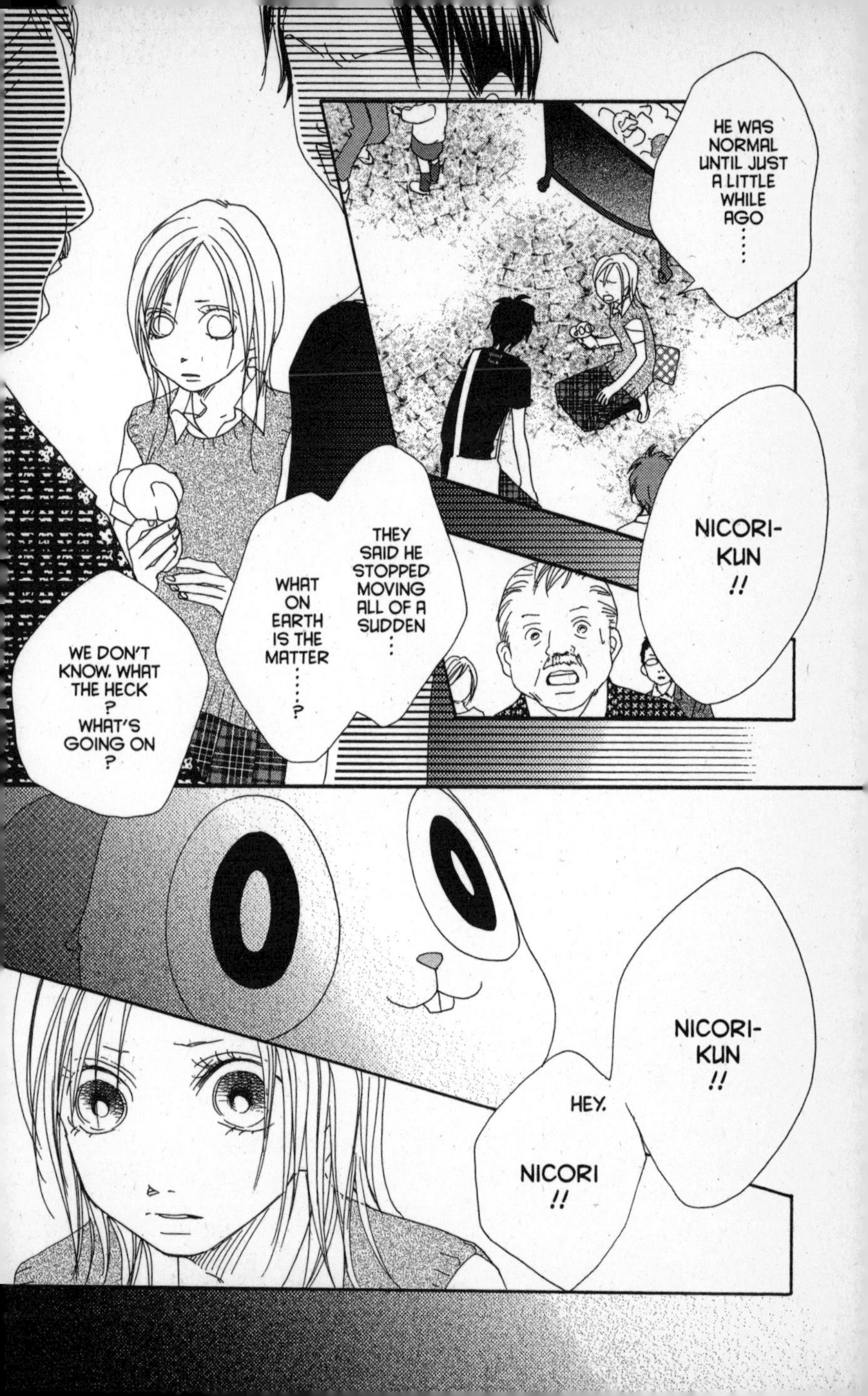
HE WAS NORMAL UNTIL JUST A LITTLE WHILE AGO.....
NICORI-KUN!!
THEY SAID HE STOPPED MOVING ALL OF A SUDDEN...
WHAT ON EARTH IS THE MATTER.....?
WE DON'T KNOW. WHAT THE HECK? WHAT'S GOING ON?
NICORI-KUN!!
HEY.
NICORI!!

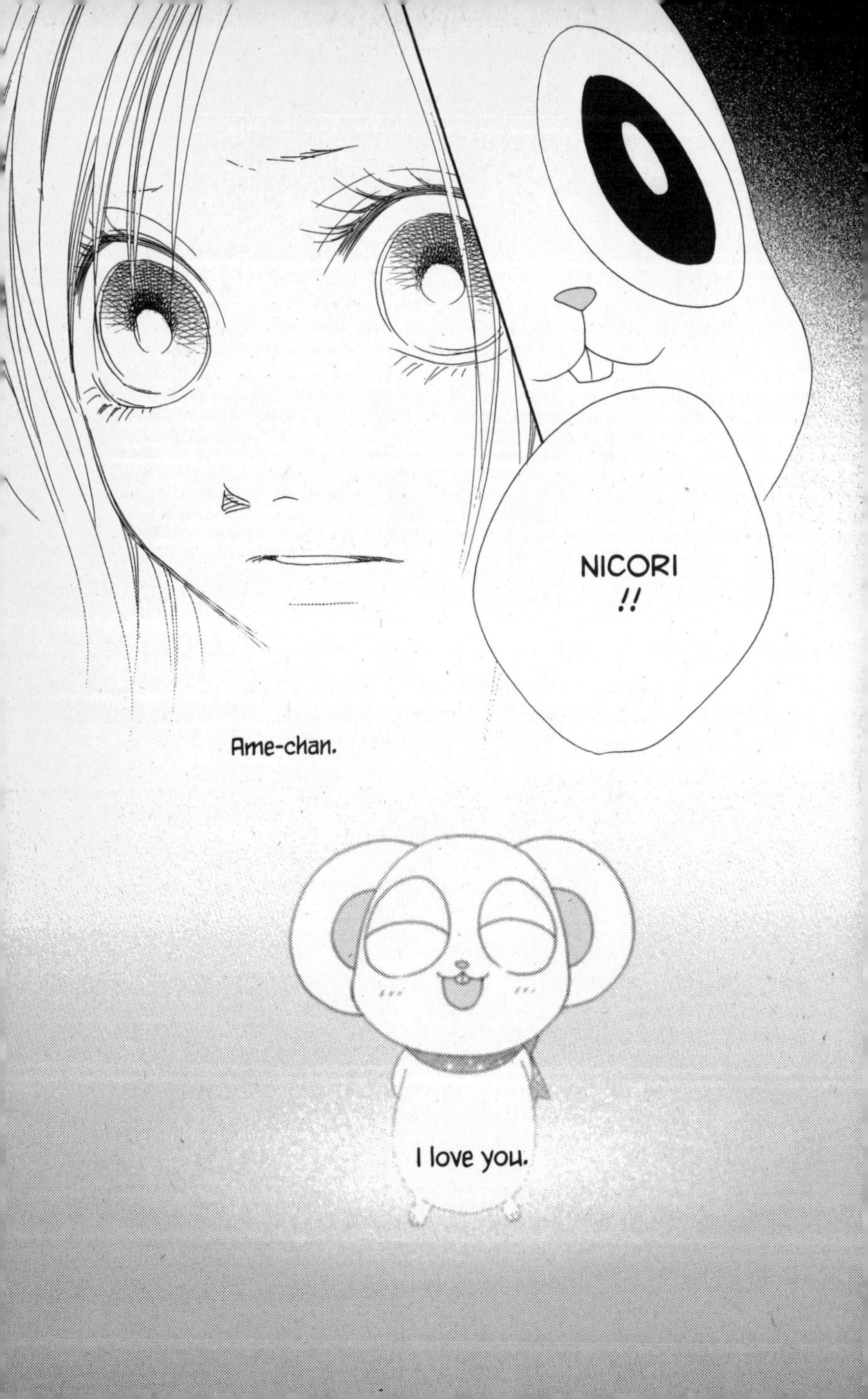
NICORI
!!
Ame-chan.
I love you.

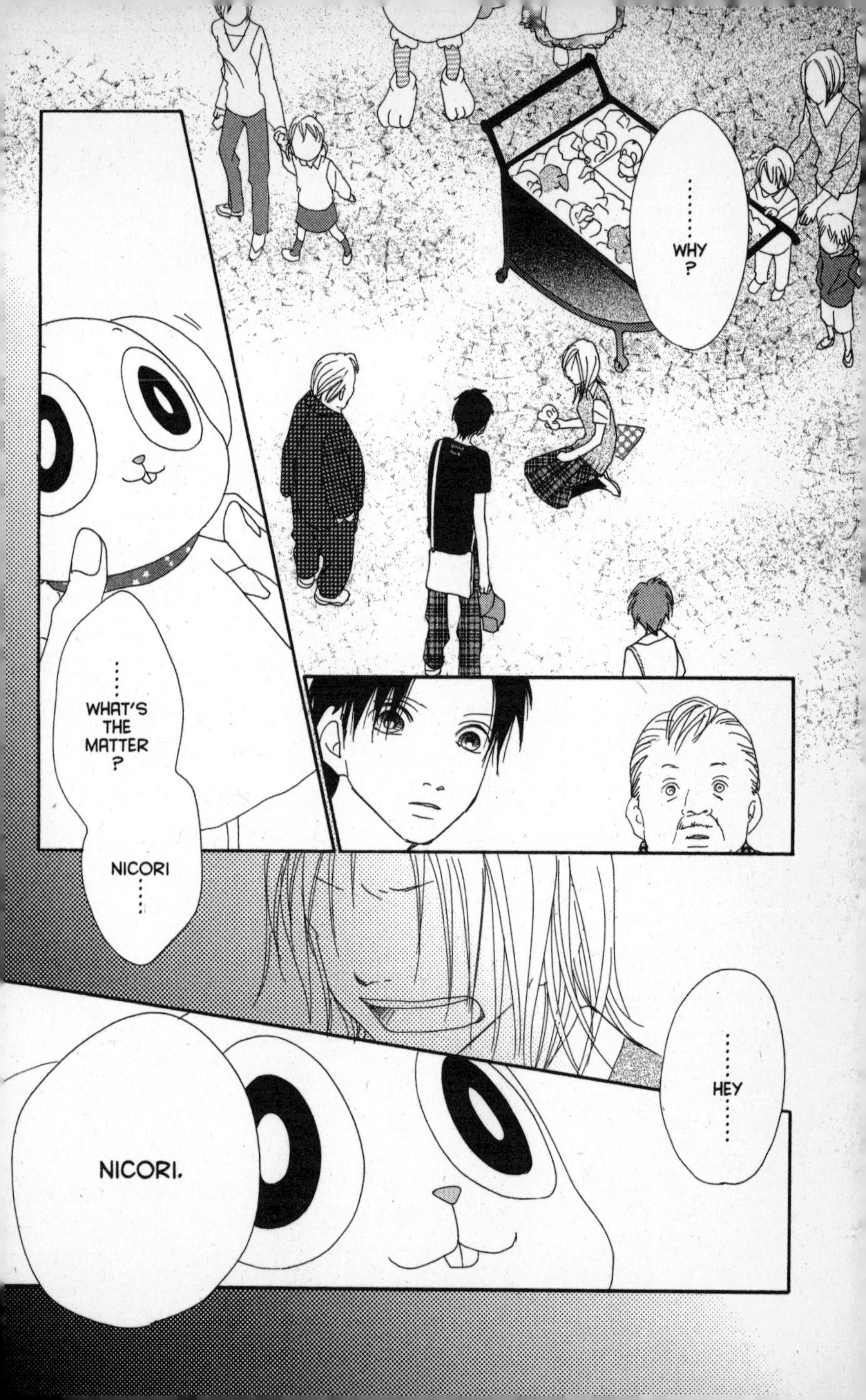
......WHY?
......WHAT'S THE MATTER?
NICORI......
......HEY......
NICORI.

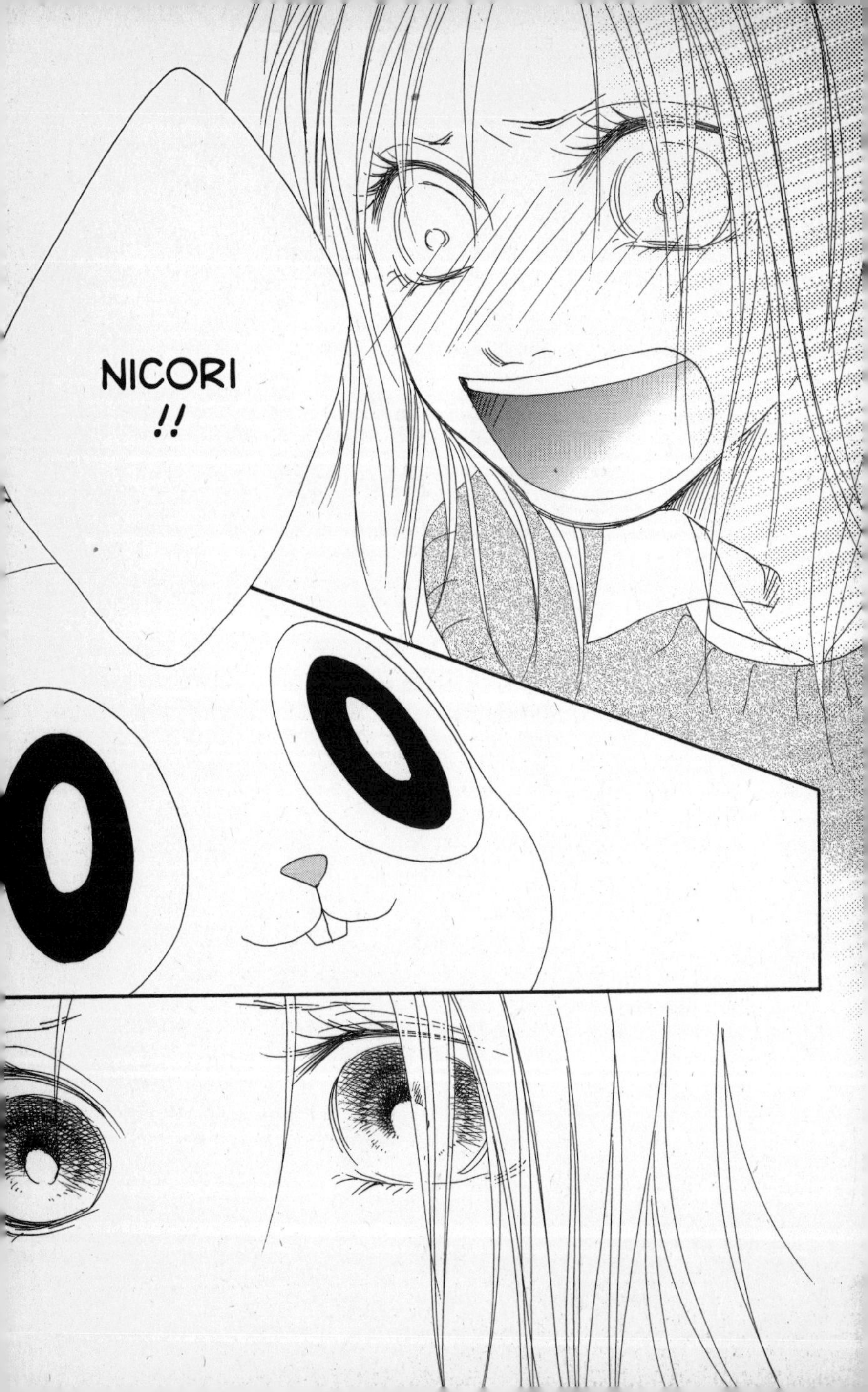
NICORI
!!

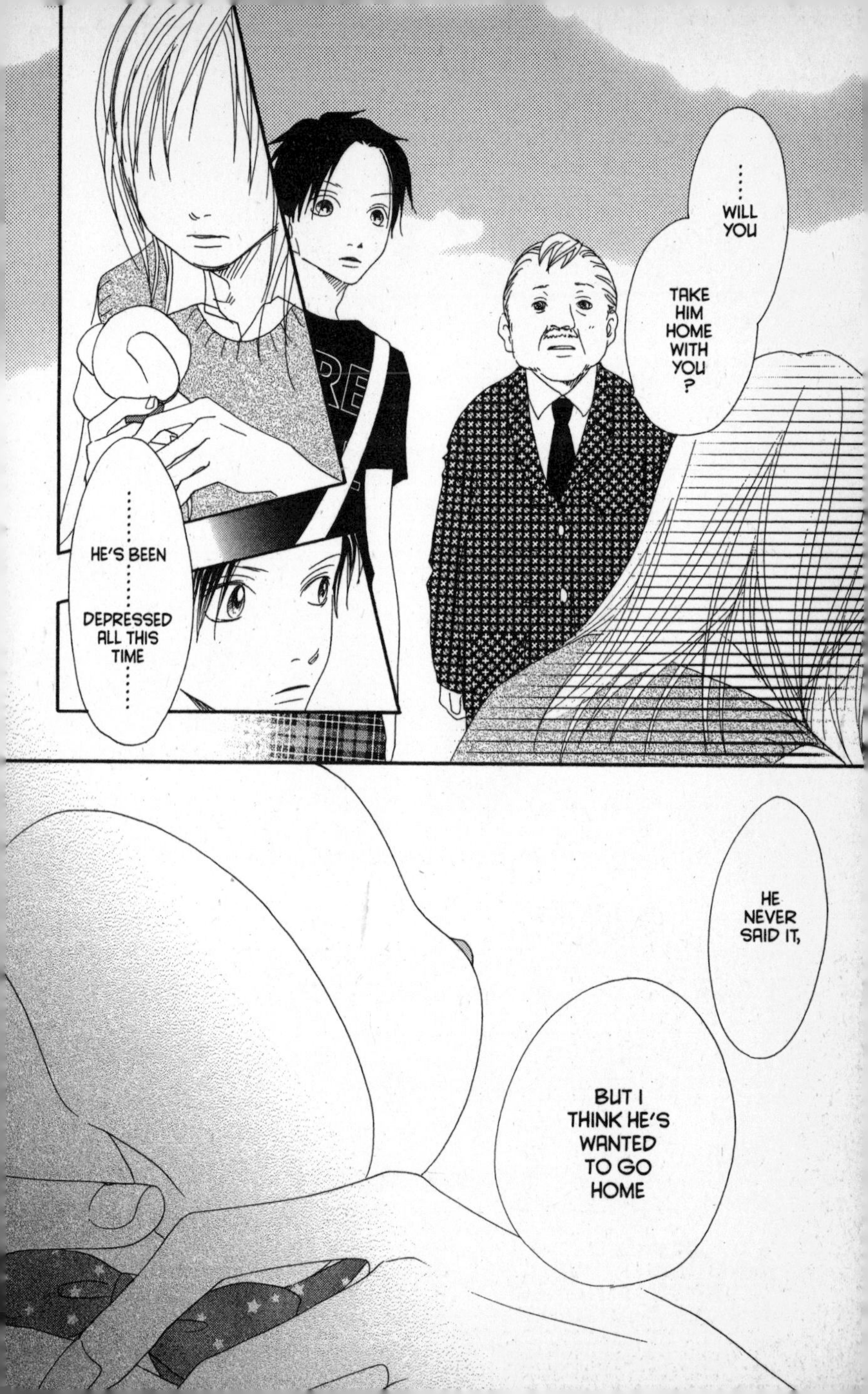
......WILL YOU TAKE HIM HOME WITH YOU?
......HE'S BEEN ......DEPRESSED ALL THIS TIME......
HE NEVER SAID IT,
BUT I THINK HE'S WANTED TO GO HOME

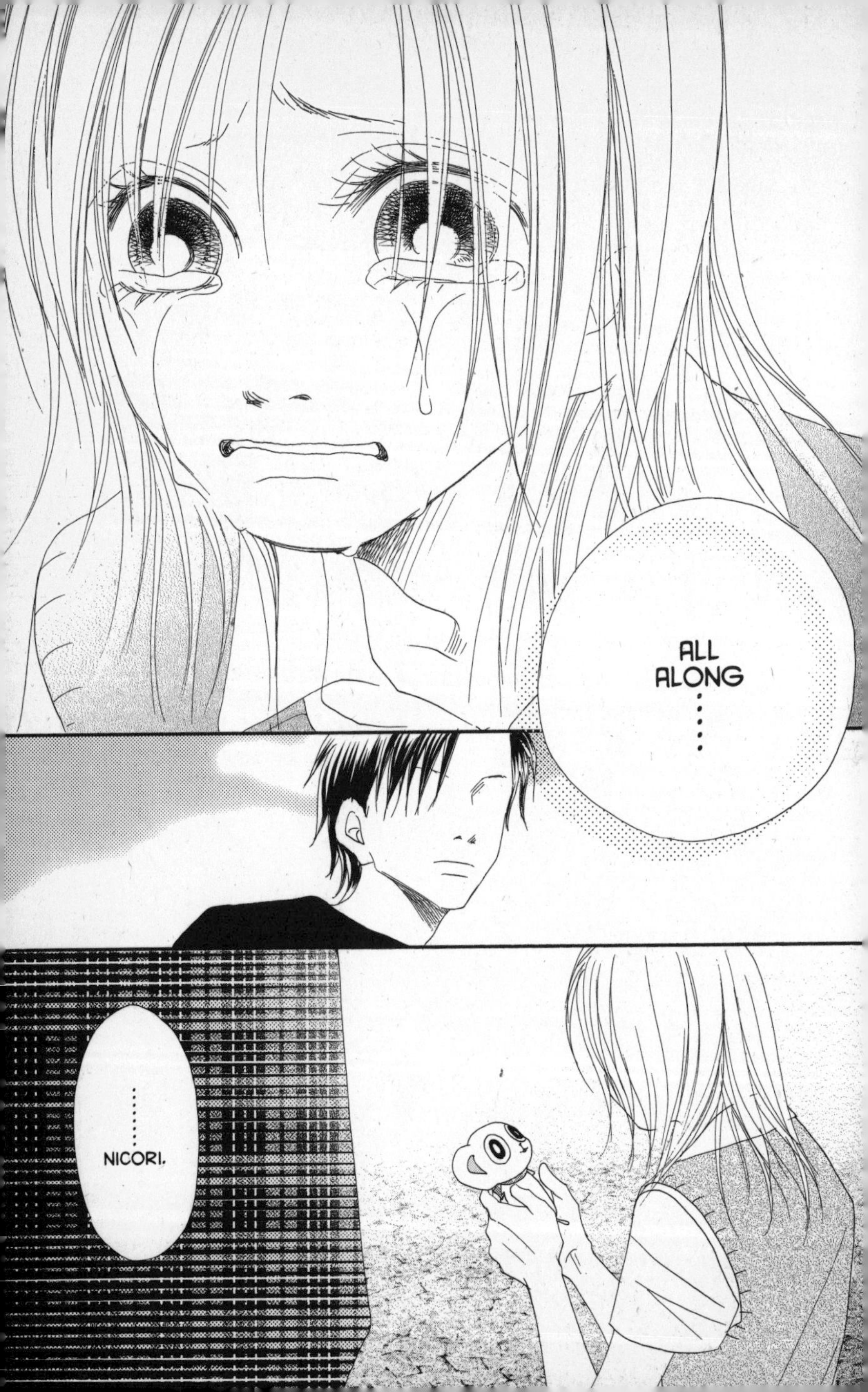
ALL ALONG......
......NICORI.

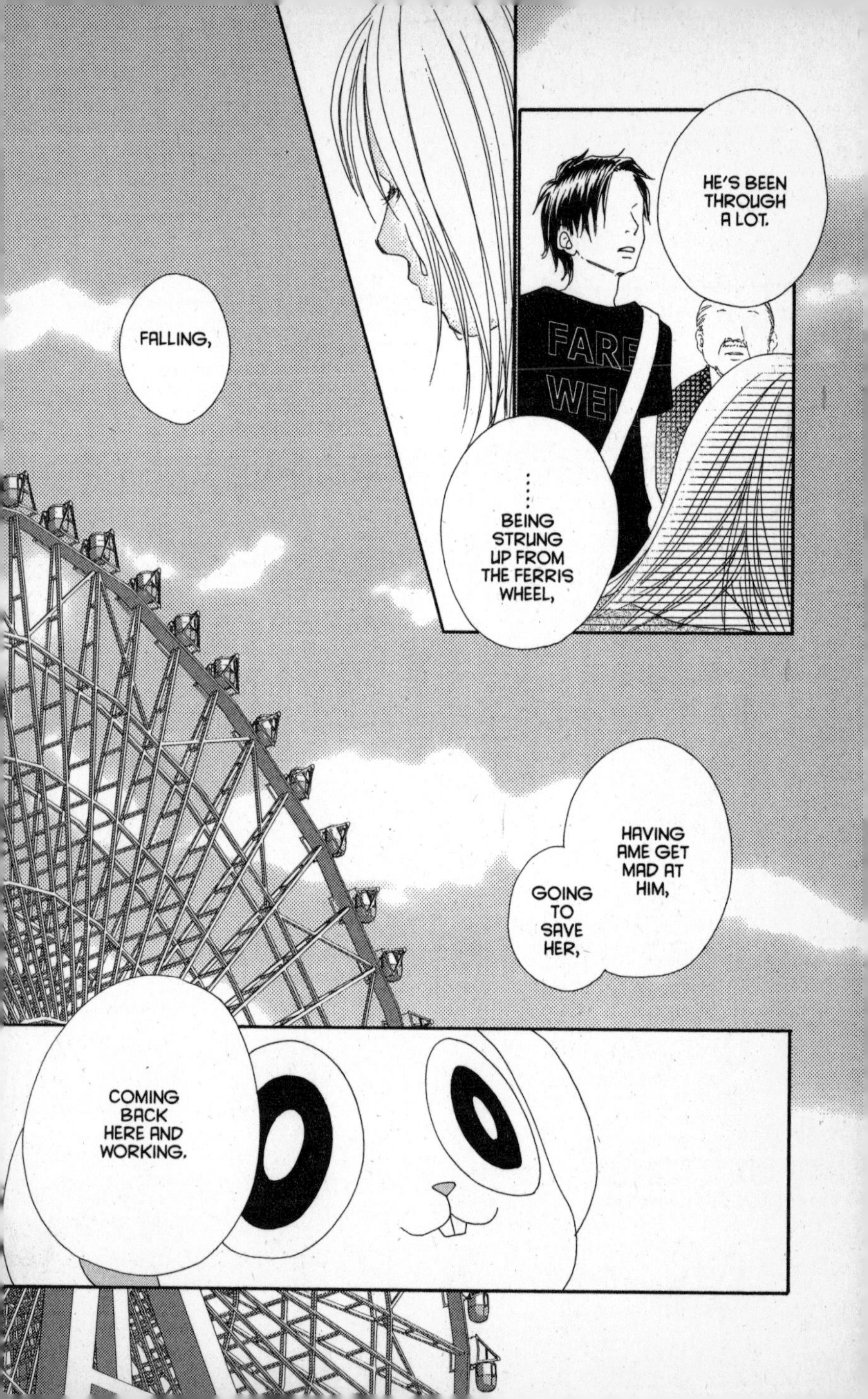
HE'S BEEN THROUGH A LOT.
FALLING,
... BEING STRUNG UP FROM THE FERRIS WHEEL,
HAVING AME GET MAD AT HIM,
GOING TO SAVE HER,
COMING BACK HERE AND WORKING.

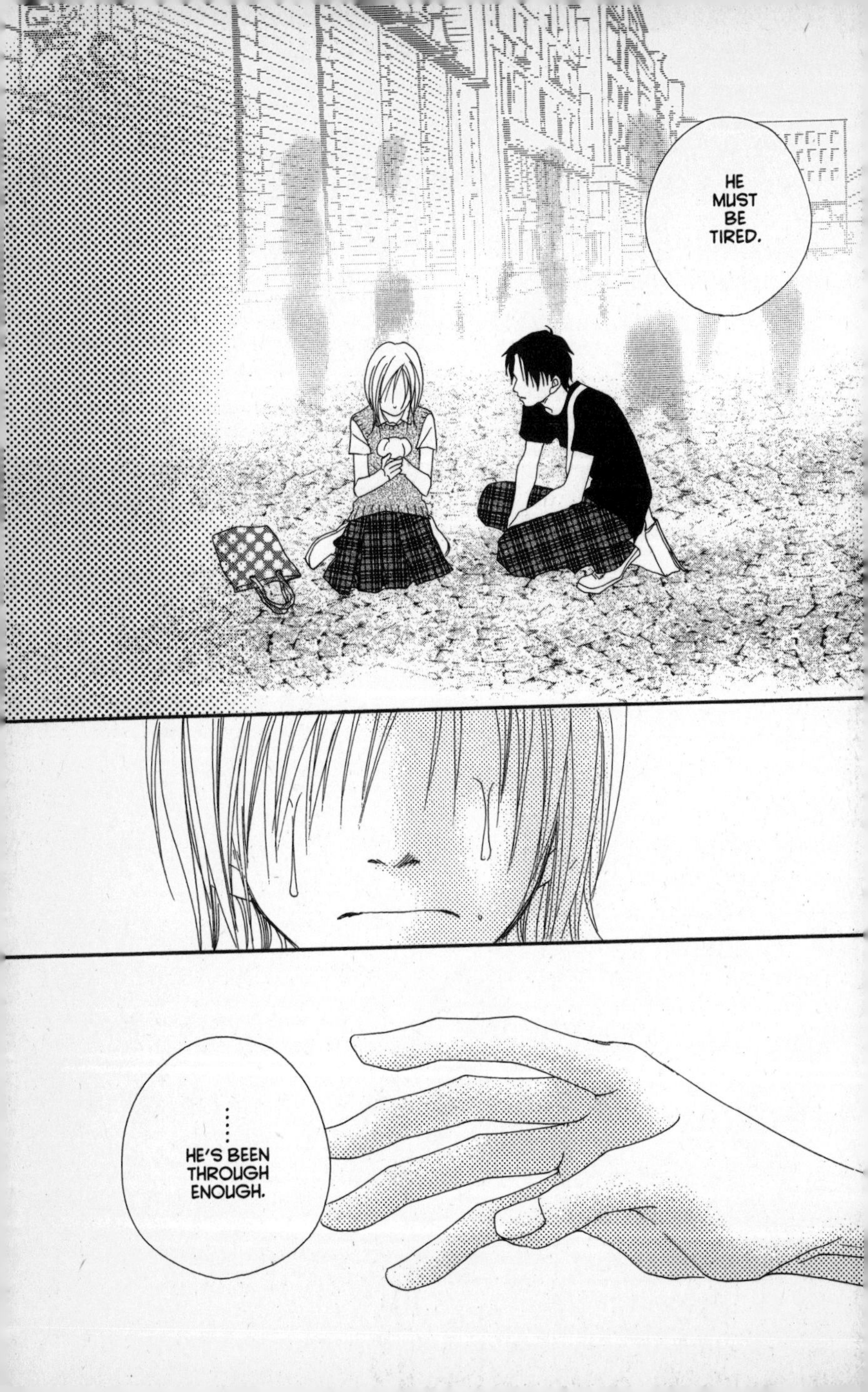
HE MUST BE TIRED.
......
HE'S BEEN THROUGH ENOUGH.

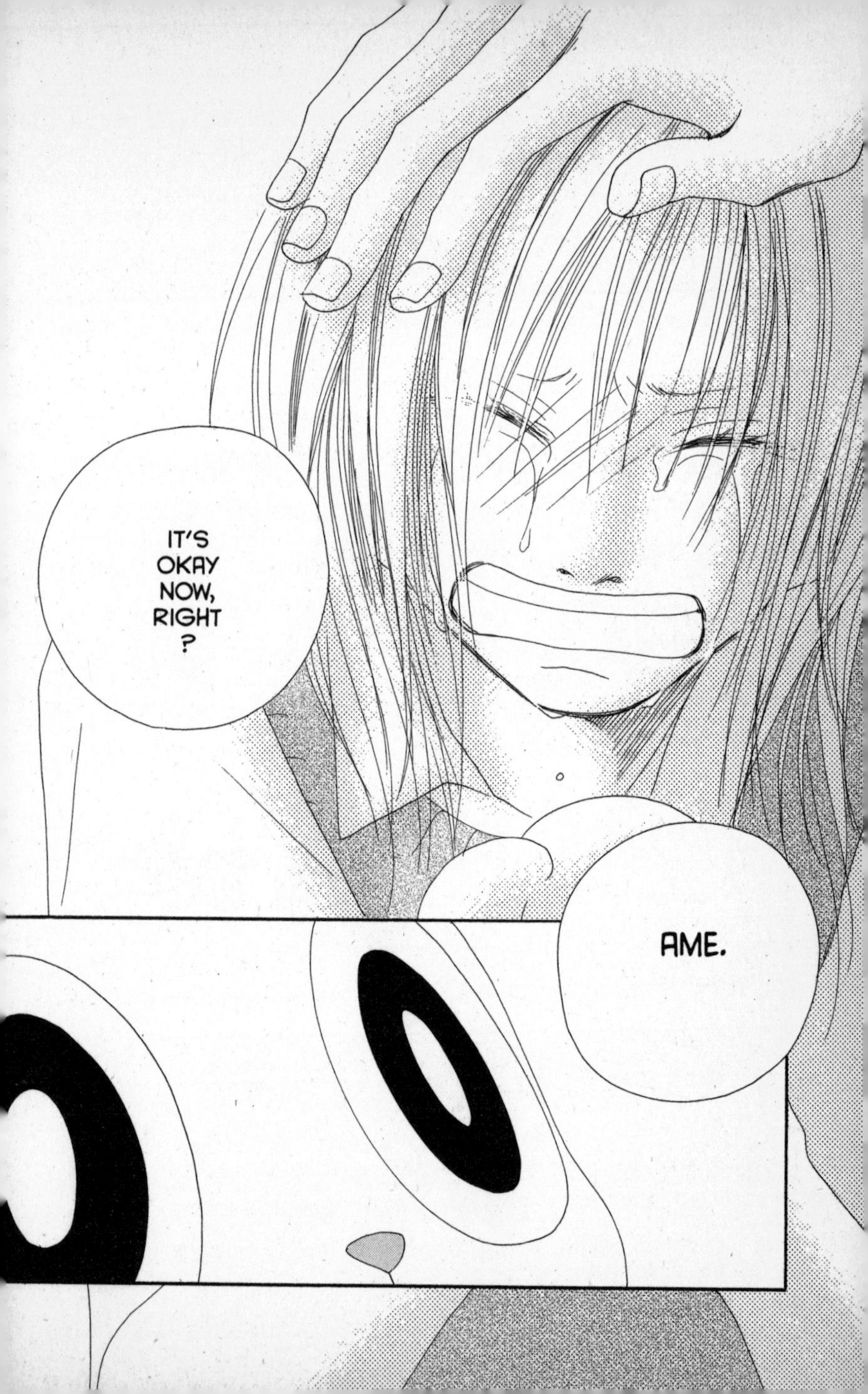
IT'S OKAY NOW, RIGHT?
AME.

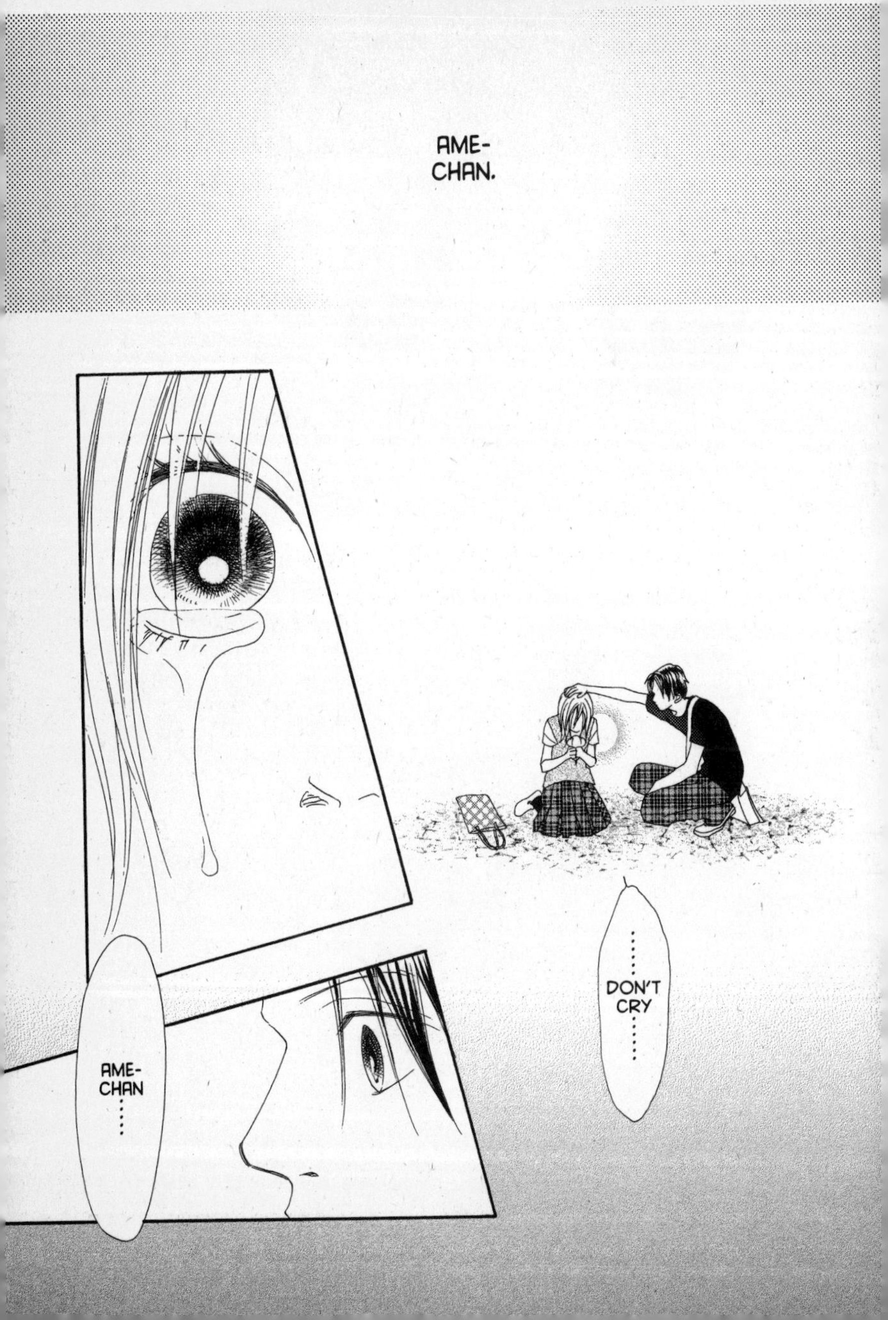
AME-CHAN.
......DON'T CRY......
AME-CHAN......

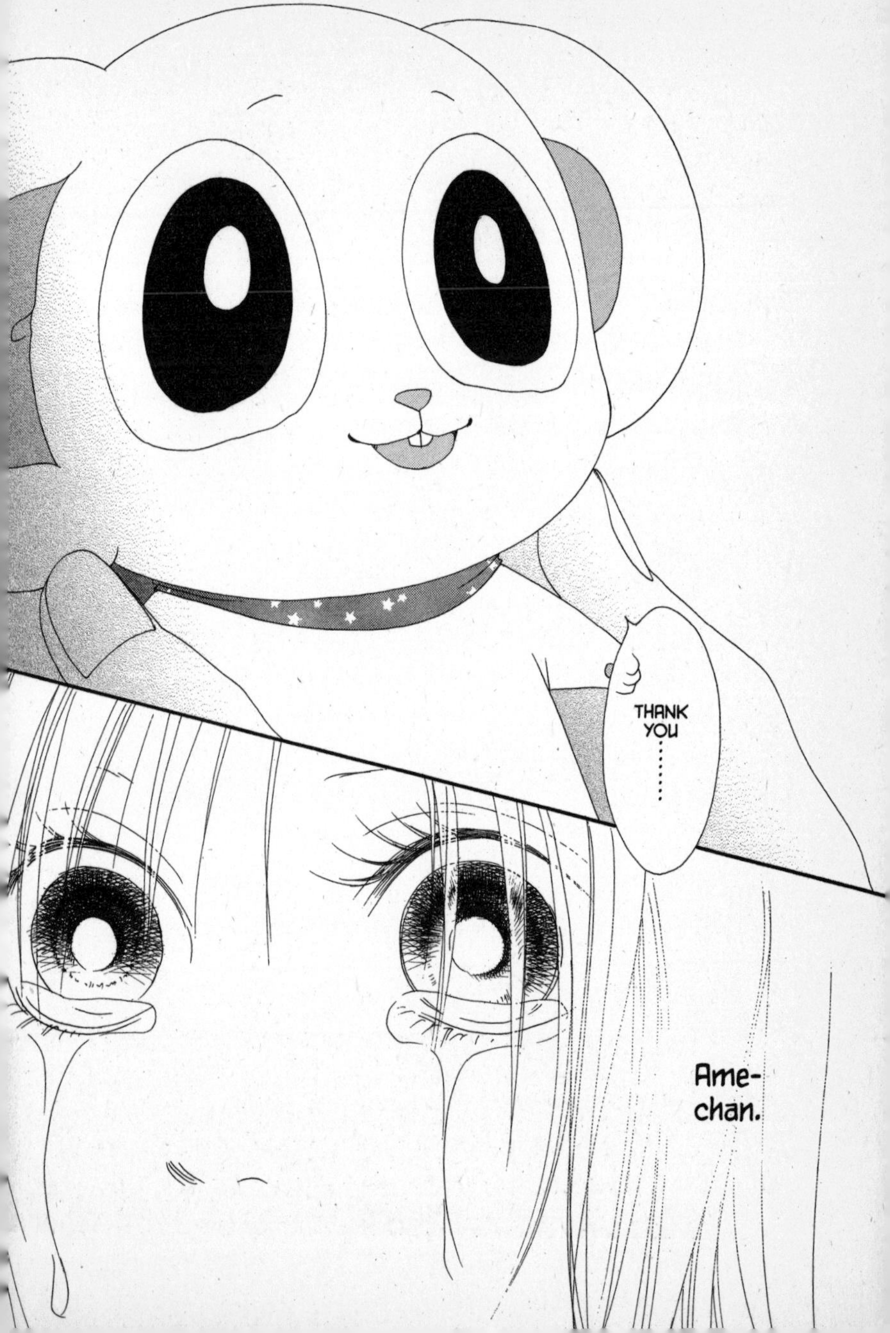
THANK YOU......
Ame-chan.

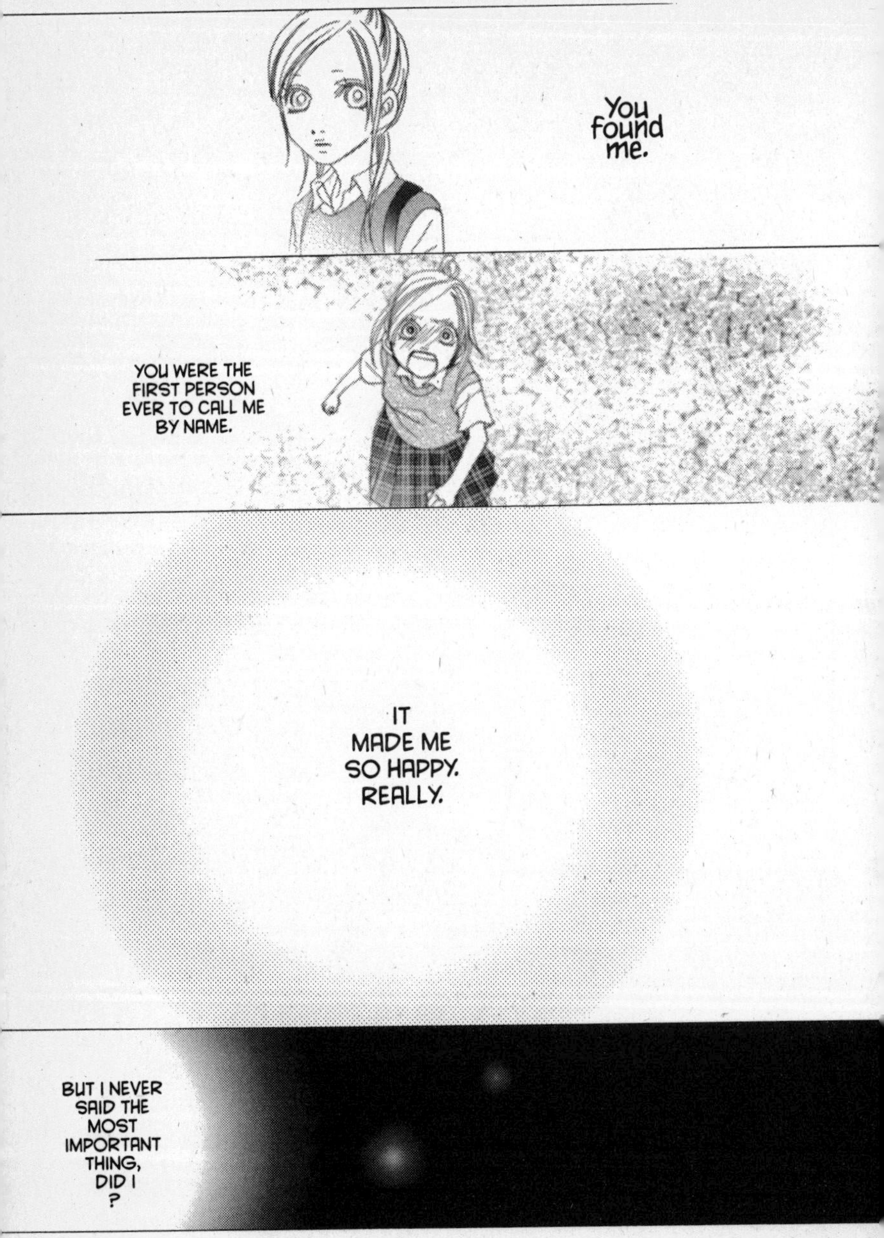
You found me.
YOU WERE THE FIRST PERSON EVER TO CALL ME BY NAME.
IT MADE ME SO HAPPY. REALLY.
BUT I NEVER SAID THE MOST IMPORTANT THING, DID I ?

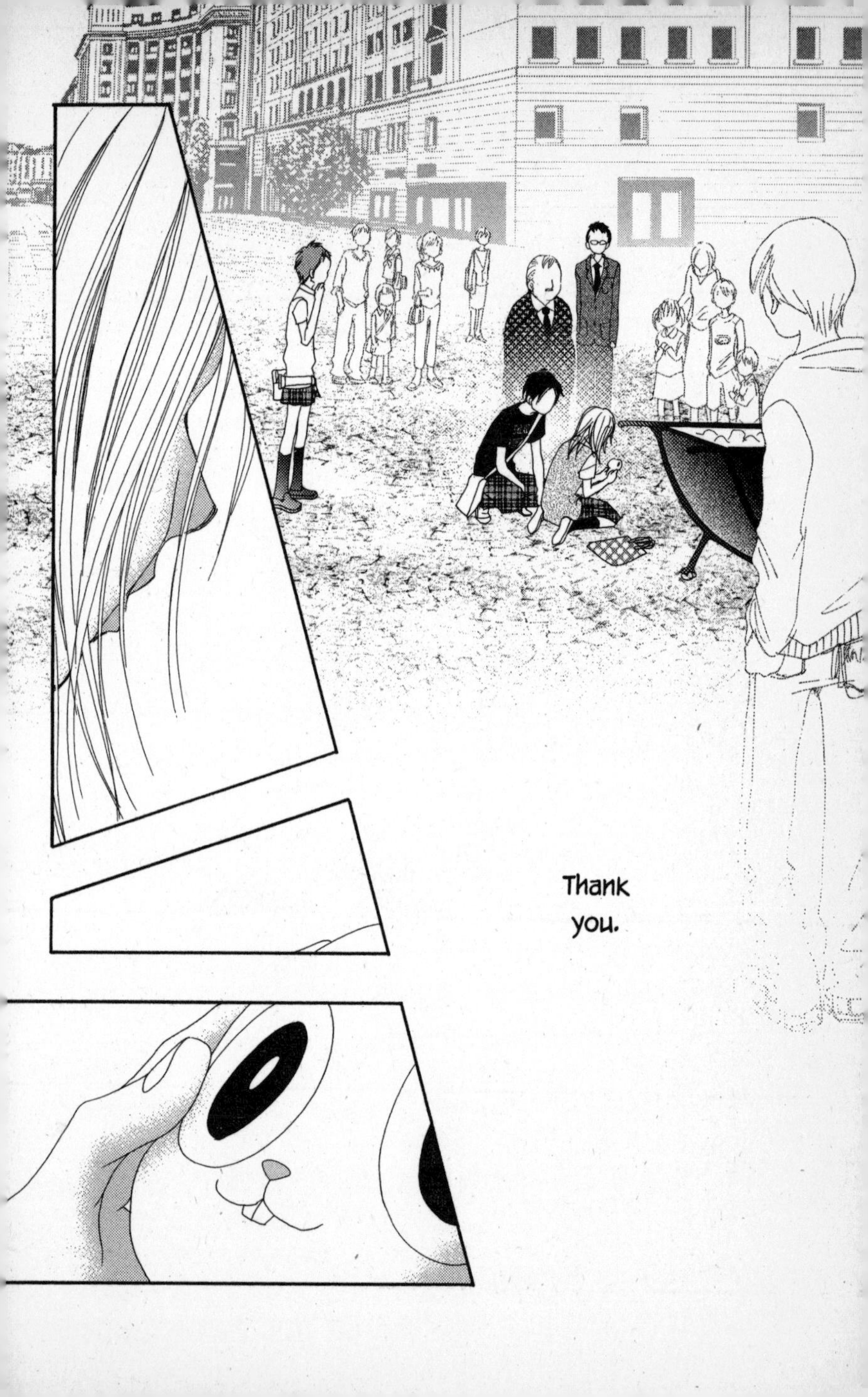
Thank you.

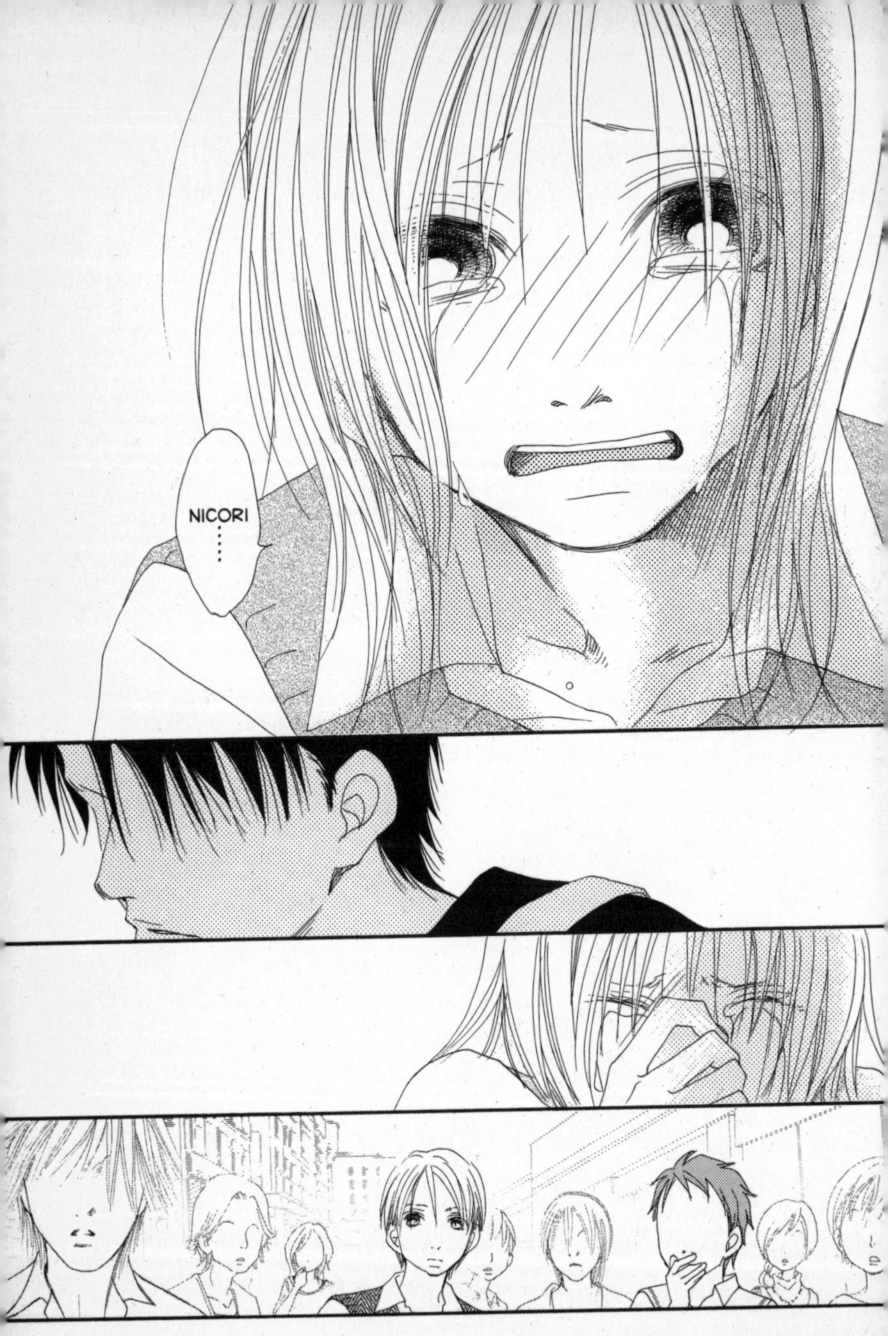
NICORI
.....

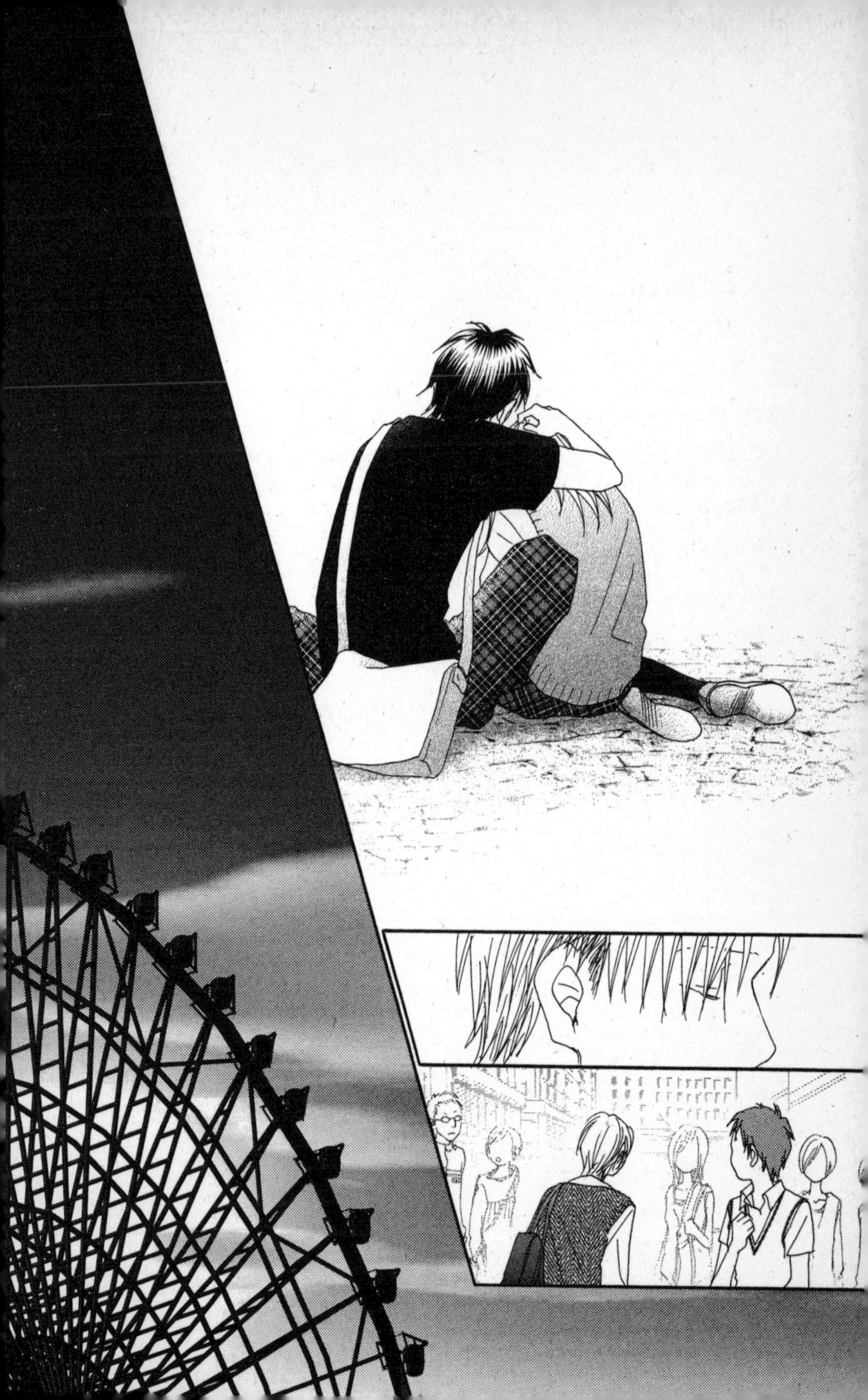

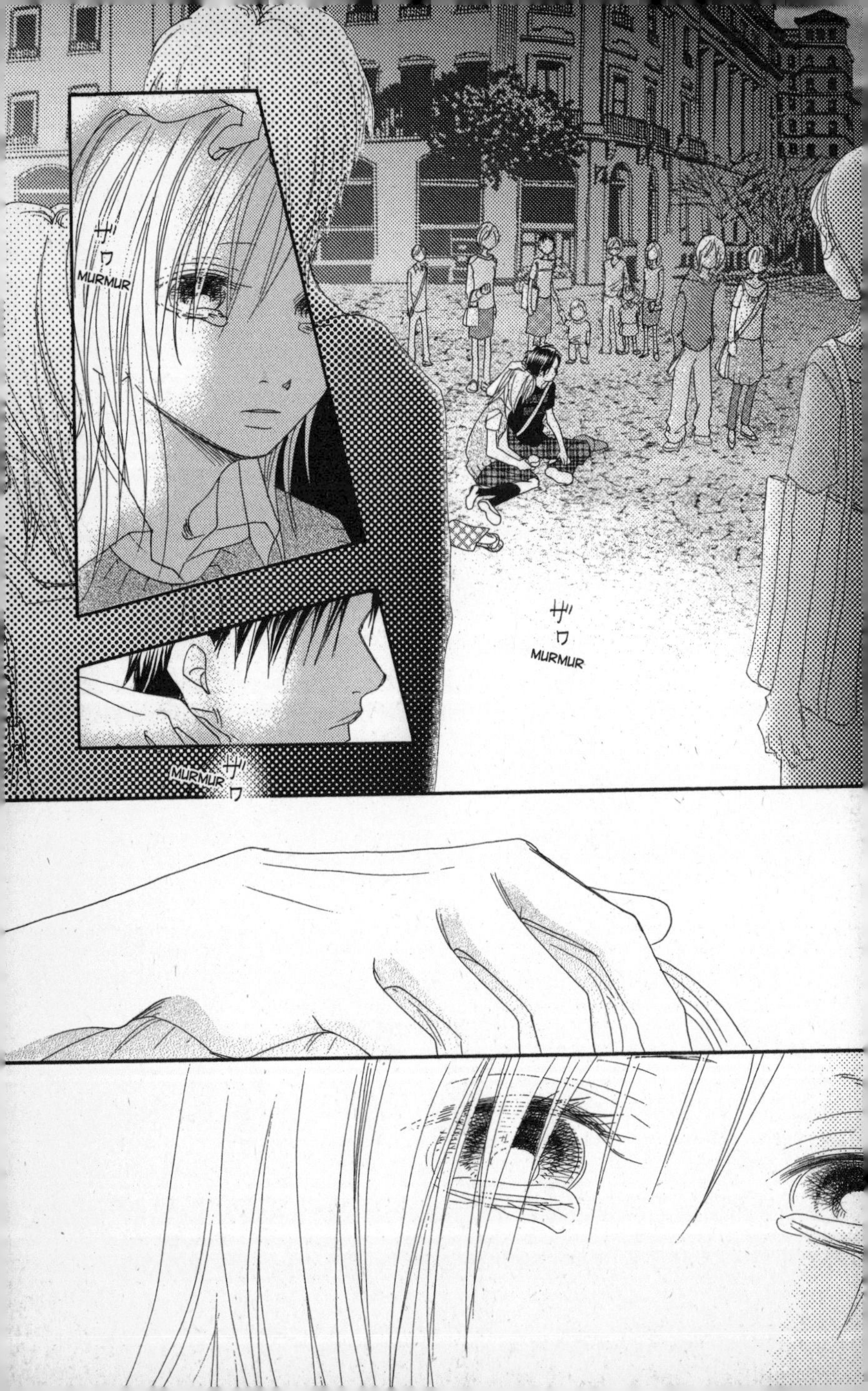
ザワ
MURMUR
ザワ
MURMUR
ザワ
MURMUR

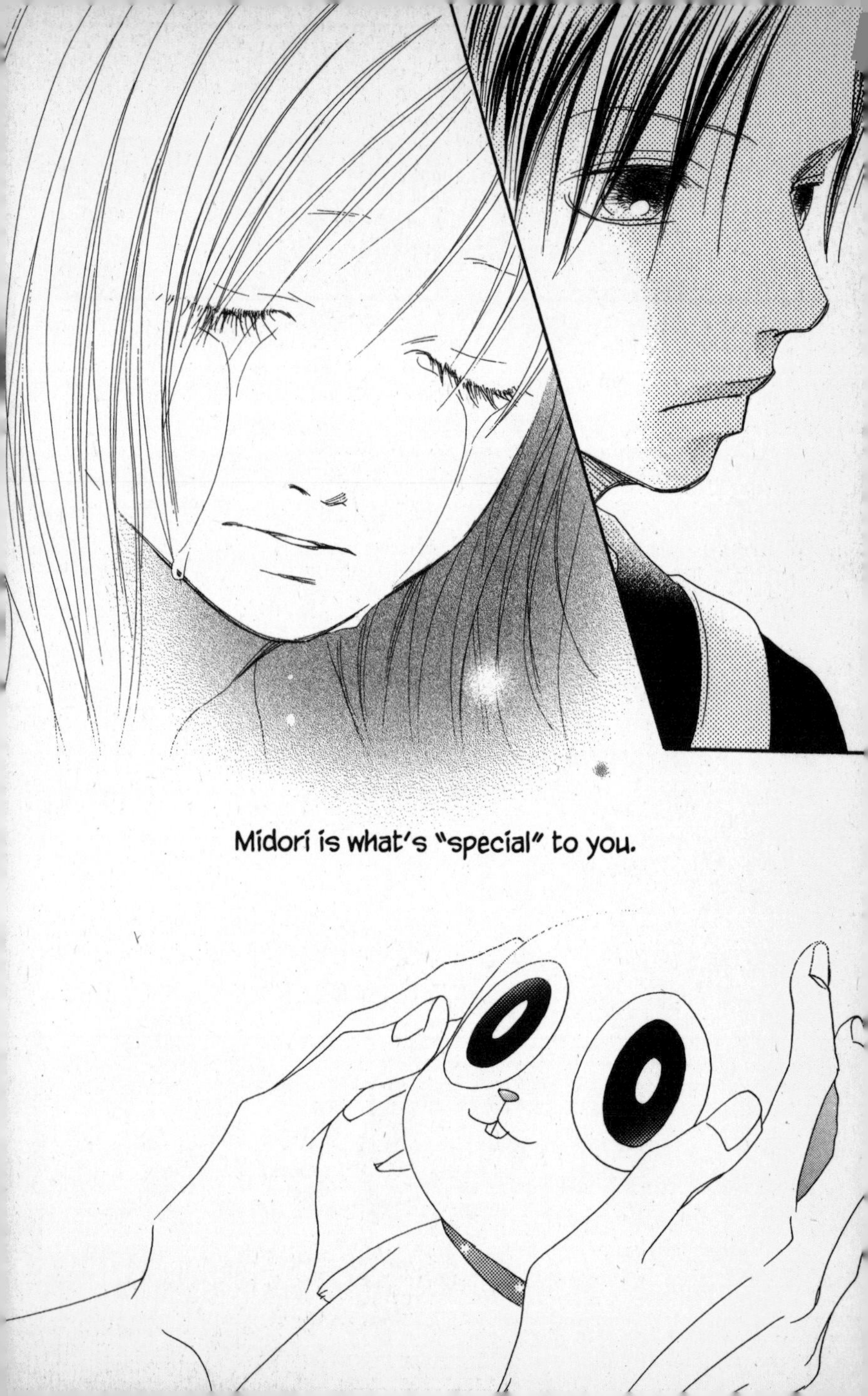
Midori is what's "special" to you.

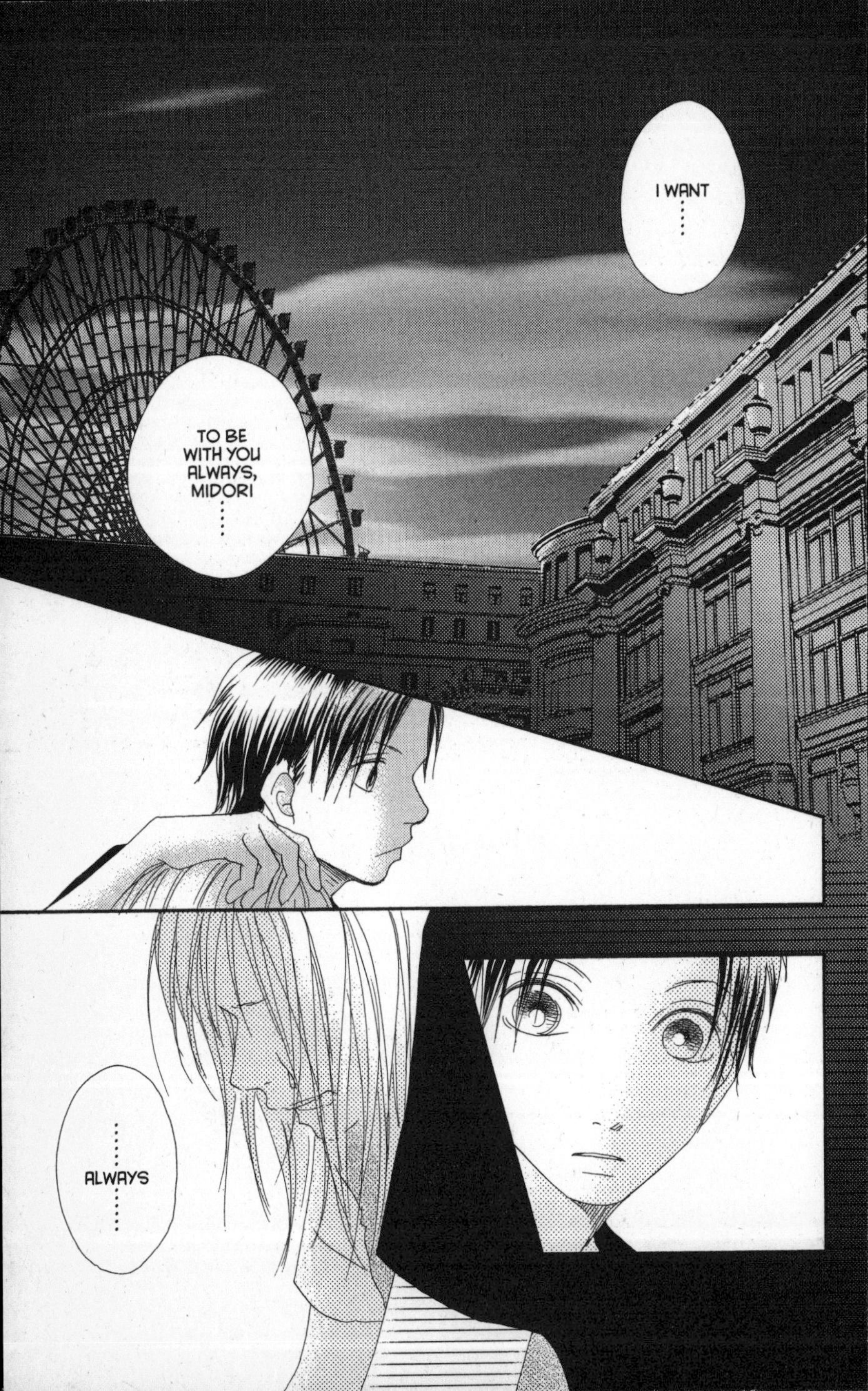
I WANT
......
TO BE WITH YOU ALWAYS, MIDORI
......
......
ALWAYS
......

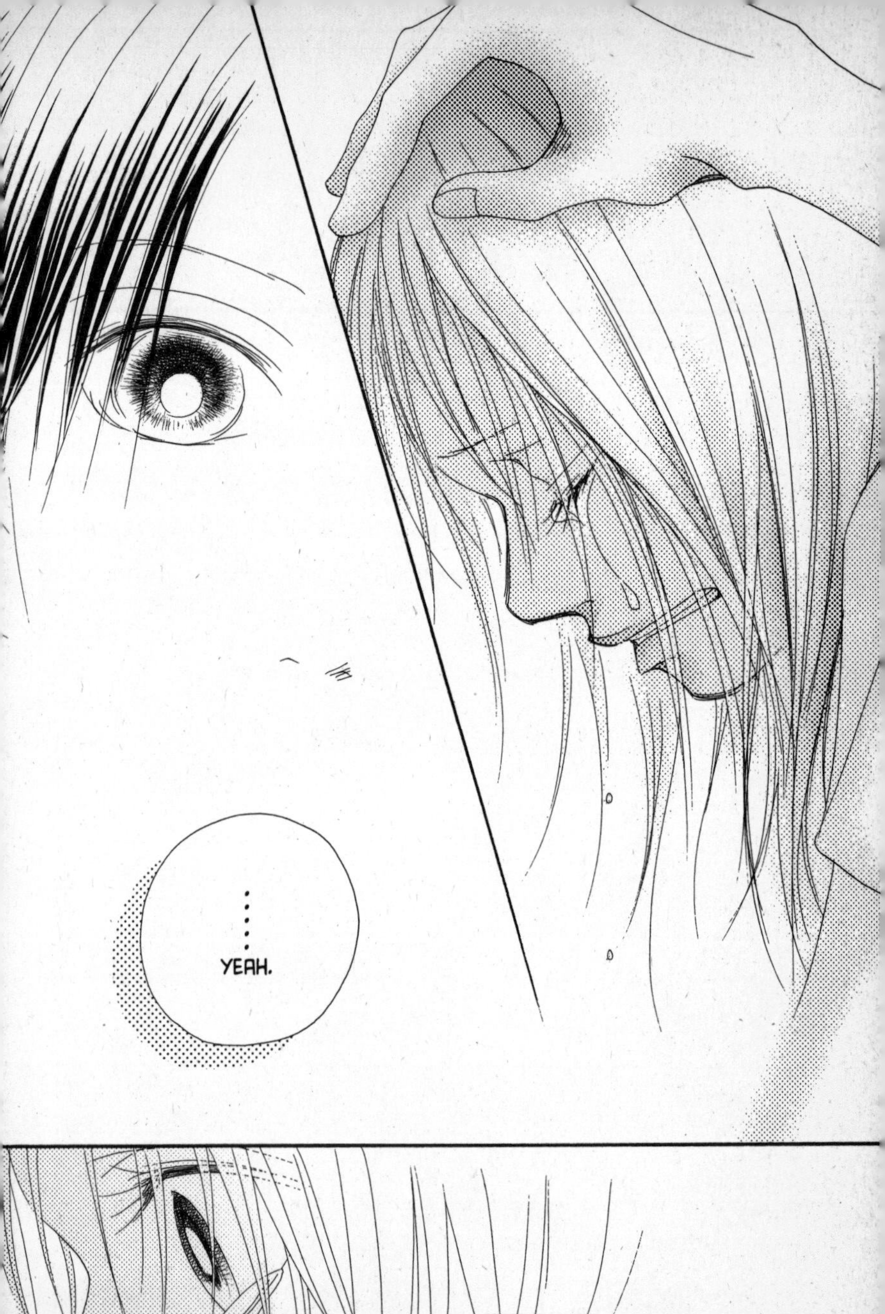

....
YEAH.

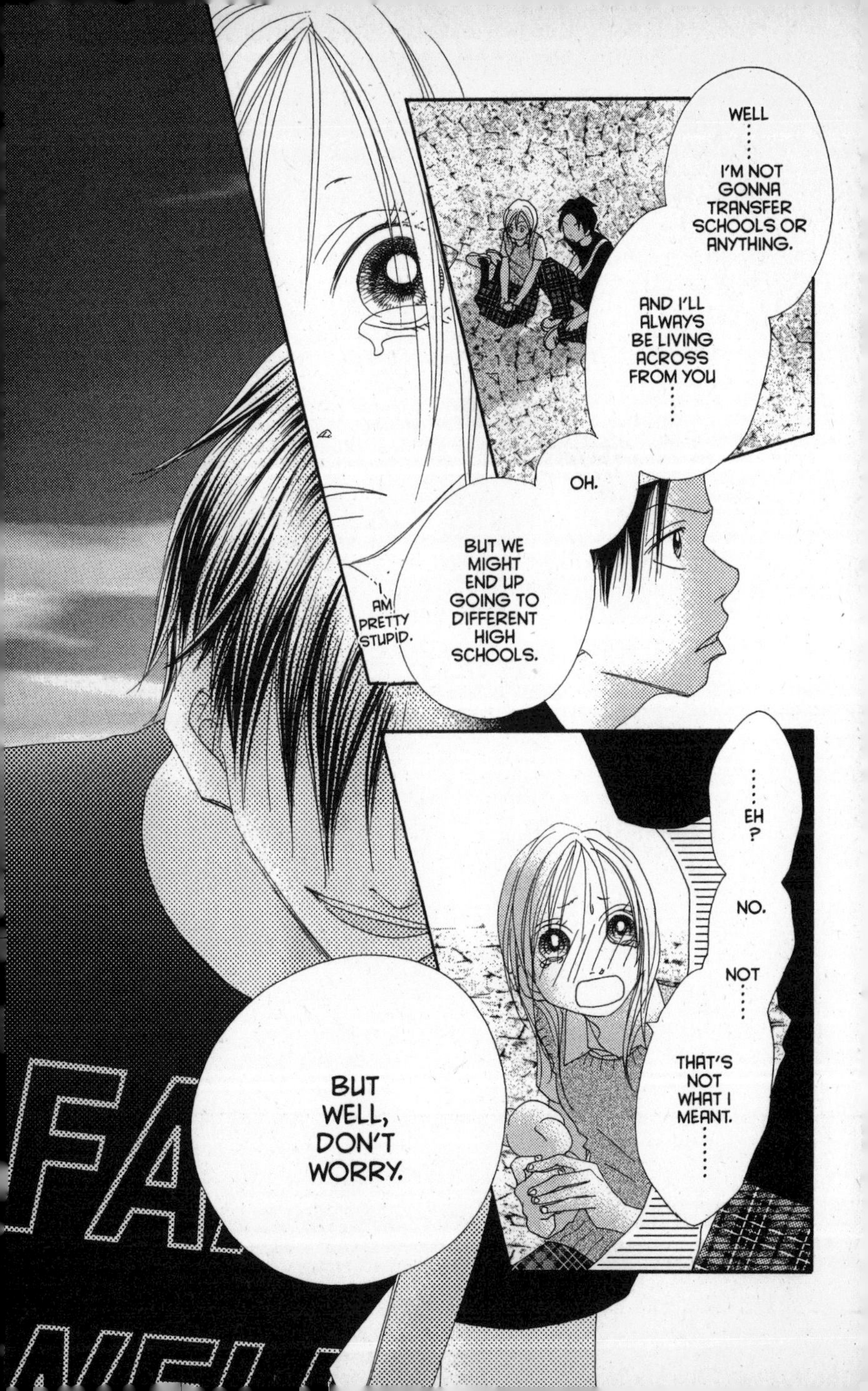
WELL ……
I'M NOT GONNA TRANSFER SCHOOLS OR ANYTHING.
AND I'LL ALWAYS BE LIVING ACROSS FROM YOU ……
OH.
BUT WE MIGHT END UP GOING TO DIFFERENT HIGH SCHOOLS.
I AM PRETTY STUPID.
……EH?
NO.
NOT……
THAT'S NOT WHAT I MEANT. ……
BUT WELL, DON'T WORRY.

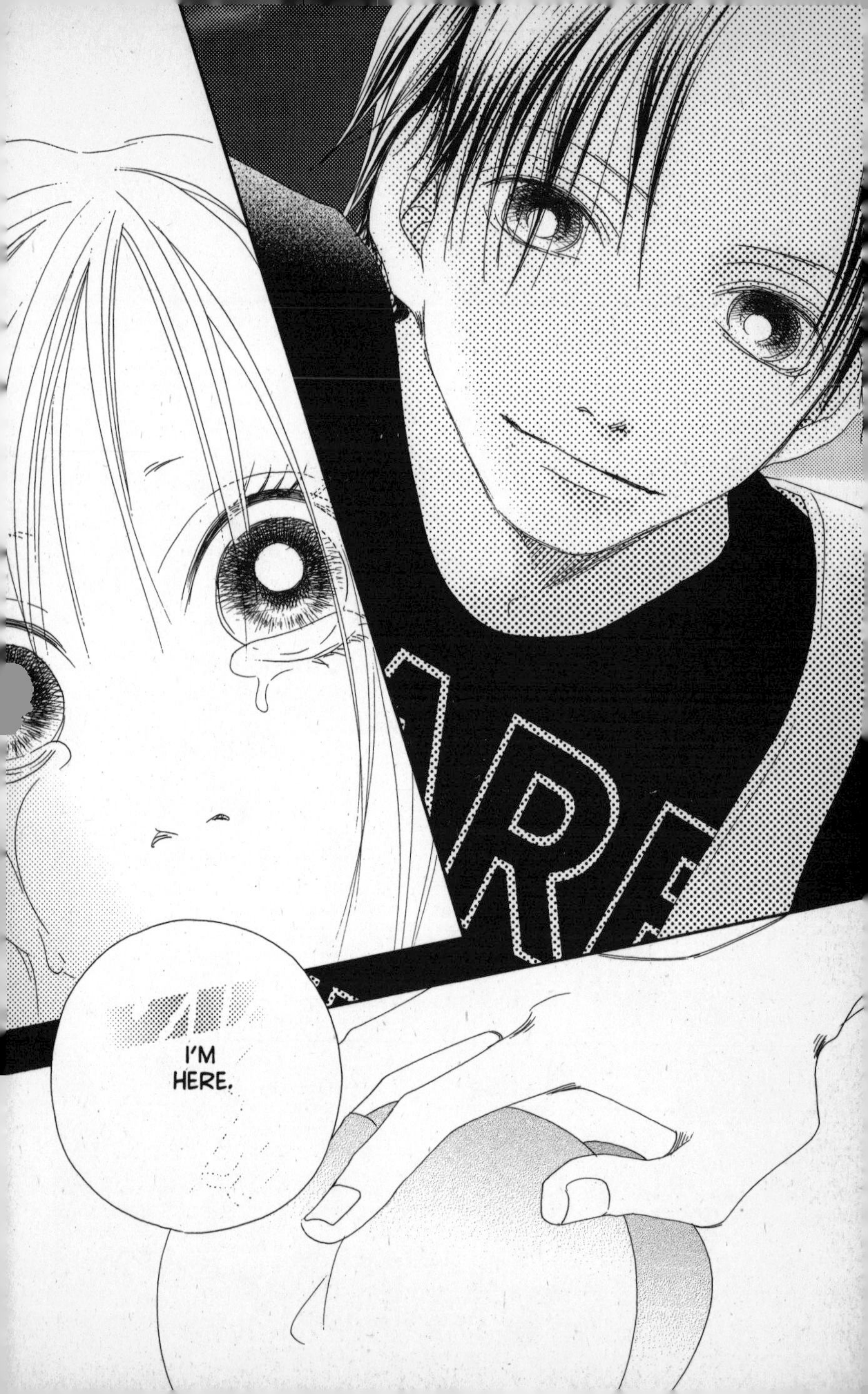
I'M HERE.

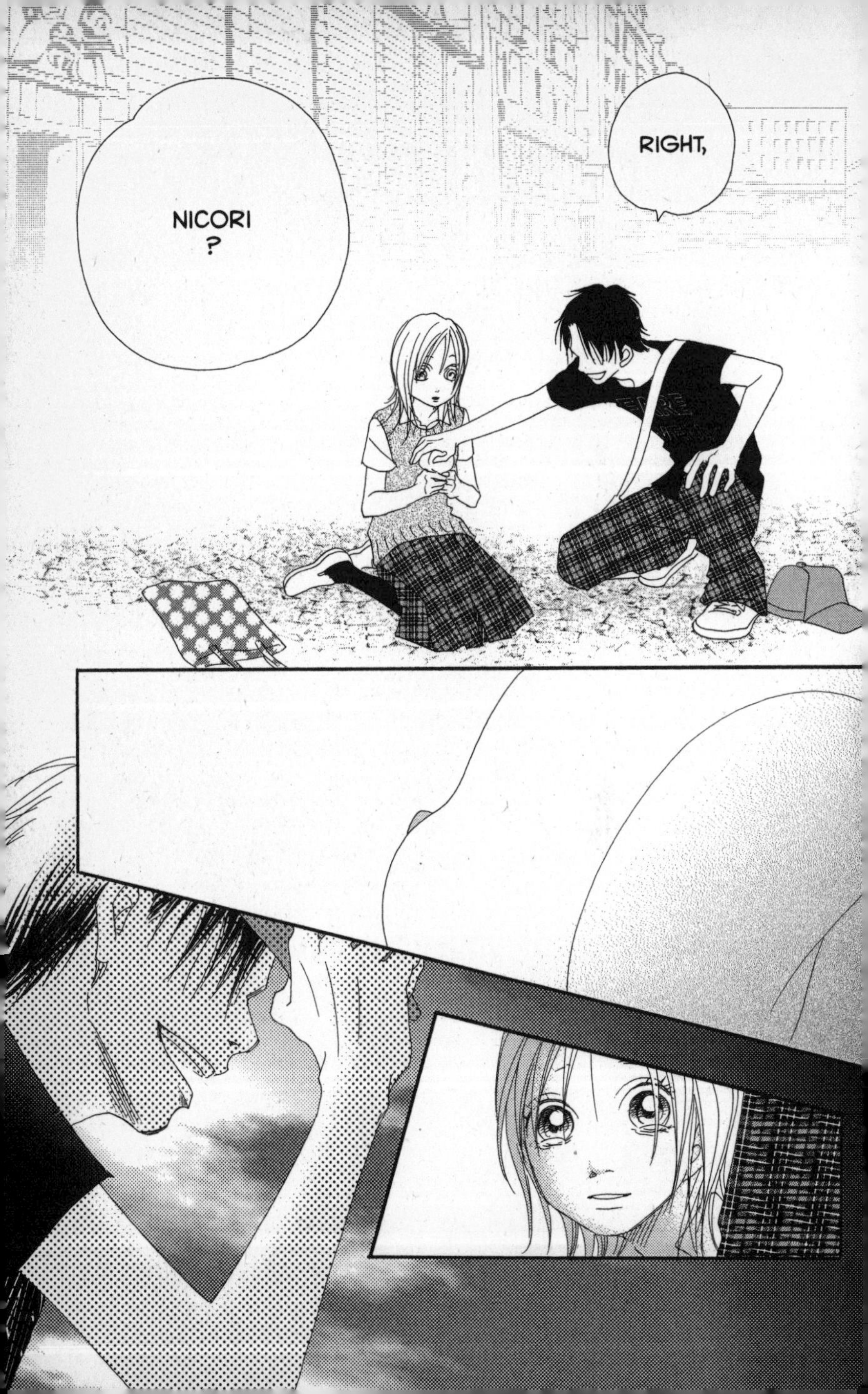
RIGHT,
NICORI ?

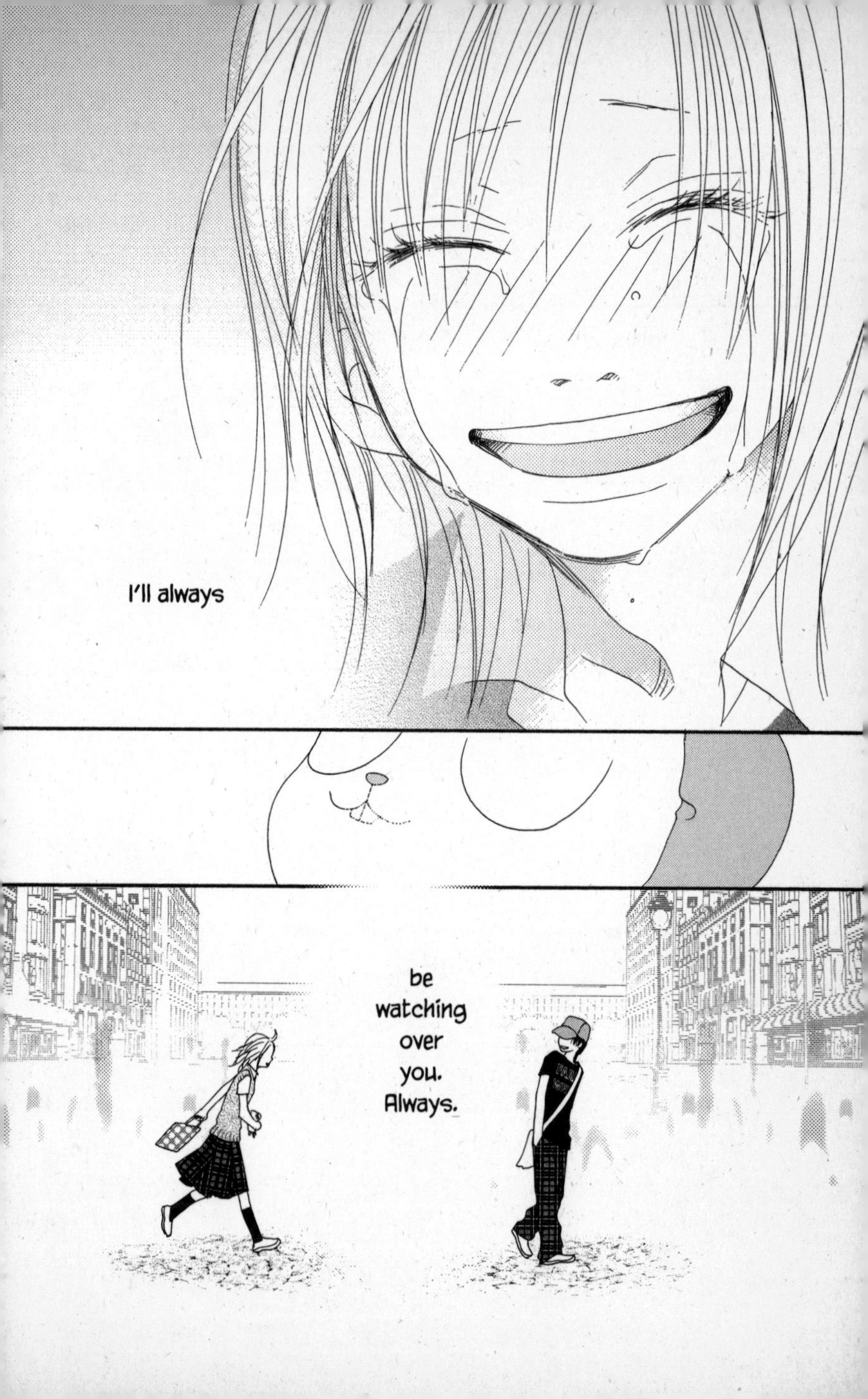
I'll always
be watching over you. Always.

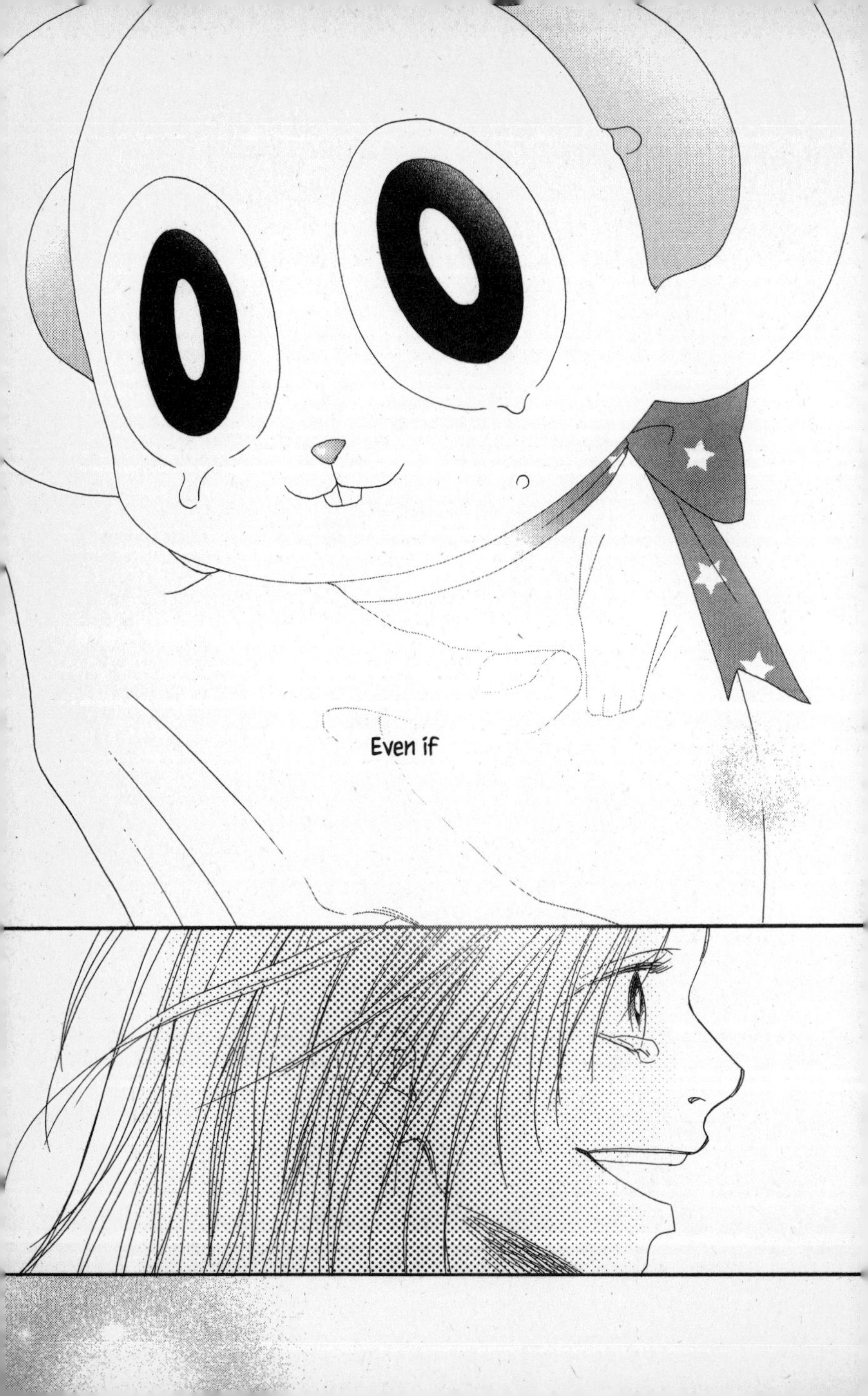
Even if

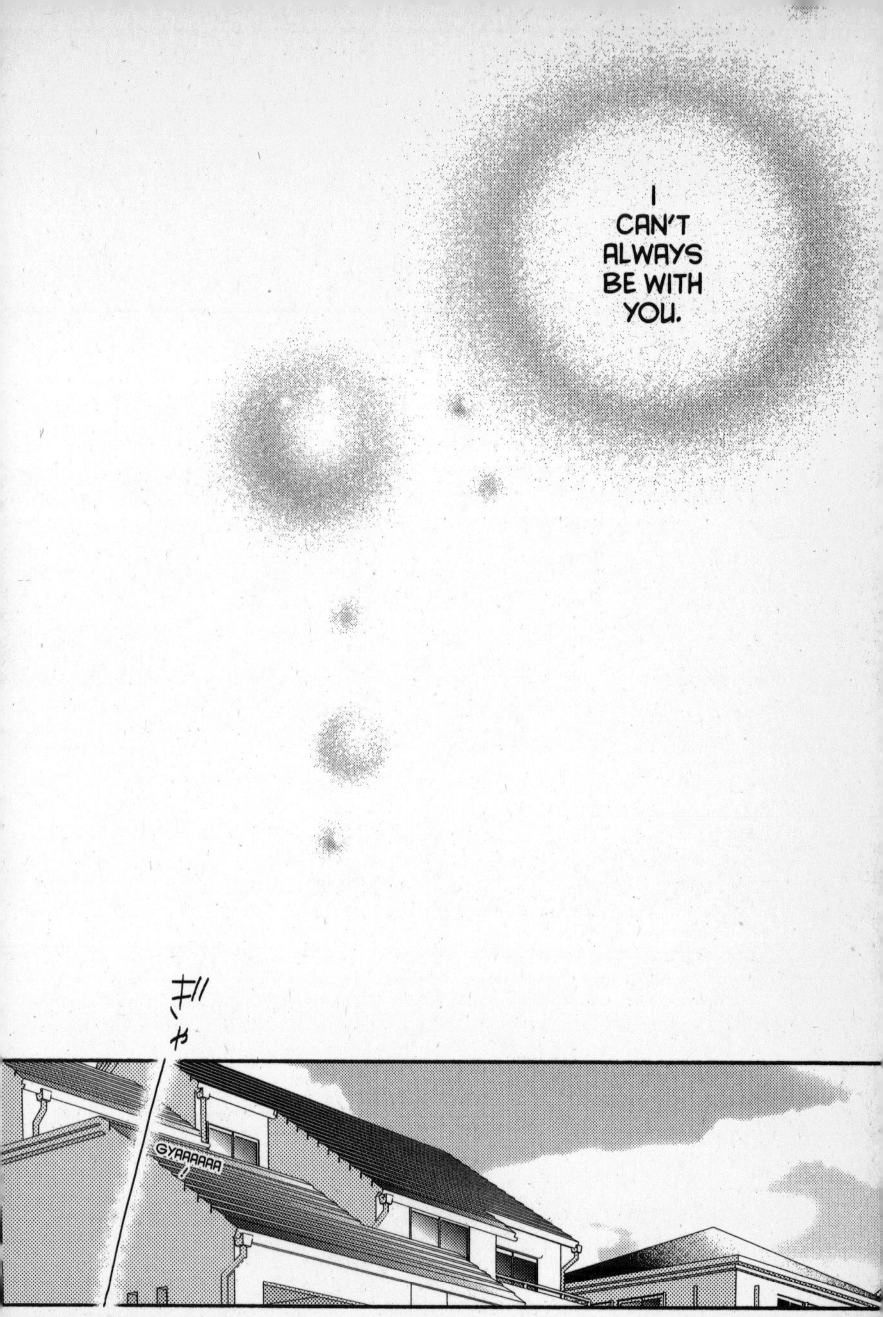
I CAN'T ALWAYS BE WITH YOU.
GYAAAAAAA!

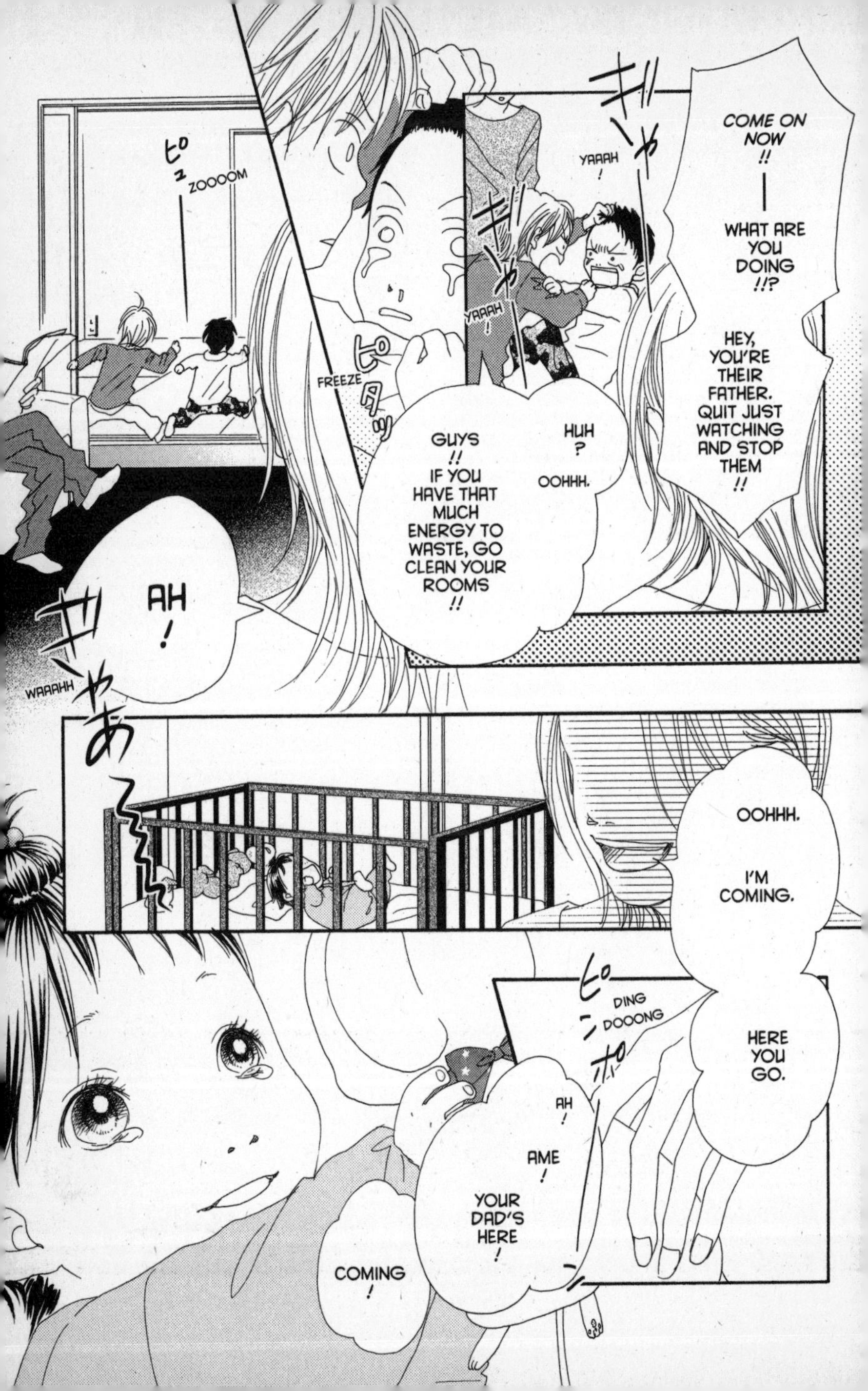
COME ON NOW!! — WHAT ARE YOU DOING!!?
HEY, YOU'RE THEIR FATHER. QUIT JUST WATCHING AND STOP THEM!!
YAAAH!
YAAAH!
HUH? OOHHH.
GUYS!! IF YOU HAVE THAT MUCH ENERGY TO WASTE, GO CLEAN YOUR ROOMS!!
FREEZE
ZOOOOM
AH!
WAAAHH
OOHHH.
I'M COMING.
DING DOOONG
HERE YOU GO.
AH!
AME!
YOUR DAD'S HERE!
COMING!

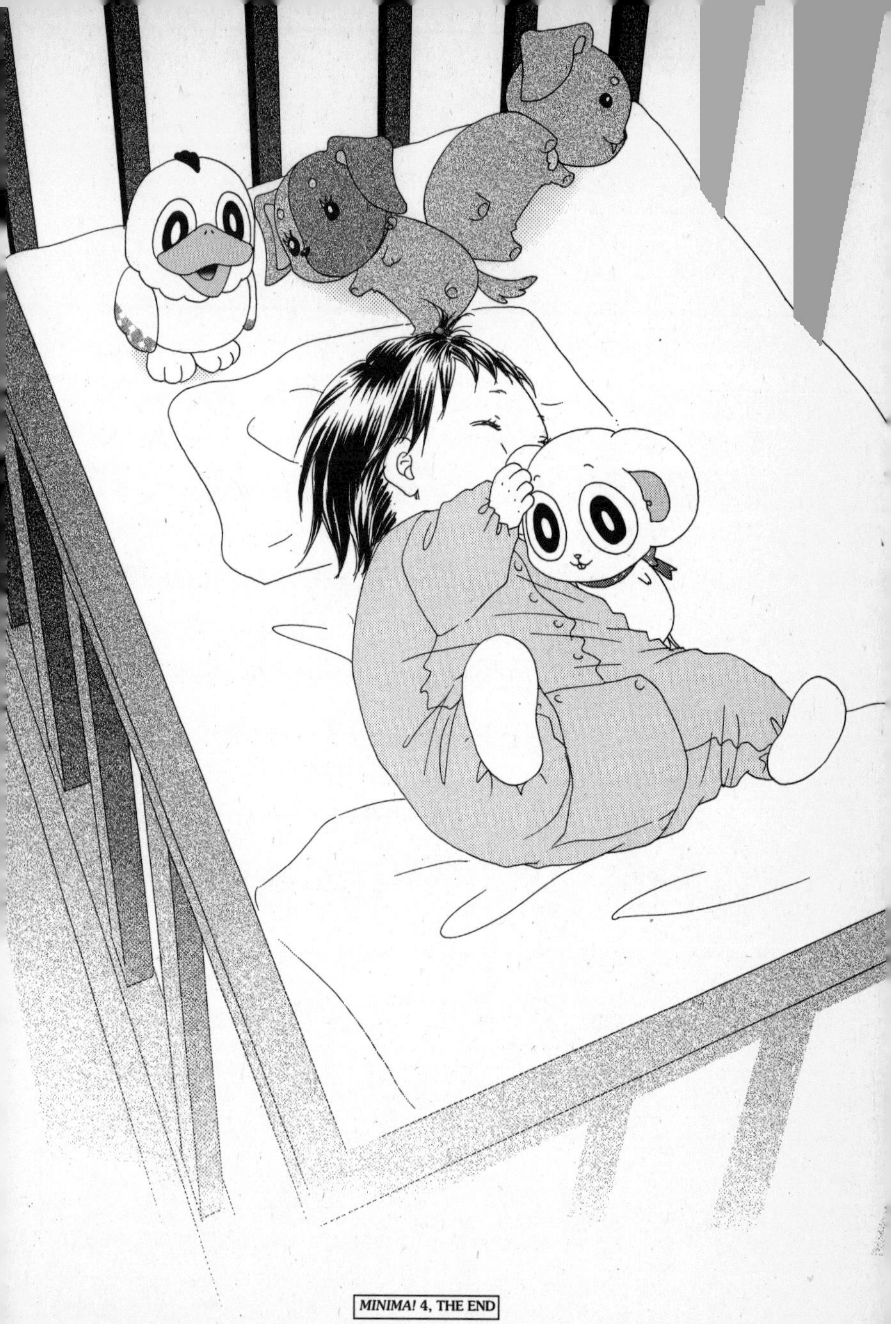

MINIMA! 4, THE END

おわり。

THE END.

つづく。

TO BE CONTINUED.

つづく。

TO BE CONTINUED.

づく。

TO BE CONTINUED.

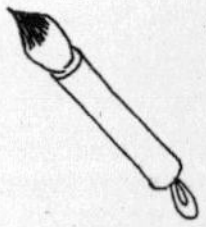

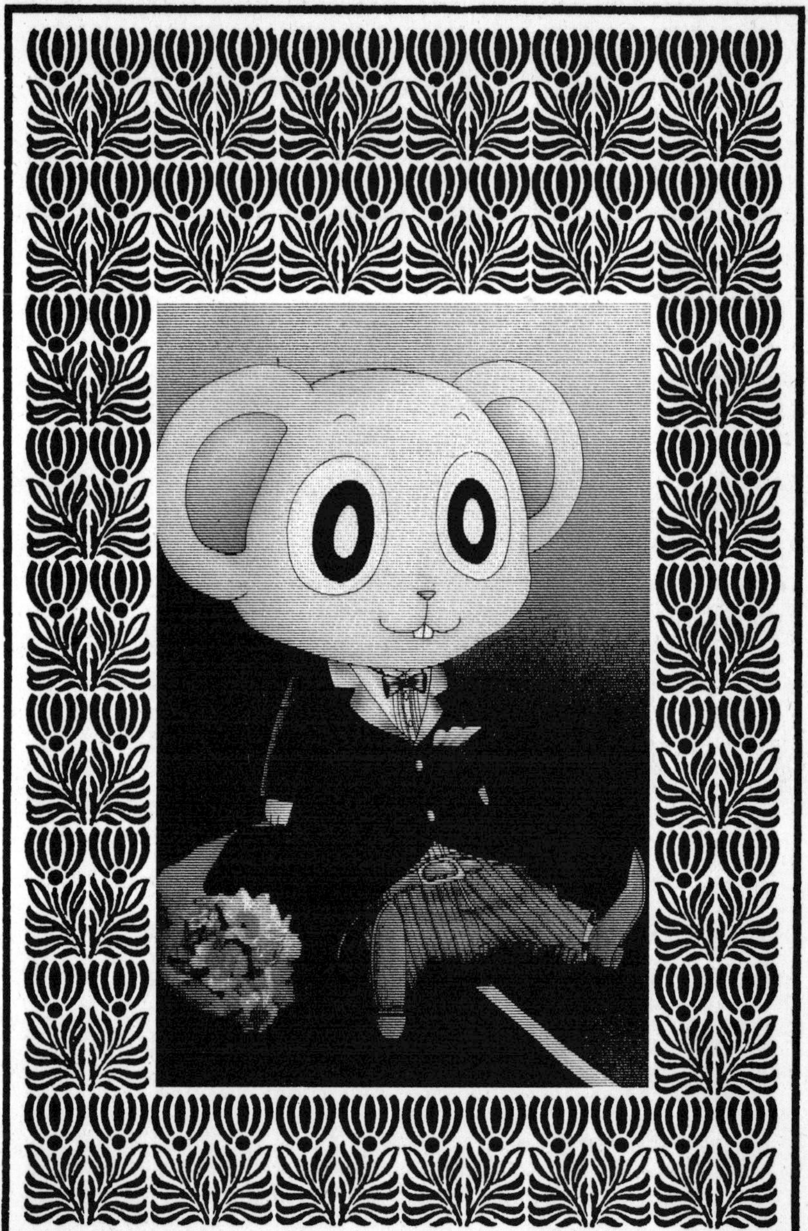

thanks!

**akimizu makoto
harui u★7**

**my family
my friends
hayakawa tomoco**

**hamano sawako
ikumi yu-ko
miyazaki asami
izawa mine**

&

you!

http://sakuraimachiko.blog101.fc2.com/

I ♥ YOU

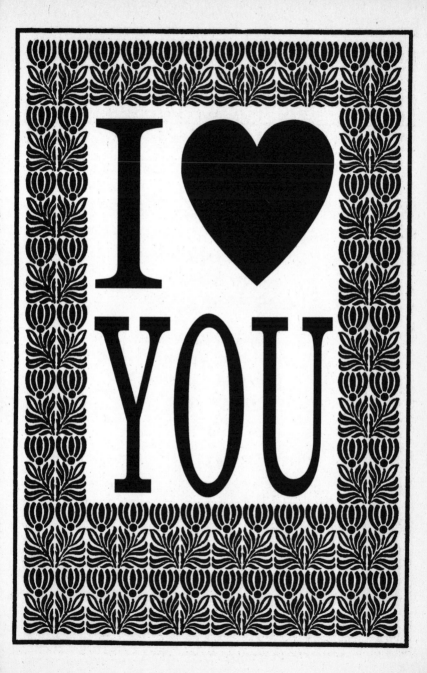

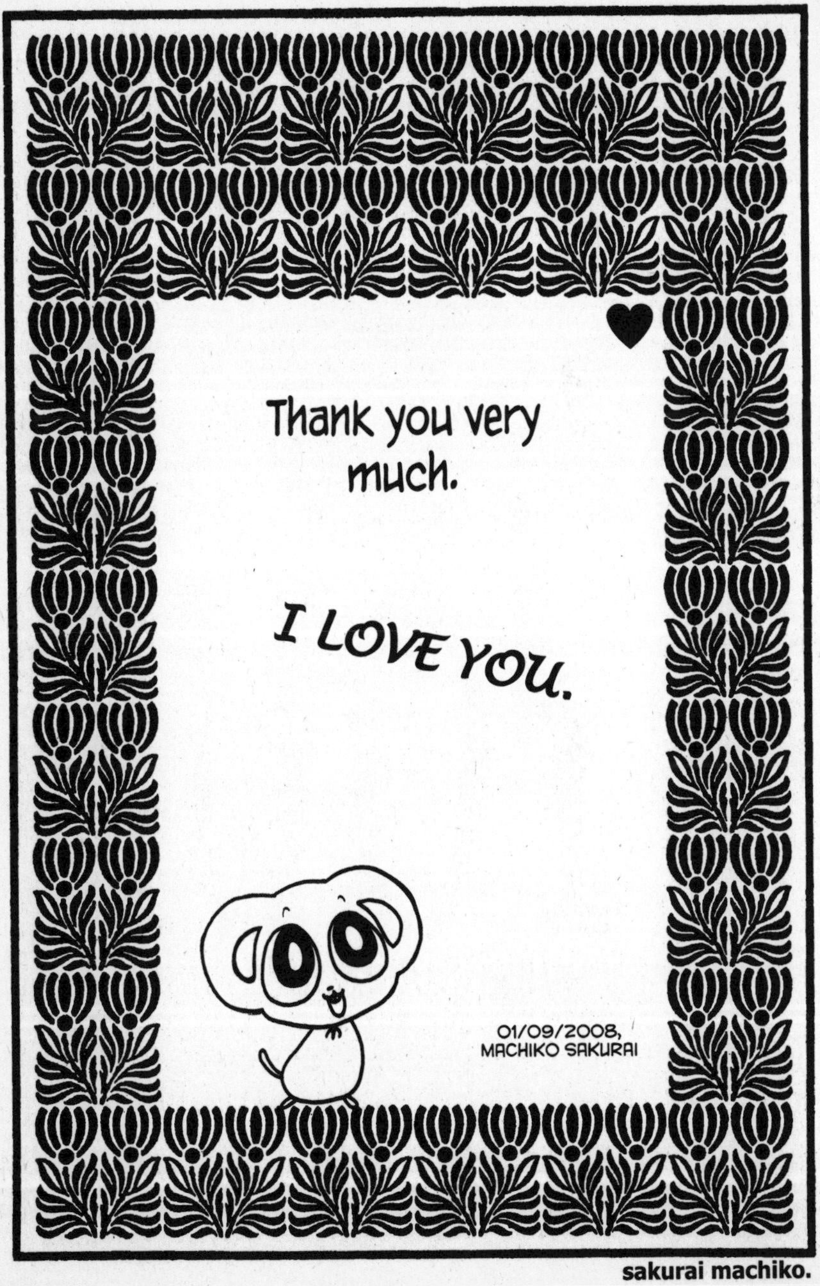
Thank you very much.
I LOVE YOU.
01/09/2008,
MACHIKO SAKURAI

sakurai machiko.

Translation Notes

Japanese is a tricky language for most Westerners, and translation is often more art than science. For your edification and reading pleasure, here are notes on some of the places where we could have gone in a different direction with our translation of the work, or where a Japanese cultural reference is used.

NEET, page 11

NEET stands for "Not currently engaged in Employment, Education, or Training," and in this case, it refers to the fact that Masamune just lies around at home doing nothing all day.

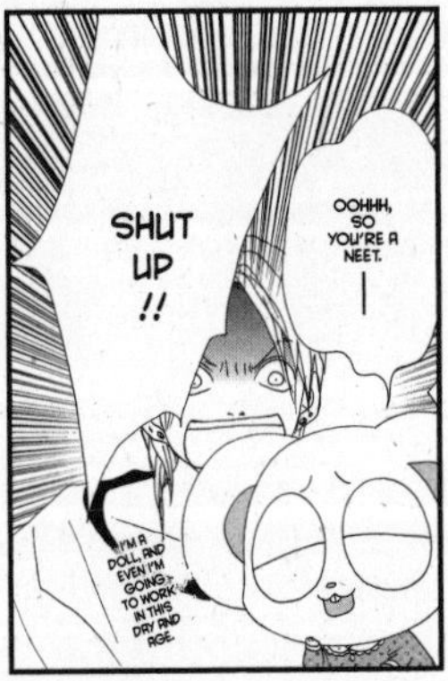
OOHHH, SO YOU'RE A NEET.
SHUT UP !!
I'M A DOLL, AND EVEN I'M GOING TO WORK IN THIS DAY AND AGE.

Different high schools, page 159

In Japan, kids have to pass exams to get into high schools. Different schools have different exams, and some are harder than others, so Midori is saying he might not be able to get into the same school as Ame, because he's not very bright.

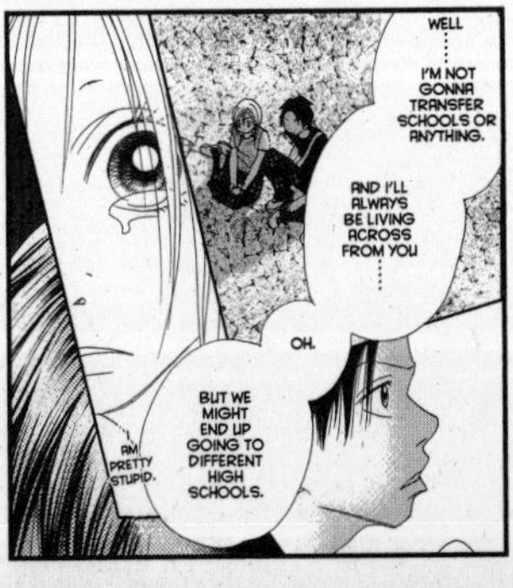
WELL...... I'M NOT GONNA TRANSFER SCHOOLS OR ANYTHING.
AND I'LL ALWAYS BE LIVING ACROSS FROM YOU......
OH.
BUT WE MIGHT END UP GOING TO DIFFERENT HIGH SCHOOLS.
AM PRETTY STUPID.

PEACH-PIT

Creators of *Dears* and *Rozen Maiden*

Everybody at Seiyo Elementary thinks that stylish and super-cool Amu has it all. But nobody knows the *real* Amu, a shy girl who wishes she had the courage to truly be herself. Changing Amu's life is going to take more than wishes and dreams—it's going to take a little magic! One morning, Amu finds a surprise in her bed: three strange little eggs. Each egg contains a Guardian Character, an angel-like being who can give her the power to be someone new. With the help of her Guardian Characters, Amu is about to discover that her true self is even more amazing than she ever dreamed.

Special extras in each volume! Read them all!

VISIT WWW.DELREYMANGA.COM TO:
- Read sample pages
- View release date calendars for upcoming volumes
- Sign up for Del Rey's free manga e-newsletter
- Find out the latest about new Del Rey Manga series

RATING T AGES 13+

  **DEL REY MANGA** デルレイ

The Otaku's Choice

STORY BY SURT LIM
ART BY HIROFUMI SUGIMOTO

A DEL REY MANGA ORIGINAL

Exploring the woods, young Kasumi encounters an ancient tree god, who bestows upon her the power of invisibility. Together with classmates who have had similar experiences, Kasumi forms the Magic Play Club, dedicated to using their powers for good while avoiding sinister forces that would exploit them.

Special extras in each volume! Read them all!

VISIT WWW.DELREYMANGA.COM TO:
- Read sample pages
- View release date calendars for upcoming volumes
- Sign up for Del Rey's free manga e-newsletter
- Find out the latest about new Del Rey Manga series

RATING T AGES 13+

The Otaku's Choice.™

Papillon

by Miwa Ueda

BUTTERFLY, SPREAD YOUR WINGS!

Ageha is a shy tomboy, but her twin sister, Hana, is the ultimate ultra-glam teen queen. Hana loves being the center of attention so much that she'll do anything to keep Ageha in her shadow. But Ageha has a plan that will change her life forever and no one, not even Hana, can hold her back. . . .

• From the creator of *Peach Girl*

Special extras in each volume! Read them all!

Kamichama Karin Chu

BY KOGE-DONBO

A GODDESS IN LOVE!

Karin is your lovable girl next door—if the girl next door also happens to be a goddess! Karin has a magic ring that gives her the power to do anything she'd like. Though what she'd like most is to live happily ever after with Kazune, the boy of her dreams. Magic brought Kazune to her, but it also has a way of complicating things. It's not easy to be a goddess and a girl in love!

• Sequel series to the fan-favorite *Kamichama Karin*

Special extras in each volume! Read them all!

STOP!!

YOU'RE GOING THE WRONG WAY!

MANGA IS A COMPLETELY DIFFERENT
TYPE OF READING EXPERIENCE.
TO START AT THE BEGINNING,
GO TO THE END!

THAT'S RIGHT! AUTHENTIC MANGA IS READ THE TRADITIONAL
JAPANESE WAY—FROM RIGHT TO LEFT, EXACTLY THE OPPOSITE
OF HOW AMERICAN BOOKS ARE READ. IT'S EASY TO FOLLOW:
JUST GO TO THE OTHER END OF THE BOOK, AND READ
EACH PAGE—AND EACH PANEL—FROM THE RIGHT SIDE
TO THE LEFT SIDE, STARTING AT THE TOP RIGHT.
NOW YOU'RE EXPERIENCING MANGA
AS IT WAS MEANT TO BE.